DAT

OPPOSING VIEWPOINTS®

EXTREMIST GROUPS

Other Books of Related Interest

OPPOSING VIEWPOINTS®
EXTREMIST GROUPS

Karen F. Balkin, *Book Editor*

Bruce Glassman, *Vice President*
Bonnie Szumski, *Publisher*
Helen Cothran, *Managing Editor*

**OPPOSING
VIEWPOINTS®
SERIES**

GREENHAVEN PRESS
An imprint of Thomson Gale, a part of The Thomson Corporation

THOMSON
★
GALE

Detroit • New York • San Francisco • San Diego • New Haven, Conn.
Waterville, Maine • London • Munich

For more information, contact
Greenhaven Press
27500 Drake Rd.
Farmington Hills, MI 48331-3535
Or you can visit our Internet site at http://www.gale.com

LIBRARY OF CONGRESS CATALOGING-IN-PUBLICATION DATA

Extremist groups / Karen F. Balkin, book editor.
   p. cm. — (Opposing viewpoints series)
  Includes bibliographical references and index.
  ISBN 0-7377-3594-5 (lib. : alk. paper) — ISBN 0-7377-3595-3 (pbk. : alk. paper)
   1. Radicals. 2. Radicalism. 3. Hate groups. I. Balkin, Karen, 1949– . II. Opposing viewpoints series (Unnumbered)
  HN49.R33E9 2005
  305.5'68—dc22

          2004054127

> "Congress shall make
> no law...abridging the
> freedom of speech, or of
> the press."

First Amendment to the U.S. Constitution

The basic foundation of our democracy is the First Amendment guarantee of freedom of expression. The Opposing Viewpoints Series is dedicated to the concept of this basic freedom and the idea that it is more important to practice it than to enshrine it.

Contents

Chapter 3: Do White Supremacist Groups Promote Hate and Violence?

Chapter 4: What Extremist Groups Pose a Threat Worldwide?

Why Consider Opposing Viewpoints?

"The only way in which a human being can make some approach to knowing the whole of a subject is by hearing what can be said about it by persons of every variety of opinion and studying all modes in which it can be looked at by every character of mind. No wise man ever acquired his wisdom in any mode but this."

John Stuart Mill

In our media-intensive culture it is not difficult to find differing opinions. Thousands of newspapers and magazines and dozens of radio and television talk shows resound with differing points of view. The difficulty lies in deciding which opinion to agree with and which "experts" seem the most credible. The more inundated we become with differing opinions and claims, the more essential it is to hone critical reading and thinking skills to evaluate these ideas. Opposing Viewpoints books address this problem directly by presenting stimulating debates that can be used to enhance and teach these skills. The varied opinions contained in each book examine many different aspects of a single issue. While examining these conveniently edited opposing views, readers can develop critical thinking skills such as the ability to compare and contrast authors' credibility, facts, argumentation styles, use of persuasive techniques, and other stylistic tools. In short, the Opposing Viewpoints Series is an ideal way to attain the higher-level thinking and reading skills so essential in a culture of diverse and contradictory opinions.

In addition to providing a tool for critical thinking, Opposing Viewpoints books challenge readers to question their own strongly held opinions and assumptions. Most people form their opinions on the basis of upbringing, peer pressure, and personal, cultural, or professional bias. By reading carefully balanced opposing views, readers must directly confront new ideas as well as the opinions of those with whom they disagree. This is not to simplistically argue that everyone who reads opposing views will—or should—change his or her opinion. Instead, the series enhances readers' understanding of their own views by encouraging confrontation with opposing ideas. Careful examination of others' views can lead to the readers' understanding of the logical inconsistencies in their own opinions, perspective on why they hold an opinion, and the consideration of the possibility that their opinion requires further evaluation.

Evaluating Other Opinions

To ensure that this type of examination occurs, Opposing Viewpoints books present all types of opinions. Prominent spokespeople on different sides of each issue as well as well-known professionals from many disciplines challenge the reader. An additional goal of the series is to provide a forum for other, less known, or even unpopular viewpoints. The opinion of an ordinary person who has had to make the decision to cut off life support from a terminally ill relative, for example, may be just as valuable and provide just as much insight as a medical ethicist's professional opinion. The editors have two additional purposes in including these less known views. One, the editors encourage readers to respect others' opinions—even when not enhanced by professional credibility. It is only by reading or listening to and objectively evaluating others' ideas that one can determine whether they are worthy of consideration. Two, the inclusion of such viewpoints encourages the important critical thinking skill of objectively evaluating an author's credentials and bias. This evaluation will illuminate an author's reasons for taking a particular stance on an issue and will aid in readers' evaluation of the author's ideas.

It is our hope that these books will give readers a deeper understanding of the issues debated and an appreciation of the complexity of even seemingly simple issues when good and honest people disagree. This awareness is particularly important in a democratic society such as ours in which people enter into public debate to determine the common good. Those with whom one disagrees should not be regarded as enemies but rather as people whose views deserve careful examination and may shed light on one's own.

Thomas Jefferson once said that "difference of opinion leads to inquiry, and inquiry to truth." Jefferson, a broadly educated man, argued that "if a nation expects to be ignorant and free . . . it expects what never was and never will be." As individuals and as a nation, it is imperative that we consider the opinions of others and examine them with skill and discernment. The Opposing Viewpoints Series is intended to help readers achieve this goal.

David L. Bender and Bruno Leone,
Founders

Greenhaven Press anthologies primarily consist of previously published material taken from a variety of sources, including periodicals, books, scholarly journals, newspapers, government documents, and position papers from private and public organizations. These original sources are often edited for length and to ensure their accessibility for a young adult audience. The anthology editors also change the original titles of these works in order to clearly present the main thesis of each viewpoint and to explicitly indicate the opinion presented in the viewpoint. These alterations are made in consideration of both the reading and comprehension levels of a young adult audience. Every effort is made to ensure that Greenhaven Press accurately reflects the original intent of the authors included in this anthology.

Introduction

"The Internet is allowing the White supremacy movement to reach places it never reached before—middle and upper middle-class, college bound teens."
—Mark Potok, *editor of* Intelligence Watch
for the Southern Poverty Law Center

Originally conceived as a useful tool for scientists and researchers, the Internet has become the wonder of the communications world. It is used for the legitimate purposes of exchanging information, research, and commerce. It has also been put to use as a vehicle for theft, sabotage, illegal gambling, and pornography. Extremist groups—especially white supremacists—have found the Internet to be a valuable resource in disseminating their messages of hate. Indeed, the Internet has changed the face of extremism in the United States and around the world.

In 1985 the Anti-Defamation League published "Computerized Networks of Hate," a report that described a computerized bulletin board that was created for and by white supremacists. Aryan Nations, a racist group affiliated with the pseudo-theological Identity Church hate movement, was responsible for the bulletin board. "White Pride Worldwide" was the slogan Stephen Donald Black used ten years later when, in 1995, he launched the world's first racist Web site—Stormfront. Black, a former member of the Ku Klux Klan, learned about computers while in federal prison in Texas. When he was released, he used his knowledge to create a Web site that encouraged racial separation. Referring to the Internet, Black says, "There is the potential here to reach millions. I don't know if it's the ultimate solution to developing a white rights movement in this country, but it's certainly a significant advance."

According to the Anti-Defamation League, the Aryan Nations' bulletin board served the white supremacist movement in the same ways that Stormfront did in its early days—and still does—and that more sophisticated Web sites do today: They were all designed to attract young people to the hate movement, stir up hatred against the enemies of the white race, help earn money for the movement through advertising and donations, provide a means to circulate secret, coded messages among extremists, and bypass the laws that nations have passed to stop hate literature from coming into their countries. Rabbi Abraham Cooper, associate dean of the Simon Wiesenthal Center, an organization that promotes religious tolerance, estimates that in 1999 there were over fourteen hundred Web sites spreading racist ideology and promoting racial or religious violence. Experts estimate that by 2001, the number had grown to as many as three thousand.

Children and teens are groups specifically targeted for influence by extremist Web sites. With their bold graphics and quick links, hate sites are created to appeal to young people. Some sites use racist rock music to pull in teens, others use word games and puzzles with white supremacist themes to catch the attention of younger Web-savvy children. "What the Net does for the [supremacist] movement is amplify its propaganda and recruiting reach," says Mark Potok, editor of *Intelligence Watch*, a publication of the extremist watchdog group Southern Poverty Law Center. "It's the perfect venue for recruiting middle-class and upper-middle-class young people. They're looking for kids to build a political movement and a revolution." In addition to influencing young people with racist propaganda, white supremacist Web sites promote violence. While it is often difficult to show a direct link between regular viewing of hate sites and actual violence perpetrated against racial or religious minorities, most racist sites encourage violence and applaud violent acts. When John Williams King, a white racist, was convicted of beating and dragging to death James Byrd, a black man, one white supremacist Web site called King an "American hero" and asked readers to "give thanks to God" for Byrd's murder. Aryan Nations' Web site originator Black claims that he does not want to incite violence with his Web site, but notes that it would be "disingenuous" of him to reject violence between the races "because history is based on wars."

Despite the proliferation of hate sites, many analysts warn against efforts to shut them down. Anthony Pratkanis, a social psychology professor at the University of California at

Santa Cruz, who has done extensive studies on propaganda and hate groups, argues that it is difficult to hold a Web site responsible for inspiring violence unless there is a provable conspiracy against a specific group. Potok comments, "You can't sue someone or prosecute them for creating an atmosphere of hate. Those things are simply protected by the First Amendment." He argues further that hate sites serve as a safety valve, allowing the majority of racists to vent their frustrations on the Web instead of in violent acts. "I don't think suppressing free speech helps," Potok says. "It actually plugs up the safety valve to some extent." Moreover, Internet service providers, not bound by the First Amendment to accept all content, can refuse any Web site they find objectionable. Filters and parental scrutiny are the best answers for parents seeking to protect their children from hate sites.

Authors in *Opposing Viewpoints: Extremist Groups* debate issues that surround the social problems created when extremist groups clash with the rest of society in the following chapters: Are Some Religious Groups Harmful? Do Some Liberal Groups Benefit Society? Do White Supremacist Groups Promote Hate and Violence? What Extremist Groups Pose a Threat Worldwide? While the views of all groups are protected in the United States, extremist groups often push the limits of the law, earning them the scrutiny of law enforcement, politicians, the media, and countless social commentators.

CHAPTER 1

Are Some Religious Groups Harmful?

Chapter Preface

Christian Identity is a religious movement that unites many white supremacist groups throughout the United States. The movement has its roots in the British-Israelism beliefs of the nineteenth century, which held that the white race, specifically the Anglo-Saxon, Celtic, Scandinavian, and Germanic peoples, are the racial descendents of the tribes of Israel and God's true chosen people. Christian Identity espouses a variant of Christian fundamentalism mixed with virulent racism and anti-Semitism that encourages violence. In the last decade Identity followers have been tied to murder, robbery, and kidnapping, and the group is on the FBI's list of most dangerous hate groups. Identity followers are frequently members of militia groups, who stockpile food and weapons preparing for a racial Armageddon.

David Nelwert, author of *In God's Country: The Patriot Movement and the Pacific Northwest*, argues that Christian Identity is the link that connects many otherwise distinct and geographically separate extremist groups. Nelwert maintains, "Adherence to [Christian Identity] is probably the single greatest common denominator among all the various fragmented factions of the radical right wing in America. It is practiced by the neo-Nazis of the Aryan Nations, by the leaders of the Militia of Montana, and by the remnants of the Ku Klux Klan in the South." Leonard Zeskind, president of the Institute for Research and Education on Human Rights and a leading analyst of white supremacist movements, agrees with Nelwert, saying that he sees "a merger of Christian nationalism with white nationalism" occurring in the United States.

Though actual numbers of Christian Identity followers are difficult to obtain, Rosemary Radford Ruether, professor of applied theology at the Garrett Evangelical Theological Seminary at Northwestern University, estimates that there are about fifty thousand hardcore adherents who would call themselves Identity Christians. However, she claims that the numbers of adherents could be growing due to the Internet. She writes, "[Identity Christians] have recently targeted alienated white youth in affluent suburbs and have considerable presence through a number of Web sites and the promotion of racist music aimed at youth." According to the Southern Poverty Law Center, an organization that monitors extremist groups, racist Web sites and extremist rock music—often with racist or anti-Semitic lyrics—are two of the most common methods hate groups use to expand their membership by reaching young people.

Christian Identity is a racist, anti-Semitic theology that is practiced by many white supremacist groups. In the following chapter authors debate the effect of religious extremist groups on the social fabric of the United States.

*"Many who call themselves Christian . . .
teach a racist theology that is not only . . .
unacceptable to mainstream Christianity,
but also poses tangible dangers to society."*

Religion Is Easily Exploited by Extremist Groups

Matthew C. Ogilvie

Racist Christian groups pose a spiritual danger to all Christians and a physical threat to everyone who does not agree with them, Matthew C. Ogilvie argues in the following viewpoint. According to Ogilvie, racist Christians use religion to justify and further their causes. Religion, he maintains, can goad people to action, for good or ill. Matthew C. Ogilvie is an assistant professor of systematic theology at the University of Dallas in Irving, Texas.

As you read, consider the following questions:
1. The combination of which two factors in racist Christianity is cause for concern, in the author's opinion?
2. According to Ogilvie, why do racist Christians preach a theology of rebellion against gun control?
3. What arguments does Ogilvie maintain are put forth by the World Church of the Creator to justify using religion as a vehicle for race ideology?

Matthew C. Ogilvie, "Children of a White God: A Study of Racist 'Christian' Theologies," *Human Nature Daily Review*, http://human-nature.com/nibbs/01/ogilvie.html, vol. 1, October 23, 2001. Reproduced by permission of the publisher and the author.

It is common knowledge that Islamic extremism has been associated with numerous terrorist attacks around the world. It remains, though, that racist Christian theologies have also animated violent movements. One key example concerns the Oklahoma City bombing. Bomber Timothy McVeigh has been connected to white supremacist movements such as White Aryan Resistance and the Christian Identity movement, both of which promote racist theology. In Australia, racist theologies have gained attention through the medium of racist politician Pauline Hanson. Apart from her generally anti-Indigenous and anti-Asian stance, Hanson has advocated giving preference to Christian migrants over those from non-Christian backgrounds. The media attention given Ms Hanson has been accompanied by an increase in race-based violence within Australia. While one acknowledges that Ms Hanson has not articulated a "race-theology" her movement has brought out many others who do present such racist religion.

The seriousness of the threat presented by supremacist groups is reflected in the US Army's approach to antiterrorism. In the prepublication edition of *Force Protection: Antiterrorism 1997*, it is noted that there exists within the United States, "an eclectic array of extremist organizations, which do not officially condone terrorism but may serve as breeding grounds for terrorist activities." Of those extremist groups, there are those that either espouse supremacist causes, or foster discrimination or the deprivation of civil rights based on race or religion. What concerns us most is the combination of the powerful factors of supremacist feeling and race discrimination with a militaristic attitude. With that combination, race-based theologies have turned from parlour talk into matters of life and death. Of much concern is that white racists, who call themselves "Christian" and who believe in a theology that gives divine justification to their beliefs, possess arsenals of high-technology weapons, the likes of which many Middle-East terrorists would be most jealous.

Racist Christians and the Pro-Gun Lobby

Racist theology has today found itself powerful and influential voices. Of these, most prominent would be David Duke, former Ku Klux Klan leader, who was elected to the Louisiana House of Representatives. Duke proclaims that he has always been a believing Christian and that an integral part of his Christianity has been a theology of racial segregation. We read in his own work that in the name of race preservation, God has commanded genocide, segregation and anti-miscegenation, and today forbids racial intermarriage and the crossing of racial boundaries. Duke's views are certainly on the fringe of Christian thinking, but he is only the visible voice of a wider movement of people whose theology conceives violence, hate, intimidation and race conflict to be in the name of God.

In studying racist theologies, one is also struck by the connection between the racist Christians and extreme elements of the pro-gun lobby. In his reflections on "Race and Christianity," Duke proceeds directly from proposing racial segregation to outlining a theology of gun possession, in which he proclaims Christ's command for his followers to possess guns. The Christian Identity movement also follows such teaching, simultaneously demanding of its followers a theology of racial separation and a belief in Christ's command for Christians to own and be ready to use the most advanced available weapons of their day, such as an M-16 assault rifle. In addition to these beliefs, we note that racist Christians generally preach a theology of rebellion against gun control, on the grounds that it is part of a "New World Order," which is supposed to be an anti-White, anti-American and anti-Christian movement. While we shall discuss these beliefs in detail below, it should suffice for our introduction to note that there are many who call themselves Christian and who teach a racist theology that is not only intellectually unacceptable to mainstream Christianity, but also poses tangible dangers to society. . . .

Biblical Fundamentalism

Racist Christianity shares with Biblical fundamentalism a naive realist approach to scripture. This parallel should not surprise us, because many, if not most or all, racist Christians align themselves to fundamentalist Churches. While we would in no way wish to implicate most fundamentalists in racism, the fact remains that the fundamentalist method is both attractive to and has had great impact on the way that racists use their sources. Besides using an exegesis by naive realism, we would note several other characteristics common to both groups.

First, racist Christians and fundamentalists hold common views on evolution. On evolution, [Baptist minister] Bob Jones presents the fundamentalist position by declaring that, "The process of the human race has not been upward from the swamp by evolution, but downward from the garden by sin." Also from a strictly creationist viewpoint, [creationist writer and lecturer John] Mackay declares that "The current cultural status of the races . . . is a direct consequence of whether the ancestors of any race worshipped the living God, or deliberately rejected Him. There is no such thing as a primitive race evolving upwards." With fundamentalists, racist Christians believe that creation can only go backwards, not forwards. Properly speaking, the fundamentalist theory of human development is of actual devolution, rather than possible evolution. Likewise, racists believe that God has made white people as they are, and that one cannot develop positively either whites or any other race. One must either maintain one's race in stasis, or face the downward spiral of ungodly devolution.

Fear of Change

The first point ties in with our second, namely, that fundamentalism and racist Christianity are extremely negative towards human creativity. Fundamentalists exercise an extreme form of Calvinism, holding that nothing that proceeds from the nature of man can be of any goodness. Taking up Calvin's idea that all proceeding from unregenerate human nature is damnable, fundamentalists hold that only that which comes from regenerated humanity, which in practice means from within the fundamentalist fold, can be of benefit to humankind. Likewise, racist Christianity holds that nothing humankind can do to or for itself can bring about effective improvement to ourselves. We have seen in this article how racists fear race-mixing and intermarriage. The underlying assumption behind such fear is that any change to humanity will inevitably be for the worse.

This racist fear of any change contradicts Christian theology that sees human stewardship of God's creation as meaning that we are co-creators with God. This belief is reflected, in part, by the Genesis creation account's statement that God has commanded humanity to fill the earth, and subdue it, which suggests making some improvements to the earth. An oft-ignored part of Christian theology also concerns the issue of procreation. Unfortunately, the furore over contraception in Catholicism has seen the theology of procreation more often ignored or misunderstood. Understood fully, procreation refers not only to biological conception, but to the whole process and life self-giving of generating, nurturing and educating a child. Procreation thus concerns the responsibility and right of parents to bring forth and take on the ongoing care of their child. Such stewardship effectively makes parents co-creators with God. We propose that Christians would have little trouble in extending this positive theology from parent-child relationships to a theology of the entire human race's co-creation with God of itself. One can thus engender a more positive outlook on divine-human relationships than those envisaged by racism or fundamentalism.

Counter-Modern Suspicion

Thirdly, both fundamentalism and racist Christianity share a counter-modern suspicion. Racists are likely to regard modern society as intolerant and dogmatic, due to its opposition to racist ideology. As modern history, biology, theology, philosophy all provide sharp and resolute criticisms of racist thinking, it is no surprise that racists should oppose all things modern. Fundamentalists are also practically defined by their opposition to modernity, especially the modern embrace of liberal culture and religion. We may be familiar with the fundamentalist hatred for liberalism, which often translates into contempt or hatred for liberals. However, there is here significant deviation of racist Christianity from fundamentalism. Regarding fundamentalism, we find upon serious reading, that despite its abhorrence of liberalism, fundamentalism most often is defined by liberalism. By this point, we mean that from the very start, Biblical fundamentalism has been defined by its opposition to matters such as evolutionary science, critical scholarship of the Bible, and liberal, pluralist morality. [Ed] Dobson and [Ed] Hindson lend support to this idea in their discussion of the history of American fundamentalism. They introduce their work [*The Fundamentalist Phenomenon*] by noting that they shall evaluate the impact of fundamentalism by reference, among other things, to its "War with Liberalism." They also admit that, to understand fundamentalism and place it in its correct perspective, they have to deal with liberalism. The term "War with Liberalism" is Dobson and Hindson's and is the title of a chapter in their book. That "war," in practical terms, defines fundamentalism. Apart from brief references to "the Fundamentals" fundamentalists are more inclined to deal with their efforts to combat what they saw as increasing corruption and anti-Christianity in an increasingly liberal Church. Dobson and Hindson effectively define the genesis of fundamentalism by its rise as a "unified, organized effort to combat its [liberalism's] influence."

Ramirez. © 1999 by Copley News Service. Reproduced by permission.

Racist Christianity, on the other hand, though as thoroughly anti-modern as fundamentalism, is opposed to modern, liberal culture for different reasons. In the first place, racism did not start as a specific reaction to increasing liberalism. Moreover, racist Christianity does not appear to have functionally defined itself so much by its opposition to new developments in society. This is not to say that racist Christianity is not a reactive, anti-modern movement in the same way as fundamentalism. Rather, racist Christianity has its own agenda, its own identity and its own objectives. The degree and manner in which it reacts to society is defined in fairly narrow terms, as opposed to fundamentalism, which has become counter-cultural in very broad terms.

Religion as a Racist Tool

The critical observer will readily agree with our observation that racist Christianity does not derive its doctrines from an impartial reading of its sources. Race theology is, more properly speaking, not a theology so much as a predetermined ideology expressed in words commonly used within Christian theology. To be truthful, racist Christianity, though using the power of religion and religious language, does not originate within a religious context, but a social and political context that uses religion for its own purposes.

We may ask why racists use religion to further their aims. The anti-Christian World Church of the Creator (WCOTC) [which now calls itself the Creativity Movement] provides candid reasons why religion is chosen as the vehicle for race ideology. In the first place, while a political party may have some influence over part of a person's life, religion dominates all parts of a person's life. The genuinely religious person will have sublated by his or her religion all of one's life decisions concerning morality, work and economy, law, education, marriage, family and community life. Another aspect of religion is that, when firmly established, it can outlast even the most dogged of political parties or social groups. While political parties last rarely longer than a century, the well-established religion can have influence for centuries after the death of its founder.

A Cover for Moral Evils

Further insight into why religion can [be] used as a racist tool comes from the master of social manipulation. In *Mein Kampf*,

[Adolf] Hitler gave his assessment of religion's significance by stating: "Verily a man cannot serve two masters. And I consider the foundation or destruction of a religion far greater than the foundation or destruction of a state, let alone a party." Hitler went on to observe that religion can be an effective cover, even for the otherwise obvious vices of those who hide beneath religion's mantle. That religion can be used as a cover for moral evils raises for us the whole question of religious freedom. We would note that the great majority of racist Christianities have originated in the United States, a nation in which freedom of religion is sacrosanct. Unfortunately, the strength of this constitutional right, along with a certain vagueness as to what exactly constitutes a "religion" has meant that, in practical terms, "freedom of religion" has meant the right to preach any form of corruption or madness, regardless of its rationality, social implications or other concerns. Various movements repeatedly find protection from criticism, public scrutiny or proactive legal action because they fall under the mantle of "free" religions. If Hitler is right in his observations on the baser side of human nature, and his wicked success gives us every reason to think so, then we have to address seriously the question of what manner of freedom we allow religions. If we are to subject racist religions to open scrutiny, and call these faiths to account, then we must abandon the popular notion of freedom of religion as a relativist right to pursue any belief system whatsoever. Rather, one would propose a more serious notion of religious freedom as freedom from state or other coercion. That is, rather than the licence to create any form of anti-social movement, one proposes that religious freedom be conceived as the right to uncoerced worship, which right brings with it the responsibility to be reasonable and rational, and responsible towards people and society.

If we turn back to why religion is so useful to racist religionists, Hitler again provides us with helpful, even if unpalatable, reflections. Religion proves potent at controlling people's actions, Hitler surmises, because "The great masses of people do not consist of philosophers; precisely for the masses, faith is often the sole foundation of a moral attitude." Later Hitler repeated the point by claiming that the great mass of humanity consists neither of philosophers nor of saints, which means that most people never access the inner efficacy that a religion can bring. Hitler, of course, knew how to harness such religion based on "faith alone" without the foundation of either clear thinking or genuine spirituality. A popular (or *folkish*) religion, whether it be theistic or not, that demands the hearts of its followers will find itself empowered to enact all manner of activities, and find a number of willing servants who will perform even the most debased of acts, if only they are in the name of God or faith.

Religion Has Great Power—for Good or Evil

We have, then, some reflections on the potency of religion and why it is used by racist Christianity. These reflections lead one to disagree somewhat with [socialist philosopher Karl] Marx, who regarded religion as the opium of the masses—a mental policeman that maintained the social order by keeping downtrodden persons submissive and passive to the oppressive drudgery of their lives. Rather than enforcing passivity, our study of racist Christianity shows that religion can be more of a stimulant than a narcotic, driving people to action, stimulating them into frenzied action, driving their thoughts and moral decisions and sometimes even goading them into homicidal actions, all in the name of God and the promise of bliss in the hereafter. One would agree with Marx, however, that religion can and does have great power over the lives of individuals and communities. That power can have a stupefying effect in keeping oppressed people passive and subservient, or it can have the converse effect of rousing people to action and giving power to an otherwise weak position.

> "Churches and church leaders must take
> this [white supremacist] movement
> seriously, particularly given its religion-
> based ideologies that promote hatred and
> violence."

Religion Can Counter Violent Extremism

David Ostendorf

Churches are countering racist Christian theology within their communities and throughout the United States, David Ostendorf, a United Church of Christ minister and the director of the Center for New Community in Oak Park, Illinois, argues in the following viewpoint. Because many racists use religion to justify their beliefs, church leaders are in a unique position to turn the tables using the positive power of religion against the hate and violence these white supremacist groups promote. He insists that leaders mobilize their congregations and their communities to fight the bigotry that masquerades as religion.

As you read, consider the following questions:
1. According to Ostendorf, what Christian heresy grew out of nineteenth-century British Israelism?
2. Why is it a serious mistake to ignore white supremacist activity, in the author's opinion?
3. What are some of the rules that Ostendorf suggests communities should follow when they respond to hate groups?

David Ostendorf, "Countering Hatred," *The Christian Century*, vol. 116, September 8, 1999, p. 861. Copyright © 1999 by the Christian Century Foundation. Reproduced by permission.

In a nine-state area of the Midwest, 272 far-right-wing organizations—including Christian Identity, Christian Patriot, neo-Nazi and Ku Klux Klan groups—ply their racist and anti-Semitic ideologies. Hundreds of other groups are known to operate nationally, involving tens of thousands of true believers and their followers. Violence can and does erupt from their ranks, as was evident in August [1999] when former Aryan Nations security officer Buford Furrow went on a shooting rampage at a Jewish day-care center in Los Angeles and then murdered a Filipino-American postal worker.

Roots of Hatred

Religion-based hatred is the engine of the violent far-right; dreams of a white Christian homeland, free of the despised "Zionist Occupation Government," is its volatile fuel. Most of these groups have roots in the racist and anti-Semitic ideology of Christian Identity, a Christian heresy that grew out of 19th-century British Israelism. (An exception to this pattern is the World Church of the Creator [Creativity Movement], organizational home of Benjamin Smith, who in July [1999] went on a shooting spree in Illinois and Indiana, targeting minorities.)

British Israelism was advanced in the U.S. by Henry Ford and given its peculiar American twist by Wesley Swift, who founded the Church of Jesus Christ Christian in 1946. William Potter Gale, a Swift convert, shaped the racist tenets of the ideology and helped birth the Posse Commitatus, the violent arm of the movement. . . .

Organized Opposition Is Needed

But a new generation of Identity leaders has emerged . . . and is advancing the racist and anti-Semitic ideology far beyond the Aryan Nation compound. In congregations scattered across the country, and in homes and other gathering places, Identity believers worship as the "true Israel," the chosen white race. A core group of Identity pastors, including Pete Peters of LaPorte, Colorado, has spread the message of the movement. In 1992 Peters gathered some of the nation's leading white supremacists and neo-Nazis at Estes Park, Colorado, for a meeting that launched the militia movement.

Because the white supremacist movement is organized in

countless communities, its opponents need to be organized. One example of an effective response to white supremacist activity is the work of clergy in Quincy, Illinois. Quincy is a Mississippi River town of 41,000 that serves as a center of commerce for the region. This past February [1999], when clergy learned that Pete Peters was planning a March "Scriptures for America" seminar in Quincy, the ministers met to plan their response.

Immediately after the meeting, a small delegation of clergy went to the motel where the seminar was scheduled to be held. The ministers told the motel managers about the nature of the event. The managers were shocked and immediately canceled it. While the motel suffered a financial loss, its owners and managers were adamant about not providing a place for racism and anti-Semitism to be brazenly taught.

The Quincy Ministerial Association did not stop there. It organized a Sunday afternoon education event, "From Hate to Community," and held it at the same motel Peters had intended to use. Participants in this seminar were encouraged to have dinner at the motel dining room as a show of support and appreciation for the managers' actions. Seventy-five religious and community leaders participated in the seminar, which was widely advertised in church bulletins and by local media.

Standing up to white-sheeted Klansmen is one thing. It can be much more difficult to counter white-shirted Identity or neo-Nazi leaders. These may be, after all, the folk with whom we work and worship, folk who are not blatantly racist and anti-Semitic, whose stance on government or guns may seem within the realm of mainstream politics. They may not even know that their movement is rooted in the ideology of Christian Identity.

Hate Groups Must Not Be Ignored

It is, in any case, a serious mistake to ignore white supremacist activity, hoping that it will simply go away. The argument that "they will just get more press if we openly oppose them" does not hold up and has costly consequences.

Media will report on white supremacist activity, regardless of how the community responds. Media will also report—and hunger for—the story of how a community organizes its responses. When communities do not respond, the likelihood of repeated or increased white supremacist activity escalates. Failing to build public, moral barriers against hate is an open invitation to hate groups. The key to diluting its expansion and appeal is naming names, and fully exposing this racist and anti-Semitic movement to the light of day.

Kansas church leaders have practiced this kind of intervention for years, and have recently pooled their experience and commitment in a coalition with civic organizations in

The Positive Effect of Religion

Americans strongly correlate religion with individual morality and behavior, considering it one of very few antidotes to the moral decline they observe in our nation today. That's particularly important since people are increasingly alarmed by what many consider a national moral crisis caused by such factors as a declining family structure, disappearing politeness and civility and rising materialism.

Americans believe that if individuals were more religious, their behavior would improve and our society would be stronger as a result. Crime, teen pregnancy, divorce, greed, uncaring parents, unfeeling neighbors—Americans believe that such problems would be mitigated if people were more religious. And to most citizens, it doesn't matter which religion it is. In fact, for over half (53%) of those surveyed, being religious means "making sure that one's behavior and day-to-day actions match one's faith," not attending religious services or even feeling the presence of God.

In short, people equate religion with personal ethics and morality. And as a result, seven in ten (70%) Americans want religion's influence on American society to grow. However, alongside this strong conviction that religion benefits society is an equally strong adherence to a respect for religious diversity that translates into a surprising tolerance of other people's beliefs and practices. This is no mere lip service on the public's part, nor is it an abstract ideal that disintegrates the moment it is tested. Americans seem to have an ingrained expectation that they will encounter people with different ideas about religion in their daily lives, and the idea of tolerance is so well accepted that it has been absorbed into daily standards for social conduct.

Deborah Wadsworth, "For Goodness' Sake: Why So Many Want Religion to Play a Greater Role in American Life," Public Agenda Survey, 2001.

Kansas City and Topeka. The Kansas Area Conference of the United Methodist Church has been particularly outspoken in countering Christian Identity and the militia movement in rural areas of the state. Kansas Ecumenical Ministries is an important partner in this effort. In cooperation with the Mainstream Coalition, Concerned Citizens of Topeka and the Jewish Community Relations Bureau, a longstanding ally in the struggle against organized hate group activity in Kansas, religious and civic leaders are exploring new strategies to curtail this movement.

Churches and church leaders must take this movement seriously, particularly given its religion-based ideologies that promote hatred and violence. The need is all the more urgent as movement leaders become adept at recruiting youth through music and other entry points. White supremacist bands travel the country, and their compact discs can be found in suburban record stores. Their links to the National Socialist movement are now complete with William Pierce's acquisition of Resistance Records, the nation's largest distributor of white supremacist music. Pierce, a neo-Nazi, is the author of *The Turner Diaries*, the book that inspired the Oklahoma City bombing.

When responding to hate groups, communities should remember these rules: Document the problem, expose the group, and stay informed about its local activities. Create a moral barrier against hate by speaking out and by organizing counter-responses. Build coalitions and seek to keep those coalitions together for the long haul to counter racism, anti-Semitism, bigotry and scapegoating. Assist the victims. Reach out to the constituencies targeted for recruitment. Target the entire community, including youth, for education and action. Remember that hate groups are not a fringe phenomenon. Seek to address broad social, economic and racial concerns.

Religious Leaders Must Stand Against Hate

Several years ago a friend participated in a peaceful protest that directly confronted a white supremacist group. Until that point the city leaders had decided to stay as far away from the group as possible. They held a unity rally and then hoped that the haters would be ignored.

Following the protest my friend, an experienced labor organizer, called me up and in an unusually subdued voice reported that she had never in her life felt the presence of evil as she did that day. She had looked around for moral support and counsel from the religious community, but found no one. No religious leaders were present to stand with her and others against the evil.

Anastasis. Resurrection. To stand against the forces of death. That's what we are called to do in the face of this hateful and violent racist movement, which often offers a twisted version of the Christian faith.

"*On campuses across this country . . . are organizations that promote the culture of Islamic terrorism and its . . . anti-American agendas.*"

Islamic Fundamentalists in the United States Pose a Serious Threat

David Horowitz

David Horowitz argues in the following viewpoint that radical Islamic fundamentalist groups organize on university campuses, promote anti-American agendas, and lure idealistic students into terrorist activities. He maintains that one such group, the Muslim Student Association (MSA), routinely invites pro-terrorist, anti-democratic speakers to campuses where it operates. Further, under the guise of social activism, the MSA encourages impressionable American students to become involved in Islamic-sponsored, anti-Western terrorism, usually directed against Israel. David Horowitz is a nationally known writer and political activist.

As you read, consider the following questions:

1. According to the author, why did the Black Panthers disintegrate in the 1970s?
2. What group does Horowitz argue has become the Black Panthers of the contemporary antiwar movement?
3. What is the purpose of the International Solidarity Campaign, in Horowitz's opinion?

When I was a college radical and anti-war activist forty years ago, I was quite the intellectual and (in my estimation) cautious and sober. Though I became an editor and then co-editor of the leading radical magazine of the Sixties, *Ramparts*, I never threw a rock during the entire era. I never joined a radical sect and never went to Communist Cuba or North Vietnam, which were then the meccas of the radical faith. Although I was a founder of an organization called the "Vietnam Solidarity Campaign," I never fooled myself that the Communist state that would result from an American defeat would be a "rice roots democracy," the way Tom Hayden and other leaders of the "New Left" movement proclaimed.

Nonetheless, before the era was over, I was lured by my desire to do humanitarian good and to further the cause of social justice into working with the Black Panthers, a group of radical gangsters who in 1974 murdered a friend of mine (the mother of three children) and a dozen other individuals besides. The project I had become involved in with the Panthers was building an elementary school.

From the vantage of the political and cultural left, my activities with the Black Panthers were neither marginal [n]or extreme. At the time, the Panthers were icons of the progressive intellectuals, symbolizing strong black leaders who were standing up for their "oppressed" community. The entire liberal culture supported them. Leading cultural figures like Garry Wills and Murray Kempton were writing praises of the Panthers in the *New York Times* Sunday magazine. Kempton even compared their leader Huey Newton to Mahatma Gandhi and Martin Luther in the *Times*' august pages. To this day *The New York Times*, *The Washington Post* and other pillars of the American political culture, celebrate the Panthers—the murderers of my friend and a dozen others—as icons of the "social struggle."

Radical Groups Promote Islamic Terrorism

Fortunately, the Panthers disintegrated in the early Seventies, dragged down by their criminal activities, internecine battles and the sordid brutality of their leaders, Huey Newton and Eldridge Cleaver. Before he died, Cleaver told a *Sixty*

Minutes audience, "If people had listened to Huey Newton and me in the Sixties, there would have been a holocaust in this country." Many radicals, among them Cleaver's most prominent promoter—*Los Angles Times* columnist Robert Scheer—looked forward to that holocaust and actively encouraged it. The Panthers were the "noble savages" of liberal compassion, symbols of the injustice that America was said to be inflicting on American blacks.

What would have happened if the Panthers had remained intact to the present? What if they had been the arm of an international terror network whose goal was the destruction of the United States? There are such groups in America today. They are radical groups who identify with the violent *jihad* [holy war] of Islamacist terror organizations like al-Qaeda, Hizbollah, Islamic Jihad and Hamas. And they have the support of a radical culture that regards America as the Great Satan, and Muslims and Arabs as the people whom America oppresses.

On campuses across this country, embedded in the leadership of every radical "anti-war" protest group, are organizations that promote the culture of Islamic terrorism and its anti-Western, anti-Israeli and anti-American agendas. One that will serve as an example for the others is the radical Muslim Student Association (MSA). The Muslim Student Association is an organization financed by the Saudis and also by student funds at every university where it operates. The ideas and enthusiasms that it promotes among impressionable college students should give every American cause for concern.

On October 22, 2000, Ahmed Shama, president of the UCLA [University of California, Los Angeles] Muslim Students Association led a crowd of demonstrators at the Israeli consulate in chants of "Death to Israel!" and "Death to the Jews!" Shama declared that [Israeli leader] Ehud Barak, [Palestinian leader] Yassir Arafat and [U.S. president] Bill Clinton were all "racist zionists." "When we see that a peace process is being negotiated between Zionists, mediated by Zionists, controlled by Zionists, and being portrayed in the media by Zionists, we come and we condemn all of you," Shama said.

Militant Islam Is a Threat to the United States

The Muslim population in this country is not like any other group, for it includes within it a substantial body of people—many times more numerous than the agents of [terrorist] Osama bin Ladin—who share with the suicide hijackers a hatred of the United States and the desire, ultimately, to transform it into a nation living under the strictures of militant Islam. Although not responsible for the atrocities [on September 11, 2001], they harbor designs for this country that warrant urgent and serious attention.

In June 1991, Siraj Wahaj, a black convert to Islam and the recipient of some of the American community's highest honors, had the privilege of becoming the first Muslim to deliver the daily prayer in the U.S. House of Representatives. On that occasion he recited from the Qur'an and appealed to the Almighty to guide American leaders "and grant them righteousness and wisdom."

A little over a year later, addressing an audience of New Jersey Muslims, the same Wahaj articulated a rather different vision from his mild and moderate invocation in the House. If only Muslims were more clever politically, he told his New Jersey listeners, they could take over the United States and replace its constitutional government with a caliphate. "If we were united and strong, we'd elect our own emir [leader] and give allegiance to him. . . . [T]ake my word, if 6–8 million Muslims unite in America, the country will come to us." In 1995, Wahaj served as a character witness for Omar Abdel Rahman in the trial that found that blind sheikh guilty of conspiracy to overthrow the government of the United States. More alarming still, the U.S. attorney for New York listed Wahaj as one of the "unindicted persons who may be alleged as co-conspirators" in the sheikh's case.

Daniel Pipes, *Commentary*, November 2001.

Pro-Terrorist Speakers

One of the invited speakers at the event was Hamid Ayloush, a member of the Council on American-Islamic Relations (CAIR), which was also an event sponsor. In his speech, Ayloush solicited contributions for the Holy Land Foundation, an organization that the Justice Department has shut down as [a] funder of al-Qaeda.

On May 26, 2001 the UCLA Muslim Student Association held a conference of Islamic radicals on the UCLA campus.

The conference featured speakers from CAIR whose founder is a supporter of the terrorist organization Hamas, and the Muslim Public Affairs council, a radical group whose executive director has justified the terrorist killing of 243 U.S. marines in Lebanon in 1983 by Hizbollah suicide bombers: "This attack, for all the pain it caused, was not in a strict sense, a terrorist operation. It was a military operation, producing no civilian casualties—exactly the kind of attack that Americans might have lauded had it been directed against Washington's enemies."

The UCLA Muslim Student Association has routinely invited pro-terrorist speakers to the UCLA campus and paid for them with student funds. At a January 21, 2001 event, nine months before 9/11, a speaker called Imam Musa, an African-American Muslim who is a staple of the anti-war rallies staged in Washington DC declared: "If you were to say that the Soviet Union was wiped off the face of the earth . . . people would have thought you were crazy, right? The people of Afghanistan didn't have the intellect or historical knowledge to know that they wasn't supposed to wipe out the Soviet Union, is that right? . . . We saw the fall of one so-called superpower, Old Sam is next."[1]

Praising Bin Laden

Prior to [the September 11, 2001, terrorist attacks] the UCLA magazine *Al-Talib* featured a cover story on [al-Qaeda leader] Osama Bin Laden titled, "The Spirit of Jihad." The editorial declares:

> When we hear someone refer to the great mujahideen Osama Bin-Ladin as a 'terrorist' we should defend our brother and refer to him as a freedom fighter; someone who has forsaken wealth and power to fight in Allah's cause and speak out against oppressors. We take these stances only to please Allah.

Two days before 9/11, *Al-Talib* co-sponsored a dinner at [the] University of California, Irvine to honor then accused (and subsequently convicted) cop-killer (and Imam [religious leader]) Jamil Al-Amin—aka H. Rap Brown. Another cop-

---

1. The Soviet Union occupied Afghanistan from 1979 to 1989.

killer favored by Muslim student groups and by the anti-war movement generally is Mumia Abu Jamal. Imam Musa spoke here as well:

> You think Zionism and Palestine is the only dictatorial power in the world. We're telling you about apartheid right here in America. . . . When you fight Old Sam, you are fighting someone that is superior in criminality and Nazism. The American criminalizer is the most skillful oppressor that the world has ever known.

The Palestinian terrorists have become the Black Panthers of the contemporary anti-war movement. The leftwing culture celebrates the suicide bombers of women and children as desperate victims of Jewish oppression. Attackers and destroyers of the Oslo peace process [between the Palestinians and Israelis] are proclaimed as heroes. Terrorists and totalitarian radicals are lionized as fighters for social justice. Israelis and Americans are condemned as Nazis.

Students Are Seduced by Terrorism

How many American college students and anti-war activists have been seduced by these poisonous elements at work in our society? It is difficult to know. But one who has already paid for it with her life is Rachel Corrie, a 24 year old undergraduate at Evergreen College in Olympia Washington, who has become known as the "Saint of Rafiah," the name of the West Bank town where she died. Evergreen is one of the many leftwing campuses in America, whose values have been turned so upside down by tenured leftists that it recently featured convicted murderer Mumia Abu Jamal as its commencement speaker. (He spoke via tape [because he is in prison]).

Rachel Corrie began her activist career as a member of the Olympia Movement for Justice and Peace, an organization formed directly after the 9/11 attack on America to oppose an American military response. Its members feared that, "America would retaliate by bombing some of the poorest and most oppressed on earth, the Afghan people."[2] Their Marxist view of the world is captured in one of the

---

2. According to the George W. Bush administration, Afghanistan harbored al-Qaeda, the terrorist group responsible for the September 11 attacks.

Movement's favored slogans: "Corporate Globalization Equals Imperialist Domination."

It was not long after she joined the Olympia Movement that Rachel Corrie was burning an American flag in the name of social justice. It was logical step for her to gravitate to an organization that would demonstrate her commitment to the cause. Through her contacts in the anti-war movement she joined the International Solidarity Campaign, whose purpose is to recruit young Americans to become human shields for Palestinian terrorists. The Solidarity Campaign's ties to terrorism became inescapable eleven days after Rachel Corrie's death when an elite anti-terror unit of the Israeli Defense Forces captured a senior Islamic Jihad terrorist, Shadi Sukiya hiding in its offices in Jenin.

Rachel Corrie was sent by International Solidarity to a town called Rafiah in the Gaza Strip to obstruct Israeli Defense Forces conducting anti-terror operations. She sat down in front of an Israeli military bulldozer, and—according to an American eyewitness—was inadvertently killed when the machine, whose driver could not see her, ran over her. . . . The *New York Times Magazine*—the same magazine that once celebrated the murderer of my friend by the Black Panthers—had a tribute to Rachel Corrie, to her humanitarian goodwill. The article was called "One Last Sit-In," to wrap the halo of Martin Luther King and the civil rights movement around her pro-terrorist activities. The *Times* article summarized the news reports of Corrie's death in these words: "23-year-old peace activist from Olympia, Wash., crushed to death by an Israeli Army bulldozer as she tried to block the demolition of a physician's home in Gaza."

4

"*Major Arab and Muslim organizations issued statements strongly condemning the [terrorist] attacks [by Arabs against the United States].*"

Most Followers of Islam in the United States Reject Terrorism

Shibley Telhami

Shibley Telhami argues in the following viewpoint that, like all Americans, Arab and Muslim Americans are horrified by the September 11, 2001, terrorist attacks on the United States and are seeking solutions to terrorism. Further, Telhami insists that a majority of Arab Americans—69 percent—are in favor of "an all-out war against countries which harbor or aid terrorists." Moreover, while many Arab Americans report racial profiling since the attacks, 54 percent believe that extra questioning of people with Middle Eastern accents or facial features by police is justified. Shibley Telhami is the Anwar Sadat Professor at the University of Maryland.

As you read, consider the following questions:

1. According to Telhami, from which countries do most Arab Americans come?
2. Who was the first sitting president to speak at conferences of Arab-American organizations, according to the author?
3. In Telhami's opinion, on what issue are Arab Americans in almost complete agreement?

Shibley Telhami, "Arab and Muslim America: A Snapshot," *The Brookings Review*, vol. 20, Winter 2002, pp. 14–15. Copyright © 2002 by The Brookings Institution. Reproduced by permission.

In a *New York Times* article appearing a week after the horror [of the terrorist attacks] that befell America on September 11, [2001,] a Muslim woman described her dilemma this way: "I am so used to thinking about myself as a New Yorker that it took me a few days to begin to see myself as a stranger might: a Muslim woman, an outsider, perhaps an enemy of the city. Before last week, I had thought of myself as a lawyer, a feminist, a wife, a sister, a friend, a woman on the street. Now I begin to see myself as a brown woman who bears a vague resemblance to the images of terrorists we see on television and in the newspapers. I can only imagine how much more difficult it is for men who look like [terrorists] Mohamed Atta or Osama bin Laden."

Excruciating moments like those the nation experienced [in] September [2001] test the identity of all Americans, but especially those whose identity may be caught in the middle. Many Arab and Muslim Americans lost loved ones and friends in the attacks in New York and Washington, and others had loved ones dispatched to Afghanistan as American soldiers to punish those who perpetrated the horror (Muslims are the largest minority religion in the U.S. armed forces). But many also had double fears for their own children. On the one hand, they shared the fears of all Americans about the new risks of terror; on the other, they were gripped by the haunting fear of their children being humiliated in school for who they are.

Two Partially Overlapping Communities

There is much that's misunderstood about Arabs and Muslims in America. Although the two communities share a great deal, they differ significantly in their make-up. Most Arabs in America are not Muslim, and most Muslims are not Arabs. Most Arab Americans came from Lebanon and Syria, in several waves of immigration beginning at the outset of the 20th century. Most Muslim Americans are African American or from South Asia. Many of the early Arab immigrants assimilated well in American society. Arab-American organizations are fond of highlighting prominent Americans of at least partial Arab descent. Ralph Nader, George Mitchell, John Sununu, Donna Shalala, Spencer Abraham, Bobby Rahal, Doug

Flutie, Jacques Nasser, Paul Anka, Frank Zappa, Paula Abdul, among many others. Like other ethnic groups in America, Arabs and Muslims have produced many successful Americans whose ethnic background is merely an afterthought.

Arab Americans now number more than 3 million, Muslims roughly 6 million (though estimates range from 3 million to 10 million). The income of Arab Americans is among the highest of any American ethnic group—second only to that of Jewish Americans. Arab Americans have become increasingly politicized over the years. According to a recent survey, proportionately more Arab Americans contribute to presidential candidates than any other ethnic group—and the groups surveyed included Asian Americans, Italian Americans, African Americans, Hispanic Americans, and Jewish Americans. Over the past decade especially, Arab-American political clout has increased. Although Arab Americans were long shunned by political candidates, President [Bill] Clinton became the first sitting president to speak at conferences of Arab-American organizations, and both President Clinton and President [George W.] Bush have normalized ongoing consultations with Arab- and Muslim-American leaders. In the fall 2000 election, presidential candidates sought the support of Arab Americans, not only for campaign contributions, but also as swing voters in key states, especially Michigan. The September 11 tragedy, coming just as Arab-American political clout was ascendant, has provided a real test for the community's role in American society and politics.

The Impact of September 11

For Arab and Muslim leaders, the terrorist crisis has been like no other. It has forced them to contemplate profoundly their identity. Are they Arabs and Muslims living in America, or are they Americans with Arab and Muslim background? The answer came within hours after the terrorist attacks. Major Arab and Muslim organizations issued statements strongly condemning the attacks, refusing to allow their typical frustrations with issues of American policy in the Middle East to become linked to their rejection of the terror. Rarely have Arab and Muslim organizations in the United States been so assertive.

The enormity of the horror, the Middle Eastern background of the terrorists, and the terrorists' attempt to use religion to justify their acts have inevitably led to episodes of discrimination against Arabs and Muslims, as well as against those, such as Sikhs, who resemble them. But the support that both Arabs and Muslims received from thousands of people and organizations far outweighed the negative reaction. Arab and Muslim organizations were flooded with letters and calls of empathy from leaders and ordinary Americans, including many Jewish Americans, for most understood that at stake were the civil liberties of all Americans.

Muslim American Leader Condemns Terrorism

The president of the American Muslim Council, Yahia Basha, has praised President [George W.] Bush for his swift, decisive steps to declare war on terrorism and simultaneously protect the Muslim American and Arab American communities from ethnic backlash following the September 11 [2001] terrorist attacks. . . .

"When the United States got attacked, we Muslim Americans felt we ourselves had been violated. We lost many people in those attacks. We are American. We are here as part of this nation," Basha said. . . .

Basha said members of the Muslim and Arab communities in the United States have stepped forward with offers to help U.S. law enforcement agencies combat the terrorist threat.

"Muslim Americans and Arab Americans have volunteered their knowledge of languages and other things to American law enforcement agencies to help them catch terrorists and fight terrorism. We support in any way we can the campaign against terrorism. I don't think any human being or religion could justify those crimes," Basha said.

He said the true teachings of Islam have nothing to do with violence and terrorism.

U.S. Department of State International Information Programs, "Muslim American Leader Condemns Terrorism," October 9, 2001.

In large part, the public reaction was a product of quick decisions and statements by President Bush and members of his cabinet, members of Congress from both parties, and local political leaders. The president in particular acted quickly to make two central points that seem to have resonated with most of the public. The first was that the terrorists did not represent Islam and that Osama bin Laden must not be allowed to turn his terror into a conflict between Islam and the West. The second was that Muslim and Arab Americans are loyal Americans whose rights must be respected. Bush's early appearance at a Washington, D.C., mosque with Muslim-American leaders underlined the message.

The President Acted Correctly

The message seems to have gotten through. Despite the fears that many Americans now associate with people of Middle-Eastern background, a survey conducted in late October [2001] by Zogby International found that most Americans view the Muslim religion positively and that the vast majority of Arabs and Muslims approve the president's handling of the crisis. (Among Arab Americans, 83 percent give President Bush a positive performance rating.) Moreover, 69 percent of Arab Americans support "an all-out war against countries which harbor or aid terrorists."

Certainly, the events of September 11 will intensify the debate within the Arab and Muslim communities in America about who they are and what their priorities should be. One thing is already clear. Although both communities have asserted their American identity as never before and although 65 percent of Arab Americans feel embarrassed because the attacks were apparently committed by people from Arab countries, their pride in their heritage has not diminished. The October survey found that 88 percent of Arab Americans are extremely proud of their heritage. So far, however, the terrorist attacks have not affected the priorities of the Arab public in America as might be expected, given Arab Americans' deep fear of discrimination.

Support for Profiling

Typically, Arab-American organizations highlight such domestic issues as secret evidence and racial profiling and such foreign policy issues as Jerusalem, Iraq, and the Palestinian-Israeli conflict. While Arab Americans, like other minorities, are involved in all American issues and are divided as Democrats and Republicans, as groups they inevitably focus on issues about which they tend to agree. The situation is no different from that of American Jews, who are also diverse, but whose organizations largely focus on issues of common interest.

Given the fear of profiling that Arab Americans had even before September, one would expect this issue to have become central for most of them since September 11. And for many it certainly has. Arab-American organizations, especially, have focused on it. But the findings of the Zogby poll among Arab Americans in October were surprising. Although 32 percent of Arab Americans reported having personally experienced discrimination in the past because of their ethnicity, and although 37 percent said they or their family members had experienced discrimination since September 11, 36 percent nevertheless supported profiling of Arab Americans, while 58 percent did not. Surprisingly, 54 percent of Arab Americans believed that law enforcement officials are justified in engaging in extra questioning and inspections of people with Middle Eastern accents or features.

Palestinian-Israeli Dispute Must Be Resolved

Though their views on profiling have been mixed since September 11, Arab Americans have been considerably more unanimous on one subject—the need to resolve the Palestinian-Israeli dispute. Seventy-eight percent of those surveyed agreed that "a U.S. commitment to settle the Israeli-Palestinian dispute would help the president's efforts in the war against terrorism." Although most Arab Americans are Christian and mostly from Lebanon and Syria—and only a minority are Palestinians—their collective consciousness has been affected by the Palestinian issue in the same way that Arab consciousness in the Middle East has been affected. In a survey I commissioned in five Arab states (Lebanon, Syria, United Arab Emirates, Saudi Arabia, and Egypt) . . . majorities in each country consistently ranked the Palestinian issue as "the single most important issue to them personally." The role of this issue in the collective consciousness of many Arabs and Muslims worldwide is akin to the role that Israel has come to play in contemporary Jewish identity.

Like all Americans since September 11, Arab and Muslim Americans are searching for solutions to terrorism. Like all Americans, they are also finding new meaning in aspects of their identity to which they might have given little thought a few short months ago.

> "*Christian nationalists seek to eviscerate the capacity of federal courts to protect the religious freedom and equality of all Americans.*"

The Religious Right Has a Harmful Agenda

Frederick Clarkson

The religious Right seeks to restore a Christian constitution that never existed, promoting their political vision of the United States as a Christian nation, Frederick Clarkson maintains in the following viewpoint. Clarkson argues that the religious Right's notion of the United States as a Christian theocracy has no historical basis and is in direct opposition to the Constitution. He contends that the religious Right is trying to undermine religious freedom in America. Frederick Clarkson is the author of *Eternal Hostility: The Struggle Between Theocracy and Democracy.* He also writes for the *Christian Science Monitor.*

As you read, consider the following questions:

1. Why is Roy Moore called "the Ten Commandments judge," in Clarkson's opinion?
2. According to the author, what would the Constitutional Restoration Act do?
3. What action does Clarkson argue was a judicial break with Christian America?

Was the United States founded as a "Christian nation"? For many conservative Christians there is no question about it. In fact, this is one of the primary ideas animating and informing the Christian right in the US. We are likely to hear a great deal about it this election year [2004]— thanks to Roy Moore, the former chief justice of the Alabama Supreme Court, who is at the center of a national campaign to alter the course of history. Depending on whom you talk to, Mr. Moore is alternately a hero, a crackpot, or a demagogue.

Whatever one's view, Moore, known to many as "the Ten Commandments judge," has come to personify a revisionist view of American history—one that, if it gains wide currency, threatens to erode the culture, and constitutional principle, of religious pluralism in the US.

Moore's story is already the stuff of legend. After being elected chief justice, he had a 5,280-pound monument to the Ten Commandments installed in the rotunda of Alabama's state judicial building in 2001. Moore insisted he had a First Amendment right to "acknowledge God" as the "moral foundation of law." The result of the inevitable lawsuit was US District Judge Myron Thompson's decision that Moore had violated the establishment clause of the First Amendment by creating "a religious sanctuary within the walls of a courthouse." When Moore refused to remove the rock, he was removed from office.

Judge Thompson got it right. But Moore and his allies see the decision as a defining moment in their campaign to "overthrow judicial tyranny." At stake over the long haul is the authority of the courts to protect individual civil rights against religious and political majoritarianism.

Constitution Restoration Act

On one front, leaders on the Christian Right are organizing Ten Commandments rallies across the country. The charismatic Moore is often the headliner. A recent rally in Dallas drew 5,000 people. Meanwhile in Congress, US Rep. Robert Aderholt and Sen. Richard Shelby, both of Alabama, have introduced a bill (written by Moore and his lawyer) that would remove jurisdiction from the federal courts over all matters involving the "acknowledgement of God" in the public arena, including school prayer, the pledge of allegiance, and the posting of the Ten Commandments in public buildings. The Constitution Restoration Act would be retroactive, apparently to undo many federal and Supreme Court decisions—such as Moore's case.

While the bill is unlikely to pass this year, it does suggest the emerging contours of the debate.[1]

Although Moore's movement has gained some political traction, its core premise has a fundamental flaw: It aims to "restore" a Christian constitution that never existed. And this presents challenges for Moore and his allies as they attempt to invoke the framers of the Constitution in support of their contemporary notions of a Biblically based society.

Last August, for example, James Dobson, head of Focus on the Family, rallied with Moore in front of the Alabama state courthouse.

"I checked yesterday with my research team," Dr. Dobson announced. "There are only two references to religion in the Constitution." The first, from the preamble, he said, refers to securing "the blessings of liberty," which, he asserted, "came from God" (although there is nothing in the document to support that view.) The other was the First Amendment's establishment clause that, he said, "has given such occasion for mischief by the Supreme Court."

Disestablishment of Christian Churches

However, Dobson's researchers missed—or ignored—Article Six of the Constitution. That's the one barring religious tests for public office and set in motion disestablishment of the Christian churches that had served as arbiters of colonial citizenship and government for 150 years.

Mainstream historian Gary Wills writes that the framers' major innovation was "disestablishment."

"No other government in the history of the world," he writes, "had launched itself without the help of officially recognized gods and their state connected ministers."

Christian Right historian Gary North agrees. The ratifica-

1. The bill did not pass.

The Religious Right's Scorecard for Congress

The graphs and tables below tell a story. They portray a Congress that is highly polarized, and they dispel two important myths:

Myth 1) There isn't much difference between the two political parties.

Myth 2) The Religious Right has grown into obscurity.

According to ratings of key organizations of the Religious Right, members of Congress who support their agenda overwhelmingly dominate the Republican Party. The following graph is based on how Christian Coalition rated the United States Senate in 2001, the most recent year their scorecards for the U.S. Senate are available.

U.S. Senate—2001
Christian Coalition Scorecard

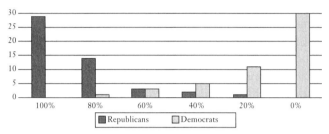

29 Senators voted with Christian Coalition 100% of the time. They were all Republican. 30 Senators received a 0 rating from Christian Coalition meaning they never voted with their issues. They were all Democrat.

U.S. House of Representatives—2001
Christian Coalition Scorecard

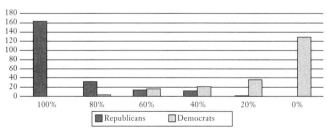

163 Republicans and 1 Democrat received scores of 100%. 32 Republicans and 3 Democrats received scores of 80%. 16 Republicans and 14 Democrats received scores of 60%. 12 Republicans and 22 Democrats received 40%. 1 Republican and 36 Democrats received 20%. 129 Democrats and no Republicans received 0.

"Scorecards: Snapshots of Congress," www.4religious-right.info, May 1, 2004.

tion of the Constitution was a "judicial break with Christian America." Article Six provided a "legal barrier to Christian theocracy" leading "directly to the rise of religious pluralism," he declares in *Political Polytheism: The Myth of Pluralism*. Indeed, history shows that the framers of the Constitution sought to establish religious equality among citizens and in government. But, as Christian nationalists seek to eviscerate the capacity of federal courts to protect the religious freedom and equality of all Americans, we can expect that one of their main tactics and goals will continue to be the revision of history itself.

> *"The religious Right has acted as an often lonely source of resistance to the complete triumph of relativism in our culture and libertinism in our behavior."*

The Religious Right Has a Beneficial Agenda

Norman Podhoretz

In the following viewpoint Norman Podhoretz insists that there is no reason to fear that the religious Right is trying to make the United States into a Christian theocracy or has any other harmful agenda. On the contrary, Podhertz argues that the religious Right offers many positive virtues. He maintains that conservative Christian communities help maintain standards of behavior and offer staunch resistance to the triumph of relativism in American culture. Norman Podhoretz is a nationally known author and former editor of *Commentary* magazine.

As you read, consider the following questions:

1. In Podhoretz's opinion, why are Jewish people more likely to fear the Christian Right than other groups?
2. According to the author, why did fundamentalist Christians become politically involved?
3. What is the basis for Podhoretz's argument that liberals are not as unhappy with the Christian Right as they profess to be?

Norman Podhoretz, "Essay: The Christian Right and Its Demonizers," *National Review*, April 3, 2000. Copyright © 2000 by National Review, Inc., 215 Lexington Avenue, New York, NY 10016. Reproduced by permission.

Who's afraid of the religious Right? Not I. And yet, as a "New York intellectual," I am precisely the type of person who is supposed to be trembling with apprehension at the baneful influence conservative Christians have gained within the Republican party and, through it, on the nation as a whole.

Of course, though to the manner born, I am not a typical New York intellectual. Most members of my breed are situated somewhere left of center, and I have long since migrated to a position on the other side of the political divide. Yet even the tiny handful of my former fellows who so much as barely tolerate my apostasy, at least in certain of its aspects, still taunt me with a classic piece of black humor: "Other than that, Mrs. Lincoln, how did you like the play?"

The "that" in the case of this "Mrs. Lincoln" refers to the alleged extremism and bigotry for which John McCain recently attacked [fundamentalists] Pat Robertson and Jerry Falwell. That speech may have destroyed McCain's chances of beating George W. Bush in the presidential primaries. And yet he was only saying out loud what is believed by vast numbers of the non-Republican-independents and crossover Democrats—on whom he had been counting to carry him to the nomination [for president in 2000].

Why then did the speech do him damage? The answer is that any gains he may have made with these voters could not compensate for the losses he sustained among others who, whether religious or not, are not strict secularists. In fact, even many Catholics seem to have resented McCain's assault on Robertson and Falwell, since they took it as an attack on the role of religion in general in our politics. On this point, the old sectarian animosities were trumped by a growing tendency among Catholics and Protestants to view seriousness about "traditional values" as more important than the specific theological etiology of that seriousness.

Fear of the Christian Right

But not, I would be willing to bet, among Jews. Now, like many New York intellectuals (though not quite so many as is often imagined), I am Jewish. This makes my attitude doubly untypical. Indeed, a good guess would be that an even higher percentage of American Jews in general than of New York intellectuals (Jewish or not) are afraid of the Christian Right.

As Jews, my coreligionists are responding in part to inherited—and well-grounded—ancestral anxieties over the prevalence of anti-Semitism in conservative Christian circles. Never mind that, in the justly celebrated quip of Irving Kristol (a New York Jewish intellectual who preceded me in the political migration from left to right), Christians in America today are less interested in persecuting Jews than in marrying their sons and daughters. This undoubtedly poses a threat to what has come to be known as "Jewish continuity." But it is surely a benign one compared with the experience of the past, when Christian hostility toward Jews more often took forms ranging from discrimination to forced conversion, expulsion, and murder.

Never mind, too, that the charges of anti-Semitism which have been made against Pat Robertson are unsustainable. True, he has written a few off-the-wall things about an alleged conspiracy between Freemasons and Jewish bankers to take over the world in the 18th century. It is also true that he has sharply criticized "Jewish intellectuals and media activists" of today for playing a part in "the assault on Christianity."

Yet unlike the crackpot theory about the 18th century, his charge against the intellectuals and media activists of Jewish origin cannot so easily be dismissed. (It is important to recognize, however, that these particular persons tend to be the ones who have been described as "non-Jewish Jews.")

Furthermore, with regard to the concerns of present-day "Jewish Jews," Robertson has been a staunch friend. He has supported Israel through thick and thin; and when the Soviet Union still existed, he contributed large sums of money to help Jews emigrate. Would that all Christians were so anti-Semitic. . . .

Anti-Semitism Has Declined Among Christians

Speaking first as a Jew, even if I shared to some degree in the paranoid interpretation of the Christian Right's agenda, I would still not be afraid of it. For quite apart from the sharp decline of anti-Semitism among Christians, there seems to me not the remotest chance that any Supreme Court—not even one composed of five Antonin Scalias and four Clarence Thomases—would read the First Amendment's prohibition of "an establishment of religion" as sanctioning this country to be declared officially Christian.

Moreover, the paranoid interpretation in this instance has no more basis in reality than paranoia does in any other situation. Evangelical and fundamentalist Christians were once content to render unto Caesar what was Caesar's and to concentrate on saving their own souls. What drew them into politics, first behind Jerry Falwell's Moral Majority and then Pat Robertson's Christian Coalition, was not any wish to impose their own views and mores on the rest of us. On the contrary: Far from being an aggressive move, it was a defensive one. They were trying to protect their own communities from the aggressions the liberal culture was committing against them, with the aid of the courts, the federal bureaucracies, and the ubiquitous media.

The Religious Right Works for Human Good

The broader evangelical tradition, from which the Christian Right emerged, proved politically self-conscious and socially reformist from its beginnings in the early nineteenth century. Though evangelicals were as ideologically diverse then as they are now, there can be little doubt that many joined (if not led) the fight against slavery and the abuse of alcohol. Although the specific issues that the Christian Right has focused upon in the 1990s have changed—abortion, homosexuality, gun control, prayer in the schools—the important point to note is that a determination to reach out and construct or reconstruct society in terms of a larger image of human good has remained constant. One does not need to agree with all or even any of the Christian Right's prescriptions in order to see how profoundly American its missionary-like activism really is.

Grant Wacker, National Humanities Center, October 2000.

In this the Christian Right failed—so dismally that some of the people who persuaded them that political activism was the only way to defend themselves are now counseling an abandonment of that particular field and a retreat into the old insularity.

But now let me put on my intellectual's hat and explain why in that capacity I do not fear the Christian Right either. Take, to begin with, the cultural backwardness—in shorthand, the William Jennings Bryan anti-intellectual streak—that repels so many of my fellow intellectuals. Where an issue like the teaching of creationism is concerned, one does not need to be an uncritical Darwinist to think the intellectuals have a point—and the recent poll showing overwhelming support for including creationism in the curriculum makes that point stronger. But what the intellectuals ignore is that there has been a reversal of roles between the Bryan and [Clarence] Darrow traditions.[1] Nowadays a far greater threat to scientific progress and cultural freedom comes from the secular Left than from the religious Right—as witness the promulgation of speech codes on the campus, and the attempts there to proscribe any deviation from the officially approved line on subjects as diverse as IQ, homosexuality, and affirmative action.

Virtues of the Religious Right

But it would be dishonest of me to suggest that my attitude toward the religious Right is merely characterized by an absence of fear. For I must confess that I think this movement has certain positive virtues.

For one thing, the conservative Christian communities have served as a reminder of the religious foundations on which this country was established and on whose capital its democratic system still draws. And for another, the religious Right has acted as an often lonely source of resistance to the complete triumph of relativism in our culture and libertinism in our behavior.

On this latter issue, I have long suspected that there is a parallel between the attitudes of many liberals today and the way the French took shelter under the American nuclear umbrella during the Cold War while simultaneously gratifying themselves with luxuriant outbursts of contempt against us. Such liberals, I think, are not quite so unhappy as they

1. William Jennings Bryan and Clarence Darrow were opposing attorneys in the Scopes trial over the teaching of evolution in schools.

profess to be that there is a force in this country whose very existence helps set limits to libertine tendencies that they themselves worry about, especially when they have children, but that they do not know how to restrain and would lack the courage to fight even if they were in command of the necessary arguments. And so they rely on the "nuclear umbrella" of the Christian Right, while denouncing it all the more loudly as they quietly benefit from its protection.

> *"The JDL [attempts to] . . . change the Jewish image through sacrifice and through all necessary means . . . even strength, force and violence."*

The Jewish Defense League Is Justified

Jewish Defense League

Jewish people have a right to defend themselves, their rights, property, institutions, and honor by any means necessary, including the most violent, the Jewish Defense League (JDL) argues in the following viewpoint. The organization maintains that its use of violence is justified by the attacks of Nazis and other anti-Semitic groups. The JDL seeks to replace the image of the Jew as weak, frightened, and incapable of fighting back with the image of a Jew who is strong, courageous, and capable of defending him or herself. The JDL is an international organization that advocates violence, if necessary, to protect Jewish people from anti-Semitism.

As you read, consider the following questions:

1. According to the JDL, what is the true solution to the Jewish problem?
2. What is the purpose of anti-Semitic hatred and contempt for Jewish people, in the JDL's opinion?
3. According to the JDL, what will ensure its success?

The Jewish Defense League [JDL] is the most controversial, yet the most effective, of all Jewish organizations. Founded in 1968 by Rabbi Meir Kahane, of blessed memory, the activist group has been responsible for bringing such issues as, but certainly not limited to, Soviet Jewry, Nazi war criminals, Jew-hatred and Jewish self-defense to the front page of every major newspaper. Headquartered in Southern California, JDL devotes its modest resources to the defense of Diaspora Jewish communities and Jewish interests in its own inimitable fashion.

There is no issue facing the Jewish people today that the JDL won't tackle and unlike the so-called "respectable" Jewish establishment organizations the JDL doesn't form committees and study what needs to be done for years on end, thus wasting precious time and accomplishing absolutely nothing! The JDL takes concrete action to solve Jewish problems.

To better understand why JDL does what it does one must read the 5 principles of the JDL to get a better appreciation of our work.

The 5 principles of the JDL are:

Ahavat Yisrael—Love of Jewry

The Jewish Defense League came into being to educate the Jewish people to the concept of Ahavat Yisrael . . . one Jewish people, indivisible and united, from which flows the love for and the feeling of pain of all Jews. It sees the need for a movement that is dedicated specifically to Jewish problems and that allocates its time, resources, energies and funds to Jews. It realizes that in the end . . . with few exceptions . . . the Jew can look to no one but another Jew for help and that the true solution to the Jewish problem is the liquidation of the Exile and the return of all Jews to Eretz Yisrael . . . the land of Israel. It sees the immediate need to place Judaism over any other "ism" and ideology and calls for the use of the yardstick: "Is it good for the Jews?"

Hadar—Dignity and Pride

JDL teaches the concept of Hadar . . . pride in and knowledge of Jewish tradition, faith, culture, land, history, strength, pain and peoplehood. Hadar is the need to have pride in Ju-

Violence Is Sometimes Necessary

The story is told of two Jews being taken out by anti-Semites to be shot. As they were both placed against the wall, blindfolds were placed over their eyes and one cried out: "The blindfold is too tight!"

At which point the other frantically whispered: "Quiet, don't make trouble . . . "

The advertisement appeared in *The New York Times* on June 24, 1969. Over a picture of a group of tough-looking pipe-wielding youngsters was the question:

Is this any way for a nice Jewish boy to behave?

The question did not wait for an answer. That followed immediately:

Maybe. Maybe there are times when there is no other way to get across to the extremist that the Jew is not quite the patsy some think he is.

Maybe there is only one way to get across a clear response to people who threaten seizure of synagogues and extortion of money. Maybe nice Jewish boys do not always get through to people who threaten to carry teachers out in pine boxes and burn down merchant's stores.

Maybe some people and organizations are *too* nice. Maybe in times of crisis Jewish boys should not be that nice. Maybe—just maybe—nice people build their own road to Auschwitz.

The text went on to state the problems that had arisen and unorthodox militant solutions to them. It ended with the words: "We are speaking of Jewish survival."

The ad was placed by the Jewish Defense League, which had decided to "make trouble," and after its appearance the Jewish community was never quite the same.

Meir Kahane, *The Story of the Jewish Defense League*, 1975.

---

daism and not allow it to be disgraced and defiled by beating and desecration of Jewish honor. This is the concept that the great Jewish leader Zev Jabotinsky attempted to instill in the oppressed and degraded masses of Eastern Europe during the holocaust over 5 decades ago. The Anti-Semite's hatred and contempt for the Jew is an attempt to degrade us. It is an attempt to instill within the Jew a feeling of inferiority. It is an attempt that all too often succeeds in promoting Jewish self-hatred and shame in an attempt to escape one's Jewishness.

Hadar is pride! Hadar is self-respect! Hadar is dignity in being a Jew!

Barzel—Iron

JDL upholds the principle of Barzel . . . iron . . . the need to both move to help Jews everywhere and to change the Jewish image through sacrifice and through all necessary means . . . even strength, force and violence. The Galut [Diaspora] image of the Jew as a weakling, as one who is easily stepped upon and who does not fight back is an image that must be changed. Not only does that image cause immediate harm to Jews but it is a self-perpetuating thing because if a Jew runs away or because a Jew allows himself to be stepped upon, he guarantees that another Jew in the future will be attacked because of the image he has perpetuated. JDL wants to create a physically strong, fearless and courageous Jew who fights back. We are changing an image born of 2000 years in Galut, an image that must be buried because it has buried us. We train ourselves for the defense of Jewish lives and rights. We learn how to fight physically, for it is better to know how and not have to than have to and not know how.

Mishmaat—Discipline and Unity

Mishmaat . . . discipline and dedication . . . creates within the Jew the knowledge that he (or she) can and will do whatever must be done, and the unity and strength of willpower to bring this into reality. It was the lack of discipline and unity that led continually to the destruction of the Jewish people. It is Jewish unity and self-discipline that will lead to the triumph of the Jewish people.

Bitachon—Faith in G-d and the Indestructability of the Jewish People

Faith in Hashem our G-d and in the greatness of the Jewish people, our Torah, our religion and our land of Israel is Bitachon. It is a faith that is built by our belief in Hashem. . . . The Jewish G-d of Hosts, and the incredible saga of Jewish history that has seen us overcome the flood of enemies that have arisen to wipe us out in every generation. It is this faith in Hashem our G-d and the permanence and survival of the

Jewish people that in turn gives faith to the ultimate success of the Jewish Defense League. No matter how difficult, no matter how impossible the task may seem . . . if it is a good task . . . if it is a holy task . . . it will succeed because it must.

The sources for the philosophy and actions of the Jewish Defense League are Jewish sources. They stem from the wellsprings of Jewish tradition and have their roots in Jewish teachings. In the Torah, the Talmud, in the teachings of our sages throughout the ages in Jewish practice throughout history, the concepts of Ahavat Yisrael, Hadar Yisrael, Barzel Yisrael, Mishmaat Yisrael and Bitachon are hallowed. At the same time an eternal debt is owed to the Jews of our era who also recognized that these concepts are indeed Jewish and who fought the assimilated Jewish tide to put them into practice. We refer to the great Zev Jabotinsky, . . . his followers and his movement of which we consider ourselves to be a spiritual part, and sitting in heaven righteously alongside Jabotinsky is the founder and eternal spiritual leader of the Jewish Defense League, Rabbi Meir Kahane. . . . May the Almighty grant us the understanding to recognize and act on our problems forthrightly and the courage to go out to battle against our enemies in the face of all obstacles . . . from within and without.

> *"[The Jewish Defense League is] a racist,*
> *terrorist, extremist, militant, Zionist hate*
> *group."*

The Jewish Defense League
Promotes Hate and Violence

Angela Valkyrie

Angela Valkyrie claims in the following viewpoint that the Jewish Defense League (JDL) is an extremist group that promotes hate and violence and whose membership is increasing daily. She maintains that the JDL is a threat to all Americans because members have a victim mentality combined with a superiority complex that leads to criminal behavior motivated by hate and fear. Angela Valkyrie writes for AlterMedia.info, a white supremacist, anti-Semitic Web site.

As you read, consider the following questions:

1. According to Valkyrie, why was Irv Rubin arrested in 1980?
2. Who was the founder of the JDL, in Valkyrie's opinion?
3. What does the author argue was the job of the Chaya Squad?

Angela Valkyrie, "The JDL: Jewish Hate Group," www.altermedia.info, November 24, 2003. Copyright © 2003 by AlterMedia. Reproduced by permission.

There is a Jewish hate group in America. No one in the media seems to want you to know that they exist. But they do exist. And, Altermedia.info USA wants you to know about them. Or more specifically, I want you to know more about them.

This Jewish extremist hate group in America is called the Jewish Defense League (JDL). They claim to have 6,000 members. They are a racist, terrorist, extremist, militant, Zionist hate group. JDL member numbers are growing in the United States every day.

Americans, especially European-Americans need to be aware of the threat the JDL are to us and to the Nation as a whole. Since the mainstream media won't give this topic the attention it deserves, I will.

In December of 2001 in Los Angeles, CA John Gordon of the L.A. U.S. attorney's office announced that two members of the Jewish Defense League had been arrested on conspiracy and terrorist charges. They had been plotting to bomb a mosque in Culver City, CA. The two suspects were identified as Irv Rubin, 56, and Earl Krugel. Irv Rubin had been the National Chairman of the JDL since 1970. This was not the first time that Irv Rubin had been in trouble with the law. Rubin had been arrested at least 50 times on other counts prior to the conspiracy and terrorism charges of December 2001.

As leader of the Jewish Defense League, Rubin had instituted civilian patrols, organized militant programs of firearms and the martial arts.

In 1980, Irv Rubin was known to be soliciting the murders of anyone he considered to be a "Nazi" in the United States. The police charged him with solicitation with murderous intent but then he was acquitted of the charges.

Jewish Defense League Founder

Two of Irv Rubin's favorite JDL slogans were, "I want every Jew, a .22," he has said. "Keep alive with a .45."

The Jewish Defense League was founded in 1968 by well-known Zionist Rabbi Meir Kahane, who left the JDL in 1985 to serve on the Israeli Parliament and then was mysteriously assassinated in 1990.

The Jewish Defense League Promotes Violence

The JDL [Jewish Defense League] was a Jewish self-defense movement that began with the limited goals of protecting orthodox Jewish neighborhoods in New York City from depredations by young black and Puerto Rican hoodlums and to protest local instances of anti-Semitism. Eventually the JDL embraced a universal program of fighting for Jewish interests worldwide. The group was self-sustaining and lacked any support from mainstream Jewish organizations in the United States or from the State of Israel. The JDL was founded in 1968 by Rabbi Meir Kahane, who began to organize young Jewish men as vigilantes to protect Jews and Jewish businesses in the Williamsburg and Crown Heights areas of Brooklyn and elsewhere in the New York City area. Within a year the group had graduated from vigilantism and demonstrations against alleged anti-Semites to burglarizing the files of the [Palestine Liberation Organization United Nations] Mission and launching attacks on Soviet diplomatic, trade, and tourism offices and personnel. According to the FBI, the JDL was responsible for at least 37 terrorist acts in the United States in the period from 1968–1983, while the International Terrorism: Attributes of Terrorist Events (ITERATE) database developed on behalf of the United States Central Intelligence Agency by Edward F. Mickolus recorded 50 such incidents from 1968–1987, making the JDL second only to the Puerto Rican FALN . . . as the major domestic terrorist group. Nonetheless the JDL is a legally incorporated political action group and has officially disavowed responsibility for any violent actions carried out by its members. Bombings accounted for 78 percent of all JDL terrorist activities; shootings accounted for 16 percent; while arson attacks, vandalism, kidnapping, threats, and verbal harassment accounted for the rest.

Sean Anderson and Stephan Sloan, *Historical Dictionary of Terrorism*, 1995.

It was Kahane who originally coined the popular JDL slogan, "every Jew a .22." He created the Kahane's Chaya Squad, a group within the JDL, whose job was to, and I quote, "instill fear in the hearts of the would-be criminals against Jews" according to Rabbi Meir Kahane. He adamantly spoke out against the intermarriage of Jews and the importance of maintaining the purity of the Jewish race.

Kahane was jailed many times for breaking the law in JDL related militant activities and was sentenced to prison before he finally decided to move his operations to Israel.

Kach Movement

After Kahane immigrated to Israel he formed the Kach movement.

The Kach movement was most famous for its platform calling for the removal of the the entire Israeli-Arab population from Israel and transferring them "elsewhere." The Kach movement under Rabbi Kahane demanded the demolition and complete annihilation of all Palestinian territories followed by unlimited Jewish-Israeli settlement and the complete and final colonization of Palestine.

Rabbi Kahane considered Israel to be the chosen nation by G-d and the exclusive owners of the Holy Land. He was a self-confirmed Zionist who loathed American Democracy. He is quoted here as having said, "Judaism is not Thomas Jefferson and the Middle East is not the Midwest.". . .

Terrorist Activities

So now you are a bit more informed about the Jewish Defense League than you were before. Now you know what the media does not want you to know.

In closing, I give you a short compiled list summarizing a few JDL activities to look over:

- The 1985 murder of Alex Odeh, director of the American Arab Anti-Discrimination Committee.
- Terrorist bombings.
- Plotting to bomb a mosque in Culver City, CA in December of 2001.
- Conspiracy and terrorism charges.
- Organized militant programs of firearms and the martial arts.
- Solicitation with murderous intent.
- Ties with Mossad, the Israeli Zionist militant extremist group.
- Explosives and stockpiled weaponry.
- Blatant hatred towards Christians, Arab-Americans, Muslims, Blacks and European-Americans. . . .
- Training Jewish children to use guns and martial arts.
- JDL slogans like; "I want every Jew, a .22" and "Keep alive with a .45."
- Mysterious assassinations.

- Convicted felons owning and handling firearms.
- Website advertising weapons courses at Camp Jabotinsky.
- Stirring up hatred by faking "anti-Semitic" activity.
- Twisting the truth and using it as propaganda.
- The JDL belief that intermarriage is forbidden because Jews must perpetuate the Jewish race by having children who are not only religiously Jewish but ethnically Jewish.
- Whole-heartedly dedicating their lives to fighting a holy war using violence, intimidation tactics and murder.
- Victim mentality scapegoating combined with a superiority complex that leads to self-righteous criminal behavior motivated by hate and fear.

With all that read, is the JDL a terrorist hate group? Decide for yourself.

Periodical Bibliography

The following articles have been selected to supplement the diverse views presented in this chapter.

Chuck Baldwin "Is America Losing Her Purpose? God Raised America to Preach Gospel, Protect Israel, Preserve Liberty," *Free Republic*, October 5, 2001.

James Dobson "The New Cost of Discipleship," *Christianity Today*, September 6, 1999.

Amy Driscoll "Religious Right Sees New Hope for Morality Agenda," *Miami Herald*, February 22, 1999.

Jonah Goldberg "Jewish Defense League Plotters Are Terrorists," TownHall.com, December 14, 2001.

Delinda C. Hanley "Freeze on Jewish Defense League Assets Called for After JDL Bomb Plot Failed," *Washington Report on Middle East Affairs*, January/February 2002.

John Hicks "The Political Substance of the Religious Right: Why the Christian Right Survives and Does Not Thrive," The American Religious Experience, 2000. http://are.as.wvu.edu.

Jewish Defense League "The Five Principles of the Jewish Defense League," 1999. www.jdl.org.

Ruqaiyyah Waris Maqsood "On the Hijacking of Islam," Islam for Today, September 16, 2001. www.islamfortoday.com.

Steven E. Miller "The New Right Wing Agenda," Common Dreams, June 13, 2003. www.commondreams.org.

Carroll Payne "What Is Islam?" *World Conflict Quarterly*, October 2001. www.globalterrorism101.com.

Daniel Pipes "Aim the War on Terror at Militant Islam," *Los Angeles Times*, January 6, 2002.

Daniel Pipes "Protecting Muslims While Rooting Out Islamists," *Daily Telegraph* (London), September 14, 2001.

Laura Montgomery Rutt "H.R. 2357—Religious Right's Newest Attempt to Destroy Democracy," *Progressive Voices*, Winter 2001.

Unitarian Universalist Association "The Religious Right's Agenda for 1999 and Beyond," July 29, 1999. www.uua.org.

Westchester Coalition for Legal Abortion "Barry Lynn: Educate Public About Religious Right Agenda," Spring 1999. www.wcla.org.

CHAPTER 2

Do Some Liberal Groups Benefit Society?

Chapter Preface

Some radical animal rights organizations such as the Animal Liberation Front (ALF) and People for the Ethical Treatment of Animals (PETA) engage in violent acts of destruction and vandalism in an effort to stop what they perceive to be the cruel exploitation of animals. Other animal rights advocacy groups such as the Animal Legal Defense Fund (ALDF) have taken a less violent—though no less radical—approach to securing the rights of animals. The ALDF is working to achieve legal status in court for all animals. By fundamentally changing their legal status, ALDF hopes to put an end to the exploitation of animals, particularly the use of animals as research subjects. Steve Ann Chambers, president of the ALDF insists, "We need to expand legal rights beyond humans." The ALDF claims that changing the legal status of animals will result in far-reaching moral, ethical, and environmental benefits to society.

The ALDF is not alone in its fight for animal rights. Twenty-five U.S. law schools now offer courses in animal rights (in the mid-1990s, there were only five offering such courses). University of Chicago professor Cass Sunstein argues that although animals are regarded as property, they can still have rights under the law and that there is significant popular support for such changes. Sunstein said, "Our culture is much more interested in protecting animals than our laws are." Steven Wise, author of *Rattling the Cage: Toward Legal Rights for Animals*, maintains that nonhuman animals, particularly primates, "have a kind of autonomy that judges should easily recognize as sufficient for legal rights." While some progress is being made, the fight for animal rights is likely to be a long one.

Some radical animal rights activist groups such as the ALDF are working to end the exploitation of animals without resorting to violence but nevertheless using what many would call extreme means. Authors in the following chapter explore the issues raised by radical animal rights activists and other extremist groups.

"The healthiest generation in history is a ripe target for the anti-science nonsense pushed by the animal rights movement."

Radical Animal Rights Groups Harm Society

Frederick K. Goodwin and Adrian R. Morrison

Radical animal rights activists misguidedly harass scientists and disrupt research critical to human and animal welfare, argue Fredrick K. Goodwin and Adrian R. Morrison in the following viewpoint. The authors maintain that even though scientists and research facilities follow the strictest animal care guidelines, they are targets of violent attacks that inspire fear among researchers and stifle scientific creativity. Frederick K. Goodwin is a former director of the National Institute of Mental Health. Adrian R. Morrison is a professor of veterinary medicine at the University of Pennsylvania.

As you read, consider the following questions:
1. According to the authors, what is the difference between the animal rights movement and animal welfare organizations?
2. Name one of the factors that Goodwin and Morrison identify as contributing to the climate of moral confusion surrounding the use of animals in research.
3. In the authors' opinion, what was the disastrous tactical error that scientists made at the outset of their encounter with the animal rights movement?

Frederick K. Goodwin and Adrian R. Morrison, "Science and Self-Doubt," *Reason*, vol. 32, October 2000, p. 22. Copyright © 2000 by the Reason Foundation, 3415 S. Sepulveda Blvd., Suite 400, Los Angeles, CA 90034, www.reason.com. Reproduced with permission.

Twenty years ago, animal research became the target of a new generation of anti-vivisectionists: the radical "animal rights" movement. That movement, which views animals as moral agents on a par with people, has promoted a profoundly confused philosophy that equates animal research with the enslavement of human beings.

Scientists responded to this movement by proposing to strengthen the standards and regulation of animal research and care. But even as the handling of research animals became ever more restricted, the animal rights campaign became ever more demanding and violent. Scientists working with animals, especially those involved in brain and behavioral research, were assaulted in their laboratories, harassed in their homes, and threatened with death.

In Europe, scientists have long been the target of actual terrorism, now identified as such by the United Kingdom. Indeed, the neuroscientist Colin Blakemore at Oxford University, who studies brain activity in cats, literally lives under siege. Police must protect his home, which has been assaulted with his frightened wife and daughters in residence. Why? He spoke out in support of the obvious necessity of using animals to advance medical science—to alleviate the suffering of human beings—and has been in danger ever since that principled act. In 1998, Blakemore and other European scientists were marked for death by animal rights terrorists, and Blakemore lived for months under round-the-clock police protection.

The United States Is the Latest Target

Although for a few years American researchers enjoyed relative peace, animal rights activists struck last spring [2000] at the University of Minnesota, causing thousands of dollars in damage. A scientist studying hearing at the University of California at San Francisco is now suffering what Blakemore has endured for years. But biomedical research is coming under another kind of siege.

There has been a campaign in New Zealand to give the great apes constitutional rights, an outgrowth of the ideas of the animal rights movement and the Great Ape Project, which seeks to award apes the same rights as those possessed by humans. Last year [1999] in Germany, the ruling Social Democratic and Green parties introduced legislation stating that animals have the right to be "respected as fellow creatures," and to be protected from "avoidable pain." Two recent developments in the United States suggest that we may be entering a dangerous era in thinking about animals.

In the first, a U.S. court recognized the legal standing of an individual to sue the federal government in order to force changes in animal-welfare regulations. In that case, the individual claimed "harm" as a result of seeing animals mistreated, in his opinion, at a roadside zoo; the plaintiff held the Department of Agriculture [USDA] responsible. However, in deciding the merits of the case, an appeals court later found that USDA was not responsible for the individual's alleged harm, and declined to order any change in the current regulations.

In the second, animal rights groups are pushing USDA to include rats and mice under the Animal Welfare Act.

Animal Rights Versus Animal Welfare

The campaign to end the use of animals in biomedical research is based upon a complete misunderstanding of how scientists work, what research requires, and what has made possible our era's outpouring of lifesaving advances in medicine. Unfortunately, neither their misunderstanding of science nor their misguided philosophy has prevented activists from becoming an increasingly powerful, militant force—one now threatening the discovery of new medical treatments and preventive strategies for serious illnesses.

To understand the animal rights movement, we must distinguish its objectives from those of animal welfare organizations. Typically, such organizations as local societies for the prevention of cruelty to animals will care for strays, teach good animal care, run neutering programs, and build animal shelters. Acting as the stewards of animals, especially those not in a position to care for themselves, these organizations uphold our traditional values of humane, caring treatment of sentient creatures.

Animal rights organizations, on the other hand, invest their energies in campaigning against various uses of animals, including research. They start with a completely different philosophy, summed up by Peter Singer, the acknowledged founder of the animal rights movement, in his 1975 book, *Animal Liberation*. Singer, now De Camp Professor of Bioethics at Princeton University, argues that sentient creatures—all those capable of feeling pain—must essentially be considered moral equivalents to human beings, certainly as equivalent to the severely brain-damaged and to human infants before the age of reasoning. Anyone who dismisses any sentient creature as merely an animal to be used for human benefit is guilty of "speciesism," a prejudice morally equivalent to racism and sexism. (Singer, who is Australian, does not base his opposition to animal research on the concept of rights; his American counterpart, University of North Carolina philosophy professor Tom Regan, does.)

PETA

On the political front, Ingrid Newkirk, the national director of People for the Ethical Treatment of Animals (PETA), asserted in 1983 that "animal liberationists do not separate out the human animal, so there is no rational basis for saying that a human being has special rights. A rat is a pig is a dog is a boy. They're all mammals." She has also said, "Six million Jews died in concentration camps, but six billion broiler chickens will die this year in slaughterhouses." Chris DeRose, who heads an organization called In Defense of Animals, said recently that even if the death of one rat would cure all disease, that death still would not be right, because we are all equal.

Despite PETA's view that broiler chickens are the moral equivalent of murdered Jews, animal rights activists decided early on to target scientific researchers, not farmers, although more than 99 percent of the animals used by people are for food (or clothing, or killed either in pounds or by hunters) and just a fraction of 1 percent for research. Singer has said that the strategic decision to level protests against science was made because farmers are organized and politically powerful (and live in rural areas, which makes them hard to get at). In contrast, scientists are not politically organized, live in urban areas, and can be hard put to explain their work in lay language.

Neuroscientists have been a frequent target. Two key fields of neuroscience, behavioral and addiction research, were highlighted in Singer's book. High-profile laboratory invasions have targeted scientists engaged in brain research. For example, PETA, which adheres to Singer's philosophy, established itself by infiltrating the laboratory of neuroscientist Edward Taub in Silver Spring, Maryland, in 1981, and "exposing" deficient laboratory conditions with photographs that purported to show animal mistreatment. Taub, however, has noted that no one else in the lab observed the conditions in the PETA photographs, and he is supported by the sworn statements of seven people, including a USDA inspector, who testified at Taub's subsequent trial. At the time, Taub was investigating how monkeys perform complex tasks with certain nerve pathways in their arms severed, work that was the basis for the subsequent development of improved methods for stroke rehabilitation.

In 1984, PETA exploited the Animal Liberation Front's invasion of the University of Pennsylvania Head Injury Research Laboratory by cleverly editing videotapes taken in the raid and using the resulting composite as a fund raising tool. In subsequent literature, PETA made it clear that alleged mistreatment of animals was not the real issue. In PETA's view, animals cannot be used to alleviate health problems of people, period. Even after more stringent government controls over animal research were in place (by 1985) Texas Tech sleep researcher John Orem suffered a raid in 1989 that resulted in $40,000 worth of damage to his laboratory. In this and other cases, however, the critical damage is to the scientist's will to continue research.

Moral Confusion

Many factors have contributed to the climate of moral confusion surrounding the use of animals in research and to the apparent willingness of many people to credit the bizarre ideas of the animal rights activists.

For one thing, we are victims of our own health care successes. We have enjoyed such a victory over infectious diseases that baby boomers and subsequent generations do not even remember polio and other dreaded infectious diseases, and have little sense of how amazing it was when antibiotics were first developed. With the eradication of so many deadly infectious diseases, antibiotics have become something that you take for incidental minor infection. The healthiest generation in history is a ripe target for the anti-science nonsense pushed by the animal rights movement.

Second, America has sustained a steady, devastating decline in scientific literacy. Our high school students consistently rank below those of other developed countries. As a result, most people, especially young people, do not understand what the scientific method is really about.

Asay. © by Charles Asay. Reproduced by permission.

Additionally, Americans today spend little time around animals other than house pets. It is worth remembering that just before World War II one in four of us lived on a farm; now it is one in 50. What do most urban and suburban kids know about animals, other than what they see in cartoons?

Such factors have helped propel the ever-tightening regulation of research, stifling the creativity that is its essence and posing a threat to the human well-being that is its goal. Many major discoveries in the history of medicine have come about by serendipity, when a scientist has had his sights trained on an entirely different topic of research. The story behind the initial discovery that lithium, an elemental substance on the periodic table, might have therapeutic benefits illustrates this serendipity and demonstrates how basic research with animals can lead to major medical advances.

In that case, Australian psychiatrist John Cade asked what might be wrong in the brains of patients with manic-depressive illness and wondered whether a substance called urea would have therapeutic value. Testing his hypothesis on guinea pigs, Cade gave them a salt form of urea, which happened to contain lithium. The guinea pigs became unexpectedly calm. Further experimentation revealed that the urea had nothing to do with this result; it was caused by the lithium—a complete surprise to Cade. Having laid his foundation with animal research, Cade extended his findings by giving lithium to manic patients, who experienced an alleviation of their manic excitement without being sedated. This single discovery has revolutionized treatment of manic-depressive illness, easing the lives of millions and saving billions of dollars along the way. At the same time, it has opened whole new productive areas for brain research.

No one could have predicted the outcome of Cade's initial experiment with urea. There was no way to list in advance what the health benefits of using guinea pigs would be. That would have required knowing the answer to a question that had not yet been asked. If one already knows the answer, research is unnecessary.

Few Studies Involve Animals

In 1976, before the animal rights controversy arose, the National Institutes of Health sponsored a study by Julius H. Comroe Jr. and R.D. Dripps to ascertain if government funding of basic biomedical research had been a good investment. The authors asked practicing cardiologists what they regarded as the 10 leading medical advances of their lifetimes; the scientists named such advances as cardiac surgery, drug treatment of hypertension, and medical treatment of cardiac insufficiency. Comroe and Dripps then traced the scientific ancestry of each of these discoveries and found that 40 percent of the studies leading to the advances originated from work in a different, seemingly unrelated field of research. Animal research was fundamental to many of these studies. Regulations that require justification of animal research in terms of its specific outcomes, rather than the clarity of the hypotheses and strength of the research design, may end much of the creative research now under way.

Less than a quarter of the studies in biomedicine involve animals (and more than 90 percent of those are rats and mice), but anyone working in the field will tell you that such animal studies are indispensable. One cannot develop an understanding of a chemical or a gene, then try to ascertain its role in a complex human organism with billions of cells and dozens of organs, without first knowing how it works in the biological systems of animals. The animal model enables a scientist to understand what is happening at a level of detail that could not be reached in humans.

The great kidney transplant pioneer Dr. Thomas E. Starzl was once asked why he used dogs in his work. He explained that, in his first series of operations, he had transplanted kidneys into a number of subjects, and that the majority of them died. After figuring out what had enabled a few to survive, he revised his techniques and operated on a similar group of subjects; a majority of them survived. In his third group of subjects, only one or two died, and in his fourth group all survived. The important point, said Starzl, was that the first three groups of subjects were dogs; the fourth group consisted of human babies. Had Starzl begun his series of experimental operations on people, he would have killed at least 15 people. Yet there are activists who believe, in the name of animal rights, that that is what Starzl should have done.

At the outset of their encounter with the animal rights movement, scientists made a disastrous tactical error. Accustomed to dealing with others by reason, and eager to meet the activists halfway, the research community adopted "The Three Rs," described as long ago as 1959 by W. Russell and R. Birch in their book, *The Principles of Humane Experimental Technique*. Scientists pledged to reduce the number of animals used, to refine their techniques, and to replace animals whenever possible. In truth, scientists are always looking for ways to reduce, refine, and replace animal use. It makes sense from the point of view of humane treatment, the economics of research and, often, science.

But this response came across as a confession of guilt. Although scientists accept high standards for the use and care of research animals, they are not engaged in some kind of "necessary evil." Appeasement is a losing game. To make concessions on a matter of principle is to concede the principle itself. Then defeat is only a matter of time, as opponents demand complete consistency with their own principle.

Rights Are a Human Concept

"Rights," the idea that the activists are working so hard to enlist in their cause, are a moral concept. Rights stem from the uniquely human capacity to choose values and principles, then act on choices and judgment. Within that context, rights are moral principles stating that, as human beings with the ability to develop and act on moral judgments, we must leave each other free to do so. That is the basis of our claim to political and personal freedom. Rattlesnakes and rats, tigers and sheep, and even our closest animal relatives, chimpanzees, exhibit no ability to comprehend, respect, or act upon rights. The "law of the jungle" is no law at all. Indeed, the concept of rights is profoundly incoherent when applied to animals. It is worse than mistaken; it dangerously subverts the concept of rights itself at a time when human rights worldwide are in need of clear articulation and defense.

Focusing on the Three Rs without exposing and refuting the underlying philosophy of animal rights proved a public relations catastrophe. The research community's basic position should have been that human beings have a right to use animals for human purposes, but also have a responsibility to use animals humanely. The more we emphasized the Three Rs, the stronger the animal rights movement became, and the more money the radical activists raised. This was occurring at the very same time that science was demonstrating noticeable improvements in the handling of laboratory animals.

It is not sufficient for the medical-scientific community to expose the fundamental flaws in the philosophy of animal rights. It must be able to respond to the movement's other, more utilitarian, arguments against the use of animals in research.

Activists' Arguments Are Weak

Activists assert that animal research is cruel. But their argument misses the point that experimenters usually want to disturb the animal as little as possible, since their goal is to study its natural response to whatever is being tested. An estimated 7 percent of research does employ procedures causing pain in order to understand pain mechanisms in the central nervous system. This kind of experimentation has enabled us to develop effective painkillers.

Activists claim that animal experiments are duplicative. The reality is that today only one out of four grant requests is funded, a highly competitive situation that makes duplicative research scarce. But research does have to be replicated before the results are accepted; and progress usually arises from a series of small discoveries, all elaborating on or overlapping one another. When activists talk about duplication, they betray a fundamental misunderstanding of how science progresses. Nor do they understand scientists. What highly trained, creative individual wants to do exactly what someone has already done?

Activists urge prevention rather than treatment. They say we should urge people to adopt measures such as an altered diet or increased exercise to prevent major illness, so that we would not need so many new treatments. But much of what we have discovered about preventive measures has itself resulted from animal research. You cannot get most cancers to grow in a test tube; you need whole animal studies.

Activists argue that we should use alternatives to animal research. A favorite example is computer simulations. But where do they think the data that are entered into computers come from? To get real answers, one has to feed computers real physiological data. There is an argument that researchers should use PET scans, which can provide an image of how a living human organ is functioning, as a way of avoiding the use of animals. It took Lou Sokoloff at the National Institute of Mental Health eight years of animal research to develop the PET scan methodology. . . .

Moral Self-Doubt

We live in an age of moral self-doubt. Some scientists and other individuals associated with biomedical research in supportive roles have begun to feel guilt over their use of animals. That has spawned a group calling itself the "troubled middle" (a rather presumptuous phrase, suggesting that only they care about the issues raised by animal research). Indeed, a whole industry has grown up around this sense of guilt, with constant, somewhat repetitive conferences focusing on how to oversee research, how to be the perfect member of an Institutional Animal Care and Use Committee, and how to find alternatives to using animals. These topics are not unworthy, but the conferences give short shrift to the perspectives of working scientists, who rarely appear as major speakers.

Progress toward increased human well-being cannot flourish amid such self-doubt. Scientists and members of the public who support their work must recognize that they are engaged in a struggle for minds. Their own minds therefore must be clear about what justifies animal research when necessary: that human beings are special. Researchers and others must appreciate the value of such work, and must be ready to state unequivocally and publicly that human life comes first. We who work with animals, and those who support the benefits of that work, have made a moral choice, and we must be willing to stand by it.

"By performing illegal actions the Band [of Mercy] was able to directly save the lives of animals by destroying the tool of torture and death."

Radical Animal Activism Is Justified

Noel Molland

In the following viewpoint Noel Molland maintains that radical animal activism is justified because conventional legal methods do not bring about desired changes in people's thinking or behavior toward animals. He insists that saving animal lives is as important as saving human lives. Molland claims that destroying property and frightening people is often the most effective way to make the public understand the revolutionary nature of the animal rights movement. Noel Molland is a contributor to *No Compromise*, the publication of No Compromise, a direct action animal liberation organization.

As you read, consider the following questions:
1. According to Molland, what group did John Prestidge found in 1964?
2. Why was the Band of Mercy formed, in the author's opinion?
3. Why does Molland argue that the Hoechst Pharmaceutical building had to be destroyed?

It is hard, if not impossible, to say when the Animal/Earth Liberation movement first started. A study of the subject literally takes you back thousands of years to 200 B.C. when people like Pythagoras advocated vegetarianism & animal compassion on spiritual grounds, and to the 1st century A.D. when Plutarch wrote what is widely regarded as the first animal rights literature.

However, the reader will be delighted to know that I am not going to bore you to death with 2000 years of waffle. Instead, I merely intend to look at what occurred 30 years ago this year [2002]. But first, to fully understand the events of 30 years ago, we must look slightly further back than that, to the events of 1964.

During the 19th and 20th centuries Britain saw a wealth of Animal Welfare and Rights groups established. However, these groups by and large relied upon the parliamentary way of legal reform to achieve their aims. This process was incredibly slow and achievements were minor. Even the 1911 Animal Protection Act treated animals as property and offered no protection to wild-born creatures. By the mid-nineteen sixties people started to look around for other ways of campaigning and in 1964 John Prestidge found that new style.

The Hunt Saboteurs Association

In 1964 in Brixham, Devon, England, John Prestidge founded a group that would actively oppose blood sports. Rather than campaigning for parliamentary reforms, John's new group was prepared to directly go out into the fields of Britain and do everything they could, within the law, to prevent the killing of British wildlife: John founded the Hunt Saboteurs Association (H.S.A.).

The popularity of this new form of campaigning was instant. Just a year after the H.S.A. was founded, hunt saboteur groups were active across the English Westcountry in Devon, Somerset and Bristol. Groups also started to emerge outside of the Westcountry in places like Birmingham, Hampshire and Surrey.

Originally a single Devon-based group, the H.S.A. soon became a national network of dedicated activists using lawful methods to disrupt blood-junkies of Britain and to prevent the "green and pleasant lands" from literally becoming the killing fields.

And so it was, in 1971, as part of the ever-expanding H.S.A. network, a new hunt sab [saboteurs] group was formed in Luton. The group was founded by a law student named Ronnie Lee. The Luton hunt sabs, like a lot of other hunt sab groups, soon became very successful in saving the lives of animals. Many a hunt soon found their sadistic day's entertainment ruined by the Luton Gang.

However, despite the success of the Luton hunt sabs in the field, it soon became apparent to some people within the groups that the strictly legal actions of the H.S.A. could only ever go so far to preventing animal suffering. The problem was that if a hunt is allowed to be active, no matter how good a hunt sab group may be, there is a chance that an animal may be harmed or killed.

Even if the sabs do manage to prevent an animal from being killed, the fear the animal goes through whilst being hunted is tremendous. Contemporary vet reports, gathered at the end of the 20th century, have revealed animals do suffer incredible stress whilst being hunted.

The Hunt Must Never Begin

It was out of this recognition (that strictly legal hunt sabotage couldn't totally prevent the suffering of an animal) that Ronnie Lee and a few close friends started to look around for other ways to help prevent suffering. They realized that the only real way to prevent any sort of suffering is to assure that the hunt is never allowed to become active in the first place. As soon as an animal is being chased, she is psychologically suffering as she fears for her life. Therefore she has to be assured that 'the chase' is never allowed to start in the first place. With this aim in mind, Ronnie Lee, Cliff Goodman and possibly two or three other people, decided to form the Band of Mercy in 1972.

The name the Band of Mercy was chosen because it had been the name of an earlier animal liberation direct action group. During the 19th century, an anti-slavery activist named Catherine Smithies had set up a youth wing to the RSPCA [Royal Society for the Prevention of Cruelty to Animals] called the Bands of Mercy. By and large these youth groups were just normal young supporters of the RSPCA who told stories of heroic animal deeds and who took oaths of compassion to the animals. However some of these young Victorian animal rights activists were a little more zealous than others and went around sabotaging hunting rifles. The activities of the Victorian Bands of Mercy became so great that there was even a theatrical play written during which a group of children sabotages a hunting rifle.

For Ronnie Lee and his companions the Victorian Bands of Mercy were a fine example of direct action, so they decided to adopt their not-strictly-legal approach to saving lives.

Initially, the Band of Mercy concentrated on small actions directed against the hunt during the cub-hunting season. Cub hunting is when young hounds are taught to tear young fox cubs apart in order for the hound to get the taste for killing.

The initial actions of the Band of Mercy were very simple and were basically designed around the idea of disabling the hunt vehicles in order to slow down or even stop the hunt from carrying out its murderous activities.

However, the Band of Mercy was very clear from the beginning that it was not merely carrying out acts of wanton vandalism against those whom they opposed but instead their actions were designed around the idea of 'active compassion'. To this aim the Band would always leave a message to the hunters explaining why the Band had carried out their actions, the logic of animal liberation and to show that there was nothing personal against any one individual person.

Illegal Direct Action

The success of the Band of Mercy was soon clear. By carrying out illegal direct action, the Band was able to prevent the hunts. By preventing the hunts from ever becoming active, the Band was safe in the knowledge that not only have they saved the lives of innocent animals, but they had also prevented the psychological suffering of 'the chase'.

Recognizing their true potential for the prevention of animal suffering, the Band then started to think about ways to expand and develop their campaigns. Following on from their early successes the Band soon became much more daring. Towards the end of 1973, the Band learnt about the construction of a new vivisection laboratory. The research laboratory was being built near Milton Keynes for a company called Hoechst Pharmaceutical.

Breaking the Law Is Not Inappropriate

The overall attempt at creating any type of change, socially or politically, should be looked at as a puzzle, because just like a puzzle we need certain pieces to come together and become whole in order to be successful. Specific to animal liberation, we need those out there spreading the word about animal suffering and clueing the general public in on the vegan lifestyle, to create an overall consciousness. We need those on the legal front enforcing the acknowledgment of animals within the law and looking to ban such inhumane, legal events and practices such as the circus and racing, fur trapping and farming. Amongst the other puzzle pieces that I've neglected to mention as examples of necessary pieces in order for the proper connections to be made that will bring about change and bring this movement to success is directly acting on behalf of the animals or yes, breaking the law. We need those out there breaking the law to bring immediate attention to an extreme situation. We need to present that the extreme situation that the animals are in, does call for extreme measures to be taken on their behalf.

I feel that breaking the law should not be looked at as inappropriate even though it may be seen as such by the vast majority. Those willing to take a stand as the voice for the voiceless, those who value life over property, should look at the concept of breaking the law as secondary to the action itself. What can be accomplished and the necessary aspect of the action itself is what is primary. The fact that a law enacted by the state will be broken posing possible consequences should merely serve as the risk involved when taking such actions.

"Interview with Animal Rights Activist, Peter Schnell," *Liberation Magazine*, April 4, 2003.

Having learnt about its existence, two of the Band's activists visited the vivisection lab building site a few times whilst trying to decide the best course of action to be taken. Together these activists realized that if they could prevent the building from ever being completed, then they could prevent the suffering of animals destined to be tortured within its four walls. The Band had to assure the construction could never be finished and eventually decided that the best way to destroy the construction was through the use of arson.

By destroying the building, the Band would prevent the vivisectors from ever being able to start their brand of sadistic 'science'. And even if the damage caused by the fire could be repaired, the restoration work would all cost money that would have to be paid for by Hoechst Pharmaceutical (thus meaning less money to spend on torturing animals).

On November 10th, 1973, the Band of Mercy conducted its first ever action against the vivisection industry. Two activists gained access into the half completed building at Milton Keynes. Once inside the activists set fire to the building. This action was a double watershed for the movement as it was not only the Band's first action against the vivisection industry; it was also the Band's first use of arson.

In that first fire an amazing £26,000 worth of damage was caused. More incredible was six days later, the Band of Mercy returned and started another fire in the same building causing a further £20,000 damage.

To make sure everyone knew why the building was set alight, the Band of Mercy sent a message to the press. The statement read:

"The building was set fire to in an effort to prevent the torture and murder of our animal brothers and sisters by evil experiments. We are a non-violent guerrilla organization dedicated to the liberation of animals from all forms of cruelty and persecution at the hands of mankind. Our actions will continue until our aims are achieved".

After the Milton Keynes arson, the next major action occurred in June 1974 when the Band turned its attention to the bloody seal cull of the Wash along the Norfolk coast.

Stopping the Seal Cull

The seal cull was an annual event and involved hunters going out in two Home Office licensed boats and butchering seals. Seal culling is a bloody attack and the seal has no hope of escape. Knowing how sick the seal cull is the Band obviously wanted to prevent the cull from ever starting. With the goal of preventing the cull from ever starting and regarding the success in the use of arson in the November

1973 action, the Band once again decided to use arson as a campaign tool to destroy the tools of animal murder.

In June 1974 the Band of Mercy set out [on] their second major action. Under the cover of darkness, two activists sought out the Home Office licensed boats. Having found the boats, these transporters of death were then set alight. One of the boats was sadly only slightly damaged by the fire; the other however, was totally destroyed.

After conducting this June 1974 action, the Band of Mercy decided that this time they wouldn't leave a message claiming responsibility. Instead they wanted to leave the sealers wondering what on earth had happened, if those responsible would return and if someone else provided two new boats, if these new vessels would meet with the same fiery fate.

That year there was no seal cull at all due to the actions of the Band of Mercy. Also, besides totally halting the seal cull for that year, there was another knock on effect. Because of the fire, the owner of the two Home Office licensed boats went out of business. And having seen one person's business totally destroyed by the actions of these anonymous arsonists, no one was keen to invest the money into a new business that might very well go the same way. Because of this fear no one has ever attempted to re-start a seal culling business and there has never been a seal cull at the Wash since. Because of the actions of two activists, countless numbers of seals have been saved from the bloody annual seal cull.

Looking back on the June 1974 action it is clear for everyone to see that what happened was an amazing success. Not only were de facto seals saved at the time, but generations of seals to come have also been saved from the seal cullers. Sadly, however, despite the fact the Band of Mercy was saving lives and preventing suffering, not everyone in the animal liberation movement approved of their tactics.

In July 1974 a member of the Hunt Saboteurs Association offered a reward of £250 for information that would inform upon the Band of Mercy. Speaking on behalf of the local sab group the person represented, the spokesperson told the press, "We approve of their ideals, but are opposed to their methods."

How anyone can say they approve of a person's ideals and then side against them by offering a reward for their capture is a total mystery. Fortunately, despite this act of treachery, the Band of Mercy had by now realized its power. By performing illegal actions the Band was able to directly save the lives of animals by destroying the tool of torture and death. Even if the weaker members of the movement rejected the Band's ideas, the Band realized its work had to continue. To stop would be to let the animals down.

The First Animal Rescue

Following the anti-seal action the Band of Mercy then launched its first intensive wave of campaigning against the vivisection industry. In the months leading up to the action at the Wash, the Band of Mercy had been able to gather some inside information about vivisection laboratory animal suppliers. All of this information was gathered and stored, waiting for the day it could be used to its fullest effect. And so it was, that following the action at the Wash, the Band was able to launch straight into a wave of actions against the vivisection industry.

Between June and August 1974 the Band of Mercy launched eight raids against vivisection lab animal suppliers. The main emphasis of the actions was to cause economic sabotage by either damaging buildings or vehicles. But the Band also reached another landmark in their history by carrying out their first-ever animal rescue during this period.

The first Band of Mercy animal rescue happened in Wiltshire in the English Westcountry. A guinea pig farm was targeted and the activists managed to rescue half a dozen of the inmates. Besides being a landmark action for being the first Band of Mercy animal rescue, the action also produced an unexpected but very welcome outcome. The guinea pig farm owner was so shaken by the raid she began to fear that more activists would turn up during the night. With such a fear of the masked strangers breaking into her home, this uncaring capitalist who profited from animal torture took the only course of sensible action: she closed her business.

Besides targeting the vivisection industry, the Band of Mercy also continued to take actions against the hunt. But not wanting to limit their actions to just two forms of animal abuse, the Band also targeted chicken breeders and the firearm lobby. In July 1974, a gun shop in Marlborough was attacked and damaged. The original Victorian Bands of Mercy could surely be proud that their great deeds were being continued in a twentieth-century form.

For a small group of friends, consisting of less than half a dozen activists, the Band of Mercy was able to make a tremendous impact against the animal abusers and their presence was truly felt. Sadly, however, the Band of Mercy's luck ran out in August 1974.

In August 1974 the Band of Mercy targeted Oxford Laboratory Animal Colonies in Bicester. The first action was a success. But then the Band of Mercy made the mistake of returning to O.L.A.C. two days later (I should point out its very easy with hindsight to say it was a mistake to return, but back then it was a perfectly logical action). It was on this second raid the activists, Ronnie Lee and Cliff Goodman, were spotted by a security guard. After being spotted the police were called and Ronnie and Cliff were promptly arrested.

If the police had hoped that the arrests would bring an end to the Band of Mercy, they were very mistaken. The arrest of Ronnie Lee and Cliff Goodman gave a fresh wave of publicity to the Band of Mercy. Rather than being regarded as terrorists, many people viewed the Band as heroes. These two young men were seen as a sort of latter day Robin Hood for the animals. Ronnie and Cliff were soon canonized as the Bicester Two. Throughout the hearing daily demonstrations took place outside the court. Support for the Bicester Two was very strong and came from the most unlikely of quarters. Even Ronnie Lee's local Member of Parliament, the Free Church Minister Ivor Clemitson, joined in the campaign for their release.

Strong Public Support

Despite the strong public support for the Bicester Two, both Ronnie Lee and Cliff Goodman were given three years imprisonment. A letter published in the *Daily Telegraph* shows the anger felt at the outcome of the first animal liberation trial.

"Many would sympathize with their action against the utterly diabolical and largely unnecessary form of cruelty involved in animal experimentation. These young men, while defying the law, showed great courage, and the sentences of three years imprisonment seems unrealistic and harsh."

Now, it is said you can't keep a good Animal/Earth liberation activist down. This is certainly true in the case of Ronnie Lee. After the sentencing, Ronnie and Cliff split up. Ronnie was moved to Winchester prison and Cliff went back to Oxford prison (whilst on remand [awaiting trial] both Ronnie and Cliff were inmates of Oxford prison).

At Winchester prison Ronnie discovered that provisions for vegans in prison were less than desirable. So once at Winchester, to try and assure a decent meal and proper vegan clothing Ronnie went on a hunger strike. This hunger strike gained a great deal of media attention and once again the issue of animal liberation was being openly discussed. With the spotlight once again being focused on animal liberation Ronnie soon expanded his hunger strike demands to include issues revolving around Porton Down, the Government's chemical and biological warfare research station, where horrific animal experimentation goes on. . . .

Both Cliff Goodman and Ronnie Lee only served a third of their sentence and were both paroled after 12 months in the spring of 1976.

Being in jail had affected both of the Bicester Two, but in totally different ways. Cliff Goodman came out of prison with just one thought: he didn't want to go back inside. He decided he wasn't a revolutionary and wanted to stick to strictly legal campaigning in the future. Sadly, whilst in prison, Cliff decided to turn informer and gave the police a great deal of information about the use of radios by the Band of Mercy. For this act of treachery, Cliff was given the title of the movement's first 'grass' (police informer).

The Birth of the Animal Liberation Front

Ronnie, on the other hand, was given a new sense of determination and realized there was widespread public support for animal liberation illegal direct action. Whilst in prison Ronnie read widely on the subject of the labor movement.

With this knowledge and his pure determination, he started to plan a more revolutionary animal liberation group, a group that could indeed achieve animal liberation. . . .

Upon his release Ronnie gathered together the remains of the Band of Mercy. He was also able to find a couple dozen more new recruits for the illegal direct action animal liberation movement. Under Ronnie's gaze the new gathering (of approximately 30 people) was able to plan its future. With Ronnie as a leading light, the group could develop and expand the work of the Band of Mercy. This was a revolutionary group and everyone knew it.

The only problem for the group was the name the Band of Mercy. The name was no longer appropriate. It didn't fit the new revolutionary feel. A new name was needed. A name that would haunt the animal abusers. A name whose very mention could symbolize a whole ideology of a revolutionary movement. A name that was more than a name. With all this in mind Ronnie selected the name the Animal Liberation Front; the A.L.F.

"Latent violence is behind every law, every rule, and every requirement in any collectivist undertaking."

Socialists Encourage Violent Extremism

Brian Paterson

Socialism, Brian Paterson argues in the following viewpoint, is a political system based on violence and coercion. According to Paterson, socialism creates no new wealth or property but rather redistributes what already exists. He insists that the forced redistribution of wealth inherent in socialism makes it a poor choice for the twenty-first century. Brian Paterson is a mainframe and PC computer programmer who originated and maintains the www.screwedupworld.com Web site.

As you read, consider the following questions:
1. In the author's opinion, why do some people consider capitalism a universal monster?
2. According to Paterson, in a socialist society, what will happen if you ignore a command to redistribute your wealth?
3. What new political ideas did the Enlightenment offer the Western public forum, in Paterson's opinion?

Although in many ways I do not fit the sensitive, New-Age guy profile, I do enjoy reading some authors of a transformational or modern philosophical bent. And over the years, I've noticed that many New-Age type people whom I either read about or talk with seem to accept some form of collectivism as a given in progressive thinking.

This was brought home to me while reading an article in *Yoga Journal* by someone who was emphasizing to readers that their life challenges were their own and not the cause of some external force. In making his point, he put forth a list of things to which people commonly attribute their unhappiness (spouse, job, boss, etc.) and concluded that list with, "no, not even Capitalism is to blame". And it wasn't intended sarcastically.

The columnist's easy use of Capitalism as a universal monster struck me as rather odd. I do know that references to the goodness of collectivism are common in New-Age or "progressive" writings and I would be the first to agree that having less attachment to material things and sharing freely with others is undoubtedly a more evolved outlook.

Nothing New Is Created

But collectivism—Socialism—does neither. First of all, it stresses enormous attachment to (usually others') possessions and emanates from the very un-New-Age outlook of "scarcity" thinking. Socialism rarely creates anything new; rather it looks at what free people have already created and redistributes it, according to what is popular at the time.

Secondly, it is a system based entirely on coercion and violence—forcing other people at gunpoint to do things with their possessions and their livelihoods that they would not have done by choice. Over-the-top hyperbole, you say? Try ignoring a command to redistribute your wealth. If you do so long enough, people will eventually come to your house with guns, take you away and incarcerate you. We call it going to prison for tax evasion.

That latent violence is behind every law, every rule, and every requirement in any collectivist undertaking. And it has been my experience that, just as Mom always said, any matter brought to bear through violence or the threat thereof, is only a short-term solution at best. No matter how noble the cause—whether you are planning to cure cancer or distribute food—taking people's money at gunpoint is not a morally sound long-term proposition. And, no, the fact that you get to vote on it doesn't make it any more so.

Socialism Creates Terror

The left's vision was man as a selfless slave of the state, and the state as the omniscient manager of the economy. However, instead of prosperity, happiness and freedom, Communism and Socialism produced nothing but poverty, misery and terror (witness Soviet Russia, North Korea and Cuba, among others). Their system had to fail, because it was based on a lie. You cannot create freedom and happiness by destroying individual rights; and you cannot create prosperity by negating the mind and evading the laws of economics.

Edwin A. Locke, *Capitalism Magazine*, May 1, 2002.

If I were to suggest that you should be forced to work unpaid for two days each week but you get to vote on where, you would be outraged. You would correctly call it slavery. Yet when I propose that you can work wherever you like, but I will take the fruits of two (or three) days from each week's labor, you wouldn't bat an eye. You would correctly call it taxation. Then, when that money is handed out to a properly anointed cause, those doing the handing can proclaim what a generous people we are, never addressing the awkward fact that the money was in fact "contributed" more out of the wish to avoid federal prison rather than anything resembling authentic generosity.

Individuals Choose What Works

If people voluntarily choose to live and share in a communal situation, I think that's great. I personally would become highly annoyed living in close quarters with a group and having to vote on everything that happens. But, thanks to the wisdom of our forefathers when they created a Constitutional Republic, you don't have to live my way either.

As opposed to in a simple majority-rule democracy, you can choose what works for you with the comforting knowledge that it cannot ever be voted on by people you don't even know. And that actually sounds pretty progressive to me. For although we may take it as self evident today, it was at that time truly new thought born of the Enlightenment movement in Europe. The importance of that can't be over-emphasized—that rather than a new spin on old ideas, it was thought that had never before happened in the Western public forum.

So, modern pundits notwithstanding maybe the "new" ideas of the 1970's are actually more rooted in weary Marxism of the 1870's than in the authentically new age thinking of the 1770's.

"Without a mass Marxist party offering clear socialist alternatives to capitalism people will turn to all sorts of strange actions and ideas for answers."

Socialism Would Benefit Society

John Fisher

The reconstruction of society along socialist lines will end the anger and cynicism of youth caused by the violence and destructiveness of capitalism, John Fisher claims in the following viewpoint. Fisher argues that young people who reject American culture by embracing radical religious views are seeking an alternative to the decaying values of capitalism that only socialism can provide. Further, he maintains that the benefits of socialism offer young people a future that capitalism cannot match. John Fisher is an executive member of the Socialist Alliance, a socialist organization in England.

As you read, consider the following questions:

1. In Fisher's opinion, why are Marxists not surprised by the actions of John Walker and Charles Bishop?
2. According to the author, why were Walker and Bishop attracted to religious fanaticism?
3. Who will guide the forward movement of humanity as a whole, in Fisher's opinion?

John Fisher, "Domestic Symptoms of Capitalism in Decay," *Youth for International Socialism*, www.newyouth.com, January 7, 2002. Copyright © 2002 by Wellred. Reproduced by permission.

Recently an American by the name of John Walker was found in the ranks of the [Muslim fundamentalist] Taliban. A young boy, Charles Bishop, also recently flew a small plane into a tall Florida office building. In his pocket was found a hand written note expressing support for [Arab terrorist Osama] bin Laden. To many these occurrences are shocking, to Marxists they are no surprise. Global capitalism is in the epoch of its senile decay. Not even suburban America is safe from the cancer of this rotten system.

Unknowingly the two mentioned individuals have expressed discontent not just with American culture, but with capitalism as a whole. They have rejected American society, but have embraced reactionary religious fanaticism. Without a clear alternative to the problems and filth capitalism has created they have turned into the shock troops of reaction. Without a mass Marxist party offering clear socialist alternatives to capitalism people will turn to all sorts of strange actions and ideas for answers.

Angry Youth

Why though is the rottenness of capitalism popping up so close to home? Today's suburban kids have "everything they need, they go to school, they have their TVs, their video games, their music."

Young Americans and Western Europeans are angry. But again, why? The apologists of capital say, "what is wrong with these kids, they have everything they want!" They're angry because the system of capitalism offers them no real future. On the news they see wars raging in ex-colonial nations thanks to the consequences of imperialism. In their own country they see mass violence, such as school shootings (yet another product of the American culture created by a decaying capitalism). In their own homes they see their parents at each other's throats over money, it is no wonder violence and anger is all the "rage" in the West among the youth. Multiply this scenario by millions with thousands of different variations and it is no surprise the cancer of capitalism is popping up in the intestines of the beast itself.

How does this end? How does the anger and cynicism of the youth end? It will end along with the rotten system which created it—capitalism. The answer is not the injection of hypocritical religious morals into the schools but the conscious revolutionary reconstruction of society along socialist lines.

Socialism Offers a New Social and Economic Order

The Socialist Party strives to establish a radical democracy that places people's lives under their own control—a nonracist, classless, feminist, socialist society in which people cooperate at work, at home, and in the community.

Socialism is not mere government ownership, a welfare state, or a repressive bureaucracy. Socialism is a new social and economic order in which workers and consumers control production and community residents control their neighborhoods, homes, and schools. The production of society is used for the benefit of all humanity, not for the private profit of a few. Socialism produces a constantly renewed future by not plundering the resources of the earth.

Michigan Socialist Party, www.michigansocialist.net, 2004.

How will this happen though? Not through religious fundamentalism, not through any sort of reforms even. It will end through the building of a mass party of the proletariat. Only through the conscious efforts of the working class guided by an aware Marxist leadership will the socialist reconstruction of society be possible and with that the movement forward of humanity as a whole.

"The FBI now considers . . . 'ecoterrorism'
. . . to be America's most serious form of
domestic terror."

Radical Environmentalists Are Terrorists

Brad Knickerbocker

Brad Knickerbocker argues in the following viewpoint that attacks by radical environmentalists such as the Earth Liberation Front (ELF) are now considered serious acts of terrorism. While ELF's acts of vandalism and arson have not yet physically hurt anyone, Knickerbocker contends that the group has threatened to use guns if necessary to achieve its ends. Moreover, the U.S. government defines terrorism as the "unlawful use of force and violence against persons or property," which clearly includes ELF acts such as burning down construction projects and blowing up SUVs. Brad Knickerbocker is a staff writer for the *Christian Science Monitor*.

As you read, consider the following questions:
1. According to Knickerbocker, until the San Diego fire, what was ELF's largest attack?
2. Why is it difficult to arrest or prosecute ELF ecoterrorists, in the author's opinion?
3. In Knickerbocker's opinion, how do mainstream environmentalists regard ELF's tactics?

Environmental activism's darker side is turning from wild nature to the urban jungle. Among its targets: posh housing developments, car dealerships hawking sport utility vehicles, and military-recruiting stations.

The latest attack came [in early August 2003] when a large condominium project under construction in an upscale San Diego neighborhood burned to the ground. A banner stretched across the charred site read: "If you build it—we will burn it. The E.L.F.s are mad." In e-mails to regional newspapers, the Earth Liberation Front (ELF) claimed responsibility for the conflagration that also damaged nearby homes.

Domestic Terrorism

Property damage in the name of environmental protection dates back to the "monkey wrenching" advocated by groups like Earth First. But trashing logging trucks and driving spikes into old-growth trees pales in comparison to recent events—arson and vandalism of luxury homes, and violent assaults on the symbols of urban sprawl. SUVs have been vandalized or firebombed in Santa Cruz, Calif., Eugene, Ore., and Erie, Pa. At the US Navy recruiting headquarters in Montgomery, Ala., cars were spray painted with antiwar messages and a truck was set on fire. The FBI now considers such attacks—dubbed "ecoterrorism"—to be America's most serious form of domestic terror.

Still, it's not clear why activists targeted the San Diego apartments. Despite the size of the complex—at 1,500 units, it's one of southern California's largest apartment-construction projects—the La Jolla Crossroads was hardly controversial, raising nary an eyebrow when plans came before city officials a few years back.

"It wasn't a big item on our radar," says Richard Miller, chair of the local Sierra Club chapter. The condos did take up open space and will of course contribute to urban growth and traffic, Mr. Miller says. But on the other hand, the project met environmentalists' goals, providing housing for hundreds of people in a fairly small space and setting aside apartments for poor and middle-income residents.

Until the San Diego fire, the largest such attack was the 1998 burning of a new ski resort in Vail, Colo., which critics

Earth Liberation Actions in 2002

The total direct actions for Earth liberation that occurred in 2002 were 53, down from 65 in 2001, an 18% decrease. January was by far the busiest month with 10 actions recorded.

There were 49 actions in the US, in 16 different states, and 4 in Canada, in 2 provinces. Oregon was the most active state with 10 actions recorded, followed by Virginia with 7. California had 6 and Pennsylvania recorded 5. . . .

New developments dominated the issues focused on with 13 actions taken against various new homes and building projects. Forest issues accounted for 10 actions while cars and SUVs took 8. 91 vehicles were targeted.

Monthly Totals		States/Provinces	
January	10	AZ	01
February	02	CA	06
March	02	CO	02
April	05	IN	01
May	02	KY	01
June	05	MA	02
July	06	ME	01
August	04	MI	01
September	06	MN	04
October	06	MT	01
November	01	OR	10
December	04	PA	05
		TX	01
		UT	02
		VA	07
		WA	04
		BC	03
		ONT	01

Issues

development	13
forest/environment related	10
cars & SUVs	08
GMO	06
police & government	06
powerlines	05
corporate	01
education	01
golf	01
olympics	01
sexism	01

North American Animal Liberation Front press office, 2002.

had said would eliminate a vast habitat for the threatened Canada lynx.

The fundamental factor behind the ELF—apparently the main motivator of such attacks—is that "the profit motive caused and reinforced by the capitalist society is destroying all life on this planet," according to the ELF website. "The only way, at this point in time, to stop that continued destruction of life is to . . . take the profit motive out of killing."

Violence Is Allowed

ELF "guidelines" include taking "all necessary precautions against harming any animal, human and non-human." But they also include a call to "inflict economic damage on those profiting from the destruction and exploitation of the natural environment."

An ELF "communiqué" taking responsibility for last September's [2002] firebombing of a US Forest Service research station in Pennsylvania declared: "While innocent life will never be harmed in any action we undertake, where it is necessary, we will no longer hesitate to pick up the gun to implement justice, and provide the needed protection for our planet that decades of legal battles, pleading, protest, and economic sabotage have failed . . . to achieve."

The group's website includes a 37-page how-to manual titled "Setting Fires With Electrical Timers."

The ELF is an ideological cousin to the Animal Liberation Front (ALF), a group that began in England about 12 years ago as a more radical alternative to Earth First. The ELF claimed its first "action" in the United States in 1997—releasing wild horses and torching a US Bureau of Land Management corral near Burns, Ore.

Since then, it's claimed credit for what it says are hundreds of attacks and some $50 million in damages. The FBI does not dispute those figures.

Few Arrests

Few arrests or prosecutions have followed from the violent actions of environmentalists or animal-rights advocates—and, indeed, most such crimes remain unsolved. One "eco-terrorist" on the FBI's "wanted" list is Michael James Scarpitti, accused of torching concrete mixing trucks and Oregon logging equipment.

The ELF has no central location, leadership, or hierarchy. It's organized into autonomous cells that work independently and anonymously. Its "communiqués" and website are managed by supporters without clear links to ELF crimes.

While mainstream environmentalists generally reject ELF tactics, some activists object to the portrayal of the group's assaults on property as "terrorism": So far, at least, the vandalism, even the violence, has not caused any death or major injury.

But the federal government defines "terrorism" as "the unlawful use of force and violence against persons or property to intimidate or coerce a government, the civilian population, or any segment thereof, in furtherance of political or social objectives"—a definition that would appear to match the aims and activities of the ELF.

"Acts of [environmental sabotage] are entirely justified and are, indeed, both necessary and effective."

Ecoterrorism Is Justified

Emily Kumpel

Radical environmentalism is justified because less violent tactics have not proven effective in stopping the destruction of the environment, Emily Kumpel argues in the following viewpoint. She insists that many radical environmentalists address the immediate need to protect what is left of the environment at any cost. Although Kumpel is uncomfortable with the destructiveness of ecoterrorist acts, she supports them because they effect necessary change. Emily Kumpel is a student at Johns Hopkins University.

As you read, consider the following questions:
1. What is deep ecology, in the author's opinion?
2. What is the central goal behind ecoterror, according to the author?
3. Why have strategies to crack down on ecoterrorism not worked, according to Kumpel?

Emily Kumpel, "In Defense of Radical Environmentalism," www.takingitglobal.org, August 18, 2002. Copyright © 2002 by Taking It Global. Reproduced by permission.

The immediate danger facing the environment and the human cause of this destruction are clear to many activists around the globe. Also acknowledged is that something must be done. However, there are many different types of environmentalists out there with a wide range of tactics and philosophies used to justify their actions and guide them in their defense of the wild. One movement of extreme environmental activism has been dubbed "ecoterrorism" or "ecotage". Ecoterrorism is defined in the dictionary as "terrorism or sabotage committed in the name of environmental causes," while these groups themselves describe it as nonviolent direct action. According to the FBI, ecoterrorism is "the use or threatened use of violence of a criminal nature against innocent victims or property by an environmentally-oriented, subnational group for environmental-political reasons, or aimed at an audience beyond the target, often of a symbolic nature." David Foreman, the founder of a self-described "radical" environmental group Earth First!, asserts that, "We can have big wilderness, and we can reintroduce extirpated species, but unless the fact that there are way too many people on the earth is dealt with, unless the idea that the world is a resource for us to use is dealt with, unless humans can find their way home again, then the problems will continue."

Many ecoterrorists ascribe to what is known as deep ecology, and their actions address the immediate need to protect what is left—preventing, for example, the logging of a particular forest or the death of a single whale—as well as suggesting a change in the fundamental way we think of ourselves and of our place in nature. As Foreman explained, ". . . we had to offer a fundamental challenge to Western civilization." The group's motto is "No compromise in defense of Mother Earth."

Earth First! uses "confrontation, guerrilla theater, direct action and civil disobedience to fight for wild places and life processes." While they do not actually "condone or condemn monkey wrenching, ecotage, or other forms of property destruction," they do provide a network for activists to discuss creative ways of opposing environmental destruction. According to Bill McKibben, "Earth First! and the few other groups like it have a purpose, and that purpose is defense of the wild, the natural, the nonhuman." However, there is a line between civil disobedience and nonviolent direct action in that the latter includes monkey wrenching and criminal destruction of property. Other groups, such as the Earth Liberation Front (ELF), which broke off from Earth First! when others wanted to "mainstream" the group, and the Animal Liberation Front (ALF) are well known for their acts of ecotage. According to the FBI, the ELF and the ALF are "serious terrorist threats(s)." Tactics include disabling logging machinery, placing activists in front of whaling ships, destroying airstrips, spiking trees, and arson.

Deep Ecology Is a Defense

How do these environmentalists justify destroying human creations for the sake of a single living thing or small forest? This movement finds its defense in deep ecology and ecocentric ethics, major religions and new age philosophy, and, sometimes, conventional wisdom.

In defense of ecoterrorism, I will put forward that these actions are dictated by the Earth Liberation Front Guidelines, which are as follows: "1. To inflict economic damage on those profiting from the destruction and exploitation of the natural environment. 2. To reveal and educate the public on the atrocities committed against the earth and all species that populate it. 3. To take all necessary precautions against harming any animal, human and non-human."

The central goal behind ecoterror beliefs is to shift the focus away from humans and onto the entire ecosystem. McKibben describes Earth First! as "one of the purest examples of putting the rest of creation ahead of exclusively human needs." Changing the anthropocentric view of the environment is the heart of many environmental philosophies. However, these philosophies often dictate only how we think, not our actions. Ecoterrorists take this to heart and use traditionally drastic measures to accomplish their goals.

First, we as humans are not superior and therefore either all living things should be treated the same, or the whole of the community should come before the good of the individual. The first is a biotic view of ecology, incorporating Albert

Schweitzer's notion of a "reverence for life." In resolving conflicts between man and nature, he suggests this order: 1. self-defense 2. proportionality 3. minimum wrong 4. distributive justice 5. restitutive justice. Ecoterrorists protect the life of both living beings and natural systems from human destruction when the human destruction is a function of our wants, not our needs. In Colorado, for example, ecoterrorists committed an incredibly costly act of ecotage, burning five buildings at the Vail Ski Resort in 1998. The ski resort was constructed despite the outcries of the public and environmentalists, as the company clear-cut what was supposed to remain untouched wilderness. While human property was destroyed, no humans or other living things were harmed. "They ask, why is more ski terrain, miles of roads, bathrooms and a warming house more important than the habitat of creatures man has already pushed to the brink of extinction?" This protection by ecotage—while extreme by many standards—is justified by Schweitzer's system. Humans had no claim to self-defense, the proportional gain for our species was not enough, there was no way to do a minimum wrong, and there is so little land left that there is no fair way to make up the destruction in another area. And, if we accept that all life should be respected and cared for, then we should do all we can to protect life from human destruction.

Earth Liberation Front Guidelines

1. To cause as much economic damage as possible to a given entity that is profiting off the destruction of the natural environment and life for selfish greed and profit,

2. To educate the public on the atrocities committed against the environment and life,

3. To take all necessary precautions against harming life.

North American Earth Liberation Front press office, 2001.

In one of the most well known defenses of environmentalism, Aldo Leopold upholds that, "A thing is right when it tends to preserve the integrity, stability, and beauty of the biotic community. It is wrong when it tends otherwise." We have an obligation to uphold the stability of the system. Ecoterrorism serves to protect the biotic community using methods that, while destroying human creations, still do not benefit the community. Human creations are not included as a part of this biotic community, and most methods of ecotage in the environmental movement serve to protect wild areas from human expansion. Any infringement by humans into this area would disrupt our ecosystem's integrity, stability, and beauty; therefore, it is wrong. Ecoterrorist acts are consequently right because they protect those values.

The Land Ethic View

The land ethic view of environmental philosophy incorporates both living and nonliving entities, and it puts the stability of the community above individual lives. In this belief, humans have no superiority in nature, and we, as humans, are responsible for righting our wrongs—for example, reintroducing species to an area if we caused their extinction. The strongest criticism of this approach is also the strongest support for ecotage; it "condones sacrificing the good of individuals to the good of the whole," which is indeed just what the movement is doing. Bill McKibben also suggests that "individual suffering—animal or human—might be less important that the suffering of species, ecosystems, the planet."

The FBI considers these ecoterrorist organizations to be domestic terrorist groups, and many mainstream environmentalists working to protect the same wilderness areas are opposed to monkey wrenching. Environmentalists, politicians, business leaders, and the public alike have all brought up many arguments against the use of ecotage. Some argue that we as humans are a part of nature and our evolution has led us to superiority over the rest of the environment. Therefore we should be in control of the environment, letting our own natural evolution take its course. By downsizing our lives to preserve the environment we are going against the natural course of things.

Ecoterrorists (and others) reply that we are addicted to consumerism as well as growth and expansion. Just because that is the way it has always been does not mean that it is right; evolution changes things. Perhaps our evolution is not in taking control of the earth, but in learning to stop our growing and settle down. [David] Orr states that economic growth is the target of our society because growth is "the normal state of things." However, our natural resources are finite, and can only hold so many people and offer so much, therefore, economic growth has to be finite at some point as well. People, especially workers, do things because that's just the way it is and how it's always been "And we don't want to change," McKibben suggests. "Jim wants to log as he always has. I want to be able to drive as I always have and go on living in the large house I live in and so on." As a result we have begun to decline as human beings by staying the same, because material goods are no longer fulfilling and there is no more meaningful work left to be done. The cultural sickness dubbed "affluenza" is used to describe our addiction to material goods and the absurdity of it all. Ecotage contributes to reducing our lifestyles and the material goods and lifestyles within. . . .

Extreme Action Is Not Pragmatic

Others, especially more traditional environmentalists, argue that extreme action is simply not pragmatic in the society in which we live. According to this argument, ecoterrorism ignores the culture and the political system we work in, and we cannot just disregard that. They argue that ecoterrorists make it hard for other environmental activists working from within the system because they lose respect for all other environmental causes. In our current political system, there are so many things that are going on in voter's minds and environmentalism is only one of many. Equating environmentalism with extremism is not going to help gain any votes.

However, according to an ABC reporter who investigated the ecotage movement, ecoterrorists have exhausted all of the traditional options before turning to destruction. ". . . though there are many many environmental groups out there who use traditional approaches like lobbying Congress and protesting timber sales, ELF regards mainstream groups as sell-outs, and corporate puppets . . . they saw these techniques fail time and time again to stop the march of industry on nature." The Earth First! website asks readers if they are tired of, "namby-pamby environmental groups" and "overpaid corporate environmentalists who suck up to bureaucrats and industry." Ecoterrorists are not looking to uphold the system and work within it, but are instead looking to change people's attitudes and see extreme actions as the only way to both protect the immediate needs of the environment and drastically inspire a change of attitude. These acts probably do make environmentalists as a whole lose credibility in the political and economic world, though ecoterrorists argue that the political, economic, and moral world we currently live in is what itself needs to be changed and working within the system will not accomplish that.

Ecoterrorism does challenge the way we think about the system and many activists' view of how to work within the system. Yet their methods have proven effective in saving individual wild lands and living beings.

Another argument against ecoterrorism is that even though many activists say that they aren't harming human lives, destruction of property is destroying people's jobs and is therefore destroying livelihoods. A contributor to *Nature* magazine described Earth First!'s methods as showing a "deep insensitivity to human suffering." One of the newer arguments against ecotage in the United States [after the September 11, 2001, terrorist attacks] is that if foreign terrorism is not acceptable, then domestic terrorism like ecotage is not acceptable either. Some environmentalists are even accused of "environmental fascism."

Environmental Destruction

But many also recognize that the environmental destruction that humans are creating because of our view of the earth as a resource for our own use is threatening our health and that of our children. Richard Falk calls for tougher strategies in order to produce results, suggesting that we, "engage concrete sources of resistance, including human depravity and greed . . . moral concern is serious only if it includes active participation in ongoing struggles against injustice and suffering." McKibben says of deep ecology's reductionist approach, ". . . they are extreme solutions, but we live in an extreme time. . . . If industrial civilization is ending nature, it is not utter silliness to talk about ending—or, at least, transforming—industrial civilization," and that "the thinking is more radical than the action." Many actions we collectively take, such as the nuclear arms buildup and our cultural obsession with fast food and Coca-Cola, are all considered irrational, yet we do it. So why not ecoterrorism? Links have been made between slavery and today's exploitation of natural resources such as fossil fuels and animals. Radical actions ended slavery, and radicalism powered the civil rights movement, native independence, and many other great progressive moves throughout history. So why not ecoterrorism? Nature is dying, according to McKibben, and he urges us to give the end of nature our best fight. "We are different from the rest of the natural order, for the single reason that we possess the possibility of self-restraint, or choosing some other way."

And the suggestions to crackdown on ecoterrorism post 9-11 have not worked. Richard Berman, the executive director of the Center for Consumer Freedom, asked Congress to cut funding to ecoterrorist groups, much like it did to the Al Qaeda network [responsible for the September 11 attacks]. He asked that their nonprofit status be taken away, or that groups like People for the Ethical Treatment of Animals and Physicians Committee for Responsible Medicine that have supposedly given support to ecoterrorist groups in the past be reprimanded in some way. However, this proposal did not gain much support. So far, the ELF and ALF members have been very effective in avoiding the authorities because they are so decentralized and act within cells of one to several members. Funding does not seem to be a key issue for the group.

While ecoterrorists describe themselves as subscribers to deep ecology, I find that the strongest arguments to justify their actions instead come from a mixture of many environmental philosophies. Indeed, based on any view of the environment that puts the emphasis away from humans, I find it hard not to support the use of ecoterrorism to prevent destruction.

Ecoterrorism Is Justified

Yet I also feel myself so entrenched in this system of the way it has always been that I find it hard to advocate acts of sabotage against the political and economic structure of our world.

I think that acts of ecotage are entirely justified and are, indeed, both necessary and effective, yet I cannot imagine myself being able to actually commit ecoterrorism. Looking at radical animal rights groups like People for the Ethical Treatment of Animals, I entirely disagree with most of their tactics, and yet, it was their tactics that caused me to become vegan. Like many supporters of "extreme" environmental activists, I may disagree with the destructive and damaging nature of such tactics, yet I cannot argue with their effectiveness.

Periodical Bibliography

The following articles have been selected to supplement the diverse views presented in this chapter.

Diane Alden	"Destroyer of Worlds," NewsMax.com, August 18, 2001.
Alex Callinicos	"The Case for Revolutionary Socialism," *Z Magazine*, December 7, 2003.
Brian Carnell	"Extent of Animal Rights Extremism in the United States," AnimalRights.net, May 14, 2000.
Dan Gabriel	"Extremist Groups Target Businesses and People," *Insight on the News*, May 28, 2001.
William T. Johnson	"The Bible on Environmental Conservation: A 21st Century Prescription," *Electronic Green Journal*, 2000.
Patrik Jonsson	"Tracing an Animal-Rights Philosophy," *Christian Science Monitor*, October 9, 2001.
Roger Kimball	"The Death of Socialism," *New Criterion*, April 2002.
Edwin A. Locke	"Anti-Globalization: The Left's Violent Assault on Global Prosperity," *Capitalism Magazine*, May 1, 2002.
Adrian R. Morrison	"Personal Reflections on the Animal-Rights Phenomenon," *Perspectives in Biology and Medicine*, Winter 2001.
Jim Motavalli	"A Movement to Grant Legal Protections to Animals Is Gathering Force," Environmental News Network, May 2, 2003. www.enn.com.
Ralph Nader	"Corporate Socialism," *Washington Post*, July 18, 2002.
William P. Orth	"U.S. Workers Face a No-Win Situation: Less Hours, Less Pay, More Work," *Socialist*, October 2003.
Dennis Prager	"Socialism Kills," TownHall.com, September 2, 2003.
Southern Poverty Law Center	"From Push to Shove," *Intelligence Report*, 2003.
Workers World	"Which Road to Socialism?" December 25, 2003. www.workers.org.

CHAPTER 3

Do White Supremacist Groups Promote Hate and Violence?

Chapter Preface

White supremacist organizations such as the Ku Klux Klan, the National Alliance, and the Creativity Movement (formerly the World Church of the Creator) have been male dominated since their founding. Women involved in these organizations have traditionally played supportive, usually subservient roles to men in the group. The division of roles along gender lines was clear: men were active in the group while women stayed home and bore and raised children. Indeed, women were usually recruited to these groups for the purpose of carrying the next generation of the white race. For many white supremacist women, this homebound, reproductive role was enough. However, late in the twentieth century women began to take more active, often violent roles in supremacist groups. Women for Aryan Unity, a women's white supremacist organization, now encourages women "to stand by their men and take up their weapons and battle cry if the men should fall." Women's roles in supremacist organizations have evolved to include the active promotion of hate and violence. Kirsten Kaiser, married for nine years to a member of the neo-Nazi National Alliance says, "It seems to me that the true believers, the women, are even more violent than the men."

Kathleen M. Blee, author of *Inside Organized Racism: Women in the Hate Movement*, maintains that while some women have drifted into racist organizations—usually because of their involvement with a man who has ties to the group—many women have sought out white supremacy organizations on their own. She contends that they are just as resolute in their commitment to racism as men in such groups and just as ready to turn to violence. Blee argues that "in a number of groups women are not only cheerleaders, but are active participants and planners." Further, her research has shown that racist groups that attract younger people—skinheads and neo-Nazis, for example—are more likely to attract women who want an active role. Blee insists, "These young women expect to be part of the violence of these groups."

Mark Potok of the Southern Poverty Law Center, an organization that tracks U.S. extremist group activity, concurs with Blee. His research shows that racist groups are actively recruiting young women who are not afraid of violence. He explains, "There is so much talk within the movement about the difficulty of finding good Aryan female warriors, that now it is being acted upon." Lisa Tuner, founder of the Women's Frontier, an offshoot of the neo-Nazi World Church of the Creator, notes, "Everyone is starting to realize that if we are going to overcome in this struggle, we are going to have to do it together—man and woman—side by side."

Women in white supremacist organizations have proven that they can be just as steadfast in the promotion of the racist cause as their male counterparts. In the following chapter authors debate whether white supremacist groups promote hate and violence.

"The 'race war' advocates are now reaching high schools, colleges and official military units through the Internet."

White Supremacist Groups Promote Hate and Violence

Carl Rowan

Carl Rowan was a syndicated columnist and authored *The Coming Race War in America*. In the following viewpoint taken from a 1999 column, he argues that the dire predictions he made in his 1996 book about the dangers posed by white supremacists are coming true. According to Rowan, white supremacists now promote hate and violence against minorities more and more efficiently using the Internet. Moreover, he maintains, these hate-mongers are amassing illegal arms with which to conduct a race war in America.

As you read, consider the following questions:

1. How did Richard Butler respond after Buford O. Furrow shot five people at a Jewish community center in 1999, as related by the author?
2. What "one-man forays" does Rowan describe?
3. Why does Rowan think his "alarmist" book is even more pertinent today?

Carl Rowan, "The Creeping Race War," *Liberal Opinion Week*, vol. 10, August 30, 1999, p. 10. Copyright © 1999 by North American Syndicate. Reproduced by permission.

[In 1999] after Buford O. Furrow shot five people at a Jewish community center in Los Angeles and gunned down postal worker Joseph Ileto because "he was nonwhite and worked for the federal government," the white supremacist leader of the Idaho-based Aryan Nations said of Furrow: "He was a good soldier."

"I cannot condemn what he did. He was very respected among us," added Richard Butler, leader of a group that is notorious for advocating violence as a means of making the United States an all-white nation.

Not an Aberration

Butler's words suggest that Furrow was not just a deranged loner when he launched his attack on Jews and nonwhites. Just as Benjamin Nathaniel Smith was more than a loner when he staged a shooting attack on Jews, blacks and Asians in Illinois and Indiana over the [1999] Fourth of July weekend. Just as Timothy J. McVeigh and Terry L. Nichols were not just "lone wolf" nuts when they perpetrated the 1995 bombing of the Alfred P. Murrah federal building in Oklahoma City, killing 168 people.

The bigots within America who hate blacks, Jews, "foreigners," immigrants, Muslims and the federal government are carrying out an unholy war, but it is a war of snipers, isolated shootings and bombings, and one-man forays so far. It may soon become more organized—and worse.

So it is wise that Columbine High School in Colorado reopens this week [in August 1999] under conditions of heightened security. It is prudent that schools across America have taken steps to prevent outbursts of violence by those caught in the dark clutches of the haters. It would be well for the rest of us to be on guard.

A Race War

In 1996, I published a book warning that this society was imperiled by white racists who threatened to kill Jews, deport or kill blacks, wage war on unfavorable judges and federal facilities, and eventually provoke a tragic race war. I made the mistake of titling that book *The Coming Race War in America*, thus scaring the hell out of many reviewers and people who

Anti-Semitic Incidents Year-by-Year National Totals 1980–1999

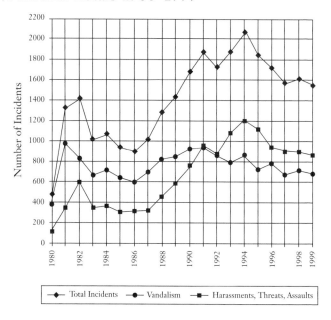

The number of anti-Semitic incidents documented by the Anti-Defamation League (ADL) fell to a total of 1,547 incidents from 1,611 in 1998, a 4 percent decrease. Of the instances of anti-Semitism in 1999, there were 868 cases of harassment (down 3 percent from 896 in 1998), and 679 acts of vandalism (down 5 percent from 715 in 1998). Harassment and vandalism incidents represent 56 percent and 44 percent of the total incidents, respectively, which represents the same proportion as in 1998. ADL's 1998 *Audit* reported 896 incidents of harassment (56 percent of the total) and 715 (44 percent) instances of anti-Semitic vandalism.

Anti-Defamation League, "1999 Audit of Anti-Semitic Incidents," 1999.

branded it "alarmist" without reading it. I cited the 800 or so "militias" and the assorted venomous groups in America that had made as their "bible" a book by William Pierce called *The Turner Diaries*, in which the script for the Oklahoma City bombing was set forth in chilling detail. That book also set forth a plan for the extermination of blacks, Jews and unwanted immigrants.

My "alarmist" book is more pertinent, its documentation

more chilling, today than it was in 1996, because the haters have their war more on track. I am more alarmed now that I have seen Tom Metzger, leader of California's White Aryan Resistance (WAR), declare, "Good hunting, lone wolves" as he calls for a second civil war in exhorting his soldiers to act "in any way you see fit" against immigrants. The "crazy" single killers all have commanders giving orders.

Since 1995, the FBI and other law enforcement agencies have moved against the Viper Militia and other paramilitary groups that were amassing illegal arms and clearly constituted a threat of violence. That provoked a movement away from group actions. To foil FBI and police infiltrators, as I predicted in my book, the move has been to "lone wolf" and "good soldier" violence, with Internet and telephone messages and books by Pierce and other racists setting forth the battle cries and the targets.

The "race war" advocates are now reaching high schools, colleges and official military units through the Internet in ways they never could through books and pamphlets. Thus they have exposed us all to the threat of sudden death.

The problem America faces is far beyond the need to get psychiatrists to a small number of "sick" souls. It is not enough for schools, synagogues, black churches and nonwhite facilities to increase security. We must somehow get all of white America out of denial about the magnitude of "Christian Identity" racism and madness in this society.

The "disciples" and "soldiers" of Butler and Metzger will kill anyone—anyone—they think stands in the way of their Aryan America. Their race war is on. We can waste no time learning more about who they are and where they next plan to strike. And our law enforcement people must act accordingly.

> "*[Morris] Dees focuses on the Klan and other white supremacy groups who's bark is worse than its bite 'to raise more money for the [Southern Poverty Law] center.'*"

The Danger from White Supremacist Groups Is Exaggerated

Adrian H. Krieg

Adrian H. Krieg argues in the following viewpoint that the Southern Poverty Law Center (SPLC) and other watchdog groups exaggerate the danger posed by white supremacists in order to enrich themselves. He maintains that by inflating the membership numbers of the Klu Klux Klan and other white supremacist groups, the SPLC can raise large amounts of money from frightened whites, especially Jewish people. Krieg insists that most of the groups targeted by the SPLC pose no real danger and are being harassed because of their political beliefs. Adrian H. Krieg is a political writer and historian.

As you read, consider the following questions:
1. Why does Krieg maintain that hate pays?
2. Why does the SPLC consider white, Anglo-Saxon males to be the primary purveyors of hate, according to the author?
3. What group does Krieg claim is the largest contributor to the SPLC?

Would be "Do Gooders" seem pressed to contribute to organizations that inform us of their profound well-meaning actions to save society from the evil political right. This has become one of the most profitable business enterprises in the nation. Having taken note of this, it seems to me that people of particularly poor judgment are the most insistent that we support their causes. Assuredly we find these people as the most fanatical members of our society; their religion is one of hate, they hate everything that contradicts their politically left dogma. A substantial number of businesses have grown out of this, which can be said . . . now constitute an entire industry, in many cases of extorting funds from innocent bystanders for the sole purpose of self enrichment. The Simon Wiesenthal Center and the JDL [Jewish Defense League], along with the World Jewish Congress [WJC], come to mind. One of the most successful and most profitable of all of this lot is The Southern Poverty Law Center [SPLC] of Montgomery, Alabama. Two things strike me as ironic: the name and location.

We must first come to the realization that the name seems to indicate some method of fighting poverty and that this is nothing but a ruse. In their 1998 Form 990 IRS return we learn that on line 26 "other salaries and wages" all four columns combined total $6,970,322.00 for total payroll, and a whopping $1,465,130.00 in pension and other benefits. (Line 27 & 28) We learn on the same page that the aggregate expenses for 1998 were $41,550,243.00, no paltry sum that! . . .

We do learn that their extremely well paid executive staffs earns from $65,192.00 up to $272,047.00, with an additional $6,972.00 in direct benefits. I wonder seriously how anyone can justify the trappings of pretending to save the poor and wretched on a salary that is almost twelve times the national average income. In fact, if you are a management job seeker, at least one with limited moral and ethical education, you might find that working for a firm that compensates its average executive staff with $163,683.00 to be an excellent idea. After all, seven times the average national income seems like a good deal especially when you live in Alabama that is on the bottom of [the] national food chain in income.

Just exactly what is it the SPLC does? Well, this is a somewhat nebulous issue since they expend close to fifty percent of their income on advertising and the raising of additional funds, and a large chunk in payroll. When I said, "Hate Pays" I was not kidding; direct public support to SPLC in 1998 was over 27 million dollars.

Government Contracts

To make things worse we learn that revenues from government contracts amounted to $88,692.00, and in addition other income was interest on savings $163,789.00 and dividends from securities of $214,024.00. I don't exactly know how much money you need to have invested to earn $370,000.00 plus in just interest, but I am sure that it's more than one million. We learn from the offices of Senator Strom Thurmond that SPLC had a budget of $9.5 million for 1999.

Just exactly what they did for the government worth over eighty-eight thousand dollars does however interest me. One contract was the US Air Force AFSCO command Hurlburt Field FL by special order executed by Rochelle D. Wiegman Lt. Col. USAF dated July 03/96. It was to Joe Roy editor of *Klanwatch*, one of SPLC printed organs. Now I have reviewed the entire published SPLC['s] list of so-called "Hate Groups" includ[ed in] *Klanwatch*, and find the information contained therein at least in part fabrication. *Klanwatch* lists 138 Ku Klux Klan organizations under 36 various names. Not one address is listed. Not the name of one individual member. All the information provided consists of the name of a town and state, something that any grade school student could put together. Another contract also from the Air Force was again at Hurlburt Field this time with USAF-SOS Special Operations School. They give classes 8 times a year on average 4.5 days and had Mr. Joe Roy speak twice as a "recognized area expert on domestic right wing extremist groups." I for one would be more than just interested [in] what was contained in Mr. Roy's talk "Threat in the United States". Moreover, why the US Air Force is at all involved with what is constitutionally a domestic state police matter could be explained at the very same time. And while we're at it if the Air Force does not know what the "Threats in the United States" are they must be in the wrong business. I thought that this is exactly what the FBI is supposed to protect us from domestically, and the Air Force internationally. It is my understanding that there is a present lawsuit by Dr. Robert Clarkson against the U.S. Air Force for illegal use of SPLC documentation in brainwashing our troops. Three past employees of SPLC, Mr. Balske, Deborah Ellis and Denis Sweet, a past Alabama legislator, all say that [Morris] Dees focuses on the Klan and other white supremacy groups who's bark is worse than its bite "to raise more money for the center". Going after the Klan has brought in millions of dollars, from across the nation. The fact that total Klan membership nationally is below 5000—less than .0035% of the population—seems not to play any part in money raising or in contributing decisions.

This then brings us to the militias that are another *cause de celebrant* for SPLC. The fact that 95% of these militias are benign simply is not part of the equation. While government agencies (FBI, BATF [Bureau of Alcohol, Tobacco and Firearms]) need to create villains to sustain their bloated budgets, SPLC working, often hand in glove with them, requires hate groups to obtain ever more contributions. That the successes of both government agencies and the private sector hate mongers have been more than just successful goes without saying. How many so-called hate groups are partially or wholly financed by various government agencies is also a matter of some conjecture. Often in joint and apparently orchestrated effort they persue the very same outcome. . . .

Hate Crimes

Hate Crimes [are] the latest of a long line of corrosive ideas pushed by the SPLC as well as the political left. George Orwell was first to write on the topic, first in an essay and then in his book *1984* calling it news-speak, a process of through language influencing a pre-plan[n]ed outcome, and of controlling people. We have already instituted a national practice of PC (Political Correctness) that is in fact Cultural Marxism. (CM) Through these processes the left has demonized any historic fact that does not meet the outcome goals of the political left and their academic stooges. In this cause history is being rewritten, consider movies and books like

Roots, *Amistad* and *Pocahontas*, historically not just inaccurate but totally wrong.

They represent the plagiarizing of history for the purpose of social change. This is taking place in our entire society in every venue. Even our language is under attack. Gay, Assault Rifle, Cop Killer Bullet, Peacekeepers, Hippie, Hispanic, Homophobic, Choice, Saturday Night Special, all these words have been created by leftist foundations so that issues can be twisted to their side of the argument. But of greater interest is the fact that none of those words and phrases they have created make any sense, nor are they definable in a lexicographer vernacular.

SPLC can well be categorized as a Dees enterprise. Morris Dees is from Shorter, Alabama. He studied at the University of Alabama School of Commerce. Together with Millary Fuller he set up Fuller & Dees Hart Dixie Products, giving him the "good old boy" appearance. The name was then changed to Fuller & Dees Marketing Group. After his marriage to Maureen he sold his 89% interest in the company to the Los Angeles Mirror Corp. for $5,150,000.00. . . .

Much amazing and confounding information can be learned from the SPLC Internet site. Things I did not know until today when I reviewed the site. First of all it appears that White Anglo Saxon males are the primary purveyors of hate because in the entire list of claimed hate groups no female, Hispanic, Homosexual, or Oriental hate groups appear; now that in itself is amazing. Can there be any doubt that such exist? Of 457 "Hate Groups" listed, 21 are claimed to be "Black Separatist" but when you go through the list you find only The House of David, and Nation of Islam listed. In fact a careful review of the entire list [reveals] listed groups that were obviously placed on the list to inflate the numbers. I know of one on the list who has just entered a lawsuit against SPLC, and one that is definitely not a Hate Group, but rather a newspaper with a circulation of over 10,000 and many that are mere figments of SPLC's imagination.

Benign Organizations Are Listed

Since no addresses are given it is impossible to validate the list, addresses which were in my opinion left off for a very good reason. Furthermore there are numerous organizations listed with rather benign names and purpose; among these are over 15 organizations containing the word Christian. A large number of Baptist and other Churches, Publishers, as well as numerous patriotic and conservative organizations are listed. The NAACP [National Association for the Advancement of Colored People] is not listed but the NAAWP (National Association for the Advancement of White People) is. . . . It only applies to Anglo Saxon males. No one else need apply!

All this in my opinion is for no other reason than to garnish funds from people stupid enough to contribute to SPLC.

Racist Groups Pose Little Danger

They collect millions of dollars for their crusades against hate groups, but do so-called "watchdog" organizations exaggerate the dangers posed by neo-Nazis and other racist movements? Laird Wilcox thinks so. A Kansas author and editor who has spent decades researching what he calls "fringe" groups, Mr. Wilcox says the total numbers of active, organized extremists on the right is not much more than 10,000.

"Because of their nature, it's very difficult to come up with firm numbers" for such groups, Mr. Wilcox says, but estimates "the militias are probably 5,000 or 6,000 people. The Ku Klux Klan are down to about 3,000 people. And the combined membership of all neo-Nazi groups are probably just 1,500 to 2,000."

In a nation of more than 270 million people, the small size of such fringe groups represents a tiny danger, yet they are the target of what Mr. Wilcox calls an "industry" of watchdog groups.

Robert Stacy McCain, *The Washington Times*, May 9, 2000.

There may also be found on the site a listing of "Hate Crimes" commited in 1999. Unfortunately the site is structured in such a way that makes it impossible to pull up the whole list. Having made a perfunctory examination of that list it revealed that tricks were used to inflate the numbers. The following acts are now "Hate Crimes": Having a Rally, having a Rally that was called off, meetings, and Un-described graffiti on a wall, a message chalked on a sidewalk, shouting a racial slur, the distribution of leaflets, false statement made about a non-existent swastika. Well it won't be long before Mr. Dees and co. will have their thought police review everyone's dreams to make sure that they are in compliance with their strange ideas of right and wrong.

We should at this point consider the vast amounts of money being diverted from real Christian charity to the poor and needy in order to keep Dees and co. living in the outrageously opulent style to which they have become accustomed.

Just exactly how large is the mom and pop hate mongering at SPLC? Their 1998 Income Tax Return shows net assets of $136,768,758.00. . . . The SPLC is one huge money machine, operating for the sole purpose of keeping Morris and f[r]iends in the high style of Living, and to afford him the funds for his numerous trysts. The palace out of which they operate in Montgomery. Alabama makes the average corporate headquarters look like a piker. Why do I call these people who claim to educate the public, schools, teachers and others about hate, a hate group? The reason is that they use hate as a weapon to induce innocent fools into giving them money. Consider that at 5% interest they would make an income of $680,000.00 just on their net assets. According to Randall Williams, a disgruntled ex-employee of SPLC, "Our donor base was anchored by wealthy Jewish contributors on the East and West coasts, and they gave big bucks. We were able to take in $3 million more a year than we could spend. Still Morris continued to send out fund raising letters about the 'Klan Menace' and the money kept po[u]ring in."

SPLC Is a Wealthy Organization

In a headline Feb. 13 1994, in the *Montgomery Advertiser* we learn, "Charity of Riches—they're drowning in their own affluence." The article goes on to explain that SPLC is raising so much money that they can not spend enough of it to keep their books on an even keel. In 1994 SPLC already had a $52 million cash reserve. They would be surprised how right they were if they saw that the cash reserve had grown to over $130 million, a growth of almost 300% in 1998. All this sort of makes me think that there should be an IRS rule about how much a 501c tax ex[em]pt corporation is allowed to retain as unused surplus; after all there are such rules for private corporations.

A close look at the SPLC indicates an organization that is essentially run for and by one man Morris Dees. Many of his avid supporters, some 600,000, see Dees as a hero. Since the bulk of his support comes from the Jewish communities in New York City, Los Angeles and Chicago, very far away from Montgomery, you can begin to grasp the reason for it.

Attacks by SPLC have been on numerous individuals under false pretence. Eustace Mullins is a well-known author and friend living in Saunton, Virginia. Now I am sure that there may be some people who disagree with Mullins but that does not make his publishing company, Revelation Books, a hate group. In fact, attacking an elderly author of dozens of widely circulated books and listing that publishing company as "Hate Group" is the act of hate. Mullins was a confidant of Ezra Pound who was the greatest American poet of the 20th century. The very first book he produced was at the suggestion of Ezra Pound; *The Secrets of the Federal Reserve* is considered the lexicon of all the books written on the FRS [federal reserve system]. How a publishing company with one sole employee, its author, constitutes a group is likewise never once explained. Far from being alone, the *Jubilee Newspaper* is listed under Identity whatever that is. How a newspaper can be classed as "Hate Group" is never explained, and the fact that it is a newspaper is omitted from the listing. I have no doubt that within short order SPLC will find some way to get my name on the list, because everyone who at one time or another criticized SPLC or Dees has wound up listed.

Phony Listings

As I have surmised, the entire listings are phony; it is inflated for one and only one purpose: to raise money and get unknowing people's support. Just consider some of the listed groups: American Nationalist Party, Christian Defense League, European American Education Assoc, Christian Bible Ministry, Christian Research, Land of Peace, and, yes, you guessed it *America First*. Who's missing? The Jewish

Defense League, The ADL [Anti-Defamatian League], the NAACP, the JDL, the WJC, NOW [National Organization for Women]. Like I said, if you're Jewish, Black, Hispanic, Oriental or female you couldn't be a "Hate Group" in Mr. Dees's lexicon.

How does SPLC get suckers to send them money? Well there's the Wall of Tolerance. It is to be constructed in Montgomery, Al. For a mere $35.00 your name will be listed on the wall. Or you can for the mere amount of $25.00 obtain SPLC publications for the next two years. Naturally, every letter, brochure, and flier tells the potential contributor that all payments are totally tax deductible. Then there's *Klanwatch* & Militia Task Force, who produces a brochure with lots of pictures including a photo of the Oklahoma City bombing, which was proven not to be in any way connected to any group. Then we have Teaching Tolerance as a program for schools and teachers, which is nothing, less than a concerted effort at multi-culturalism, one of the processes of destroying national [cohesion]. They sell programs to school systems. To date 50,000 of our schools have purchased this propaganda. Through the use of a very wide brush SPLC paints numerous political and social groups into their hate arsenal. Per example they use NEO- as a catch syllable to link different groups with whom they disagree. In Propaganda, that is simply called LINKAGE. Neo-Nazis, Neo-Confederates, and Neo-Conservatives are often linked in the same paragraph. Their most effective method of fundraising is through the use of specific letters on single topics to explicit groups. In this way Jews in NYC, LA and Chicago is their largest single contributory segment.

> *"Nature tells us to take care of our own kind and only our own kind. We do not regard any of the mud races to be our own kind."*

Racial Hatred Is Necessary to Save the White Race

Matthew Hale

Matthew Hale is the Pontifex Maximus (supreme leader) of the World Church of the Creator (now renamed the Creativity Movement). In the following viewpoint he argues that the white race, which he claims is responsible for all that is worthwhile in the world, is in danger of being destroyed by people of color. Hale contends that the law of nature dictates that people must love and protect their own kind, which for white people means promoting white interests above those of minorities. According to Hale, white people should hate the "mud races" in order to protect their own race.

As you read, consider the following questions:

1. In what way is Christianity destructive, according to Hale?
2. Why does Hale single out Jews as special enemies?
3. How does Hale propose to change white thinking on issues of race?

Matthew Hale, "Frequently Asked Questions," www.wcotc.com, 2001. Copyright © 2001 by The World Church of the Creator. Reproduced by permission.

*W*ho is the "Creator"?

The White Race. White people are the creators of all worthwhile culture and civilization. Also, believers in our racial religion are called Creators.

If you were to sum up the objective of your religion, Creativity, in one sentence what would that be?

That objective would be: The Survival, Expansion and Advancement of the White Race.

Why is that so important?

It is a matter of priorities. Our religion is based on the ultimate of all truths: The Eternal Laws of Nature. Nature tells each species to expand and upgrade itself to the utmost of its abilities. Since the White Race is Nature's finest achievement and since we encompass the White Race, there can hardly be any other goal that even compares in importance.

As a rule, racists and anti-Semites reject those labels. You embrace them. Why?

Because the first prerequisite to our attaining victory is to be completely honest about what we are and what we are not. We are racists because we believe in Race. We are anti-Semites because we oppose the Jews.

Isn't your religion based on hate?

No, on the contrary, it is based on love—love for the White Race. Besides being based on the Eternal Laws of Nature, Creativity furthermore is based on the lessons of history, on logic and common sense.

The World Church of the Creator is often described with words like "hate monger," "hate organization," "hate speech." Is this fair?

No, it isn't fair since every organization—whatever it may be—hates something or someone. Since other organizations aren't labeled "hate" groups, etc., why should we be singled out like this? We don't exist out of hatred for the other races but out of love for our own Race.

But isn't it part and parcel of your religion to hate the Jews, blacks and other colored people?

True, but if you love and want to defend those whom you love, your own family, your own White Race; then hate for your enemies comes natural and is inevitable. Love and hate are two sides of the same coin. Only a hypocrite and a liar will go into battle against his enemies proclaiming love.

ould not be the same as that to our parents. Our rela-
p to members of the White Race would not be the
s to members of the black race, for instance and we
not expect the same kind of response. The number of
es that could be quoted are endless, and on closer
, it is a completely unworkable principle. . . .

to Charity

*you limit your interest in the benefiting of the White Race
ren't you interested in all of humanity?*

re tells us to take care of our own kind and only our
d. We do not regard any of the mud races to be our
d. They may be sub-species of some common ances-
hey may not. In any case, we regard the White Race
g risen to the very top of the human scale, with vary-
luations of subhuman species below us. The niggers,
tedly, are at the very bottom of the ladder, not far
honkeys and chimpanzees.

*ouldn't your program be more charitable and help the
es advance, while at the same time promoting the White*

nswer to this rather tricky question is a most em-
NO!" We have no intention of helping the mud
sper, multiply, and crowd us off the limited space of
et.

ot?

swering this question, we again go back to the basic
Nature, which show that each species or sub-species
atural enemies, and it is a cold hard fact of life that
deadly enemies of the White Race are first of all the
secondarily, all the other mud races who are com-
r food and living space on this limited planet. We
two hard choices: (a) of either race-mixing and
ating with the mud peoples of the world, and
dragging down and destroying the White Race, or
e course that the World Church of the Creator has
namely, (b) to keep our own race pure and expand
inally inhabit all the good lands of this planet Earth.
*'t this entail a confrontation, in fact, a blood bath, in
White Race might be wiped out?*

136

---

*But weren't all the atrocities committed by Christians through-
out history done by people who were not following Christianity's
teaching of love?*

Since these killings, tortures, and persecutions were carried on by the highest leaders and authorities of the various
Churches themselves, such as the Popes, by Zwingli, Luther,
Calvin, etc., we must presume that the teachings of Christianity, which at best are ambiguous, contradictory and hypocritical, must be held responsible for producing these kinds
of people and this kind of insanity. But if we turn to the New
Testament, we find Christ himself dispensing such hateful
advice as, for example, in Luke 14:26: "If any man come to
me, and hate not his father, and mother and wife, and children, and brethren and sisters, yea and his own life also, he
cannot be my disciple." What idiotic and destructive advice!

Hate Your Enemies

What then is Creativity's final position on love and hate?

We follow the eternal wisdom of Nature's laws, which are
completely opposite to the suicidal teachings of Christianity.
Whereas Christianity says to "love your enemies" and to
hate your own kind (see, e.g., Luke 14:26), we say just the
opposite. We say that in order to survive, we must overcome
and destroy those that are a threat to our existence; namely,
our deadly enemies. At the same time, we advocate love and
protection for those that are near and dear to us: our family
and our own race, which is an extension of the family.

How does this differ from Christianity?

Christianity teaches love your enemies and hate your own
kind, while we teach exactly the opposite, namely hate and
destroy your enemies and love your own kind. Whereas
Christianity's teachings are suicidal, our creed brings out the
best creative and constructive forces inherent to the White
Race. Whereas Christians are destroyers, we are builders.

What do you mean about Christianity being a destroyer?

Christianity teaches such destructive advice as "love your
enemies," "sell all thou hast and give it to the poor," "resist
not evil," "judge not," "turn the other cheek." Anybody that
followed such suicidal advice would soon destroy themselves, their family, their race and their country.

133

If Christianity is as destructive as you say it is, how do you explain the fact that it has survived for nearly 2,000 years?

Smallpox has survived for longer than that, but the damage it has perpetrated on its victims has been devastating. Similarly, the creed and the church have survived for nearly 2,000 years, but the horrible damage it has wrought on the White Race is something else again. The Jews primary objective in concocting Christianity was to destroy their mortal enemies, the Roman Empire. In this they were successful beyond their wildest dreams. Two thousand years ago, before the advent of Christianity, the Roman Empire had reached an astoundingly high level of civilization, art, literature, law-giving, road building, language, and in dozens of other fields that are the hallmarks of progress in the White Man's civilization. Beginning with the reign of Augustus Caesar, Rome enjoyed two centuries of peace and prosperity (known as Pax Romana), the longest such span in history. As Christianity spread, and more and more poisoned the Roman mind, the good Roman citizens lost touch with reality and their minds meandered off into the "never-never land" of the spooks in the sky, fueled by fear of that humble torture chamber, HELL. The result was the collapse of the Roman Empire, and the White Race retrogressed into chaos, barbarism, and a thousand years of the Dark Ages. Poverty, ignorance and superstition were rampant. Like a monster, the Christian church fed upon and capitalized on these miseries. But the church itself grew fat and powerful. . . .

The White Race Must Be Saved

What do you believe in?

Creativity is the Eternal Laws of Nature applied to all aspects of life, including and especially our Race. In order to get the full scope and breadth of our beliefs, you must read and study *Nature's Eternal Religion* and the *White Man's Bible*.

What, in substance, is that belief?

The aim of our religion, briefly, is promoting the best interests of our race, the White Race, which we believe is the highest pinnacle of Nature's creation.

Do you have a "Golden Rule" in your religion?

Yes, we do have a Golden Rule in our religion, and it does not coincide at all with the Golden Rule in the Jewish-Christian philosophy. Our ᵁ can be summarized as follows: That wh White Race is the highest virtue; that ᵥ White Race is the ultimate sin.

Segregation Will Keep the Wh

The possibility of the White race contin will be predicated upon various methods global numbers are but a small percenta; man total, and those are rapidly dimin more genetic homelands safe from tʰ some form of segregation the White rᵃ doomed. We know this. Most of humaᵃ difference is that we have to care, becaᵤ including most of the White race, doeᵉ we bring about segregation when mar actually believe that our extinction, thoᵤ call it that, would be a good thing? Vᵢ most White folks believe that integrᵣ melange of people? The One World, ᵤ These poor dolts don't seem to want tᵤ with the Great White Race amalgamᵢ be races and racism aplenty, just no Vᵢ

Among the many first things we neeᵈ from the shadows. We must be conf and never surrender a point. We musᵗ to exist as a distinct race. Our cringᵢ White, has gone on long enough. Wᵉ that we have no enemies, and we muᵢ our enemies.

Terry W. Phillips, "The Direction Home," wᵥ December 3, 2003.

Don't you believe in the commonly ᵢ unto others as you would have them dᵢ

No, we do not, and the reason ᵢ analyze it more closely, just like ᵣ leths of the Jewish-Christian Biᵢ Rule does not make good sense. We would not treat our enemies ᵢ treat our friends. Our relationshiᵢ not be the same as to our boss. Cᵢ

Not necessarily. It is the program of the World Church of the Creator to keep expanding the White Race and crowding the mud races without necessarily engaging in any open warfare or without necessarily killing anybody. In doing so, we are only following the same principle as the colonization and westward expansion of America. During this great and productive epoch of the White Race, we kept expanding westward and onward by settling the lands that were occupied by an inferior human sub-species, namely, the Indians. It is true that there were some minor clashes, but there was not any open war of extermination. Had America not pursued this program of pushing onward and crowding the Indian, we would never have built this great stronghold of the White Race which we now call America. This is the real American way and we of the World Church of the Creator are expanding the American way on a worldwide basis.

Advance the White Race

But isn't this cruel and inhuman?

No, it is not. It is just a matter of deciding whether you would rather have your own future progeny of beautiful, intelligent White people survive and inhabit this earth, or whether you would rather see them submerged in a flood tide of mud races. In the latter case, all beauty, culture and civilization would vanish. The more we help the mud races to expand and multiply, the more we are robbing our own future generations of food, space and existence on this planet Earth. Furthermore, the mud races are doing to us that very thing in the present stage of history. They have viciously driven out and killed the White population in many countries in Africa, and I might add with the connivance and help of Jews and White traitors. Our Jewish-controlled Government right here in America is promoting the expansion and proliferation of the niggers in the United States, and shrinking the White population so that in a few generations practically all of the United States will be either completely black or mongrelized. It is strange indeed that the bleeding hearts who are so concerned about the survival of the mud races seem to be completely unconcerned about the mongrelization and destruction of the White Race, a process that is now going on before our very eyes.

But in your book Nature's Eternal Religion, *aren't you actually advocating the extermination of the Jews?*

Nowhere in our book do we ever suggest killing anybody. Our program simply is to unite the White Race for its own survival and protection, expansion and advancement. It is because the White Race has flagrantly violated Nature's Laws of looking after its own, and stupidly and foolishly instead has subsidized the expansion and proliferation of our enemies, the multitudes of mud races, that we are now on a collision course with disaster. We Creators strongly advocate that we stop this foolishness of subsidizing our enemies, and let them shift for themselves, and we take care of our own.

But wouldn't this mean the decline and perhaps the extermination of the colored races?

Perhaps it would, but that is not our responsibility, nor is it our doing. Nature has decreed that every species on the face of this earth be engaged in a struggle for survival on its own merits in competition with every other species. In no case, in no species in Nature, does the stronger and superior species voluntarily hold itself back and help subsidize a weaker and inferior species so that inferior species might crowd it from the face of the earth. No other species, that is, except the White Race, is foolishly engaging in that kind of foolish philosophy. We Creators say that this is suicidal and that we must drastically change our course. Every individual, sooner or later, dies anyway, but it is a matter of the survival of our own species, our own kind, that we are interested in. Since there is not enough land, food, and substance to support an ever exploding horde of mud races, the vital question as we stated before is: do we want our own kind to survive, or do we want the suicide of our own future generations in a world flooded by the sub-human mud races? . . .

Do you hate police and military personnel?

No. The United States Iron Heel's military and police forces are evil institutions, but we have nothing against many individual cops and soldiers, who are often the best of our Race. Indeed, many cops and soldiers are sympathetic to the pro-White cause.

Why do you use the term "niggers" in your books instead of showing some respect for the blacks and calling them "Negroes"?

This is a deliberate choice of words. As we state on page 42 in *Nature's Eternal Religion,* we must stop giving them credit and respect which they did not earn, do not deserve, and never did. Again, it is very strange that the same people who are so affronted by the niggers not getting their "proper respect" are totally unconcerned about the vicious, unwarranted attacks by the niggers and other mud races upon the White Race and will not lift a finger in the defense of their own kind. They seem to deem it quite proper that the niggers should be loyal to their race, the Jews should be loyal to their race, but when the White Man is asked to show a loyalty to his own race, he is immediately denounced, even by members of his own race, as being a racist, a bigot, a Nazi, and many other derogatory smear words that the Jews have concocted.

Jews

Why do you single out the Jews, who after all comprise less than one percent of the population of the world as your No. 1 enemy?

There are many good and valid reasons why the Jew deserves this special distinction. (a) The Jewish race, united through their Mosaic religion for thousands of years, has been for many centuries, and is today, the most powerful race on the face of the earth. (b) They not only control the news media, television networks, newspapers, and the money of the world, as of the United States, but through such power they also control the governments of the world. (c) They do, in fact, control most of the nerve centers of power in the United States and throughout the world. (d) It has been their age-old goal, not only for centuries, but for millennia, to pull down, mongrelize and destroy the White Race. (e) They have been very successful in doing this. We therefore conclude that they are a most dangerous threat to the further survival of the White Race.

Since you claim that your objectives do not include killing the Jews, just what do you propose?

It is our purpose to drive the Jews from power and eventually drive them from our shores back to Israel or whatever part of the world they choose to live in as a country of their own (perhaps also the island of Madagascar) without robbing other people of their established country.

How do you propose to do this?

By uniting and organizing the White race, and through the creed and program of the World Church of the Creator. By preaching and promoting racial loyalty among our own White Racial Comrades and making them conscious of their proud and wonderful heritage, we believe that we can mobilize the full power of the White Race and AGAIN REGAIN CONTROL OF OUR GOVERNMENT AND OUR OWN DESTINY. Once we have done that much, we believe that the fight against the Jews, the niggers and the mud races of the world is as good as won. Just distributing ten million copies of *Nature's Eternal Religion* and the *White Man's Bible* would put us well on the road to victory.

Didn't Hitler try to do the same thing and fail?

There are 500 million White people on the face of this planet. Organized and united they constitute an awesome power that would overwhelm the other peoples of the world, namely the mud races, in any kind of contest, or in any show of force. Whereas Hitler's program was similar to what we are proposing, we have learned from his failures and have made some significant changes. Whereas Hitler promoted and advocated pan-Germanism, namely, the German people as the core of his political movement, we, on the other hand, denounce Nationalism as an artificial barrier and a divisive force preventing the unification of the White Race. We promote and advocate the inclusion of all the good members of the White Race throughout the world, and propose to unite them in one solid battering ram under the banners of our religion. There are some other significant differences between our program and that of Adolf Hitler.

Why do you believe that a religious organization is a better means of accomplishing such objectives than a political party?

There are several reasons why we are convinced that we must have a religious base rather than a political party to do the job. (a) Religion embraces just about every aspect of a people's life—economies, morals, customs, law, government, education, eugenics, and above all, in our religion, the survival, expansion and advancement of our own race. (b) A political party, on the other hand, has a much narrower base. (c) Politics has a weaker appeal to an individual's loyalty. (d)

Religion, on the other hand, has a much deeper and profound influence on the entire course of his life. (e) Furthermore, history shows that religions can and do last for thousands of years, whereas practically any other human organization, whether it be government, nations, financial corporations, political parties, or whatever, are relatively short-lived, some of them existing for a few years or even less, and then fading from the scene. Of the thousands of political parties that have come and gone, few have lasted longer than perhaps fifty years and very few longer than a hundred years. In contrast to this, the Jews' Mosaic religion has lasted for several thousand years and been the keystone of the survival of the Jewish race, not to mention the horribly destructive ramifications in the lives and destruction of other nations. . . .

Changing White Thinking

What do you consider the main difficulty in winning your struggle?

The main problem we have is not overcoming the niggers and the Jews, and the mud races in general, but reeducating the perverted and twisted thinking that has poisoned the minds of the White Race over the many centuries. Despite the fact that the White Race is the most intelligent creature in the fields of logic, mathematics, science, inventions, medicine, and hundreds of other creative and productive areas, yet when it comes to the questions of race and religion, the White Race seems to be strangely stupefied as if under the influence of a mind-warping drug. And, in a way, the White Man's mind is warped as if poisoned with drugs. And this poison is the propaganda that the Jew has foisted on the White Race for all these centuries. The most potent of all these propaganda poisons that had infiltrated the White Man's thinking is the Christian religion. So, our main problem is replacing that religion with a sound racial religion for our own survival, expansion and advancement. As soon as we are able to straighten out the White Man's thinking, we can regard our problems and our struggle as good as won. Placing ten million copies of *Nature's Eternal Religion* and the *White Man's Bible* in the hands of our White Racial Comrades would be a major step in that direction. What a bargain that would be for the White Race!

How do you propose to "straighten out the White Man's thinking," as you put it?

This is the most difficult part of the task, but not at all impossible. After all, going back to Adolf Hitler, we find that he was highly successful in changing the thinking of the German people from one of communism, despair, and self-destruction, to one of vibrant creativity, constructive productivity, and re-establishing a highly constructive faith in their own people. We believe we can do the same thing for the White peoples of the United States, by widespread promotion and distribution of our books *Nature's Eternal Religion* and the *White Man's Bible*, and following that up with a strongly organized World Church of the Creator. If the Jews could organize the Christian church for the destruction of the White Race, surely the White Race can organize itself for its own survival. We can do it and we will do it!

Does Creativity believe in God?

When you ask that question, it is as vague as asking: Do you believe in "Quantity X"? There are a million different versions of "God." There is the Jewish version—a vengeful God interested only in the welfare of the Jews and repeatedly killing and destroying the Jews' enemies. There is the God of the Mohammedans, Allah; there is the "loving" God of the Christians. Women's Lib says God is a female, the niggers say he is black. Then there is the hocus-pocus about the Holy Trinity—that of the father, son and holy ghost all rolled into one. Whereas most of these versions were concocted by man to take on the image of human form, other versions like the Church of Religious Science say God is an all pervading spirit, like the ether, not in the image of man at all. These are just a few versions out of millions. Actually even members of the same religious denomination differ widely and let their imaginations run rampant. But there is not a shred of evidence to back up any of this nonsense. The sum total of all these wild proclamations is that nobody has any facts to substantiate their claims, and the sum total knowledge about any so-called God is zero. We Creators, therefore, reject all this nonsense about angels and devils and gods and all the rest of this silly spook craft. We go back to reality, and back to the Eternal Laws of Nature, about which the White Man does have an impressive fund of knowledge. . . .

Since Creativity does not believe in a Supreme Being, nor in a life in the hereafter, how can you claim to be a religion at all?

We have every legitimate right to that claim. (a) The constitution in effect prohibits any authority, religious, secular or otherwise, from delineating what is, or what is not, a religion. In short, if you claim you are a religion it is as valid as any rival religion's claim. (b) One of Webster's many definitions of religion is: "A cause, principle, system of tenets held with ardor, devotion, conscientiousness, and faith: a value held to be of supreme importance." Our faith resides in the future of the White Race and our values are set forth in *Nature's Eternal Religion*, especially the SIXTEEN COMMANDMENTS. (c) There are several major religions that are known as Nontheistic. Among these are Confucianism, Taoism, Buddhism, some sects of Hinduism, and many others. Although they contain much mysticism and hocus-pocus we don't indulge in, the point is that they, too, do not believe in a God, but rather are socioethical systems proclaiming certain moral values. Yet they have been recognized as religions for centuries, and rightfully so. There are other valid reasons why we rightfully qualify as a religion, but the above should suffice.

The Eternal Laws of Nature

What kind of religion would you call yourself?

Our religion is rooted in race, and based upon the Eternal Laws of Nature. We are, therefore, a racial religion and a natural religion. . . .

Since you do not believe in God and you do not worship anything, what is the purpose of your religion?

We have set up the loftiest and most noble goal humanly possible, namely, the Survival, Expansion and Advancement of the White Race. If the White Race isn't worth the dedication of our most ardent labors, what is? Niggers and monkeys? Imaginary, non-existent spooks in the sky? In Creativity, we have given the White Race a great and noble purpose in life. We have given the White Race a program for its own salvation and advancement for the next million years. We have given our own race a creed around which all members of our race can rally, regardless of nationality. Finally, after thousands of years of floundering, divisiveness and self-destruction, the White Race now has a meaningful constructive religion upon which it can build a better world for itself and its future progeny forever and a day. . . .

Don't you have faith in anything?

Yes, we most certainly do. . . . We have faith in the future of the White Race and its ultimate triumph. We consider that as the highest and most significant goal. The fact is we believe in anything that has valid and meaningful evidence to substantiate it. . . . We do not believe in a world of spirits and spooks and we most certainly do not believe in the Jewish Bible which was written by a gang of lying, Jewish scriptwriters. We believe "A SKEPTICAL AND INQUIRING MIND IS NO VICE. BEING GULLIBLE AND SUPERSTITIOUS IS NO VIRTUE.". . .

Since you say that the Jews occupy all the nerve centers of power, just how do you propose to drive them from power and have the White Man regain control of his destiny?

We mean to do this by building and expanding the World Church of the Creator until it penetrates the thinking and the heart and soul of all the good members of the White Race. As we have stated before, our biggest problem really is straightening out the thinking of White People. We believe that it can be done and it must be done, in fact, by building a religious movement dedicated to the survival, expansion and advancement of the White Race. We believe it is the only way that this tremendous task can be accomplished. It can be done, and it will be done.

Doesn't Creativity believe in helping others?

Yes, we do, but we are highly selective as to whom we render aid, love and affection. We most definitely do not believe in loving enemies, nor helping them. Among our enemies, we have the Jews and the mud races. We, therefore, believe in selectively helping our own kind, namely, our own White Racial Comrades. The White Man is the measure of all things, and we believe in looking at everything through the White Man's eyes, from the White Man's point of view.

The Bible Is a Hoax

Hasn't the Bible been pretty well proven by recent scientific discoveries and isn't the gap between Christianity and science rapidly deteriorating?

Most definitely not. The answer to both questions is a loud emphatic, NO! The gap between Christianity and science is as wide as the Grand Canyon. It is widening as science progresses in giant strides. The gap is irreconcilable and unbridgeable. A study of astronomy and the discovery of billions of other galaxies makes the idea of spooks in the sky a laughable absurdity. A study of geology makes the idea of a universal flood in the year 2348 B.C. a non-existent hoax. A study of Egyptian history also completely repudiates the story of the great flood. A study of authentic history further repudiates the so-called "history" the Jews have concocted for themselves in the Old Testament. Suffice it to say that the conflict is endless and an excellent set of books has been written on this subject. It comes in two volumes and is entitled *A History of the Warfare of Science with the Theology of Christendom* written by A.D. White. Unfortunately, it is now out of print and extremely hard to come by. . . .

The White Race seems to have done quite well in maintaining itself. Why are you so concerned about its survival?

The White Race used to do quite well for itself in the 15th, 16th, 17th, 18th and 19th centuries, but no more. In fact, as late as 1920, the White Race was outnumbered by the mud races of the world only in a proportion of 2 to 1. Today, scarcely two generations later, it is outnumbered by the rapidly exploding mud races of the world, by a ratio of 12 to 1. The United Nations, which is a Jew-controlled organization, gleefully reports that in another generation the White Race will be outnumbered on the face of this earth by a ratio of 49 to 1. A person has to only have an elementary grasp of mathematics to see that the White Race is now a very much endangered species, and will soon be either crowded into extinction or mongrelized into oblivion. Either way, the White Race will be gone, and with it also will vanish all the good things that it has produced, such as civilization, culture, art and all the other valuable attributes that we consider as contributing to the good life. The tragic and ironic thing about all this is that it's the White Man's ability to produce ample food, the White Man's technology, the White Man's medicine, and all the other valuable contributions created by his own ability, foolishly transferred to the parasitic mud races that has caused the present dilemma amid catastrophe. It is these valuable contributions of the White Race transferred to the mud races that has caused the latter's explosive increase. It is the unalterable goal of the World Church of the Creator to bring the White Man back to sanity and to again conserve his creativity and productivity for the benefit of his own race and his race alone. . . .

Racial Socialism

Does Creativity agree with Adolf Hitler in all respects?

Not in all respects. There are four or five major issues in which we depart from National Socialism. The main difference is we believe Nationalism, per se, was and is a divisive issue among the White Race. We instead espouse RACIAL SOCIALISM to embrace all the good White people on the face of the globe, rather than Pan-Germanism.

But didn't Hitler kill six million Jews?

No, he did not. This, along with Christianity, ranks as one of the biggest lies and biggest hoaxes in history. Privately, among themselves, the Jews published the growth of their total world population between 1938 and 1948, as increasing from approximately 16,600,000 to 17,650,000, an increase of over a million. This would be an outrageous impossibility, if it had been decimated by 6,000,000 during this same period.

If it isn't true, why would the Jews want to tell such a monstrous lie?

It has reaped tremendous dividends for them. Having worldwide monopoly of the propaganda machinery, they were able to put that lie across with little or no opposition.

What were the "tremendous dividends" for the Jews you speak of?

(a) It enabled the Jews who were the real instigators of World War II and the real culprits, to appear to be the victims, and arouse worldwide sympathy from the gullible and unsuspecting Gentiles, or Goyim, as they call them. (b) Through this world sympathy, it enabled them to loot the

Arabs of their lands in Palestine, and set up the bandit State of Israel. (c) It enabled them to loot the Germans with "restitutions" in amounts of as much as a billion dollars a year to the State of Israel. In short, this is plain blackmail and looting. (d) It enabled them to pursue a vicious program of destroying all opposition to Jewish aggression and take-over throughout the world. (e) It has provided them with a bonanza in tightening their stronghold on the peoples of the world in areas of finances, of propaganda, of governmental expansion and the spread of Jewish Communism.

So what do you propose as the answer to the Jewish problem?

The only total answer is for the White people of the world to unite and organize and regain control of their own destiny. This is the highest right in Nature. In order to do so they have to unite around something and that something must be a meaningful, significant and worthwhile creed that all the good White people of this earth can dedicate their lives to. This we have provided in the religious creed of Creativity as set forth in *Nature's Eternal Religion* and the *White Man's Bible*. In it lies the philosophy, the creed and the program for the salvation of the White Race for its own survival, expansion and advancement for all time. It is every White Man's highest moral duty to promote, advance and disseminate this lofty creed, not only for his own generation, but also to our future progeny for the next million years. Therefore let us dedicate ourselves to this noble task and go to work. . . .

What does "RAHOWA" mean?

It is our battle cry. Just as the Muslims have "jihad," we have "RAHOWA." It stands for RAcial HOly WAr.

"Whatever name you place on these [white supremacist] organizations, they are purely and simply evil. They foment hatred."

Racial Hatred Is Immoral

Doug Anstaett

White supremacist organizations such as the World Church of the Creator (now known as the Creativity Movement) encourage hate and violence against non-whites, Doug Anstaett maintains in the following viewpoint. He argues that the goal of white supremacists is total separation of the races, and if that proves impossible, they advocate annihilation of those who are different from them. Anstaett insists that decent Americans have a responsibility to condemn racial hatred whenever they encounter it because it is evil. Doug Anstaett writes for the *Newton Kansan*, a daily newspaper in Newton, Kansas.

As you read, consider the following questions:

1. In Anstaett's opinion, into what two groups do racists believe people should be divided?
2. According to the author, what types of people comprise white supremacy groups?
3. What does Anstaett report is the number one goal of the World Church of the Creator?

Hatred is not new in America. We saw it in the evil that hit Littleton, Colo., in April [1999], when 12 students and a beloved teacher died in a hail of gunfire before the two perpetrators took their own lives.

We saw it in the bombing of the Murrah Federal Building in Oklahoma City in 1995, which killed 166.

We saw it in the dragging death of a black man by thugs in Texas.

We've seen it in numerous acts of terror against those considered "different" for any number of reasons throughout America's history.

And now we've seen it again, this time in white supremacist Benjamin Nathaniel Smith's multi-state rampage in which he targeted minorities as victims, killing two and wounding at least eight others.

It's sad, but in the land of the free, there sometimes appears to be no real freedom for those who are different, especially racial minorities.

Ricky Byrdsong, a black former basketball star and Northwestern University men's basketball coach, was the first to be killed. He was playing with his children when Smith pulled out his revolver and killed him.

The second victim was a Korean student at the University of Indiana in Bloomington. He was simply taking a walk with friends.

Racists believe that people should be divided into groups that deserve to exist and those who do not.

White Supremacists Are Evil

Smith was a member of the World Church of the Creator [since renamed the Creativity Movement], a white supremacist organization that distributed anti-minority and anti-Semitic literature.

Whatever name you place on these organizations, they are purely and simply evil. They foment hatred. They encourage violence against those who are different. They seek total separation of the races, and if that's not possible, annihilation of those who aren't like them.

Typically, they are comprised of loners, losers and misfits—folks who just simply can't fit in to the mainstream of life in America.

According to the Associated Press, late last year [1998] Smith wrote a letter to the *Indiana Daily Student* newspaper.

"America," he wrote, "has become increasingly nonwhite and the constitutional rights of racial activists have increasingly been infringed upon."

Q: What's black and white and Stupid all over?

Ramirez. © 1995 by Copley News Service. Reproduced by permission.

In April [1999], Smith appeared as a witness for the World Church of the Creator's leader, Matt Hale, at a hearing before a bar association panel. He said that at times he had "considered violent acts to achieve racial goals, but Hale counseled me to act peacefully."

"Our No. 1 goal is to straighten out the white man's thinking," he said. "We're the new minority being crushed left and right. We're in a life and death struggle."

Hale, the "church's" supposed ringleader, still lives at home with his parents and spews his hatred from a room in the basement. That's an interesting "church," isn't it?

Diversity Helps America Prosper

There was a nation that separated white from black for decades. We applauded South Africa when Nelson Mandela left jail and helped his nation throw off the shackles of apartheid.

America didn't become a nation to separate itself from others. In fact, our nation has prospered because it embraced its diversity and its differences.

Every decent American should condemn acts of racial hatred in whatever form they take.

Periodical Bibliography

The following articles have been selected to supplement the diverse views presented in this chapter.

Bill Bickel	"Inside the Mind of a White Supremacist: An Interview with Matt Hale," About Crime/Punishment, October 9, 2000. www.crime.about.com.
Center for New Community	"State of Hate: White Nationalism in the Midwest 2001–2002," Winter 2001. www.newcomm.org.
CNN	"Lott: Segregation and Racism Are Immoral," December 13, 2002. www.cnn.com.
David Duke	"Is Russia the Key to White Survival?" *Duke Report*, October 2000. www.duke.org.
Sam Francis	"First, Anarcho-Tyranny Comes for the Extreme Right," *Vdare*, May 22, 2003. www.vdare.com.
Joey Haws	"Supremacist Groups Posing Greater Threat," *MSNBC News*, June 4, 2002.
Robert Stacy McCain	"Hate Debate," *Insight on the News*, June 19, 2000.
Northern California Anti-Authority (NCAA)	"NCAA Interview with Anthony Nocella," Red and Anarchist Action Network, April 26, 2004. www.raan.yardapes.net.
Terry W. Phillips	"The Direction Home," Vanguard News Network, October/November 2003. www.vanguardnewsnetwork.com.
June Preston	"Women Join Supremacy Fight," *Detroit Free Press*, September 11, 1999.
Dean Schabner	"Out of the Kitchen: Has the Women's Rights Movement Come to the Extreme Right?" ABC News, December 12, 2004. www.abcnews.com.
Ferris Shelton	"Hate Groups," Exodus Online, September 9, 2003. www.exodusnews.com.
Southern Poverty Law Center	"Militia Groups Declining, Racist Hate Groups Up," June 25, 2001.
Elie Wiesel	"How Can We Understand Their Hatred?" *Parade Magazine*, April 7, 2002.
Elizabeth Wright	"Free Speech for Some, but Not for All: The Reviled Matt Hale," *Issues and Views*, November 2000. www.issues-views.com.

CHAPTER 4

What Extremist Groups Pose a Threat Worldwide?

Chapter Preface

Twenty-first century extremist groups, especially those with political agendas, are either reviled as terrorists or hailed as freedom fighters—with the label entirely dependent on who is doing the labeling. Thus, the cliché, "One man's terrorist is another man's freedom fighter." Defining terrorism—and who is a terrorist—is crucial to understanding extremist groups, their goals and tactics. Though difficult, finding an objective, internationally agreed upon definition of terrorism is central to the struggle against it. Boaz Ganor, director of the International Policy Institute for Counter-Terrorism, a research organization that develops public policy solutions to international terrorism, insists that "without a definition of terrorism, it is impossible to formulate or enforce international agreements against terrorism."

Violent extremist groups often use an "ends justify the means" argument to win support for their activities. They claim that if they are struggling for peace and the freedom of their country, they can use any means necessary—including terrorism—and not be labeled terrorists. The problem arises when both parties involved in the conflict claim to be fighting for the same cause. For example, both Israelis and Palestinians insist that they are fighting for peace and the security of their land. Each side calls the actions of the other terrorism. Clearly whose claim to the land is more valid cannot be considered when determining which party engages in terrorism. In this case, as in so many others, the cause and justification cited by both entities are the same. The key to defining terrorism, then, is not whether the use of violence is justified. Another distinguishing element must be found.

Ganor argues that targeting civilians is the dividing line between a freedom fighter and a terrorist. The definition he proposes says that "terrorism is the intentional use of, or threat to use violence against civilians or against civilian targets, in order to attain political aims." According to Ganor's definition, only violent acts can be considered terrorism, the aim must always be political regardless of the motivation, and the target of the violence must be civilians. An objective definition such as this would allow the international community

154

to dispassionately evaluate the acts of extremist groups to determine which constituted terrorism and which were legitimate freedom-fighting activities.

An objective, internationally agreed upon definition of terrorism would go a long way toward helping nations distinguish terrorists from freedom fighters. Authors in the following chapter debate which extremist groups pose a threat worldwide. As the case of the Israelis and Palestinians shows, judging whether these extremist groups are terrorists is impossible without a clear distinction being made between terrorists and freedom fighters.

"The . . . transcript provide[s] a full and revealing picture of Al-Qaeda, showing it to be the most lethal terrorist organization anywhere in the world."

Al Qaeda Is a Worldwide Terrorist Threat

Daniel Pipes and Steven Emerson

Al Qaeda, a terrorist organization with worldwide operational reach, views the West as the ultimate enemy of Islam, Daniel Pipes and Steven Emerson argue in the following viewpoint. They maintain that as an umbrella organization that includes many militant Islamic groups, al Qaeda represents a serious terrorist threat to the world, particularly to the United States. Daniel Pipes is director of the Middle East Forum, a member of the board of the U.S. Institute of Peace, and an internationally known columnist. Steven Emerson is a nationally recognized terrorism expert and the author of *American Jihad: The Terrorists Living Among Us.*

As you read, consider the following questions:
1. According to Pipes and Emerson, a victory over what country inspired al Qaeda to attack the United States?
2. What is the ideology that keeps the various groups coordinated by al Qaeda together, in the authors' opinion?
3. What is the basis for the authors' argument that al Qaeda operatives are best thought of as soldiers, not criminals?

Editor's Note: This article was written prior to the September 11, 2001, attacks on Ameria carried out by members of Al-Qaeda.

[In May 2001,] a federal jury in New York returned a guilty verdict against the four defendants accused of plotting the terrorist bombing, [in 1998], of the U.S. embassies in Kenya and Tanzania. The successful prosecution of these murderers represents a great victory for the United States, for the principle of justice, and for the rule of law. We are all in debt to the brave and capable prosecutors.

Operational Range

Unfortunately, the trial does almost nothing to enhance the safety of Americans. The Qaeda group, headed by the notorious Osama bin Laden, which perpetrated the outrages in East Africa, will barely notice the loss of four operatives. Indeed, recent information shows that Al-Qaeda is not only planning new attacks on the U.S. but is also expanding its operational range to countries such as Jordan and Israel.

In Israel, for example, bin Laden has begun to develop a network among the terrorists of the Hamas organization. Last year [2000], Israel arrested a Hamas member named Nabil Aukel who was trained in Pakistan and then moved to Afghanistan and Kashmir to put that training into practice. He returned to Israel with well-honed skills in the remote detonation of bombs using cellular phones, and was detailed to carry out terrorist attacks in Israel.

Perhaps the real importance of the New York trial lies not in the guilty verdicts but in the extraordinary information made public through court exhibits and trial proceedings. These have given us a riveting view onto the shadowy world of Al-Qaeda—though you'd never know from following the news media, for this information was barely reported. Tens of thousands of pages from the trial transcript provide a full and revealing picture of Al-Qaeda, showing it to be the most lethal terrorist organization anywhere in the world. They demonstrate that Al-Qaeda sees the West in general, and the U.S. in particular, as the ultimate enemy of Islam. Inspired by their victory over the Soviet Union in Afghanistan in the 1980s, the leaders of Al-Qaeda aspire to a similar victory over America, hoping ultimately to bring Islamist rule here.

Toward this end, they engaged in many attacks on American targets from 1993 to 1998. One striking piece of information that came out in the trial was bin Laden's possible connection to the World Trade Center bombing in New York in 1993. A terrorist manual introduced as evidence was just an updated version of an earlier manual found in the possession of the World Trade Center defendants.

An Umbrella Organization

The court evidence shows how Al-Qaeda is an umbrella organization that includes a wide range of Islamist groups, including Hezbollah (Lebanon), Islamic Jihad (Egypt), the Armed Islamic Group (Algeria), as well as a raft of Iraqis, Sudanese, Pakistanis, Afghans and Jordanians. Each of its constituent groups has the capability to carry out its own independent recruiting and operations.

The groups coordinate through Al-Qaeda's "Shura Council," a kind of board of directors that includes representatives from the many groups. The groups meet on a regular basis in Afghanistan to review and approve proposed operations. Most of them have maintained close relationships with each other since the end of the war in Afghanistan against the Soviets. They know each other well and work together efficiently.

We learned from the trial that when operations in one place are shutdown, the rest of the network soldiers on, virtually unaffected. Even if bin Ladin himself were to be killed, this Islamist network would survive and continue to expand, sustained by its ideological adhesion. Islamism is the glue that keeps these groups together, and fired up. The court documents also revealed that although bin Laden has had a leading role in formulating and paying for Al-Qaeda, the organization did rely heavily on state sponsorship as well. For example, Sudanese President Omar Bashir himself authorized Al-Qaeda activities in his country and gave it special authority to avoid paying taxes or import duties. More remarkably, he exempted the organization from local law enforcement. Officials of the Iranian government helped arrange advanced weapons and explosives training for Al-Qaeda personnel in Lebanon where they learned, for example, how to destroy large buildings.

Perhaps the most disconcerting revelations from the trial

Wright. © 2001 by *Providence Journal-Bulletin*. Reproduced by permission of Dick Wright.

concern Al-Qaeda's entrenchment in the West. For example, its procurement network for such materiel as night vision goggles, construction equipment, cell phones, and satellite telephones was based mostly in the U.S., Britain, France, Germany, Denmark, Bosnia and Croatia. The chemicals purchased for use in the manufacture of chemical weapons came from the Czech Republic.

A Global Islamist Network

In the often long waits between terrorist attacks, Al-Qaeda's member organizations maintained operational readiness by acting under the cover of front-company businesses and non-profit, tax-deductible religious charities. These nongovernmental groups, many of them still operating, are based mainly in the U.S. and Britain, as well as in the Middle East. The Qatar Charitable Society, for example, has served as one of bin Laden's de facto banks for raising and transferring funds. Osama bin Laden also set up a tightly organized system of cells in an array of American cities, including Brooklyn, N.Y.; Orlando, Fla.; Dallas; Santa Clara, Calif.; Columbia, Mo., and Herndon, Va.

First, we should think of Al-Qaeda not as an organization dominated by one man but as a global Islamist "Internet" with gateways and access points around the world. Second, Al-Qaeda has a world-wide operational reach. Especially noteworthy is its success in the U.S. and Europe, where it recruits primarily (as this trial showed) among Muslim immigrants. The legal implications of this fact are as serious as they are delicate. Clearly, this is a major new area for law enforcement to grapple with.

Finally, this trial shows that trials alone are not enough. In conceptualizing the Al-Qaeda problem only in terms of law enforcement, the U.S. government misses the larger point: Yes, the operatives engage in crimes, but they are better thought of as soldiers, not criminals. To fight Al-Qaeda and other terrorist groups requires an understanding that they (along with some states) have silently declared war on the U.S.; in turn, we must fight them as we would in a war.

Seeing acts of terror as battles, not crimes, improves the U.S. approach to this problem. It means that, as in a conventional war, America's armed forces, not its policemen and lawyers, are primarily deployed to protect Americans. Rather than drag low-level operatives into American courtrooms, the military will defend us overseas. If a perpetrator is not precisely known, then those who are known to harbor terrorists will be punished. This way, governments and organizations that support terrorism will pay the price, not just the individuals who carry it out. This way, too, Americans will gain a safety that presently eludes them, no matter how many high-profile courtroom victories prosecutors win.

"Al Qaeda attacks are more likely to occur abroad, but the danger of this group is being exaggerated overseas as well."

The Threat of al Qaeda Is Exaggerated

John L. Scherer

John L. Scherer asserts in the following viewpoint that while small-scale terrorist attacks may occur over the next ten years, major al Qaeda attacks are over in the United States and rapidly diminishing throughout the rest of the world. Thus, he argues that the worldwide threat of terrorism perpetrated by al Qaeda—including acts of bioterrorism—is exaggerated. John L. Scherer edited the yearbook *Terrorism: An Annual Survey* in 1982–83 and the quarterly *Terrorism* from 1986 to 2001.

As you read, consider the following questions:
1. Why does the author argue that intelligence agencies are unlikely to uncover impending terrorist attacks?
2. What is the author's opinion of reports that al Qaeda plans one hundred attacks at a time?
3. In Scherer's opinion, what poses a greater threat to the food supply than terrorism?

John L. Scherer, "Is Terrorism's Threat Overblown?" *USA Today Magazine*, January 2003. Copyright © 2003 by the Society for the Advancement of Education. Reproduced by permission.

The threat of terrorism in the U.S. is not over, but [the September 11, 2001, terrorist attacks] may have been an anomaly. Intelligence agencies are unlikely to uncover an impending attack, no matter what they spend on human intelligence, because it is virtually impossible to infiltrate terrorist cells whose members are friends and relatives. At least five of the 19 [September 11] Al Qaeda hijackers came from Asir province in Saudi Arabia, and possibly eight were related.

The U.S. was not defended on 9/11. As soon as the aircraft were hijacked, helicopters armed with missiles should have risen to protect coastal cities. Two F-16s dispatched from Langley and Otis Air Force bases in Virginia and New Jersey, respectively, were too distant to reach New York and Washington, D.C., in time. On a cautionary note, the penetration of White House air space by a Cessna aircraft in June, 2002, and by several other flights since the World Trade Center and Pentagon attacks, indicates nothing much has been done.

Although there will be small-scale terrorist attacks in the U.S. in the next 10 years, major Al Qaeda operations are over. Of the more than 1,200 people arrested after 9/11, none has been charged in the conspiracy. This suggests the hijackers did not and do not have an extensive operational American network. Some intelligence officials have estimated that up to 5,000 "sleepers"—persons with connections to Al Qaeda—are living in this country, including hundreds of hard-core members, yet nothing significant has happened in more than a year. The arrests in the Buffalo, N.Y., area back up the possibility of such sleeper cells.

Al Qaeda attacks are more likely to occur abroad, but the danger of this group is being exaggerated overseas as well. Members of Al Qaeda cells have been arrested in Spain, Italy, England, Germany, Malaysia, and elsewhere, but scarcely more than a score anywhere except Pakistan.

The Threat of Terrorism Has Diminished

The threat of terrorism in the U.S. has greatly diminished, but Al Qaeda and Taliban prisoners realize they can terrorize citizens merely by "confessing" to plans to blow up bridges in California, attack schools in Texas, bomb apartments in

Florida, rob banks in the Northeast, set off a series of "dirty bombs," and have scuba divers operate in coastal areas.[1]

A recent book on Al Qaeda states that the organization plans 100 attacks at any one time. This is nonsense. There have been a handful of small-scale attacks with fatalities linked to Al Qaeda since Sept. 11, nothing near 100. These include a church bombing in Islamabad (five deaths); the explosion of a gasoline truck and bus outside a synagogue on Djerba Island, Tunisia (19 dead); a bus bombing outside the Sheraton Hotel in Karachi (14 killed); and a bombing at the U.S. consulate in Karachi (12 fatalities). Three of these incidents occurred in Pakistan. In addition, Al Qaeda links are suspected in late-2002 bombings in Bali and Kenya. The claim by Sept. 11 terrorist suspect Zacarias Moussaoui of an ongoing Al Qaeda plot in this country is a subterfuge to save himself.

Al Qaeda had planned attacks in London, Paris, Marseilles, Strasbourg, Singapore, and Rome, but most of the conspirators were arrested a short time after the Sept. 11 attacks. Meanwhile, no one had hijacked an aircraft in the U.S. using a "real" weapon in almost 15 years, although crashing planes into structures is not new. The Israelis shot down a Libyan jetliner they said was headed for a building in Tel Aviv in the 1980s. A Cessna 150 fell 50 yards short of the White House in September, 1994. French commandos prevented a jumbo jet, hijacked in Algeria by the Armed Islamic Group, from crashing into the Eiffel Tower the following December. In the mid 1990s, terrorist Ramzi Yousef plotted to have his friend Abdul Hakim Murad fly a light plane loaded with chemical weapons into CIA headquarters at Langley, Va., or to have him spray the area with poison gas. A Turkish hijacker attempted to crash an aircraft into the tomb of former Pres. Kemal Ataturk in Ankara in 1998. With enhanced security on at airports and passengers on commercial airliners who will react to any danger, this threat has diminished.

Terrorists have attacked on holidays, but authorities are now especially alert on those occasions, and the number and

1. The Taliban is a fundamentalist Islamic militia that ruled Afghanistan until ousted by the United States in 2001. The Taliban government gave asylum to Al-Qaeda terrorist leader Osama bin Laden.

violence of anniversary attacks have lessened. Al Qaeda has never staged an incident on a holiday.

Bioterrorism Attacks Are Unlikely

Chemical, biological, and nuclear (CBN) attacks are possible, but difficult and unlikely. Only one has succeeded over the last two decades—the 1995 Sarin incident on the Tokyo subway. Thousands were injured, but just six people died.

There have been no CBN attacks with mass fatalities anywhere. Terrorist "experts" simply have thought up everything terrible that can happen, and then assumed it will. Terrorists would encounter problems dispersing biological toxins. Most quickly dilute in any open space, and others need perfect weather conditions to cause mass casualties. Some biological agents, although not anthrax, are killed by exposure to ultraviolet light. The Washington, D.C., subway system has devices that can detect biological toxins. New York has the highest-density population of any American city, and for this reason might have the greatest probability of such an attack, but it also has the best-prepared public health system.

The Threat of Terrorism Is Overblown

The response of U.S. policymakers to the Sept. 11 [2001] terrorist attacks is based upon an overestimate of the threat of terrorism, and ignores the lessons that can be gained from an interdisciplinary approach to the problem, according to some think tank experts who are analyzing the issue.

"I basically think we are really overreacting to this in a fairly large way," said George Mason University economist Roger Congleton. "I think it would be useful for the press and the government to be reminded that the risks are not as gigantic as we seem to have been encouraged to believe over the last year [2001–2002]."

Christian Bourge, United Press International, August 10, 2002.

In one instance, Essid Sami Ben Khemais, a Moroccan who ran Al Qaeda's European logistics center in Milan, Italy, received a five-year prison sentence in February, 2002. His cell planned to poison Rome's water supply near the U.S. embassy on the Via Veneto. This group had 10 pounds of potassium ferro-cyanide, a chemical used to make wine and ink dye, but extracting a deadly amount of cyanide from this compound would have proved extremely difficult.

Americans are rightly concerned about a strike against a nuclear power facility, but terrorists would have to get through a series of gates and fences, bypass motion sensors, and outfight a heavily armed security force to enter a containment building. Once inside the structure, they would need to know the exact sequence to shut down a reactor. An aircraft diving at a nuclear station would have to hit a small target, nothing like the World Trade Center buildings, which rose 1,400 feet into the air. Containment vessels are 160 feet high by 130 feet wide, and storage casks are even smaller.

Politicians have proposed creating a bureau to protect food from terrorists, but no one in the U.S. has ever died from a terrorist food poisoning. In fact, the nation has experienced just one instance of tampering with agricultural produce, when members of a cult contaminated several salad bars at restaurants in Oregon. The biggest danger to the food supply would be from salmonella, E. coli 0157, clostridium botulinum, and cholera, but careless handling and improper preparation of food are far-greater menaces than terrorism.

The Department of Homeland Security Is Unnecessary

There are 168,000 public water systems in the U.S. Some serve as many as 8,000,000 people, while others as few as 25. None has ever been poisoned, although there have been attempts.

The FBI may need reorganization, especially since its failures preceding Sept. 11 resulted from officials making bad decisions. It is well-known that in mid August, 2001, officials at a flight school in Eagan, Minn., told the FBI that a French citizen of Algerian descent, Moussaoui, had offered $30,000 cash for lessons on a flight-simulator to learn how to fly a Boeing 747. He had no interest in learning how to land the plane. Moussaoui was arrested three weeks before the attacks. One week before the hijackings, French intelligence informed the FBI that he was an Islamic militant who had visited Afghanistan and had links to Al Qaeda. FBI agents could have entered Moussaoui's computer and obtained his phone records using the Federal statutes already in place, but which were ignored or forgotten by officials.

Reorganizations refuse to acknowledge that some individuals are smarter and more knowledgeable than others, and new personnel will eventually resolve these problems. The new Department of Homeland Security will disrupt normal channels of communication and create even more bureaucratic confusion. It will compete for resources with the National Security Council and it will be costly trying to coordinate 46 agencies and, judging from actual terrorist events in the U.S., wholly unnecessary. Americans must remain vigilant, of course, but there is no need to raid the Treasury or turn the country upside down pursuing phantoms.

"The PLO must engage in terrorism in order to obtain financial and diplomatic support from Arab states."

The Palestine Liberation Organization Promotes Violence and Terrorism

Paul Eidelberg

In the following viewpoint Paul Eidelberg argues that Palestinian terrorism is not a desperate response to oppression but part of the Palestine Liberation Organization's (PLO) strategy to destroy Israel. He asserts that the PLO uses terror to gain recruits and secure financial aid and diplomatic support from Arab states, which seek Israel's destruction. Moreover, Eidelberg maintains that the PLO promotes terrorism as a means of psychological warfare to weaken the Israeli will and make Israelis more likely to capitulate to Palestinian demands. Paul Eidelberg lives in Israel and is a member of the board of directors of the Freeman Center for Strategic Studies, a pro-Israel research organization.

As you read, consider the following questions:
1. In the author's opinion, why did Yasir Arafat use schools, mosques, hospitals, and other civilian structures to store arms in Lebanon?
2. According to Eidelberg, what purpose does the PLO serve in the Islamic world?
3. How is terrorism used as an instrument of economic warfare against Israel, in the author's opinion?

Paul Eidelberg, "PLO Terrorism and Grand Strategy," www.freeman.org, April 2001. Copyright © 2001 by Freeman Center for Strategic Studies. Reproduced by permission.

[Israeli] Foreign Minister Shimon Peres wants to continue the policy of negotiating with [Palestinian leader Yasir] Arafat despite on-going PLO- [Palestine Liberation Organization] Palestinian violence. Prime Minister [Ariel] Sharon rejects this policy, or so he would have us believe. The present writer will argue that negotiating with Arafat is a grave error. To explain, allow me to recall an article I wrote about the PLO back in March 1985, almost four years before Arafat renounced violence in Geneva.

1. Like all terrorist organizations, the PLO uses terror to gain recruits. Terrorist leaders know as well as Hollywood move-makers that violence and bloodshed are alluring to no small number of men. They do not harbor a softheaded view of human nature.

2. To attract recruits the PLO must of course succeed, from time to time, in killing Jews, especially in Israel. Only by murdering Jews can the PLO obtain from Saudi Arabia the financial means with which to buy arms. Only by murdering Jews can Yasir Arafat's PLO obtain diplomatic support from the Moslem world . . . above all from Egypt, the creator of the PLO and the most steadfast champion of this organization's claim to represent the so-called "Palestinian people."

3. Unlike Western politicians, Moslem leaders think in long as well as in short terms. Jewish children in Israel eventually become Jewish soldiers. Murdering one is eliminating the other. No less a "moderate" than [the late] King Hussein of Jordan urged Moslems to "kill Jews wherever you find them, kill them with your hands, with your nails and teeth."

Terrorism Is Part of a Grand Strategy

4. Now let us go a little deeper. Operating under the leadership of Yasir Arafat, another "moderate," the PLO [then ensconced] in Lebanon used schools, Mosques, hospitals, and other civilian structures for storing arms and other military purposes. The object was not only to inhibit Israeli retaliation against terrorist attacks, say on Israel's northern towns and resort areas. To the contrary, Arafat surely knew that such PLO attacks would compel Israel, at some point, to strike at the PLO's civilian sanctuaries with the consequence of killing Lebanese civilians, but of thereby alienating Amer-

ican public opinion and triggering U.S. military sanctions. Viewed in this light, terrorist attacks are instruments of grand strategy, the subject of the next consideration.

5. It was said above that the PLO must engage in terrorism in order to obtain financial and diplomatic support from Arab states. If the PLO were to go [purely] "political"—and not merely for the purpose of wresting Judea and Samaria from Israel in preparation for a mortal blow [by Arab states]—it would self-destruct; it would be of use to no one. The Islamic world uses the PLO to keep alive American fear of another Middle East war. This fear aligns the United States with Egypt and other Moslem autocracies against Israel's retention of Judea, Samaria, and Gaza [as well as] the Golan Heights. I am referring to the key strategic function of the PLO. . . .

6. Consistent therewith, Islamic autocrats have foisted on the U.S. the fiction that the "Palestinian problem" is the "core" of the Middle East conflict. PLO terrorism serves to dramatize this fiction because nothing gains the media's attention more than violence. The short-term pragmatism of American politicians enables Moslems to pander to one of America's worst instincts: the belief in "quick-fix" solutions . . . for all problems. And what is the neat solution to the so-called Palestinian problem? Simply Israel's return to her pre-1967 borders. Within those borders, however, are 600,000 [now almost 1.2 million] Moslems. These Moslems are not only related by blood to the mythical Palestinians in Judea, Samaria, and Gaza, but they identity with . . . the PLO. This unpleasant but strategically significant fact is conveniently ignored by sheltered American commentators on the Middle East [to say nothing of Shimon Peres].

PLO Terrorism Is Psychological Warfare

7. Consider, now, the impact of repeated terrorist attacks on Israeli morale [and this was written 8 years before Oslo].[1] Moslem leaders know very well the value Jews place on a single human life. . . . [Hence] one aim of terrorist attacks

---

1. According to the 1993 Oslo Accord, Israel recognized the Palestine Liberation Organization and gave them limited autonomy in return for peace and an end to Palestinian claims on Israeli land.

against the people of Israel is to break down their will and per-severance, their political sobriety and national solidarity. Jew-ish realism may give way to Jewish wishful thinking: the . . . desire for peace may move softhearted and shortsighted poli-ticians to enter into unwise and dangerous agreements. Here PLO terrorism functions as a form of psychological warfare.

Many Palestinians Support Terror

Many in the Arab world either seek Israel's destruction or con-sider suicide bombings, shootings, mortar attacks, ambushes, and other attacks—aimed not only at Israeli soldiers and set-tlers but at civilians living within Israel proper—legitimate "resistance" to Israel's occupation of much of the West Bank and Gaza Strip. Polls show that Palestinian belligerence rose as the peace process collapsed. Israelis say [Yasir] Arafat's re-jection of what they considered a generous peace offer at the 2000 Camp David summit showed that the PA [Palestinian Authority] remains committed to terror, not diplomacy. . . .

Many members of the al-Aqsa Brigades [West Bank militia], including some commanders, receive paychecks from the PA for working in one of its security services. In the spring of 2002, Israeli troops said they had found documents in Arafat's Ramallah headquarters showing that PA funds had paid for some of the brigades' terror operations, and [George W.] Bush administration officials say Arafat's reported approval of a $20,000 payment to the brigades spurred the White House to call for Arafat's removal.

Council on Foreign Relations, www.terrorismanswers.com, 2004.

8. Terrorism is also used as an instrument of economic warfare. Planting bombs in Jerusalem cannot but diminish tourism, on which Israel's economy to no small extent de-pends.

9. Finally, reluctant as the free press may be [to] say killing Jews is a religious obligation for Moslems so long as Israel remains a sovereign and independent state, ponder the words of Dr. Abdul Halim Mahmoud, rector of Cairo's al-Ashar University, theologically and politically the most in-fluential university in Islamdom: "Allah commands Moslems to fight the friends of Satan wherever they are to be found. Among the friends of Satan—indeed, among the foremost friends of Satan in the present age—are the Jews."

To begin to fathom this venomous hatred of the Jews, let us cite Professor Abd al-Rahman al-Bazzaz of the University of Baghdad: "The existence of Israel nullifies the unity of our civilization which embraces the whole region. Moreover, the existence of Israel is a flagrant challenge to our philosophy of life and a total barrier against the values and aims we aspire [to] in the world."

Support for Israel's Destruction

Not the "Palestinian problem" but the "Jewish problem" is the core of the Middle East conflict. For Islam there is but one "Final Solution" to this problem, which is why all Moslem states support the PLO Covenant calling for Israel's destruction. . . .

It is hard for men of good will to take implacable hatred seriously, which is why Adolph Hitler was chosen *Time*'s Man of the Year in 1939.

Thus my 1985 article. Only a postscript is necessary. Sharon will either make war with the PLO or succumb to its minister in the cabinet, Shimon Peres.

"Let me be very clear. I condemn the attacks carried out by terrorist groups against Israeli civilians."

The Palestine Liberation Organization Condemns Violence and Terrorism

Yasir Arafat

Until his death in 2004, Yasir Arafat was head of the Palestinian Authority, the governing body established by the Palestine Liberation Organization (PLO) in the 1990s. In the following viewpoint, first published in 2002, Arafat claims that groups who commit acts of terrorism against innocent Israeli civilians do not represent the Palestinian people or their legitimate desire for freedom. He argues further that although Palestinians are oppressed by Israelis, no degree of oppression and desperation can justify terrorist attacks. Moreover, Arafat insists that terrorism will disappear once Israelis are willing to see the Palestinian people as equals and negotiate a just peace with them.

As you read, consider the following questions:

1. What is the Palestinian vision of peace, according to Arafat?
2. What does Arafat insist is the Israelis' purpose in attacking him personally?

For the past 16 months [since November 2000], Israelis and Palestinians have been locked in a catastrophic cycle of violence, a cycle which only promises more bloodshed and fear. The cycle has led many to conclude that peace is impossible, a myth borne out of ignorance of the Palestinian position. Now is the time for the Palestinians to state clearly, and for the world to hear clearly, the Palestinian vision.

But first, let me be very clear. I condemn the attacks carried out by terrorist groups against Israeli civilians. These groups do not represent the Palestinian people or their legitimate aspirations for freedom. They are terrorist organizations, and I am determined to put an end to their activities.

The Palestinian vision of peace is an independent and viable Palestinian state on the territories occupied by Israel in 1967, living as an equal neighbor alongside Israel with peace and security for both the Israeli and Palestinian peoples. In 1988, the Palestine National Council adopted a historic resolution calling for the implementation of applicable United Nations resolutions, particularly, Resolutions 242 and 338. The Palestinians recognized Israel's right to exist on 78 percent of historical Palestine with the understanding that we would be allowed to live in freedom on the remaining 22 percent, which has been under Israeli occupation since 1967. Our commitment to that two-state solution remains unchanged, but unfortunately, also remains unreciprocated.

The Palestinian Refugee Problem

We seek true independence and full sovereignty: the right to control our own airspace, water resources and borders; to develop our own economy, to have normal commercial relations with our neighbors, and to travel freely. In short, we seek only what the free world now enjoys and only what Israel insists on for itself: the right to control our own destiny and to take our place among free nations.

In addition, we seek a fair and just solution to the plight of Palestinian refugees who for 54 years have not been permitted to return to their homes. We understand Israel's demographic concerns and understand that the right of return of Palestinian refugees, a right guaranteed under international law and United Nations Resolution 194, must be implemented in a way that takes into account such concerns. However, just as we Palestinians must be realistic with respect to Israel's demographic desires, Israelis too must be realistic in understanding that there can be no solution to the Israeli-Palestinian conflict if the legitimate rights of these innocent civilians continue to be ignored. Left unresolved, the refugee issue has the potential to undermine any permanent peace agreement between Palestinians and Israelis. How is a Palestinian refugee to understand that his or her right of return will not be honored but those of Kosovar Albanians, Afghans and East Timorese have been?

There are those who claim that I am not a partner in peace. In response, I say Israel's peace partner is, and always has been, the Palestinian people. Peace is not a signed agreement between individuals—it is reconciliation between peoples. Two peoples cannot reconcile when one demands control over the other, when one refuses to treat the other as a partner in peace, when one uses the logic of power rather than the power of logic. Israel has yet to understand that it cannot have peace while denying justice. As long as the occupation of Palestinian lands continues, as long as Palestinians are denied freedom, then the path to the "peace of the brave" that I embarked upon with my late partner [Israeli prime minister] Yitzhak Rabin, will be littered with obstacles.

The Killing of Civilians Is Never Justified

The Palestinian people have been denied their freedom for far too long and are the only people in the world still living under foreign occupation. How is it possible that the entire world can tolerate this oppression, discrimination and humiliation? The 1993 Oslo Accord, signed on the White House lawn, promised the Palestinians freedom by May 1999. Instead, since 1993, the Palestinian people have endured a doubling of Israeli settlers, expansion of illegal Israeli settlements on Palestinian land and increased restrictions on freedom of movement. How do I convince my people that Israel is serious about peace while over the past decade Israel intensified the colonization of Palestinian land from which it was ostensibly negotiating a withdrawal?

But no degree of oppression and no level of desperation can

ever justify the killing of innocent civilians. I condemn terrorism. I condemn the killing of innocent civilians, whether they are Israeli, American or Palestinian; whether they are killed by Palestinian extremists, Israeli settlers, or by the Israeli government. But condemnations do not stop terrorism. To stop terrorism, we must understand that terrorism is simply the symptom, not the disease.

No Terrorism Has Been Committed by the PLO

It is also important to differentiate between Palestine Authority violence and terrorism. While the Israeli right-wingers would have us all believe that the Palestine Authority, or in particular certain factions and forces answering to Fatah and other leading PLO factions are responsible for terrorist acts, when asked to back this contention all they can point at are legitimate acts of self-defense, i.e. gunfights with Israeli troops and armed settler gangs. The PLO renounced terrorism in 1988, and virtually without exception has stuck to this renunciation. Palestinian soldiers and police have engaged in gunfights with Israeli soldiers, police, and settler gangs, but this is legitimate self-defense as is fully endorsed and allowed by international law. The very height of Israeli *chutzpah* has been the condemnation of the assassination of Minister Rehavam Ze'evi as 'terrorism' in view of Israel's current targeted assassination policy in the Occupied Territories. Vilification campaigns notwithstanding, there has been no terrorism committed by the Palestine Authority or the forces under the command of President [Yasir] Arafat.

John Sigler, Essays and Commentary on Contemporary Middle Eastern Issues, www.eccmei.net, February 3, 2002.

The personal attacks on me currently in vogue may be highly effective in giving Israelis an excuse to ignore their own role in creating the current situation. But these attacks do little to move the peace process forward and, in fact, are not designed to. Many believe that Ariel Sharon, Israel's prime minister, given his opposition to every peace treaty Israel has ever signed, is fanning the flames of unrest in an effort to delay indefinitely a return to negotiations. Regrettably, he has done little to prove them wrong. Israeli government practices of settlement construction, home demolitions, political assassinations, closures and shameful silence in the face of Israeli settler violence and other daily humiliations are clearly not aimed at calming the situation.

The Palestinian Vision of Peace

The Palestinians have a vision of peace: it is a peace based on the complete end of the occupation and a return to Israel's 1967 borders, the sharing of all Jerusalem as one open city and as the capital of two states, Palestine and Israel. It is a warm peace between two equals enjoying mutually beneficial economic and social cooperation. Despite the brutal repression of Palestinians over the last four decades, I believe when Israel sees Palestinians as equals, and not as a subjugated people upon whom it can impose its will, such a vision can come true. Indeed it must.

Palestinians are ready to end the conflict. We are ready to sit down now with any Israeli leader, regardless of his history, to negotiate freedom for the Palestinians, a complete end of the occupation, security for Israel and creative solutions to the plight of the refugees while respecting Israel's demographic concerns. But we will only sit down as equals, not as supplicants; as partners, not as subjects; as seekers of a just and peaceful solution, not as a defeated nation grateful for whatever scraps are thrown our way. For despite Israel's overwhelming military advantage, we possess something even greater: the power of justice.

"[Basque separatists] have been blamed for killing more than 800 people . . . making it one of the most feared organisations of its kind in Europe."

Basque Separatists Promote Terrorism

Paul Sussman

The Basques, people who inhabit the Basque region in France and Spain, have long sought from both nations political and cultural autonomy. According to Paul Sussman, a writer for CNN.com Europe, the Basque separatist group ETA (Euskadi Ta Askatasuna) has engaged in a campaign of violent terrorism against the Spanish government for over thirty years. Sussman maintains in the following viewpoint that ETA is responsible for more than eight hundred murders and at least seventy kidnappings, plus countless bank robberies and acts of extortion. He argues further that ETA members have received training from terrorist groups in Libya, Lebanon, and Nicaragua, and that the organization has close ties to the Irish Republican Army.

As you read, consider the following questions:
1. According to Sussman, what is the English translation of "Euskadi Ta Askatasuna"?
2. The author reports that the Basque region straddles what two countries?
3. What has been the response of the Spanish government to Basque separatist activities?

For 32 years the Basque separatist group ETA has been fighting for an independent Basque state in northern Spain.

During that period, ETA has been blamed for killing more than 800 people, kidnapping 70 others and wounding thousands, making it one of the most feared organizations of its kind in Europe.

ETA, founded in 1959, stands for Euskadi Ta Askatasuna, Basque for "Basque Homeland and Freedom." It killed what some say was its first victim in 1968.

Since then it has waged a relentless campaign of violence against the Spanish state, targeting politicians, policemen, judges and soldiers. ETA's deadliest weapons are car bombs, which have caused numerous civilian casualties. In 1980 alone ETA was blamed for 118 deaths, and in 1995 it nearly succeeded in assassinating Jose Maria Aznar, then leader of the opposition, now Spain's prime minister.

On September 16, 1998, the organisation declared a "unilateral and indefinite" cease-fire, raising hopes that its campaign was at an end. ETA called off the cease-fire in November 1999, however, and 2000 saw a sharp escalation in violence.

Fiercely Independent

The Basque country, or Euskal Herria as it is known in Basque, straddles the western end of the Pyrenees, covering 20,664 square kilometres in northern Spain and southern France. Spain officially recognizes three Basque provinces, Alava, Guipuzcoa and Vizcaya. A fourth neighboring province, Navarra, is of Basque heritage. Separatists consider these four provinces plus three in France—Basse Navarre, Labourd and Soule—as the Basque country, with a population approaching 3 million.

The area has always possessed a fiercely independent instinct. The Basque people are the oldest indigenous ethnic group in Europe and have lived uninterrupted in the same region since the beginning of recorded history.

Their language, Euskera, which is spoken regularly by about 40 percent of Basque inhabitants, bears no relation to any other Indo-European tongue and dates back to before the Romans arrived in Spain.

For many centuries the Basques of Spain enjoyed a strong
degree of autonomy. In the Spanish Civil War, two Basque
provinces—Guipuzcoa and Vizcaya—fought against Gen.
Francisco Franco, while the provinces of Alava and Navarra
fought for Franco. Under Franco's dictatorship (1939–75),
most of the Basque region had its remaining autonomy rescinded. Its culture, people and language were suppressed.

ETA and its demands for an independent Basque state
arose in 1959 in the midst of this suppression.

Kidnapping and Bank Robbery Finance the ETA

ETA has focused its activities on the Spanish side of the border. For many years France provided a safe haven for ETA
members, a situation that began to change in the mid-1980s.

The organisation finances its campaign through kidnapping, bank robbery and a so-called "revolutionary tax" on
Basque businesses—a payment that is widely regarded as
plain extortion. No one knows how many businesses make
these payments.

According to the counter-terrorism office of the U.S.
State Department, ETA members have received training in

Libya, Lebanon and Nicaragua, while the group also enjoys close links with the Irish Republican Army (the Good Friday peace accord influenced ETA to call its cease-fire in 1998).

Active support for ETA is limited, and although no accurate figures are available, its membership is not thought to number more than a few hundred. It is believed to operate in small commando cells of about five people each. The party that many believe to be its political wing, Herri Batasuna (founded in 1978), rarely scores higher than 20 percent in local elections, considerably less than the more moderate Basque Nationalist Party (PNV).

While many Basques support independence—up to 40 percent, according to PNV leader Xabier Arzalluz—the vast majority of Basques oppose the use of violence.

The response of the Spanish government to ETA's activities has been two-pronged.

On one hand Spain has sought to accommodate the region's strong sense of local identity. Since the early 1980s, the Basque provinces of Alava, Guipuzcoa and Vizcaya have been recognised as an autonomous region known as Pais Vasco, with its own parliament and police force, and with Euskera as the official language.

Violence Continues

At the same time Madrid has cracked down hard on anyone suspected of being an ETA member.

From 1983–87, a shadowy organisation called the Anti-Terrorist Liberation Group (or GAL, from its Spanish name), was blamed for killing 27 suspected ETA members. This later proved to be a major scandal for Socialist Prime Minister Felipe Gonzalez, who was in power from 1982–96. One of his interior ministers served time in jail for his role in a kidnapping carried out by GAL.

In 1997, 23 leaders of Herri Batasuna were arrested and jailed for collaborating with ETA.

Despite the crackdowns and widespread public condemnation of its activities, ETA has continued its campaign of violence. Inaki Azcuna, the mayor of Bilbao, said: "We have too many attacks and not enough dialogue."

It is a situation which, at present, shows no sign of changing.

> *"While the political rights of the Basque Country remain denied . . . while the renovated tracks of fascism remain, ETA will keep on practising armed struggle."*

Basque Separatists Promote Nonviolent Political Change

Euskadi Ta Askatasuna

The Basques are an ethnic group inhabiting the Basque regions in northern Spain and southern France. They seek political and cultural autonomy. Euskadi Ta Askatasuna (ETA), the Basque separatist party, argues in the following viewpoint that violence against Spain and France is justified because the Spanish and French governments have failed to recognize the Basques culturally and politically. ETA insists that it has tried repeatedly over the past forty years to end its armed conflict with Spain, but Spain's refusal to give the Basques the autonomy they desire makes peace impossible.

As you read, consider the following questions:

1. What does ETA argue is the response of Spain and France to their proposals for a political solution to violence?
2. According to ETA, what has the development of Europe in the past few years shown the Basques?
3. With whom does ETA declare its solidarity?

Euskadi Ta Askatasuna, "ETA's Statement to the Institutions and Citizens of Europe," www.baskinfo.org, June 11, 2002. Copyright © 2002 by Baskenland Informatie Centrum. Reproduced by permission.

On 11th June 1995, [Euskadi Ta Askatasuna, the Basque separatist party] (ETA) sent a statement to the European public opinion for the first time. In that document this organisation explained the contents of a peace proposal—known as the Democratic Alternative—that we had published some months earlier and we requested to put pressure on the Spanish government to force them to change their uncompromising attitude.

Seven years later, the Spanish government has been in charge of the Presidency of the European Union for six months. That period will finish [in 2002] with the meeting of the leaders of the member-states in Seville (Andalusia).

Spanish fascism, French jacobinism, the building of Europe and the Globalisation: the Basque Country [is] in a tight spot.

The conflict that sets the Basque Country against Spain and France continues. Despite the power changes in the governments of Spain and France, despite the important steps towards the building of Europe, there is no indication that both oppressive states will give up the colonisation and oppression we endure in the Basque Country.

On the contrary, the Spanish government has imposed a state of siege in the Basque Country: ban on newspapers, increase in the amount of arbitrary detentions, ban on political organisations and groups of the popular movement and the legalisation of savage tortures. Subsequent to the [Arab terrorist] attacks of September 11th, [2001,] they have tried to achieve the complicity of the European institutions. In addition, taking advantage of its economic power—as in the filthiest times of the Spanish imperialism—they had increased the pressure on the countries "under their influence". Nowadays, the fascism and the restructuring of the Empire are the main features of the Spanish policy.

Increased Repression

During these years, one of the only changes has been the high speed acquired by the renovated Era of the Globalisation. In connection with the undergoing worldwide economic transformation, the building of Europe is just another part of the puzzle. The creation of a giant market has hampered the development and establishment of a social Europe.

After having created and reinforced the economic foundations of the single European market, the leading powers have [taken] the place left to the citizens and started to build on it. The speed of the European process is being marked by the capital and their financial needs. The Europe of the citizens, Europe's social chart and the Europe of the peoples were abandoned a long time ago.

On the other hand, the gap between the citizens and the European institutions is widening, as they recognise too. To avoid it, the European institutions are taking some measures. Against the Basque Country and especially against all the popular organisations that fight for the rights of the Basque Country, the measures they promote are different: the Schengen Space for the police control, the Watson law and the right to veto of Spain and France. In return for political proposals for a solution, more and more repression; that is our reality.

Meanwhile, the Basque citizens still make up a group of second-class citizens, trapped in the institutional nets of Spain's parliamentary monarchy and France's republic. Our rights remained kidnapped; by "kidnapped" we mean a group of citizens free to say whatever, but whose right to decide is undermined within both political systems. Furthermore, according to a new law Spain is planning to adopt, the Basque citizens will not be allowed even to say what they think!

No Future for the Basque Country

The Basque Country has got no future in the current Europe of the States. Lots of majestic sentences, lots of "democratic" rights, but during the last years the building of Europe has just shown us clearly that we do not have the right to think and to act as a people. To prevent the Basques from acting as such, the republic of France uses its false grandness and equity and Spain the democratic label given by Europe for the last twenty years. In the modern reservation for natives they built for us, we are told wickedly we shall only be as souvenirs for the tourists and for the history books; in fact, limited rights that can only be used in a reservation under their control. Up to now, the magnificent future offered by all the governments in Spain and France to the Basques

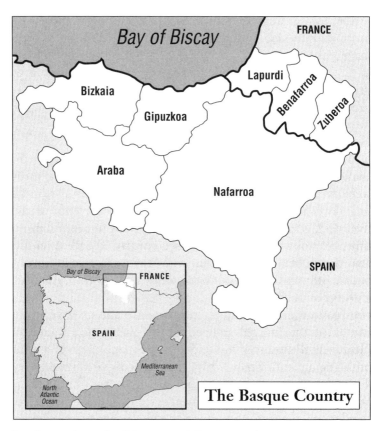

The Basque Country

has been that of a "democratic" segregation.

In addition, the republic of France and the "democracy" of Spain have built the future behind the Basque citizens' back; and, however, how many are the Basques who lost their lives in the Basque Country fighting in the resistance against the Nazis? How many are those who died in the war against the Spanish fascists? And, finally, we got paid, through their oppression and abuse.

The governments of Spain and France go against History.

ETA confirms its proposition to set the conflict on democratic grounds.

Concrete Proposals to End the Armed Conflict

ETA has usually said that there are ways to overcome the oppression and the armed conflict. Moreover, ETA has launched concrete proposals for the last forty years.

- In 1976, at the time the "Spanish democracy" was being born, the KAS Alternative [eight negotiating points for political recognition] was offered.
- In 1989, the talks in Algiers took place but the lack of political courage of the political party in power undermined the process.
- In 1995, ETA published a concrete proposal we called the Democratic Alternative [a negotiated solution to end violence].
- Later, ETA has left clear its goodwill to overcome the armed conflict through democratic ways in 1996 with a one-week initiative, or in the initiative of 1998.

In fact, we must assert proudly that ETA's strategic objectives remain the independence and socialism, but, at the same time, we make proposals linked to the reality to overcome the armed conflict. ETA will never speak in the name of our people. The members of ETA, instead of being terrorists, are a group of Basque citizens who are tightly tied to their society. Nowadays, ETA keeps on using the armed struggle in favour of the fundamental rights of the Basque Country. However, if those rights are guaranteed, ETA has repeated once and again that it will respect the decision of our people. The respect to our self-determination and to our territory. Both concepts must be guaranteed by a Democratic Process; that is the only condition demanded by ETA to overcome the current armed conflict. In fact, it could also be summed up in the slogan "Give the word to the People and respect it", the fundamentals of the Democratic Alternative. That's the only key to the problem. In addition, we must remember that in 1997, due to a campaign to become known [as] the Democratic Alternative, the judicial-repressive machinery of the Spanish government imprisoned the whole leadership of Herri Batasuna [the Basque left nationalist party]. So, what can we expect from the "democratic" propositions of our two neighbouring states? That is ETA's question to the citizens and institutions of Europe. At this moment in time, the juridical-political structuring of a new Europe is taking place; the European Institutions should know that the building of that Europe would be hampered if they were unable to reply with political courage to the existing conflicts and disputes. The responsibility would be yours too.

Solidarity with Oppressed People

[We are] in favour of a plural world and a fair society [we want to be] free to build the future. We would like to declare our solidarity to all the citizens who are worldwide fighting against injustice. . . .

ETA wants to confirm to the institutions, social agents and citizens of Europe its willingness to overcome the armed struggle. The Basque citizens should discuss, think over and say, without pressures, which is the Basque Country they want and which position in Europe they wish. While the Basque Country is doomed to die, ETA will keep on struggling. As ETA asserts its willingness to overcome the armed struggle, we also confirm that the only way against the obstinacy and arrogance of both oppressing states is the struggle. In any case, peace will only be brought by justice. While the political rights of the Basque Country remain denied; while the willingness to talk and negotiate remain deceitful; while the plans to ban the citizens' organisations, groups and initiatives continue; while there is no willingness to punish their use of torture and other atrocities; while the only truth is that of their despicable media; that is, while the renovated tracks of fascism remain, ETA will keep on practising armed struggle, as for the last four decades. Because the self-defence is our right. The struggle against injustice unites us, the dream of a fair society in the future too.

Efforts to Change

ETA requests to the European Institutions to make efforts to change the attitude of the Spanish and French governments. It requests to the social agents to come to the Basque Country, to meet all the agents here, to analyse the situation in its entirety and, in their working field to spread a view based on reality; because many media in Europe just transmit the view of the despicable Spanish media. We must take steps to set the conflict on democratic grounds. It is about time for each one to assume his/her own responsibility. ETA assumed its own one a long time ago.

Periodical Bibliography

The following articles have been selected to supplement the diverse views presented in this chapter.

David Bedein
"Your Taxes for PLO Propaganda," FrontPageMag.com, October 29, 2003.

Louis René Beres
"The Difference Between Murderers and Freedom Fighters," Freeman Center for Strategic Studies, January 29, 2004. www.freeman.org.

Michael Borop
"Focus: Basque Separatism," *World Sites Atlas*, May 15, 1999.

Christian Bourge
"Terror Threat Overblown, Says Expert," *United Press International*, 10, 2002.

J.T. Caruso
"Al-Qaeda International," Testimony before the Subcommittee on International Operations and Terrorism, Committee on Foreign Relations, U.S. Senate, December 18, 2001. www.fbi.gov.

Rod Dreher
"The PLO Man," *National Review Online*, April 3, 2002. www.nationalreview.com.

Michael Elliot
"Hate Club: Al-Qaeda's Web of Terror," *Time*, November 4, 2001.

Adam Entous
"U.S. Says Relations to PLO Tied to Terror Fight," *Miami Herald*, April 16, 2002.

Joel S. Fishman
"Ten Years Since Oslo: The PLO's 'People's War' Strategy and Israel's Inadequate Response," Jerusalem Center for Public Affairs, September 1–15, 2003. www.jcpa.org.

Reyko Huang
"In the Spotlight: Basque Fatherland and Liberty (ETA)," Center for Defense Information, May 23, 2002. www.cdi.org.

Kamel Jaber
"The Two Intifadas: PLO Activist Interview," From Occupied Palestine, November 4, 2003. www.fromoccupiedpalestine.org.

NewsMax.com
"Terrorism Nuclear Threat Real," February 1, 2002. www.newsmax.com.

Daniel Pipes
"Arafat's Suicide Factory," *New York Post*, December 9, 2001.

Republican Study Committee
"Tactics of Palestine Terrorism," September 11, 2003. www.house.gov/burton/RSC.

James Ridgeway   "Al Qaeda Duped?" *Village Voice*, November 16, 2001.

Lara Sukhtian   "PLO Taps New Prime Minister," *Washington Times*, September 8, 2003.

Time International   "Fear and Loathing Return: After a Long Truce, Spain's Basque Terrorists Resume Their Attempts to Bomb Their Way to Independence," January 31, 2000.

Wall Street Journal   "Iraq and al Qaeda," September 22, 2003.

For Further Discussion

Chapter 1

1. Matthew C. Ogilvie insists that racists use religion to justify their hate and violence. David Ostendorf maintains that the positive power of religion is the best weapon against bigotry. In your opinion, is religion a force for good or evil? Explain, citing from the viewpoints.

2. David Horowitz argues that Islamic fundamentalist groups on American college campuses pose a serious threat because they promote an anti-American agenda and lure students into terrorist activities. Shibley Telhami insists that most Arab and Muslim Americans were horrified by the Arab terrorist attacks on September 11, 2001, and are loyal to the United States. In your opinion, which argument is stronger?

3. The religious Right's notion of the United States as a Christian theocracy has no historical basis, according to Frederick Clarkson. He argues further that it is part of a harmful agenda that includes a variety of social and political issues. Norman Podhoretz, however, insists that there is nothing to fear from the religious Right because the group now embraces diverse religious views. In your opinion, which author is more convincing?

4. The Jewish Defense League insists that Jewish people have a right to use force and violence to defend themselves against threats from Nazis and other anti-Semitic groups. Angela Valkyrie claims that the Jewish Defense League is a violent terrorist group that threatens European Americans without provocation. Are there always other options besides violence to fight oppression and injustice? Explain, citing from the viewpoints.

Chapter 2

1. Fredrick K. Goodwin and Adrian R. Morrison argue that when radical animal rights groups harass scientists, they have a devastating effect on scientific creativity and medical research. Noel Molland, however, claims that violent action by radical animal rights groups is justified because peaceful methods do not get results. In your opinion, is using illegal means to achieve a noble goal ever justified? Explain.

2. Brian Paterson insists that socialism encourages violence and uses force to achieve its end of income redistribution. John Fisher argues that socialism is the cure for the violence and de-

structiveness of capitalism. Which argument is more persuasive? Cite from the viewpoints in your answer.

3. Brad Knickerbocker argues that radical environmentalists are terrorists. Emily Kumpel claims that ecoterrorism is sometimes necessary because it gets results. In your opinion, will the violent actions of radical environmental groups make the general public more or less sympathetic to environmentalism in general? Explain.

Chapter 3

1. Carol Rowan argues that white supremacist groups are violent and dangerous. Adrian H. Krieg, however, insists that the size of white supremacist organizations and the danger they pose is exaggerated by watchdog groups to encourage contributions from rich liberals. Which argument is more persuasive? Why?

2. Matthew Hale claims that it is permissible to hate non-Christians and nonwhites because they will ultimately destroy the white race. Doug Anstaett argues that white supremacist groups are evil and should be opposed by decent Americans. In your opinion, can a person be a decent American and still hate non-Christians and nonwhites? Explain, citing from the viewpoints.

Chapter 4

1. Daniel Pipes and Steven Emerson argue that al Qaeda is the most lethal terrorist organization in the world and a threat to all non-Islamic nations. They maintain that al Qaeda's acts of terrorism must be treated as wartime battles not crimes. John L. Scherer, however, insists that the threat of al Qaeda is exaggerated and that reasonable vigilance will provide adequate safety. In your opinion, which is more dangerous—overreacting to threats of terrorism or underreacting? Explain.

2. Paul Eidelberg asserts that the PLO promotes violence and terrorism as part of its strategy to destroy Israel. Yasir Arafat insists that the PLO condemns terrorism and the killing of innocent civilians and wants only peace and justice. Eidelberg is an Israeli and Arafat is the head of the Palestinian Authority. In your opinion, how does each author's nationality affect his argument?

3. Paul Sussman maintains that the ETA is a terrorist group that uses murder, kidnapping, and bank robbery to achieve its goal of a free Basque state and is unlikely to stop its violent approach. ETA argues that its violence is justified because Spain and France have failed to recognize the Basques culturally and politically. Further, ETA insists that it would stop its attacks if the Spanish government would end its repressive policies. In your opinion, is terrorism justifiable in the fight for freedom? Explain.

Organizations to Contact

The editors have compiled the following list of organizations concerned with the issues debated in this book. The descriptions are derived from materials provided by the organizations. All have publications or information available for interested readers. The list was compiled on the date of publication of the present volume; names, addresses, phone and fax numbers, and e-mail and Internet addresses may change. Be aware that many organizations take several weeks or longer to respond to inquiries, so allow as much time as possible.

American-Arab Anti-Discrimination Committee
4201 Connecticut Ave. NW, Suite 300, Washington, DC 20008
(202) 244-2990 • fax: (202) 244-3196
e-mail: adc@adc.org • Web site: www.adc.org

The committee fights anti-Arab stereotyping in the media and discrimination and hate crimes against Arab Americans. It publishes a series of issue papers and a number of books, including the two-volume *Taking Root/Bearing Fruit: The Arab-American Experience.*

American Civil Liberties Union (ACLU)
125 Broad St., 18th Fl., New York, NY 10004
(212) 549-2585
e-mail: aclu@aclu.org • Web site: www.aclu.org

The ACLU is a national organization that works to defend Americans' civil rights guaranteed in the U.S. Constitution. The ACLU publishes the semiannual newsletter *Civil Liberties Alert* as well as the briefing papers "Hate Speech on Campus" and "Racial Justice."

B'nai B'rith Canada
15 Hove St., Toronto, ON M3H 4Y8 Canada
(416) 633-6224 • fax: (416) 630-2159
e-mail: bnb@bnaibrith.ca • Web site: www.bnaibrith.ca

Affiliated with the American Anti-Defamation League, this organization works to stop the defamation of Jews and to ensure fair treatment for all Canadian citizens. It monitors violent extremist groups and advocates antiterrorism measures in Canada, and it publishes the annual *Review of Anti-Semitism in Canada.*

Center for Democratic Renewal
PO Box 50469, Atlanta, GA 30302
(404) 221-0025 • fax: (404) 221-0045
e-mail: info@cdr.org • Web site: www.thecdr.org

Formerly known as the National Anti-Klan Network, this non-profit organization monitors hate group activity and white supremacist activity in America and opposes bias-motivated violence. It publishes the bimonthly *Monitor* magazine, the report *The Fourth Wave: A Continuing Conspiracy to Burn Black Churches*, and the book *When Hate Groups Come to Town*.

Christian Coalition of America
PO Box 37030, Washington, DC 20003
(202) 479-6900 • fax: (202) 479-4260
e-mail: coalition@cc.org • Web site: www.cc.org
The Christian Coalition was founded in 1989 to give Christians a voice in government. The organization's goals include strengthening the family, protecting innocent human life, and protecting religious freedom.

Communist Party USA
235 W. Twenty-third St., New York, NY 10011
(212) 989-4994 • fax: (212) 229-1713
e-mail: CPUSA@cpusa.org • Web site: www.cpusa.org
The Communist Party USA is a Marxist-Leninist working-class party that unites black, brown, and white, men and women, and youth and seniors. The party speaks from a working-class perspective and supports labor and all militant movements for social progress. The Communist Party USA publishes the periodical *People's Weekly World*.

Council on American-Islamic Relations (CAIR)
453 New Jersey Ave. SE, Washington, DC 20005
(202) 488-8787 • fax: (202) 488-0833
e-mail: cair@cair-net.org • Web site: www.cair-net.org
CAIR is a nonprofit membership organization dedicated to presenting an Islamic perspective on public policy issues and to challenging the misrepresentation of Islam and Muslims. It fights discrimination against Muslims in America and lobbies political leaders on issues related to Islam and Muslims. Its publications include the quarterly newsletter *CAIR News* as well as the periodic *Action Alert*.

Earth First!
PO Box 20, Arcata, CA 95518
(707) 825-6598
e-mail: greg@EarthFirst.org • Web site: www.earthfirst.org

Earth First! believes that the earth's ecology has become seriously degraded and advocates direct action in order to stop the destruction of the environment. The organization publishes the *Earth First! Journal*.

Greenpeace USA

702 H St. NW, Suite 300, Washington, DC
(202) 462-1177 • fax: (202) 462-4507
e-mail: greenpeaceusa@wdc.greenpeace.org
Web site: www.greenpeace.org

This international environmental organization consists of conservationists who believe that verbal protests against threats to the environment are inadequate and advocates direct action instead. It publishes the quarterly newsletter *Greenpeace* and periodic *Greenpeace Reports*.

Jewish Defense League (JDL)

PO Box 480370, Los Angeles, CA 90048
(818) 980-8535 • fax: (781) 634-0338
e-mail: jdljdl@aol.com • Web site: www.jdl.org

The league is an activist organization that works to raise awareness of anti-Semitism and the neo-Nazi movement. The JDL Web site features news and updates on hate groups and activism as well as information on Jewish culture.

National Association for the Advancement of Colored People (NAACP)

4805 Mt. Hope Dr., Baltimore, MD 21215-3297
(877) NAACP-98 • fax: (410) 486-9255
e-mail: washingtonbureau@naacpnet.org
Web site: www.naacp.org

The NAACP is the oldest and largest civil rights organization in the United States. Its principal objective is to ensure the political, educational, social, and economic equality of minorities. It publishes the magazine *Crisis* ten times a year as well as a variety of newsletters, books, and pamphlets.

People for the American Way Foundation

2000 M St. NW, Suite 400, Washington, DC 20036
(800) 326-7329
e-mail: pfaw@pfaw.org • Web site: www.pfaw.org

People for the American Way Foundation opposes the political agenda of the religious Right. Through public education, lobbying, and legal advocacy, the foundation works to defend equal rights.

The foundation publishes *Hostile Climate*, a report detailing intolerant incidents directed against gays and lesbians, and organizes the Students Talk About Race (STAR) program, which trains college students to lead high school discussions on intergroup relations.

People for the Ethical Treatment of Animals (PETA)
501 Front St., Norfolk, VA 23510
(757) 622-7382 • fax: (757) 622-0457
e-mail: info@peta.org • Web site: www.peta-online.org

An international animal rights organization, PETA is dedicated to establishing and protecting the rights of all animals. It focuses on four areas: factory farms, research laboratories, the fur trade, and the entertainment industry. PETA promotes public education, cruelty investigations, animal rescue, and celebrity videos, and it publishes *Animal Times, Grrr!* (a magazine for children), various fact sheets, brochures, and flyers.

Prejudice Institute
2743 Maryland Ave., Baltimore, MD 21218
(410) 243-6987
e-mail: prejinst@aol.com • Web site: www.prejudiceinstitute.org

The Prejudice Institute is a national research center concerned with violence and intimidation motivated by prejudice. It conducts research, supplies information on model programs and legislation, and provides education and training to combat prejudicial violence. The Prejudice Institute publishes research reports, bibliographies, and the quarterly newsletter *Forum*.

Southern Poverty Law Center/Klanwatch Project
400 Washington Ave., Montgomery, AL 36102
(334) 956-8200
Web site: www.splcenter.org

The center litigates civil cases to protect the rights of poor people, particularly when those rights are threatened by white supremacist groups. The affiliated Klanwatch Project and the Militia Task Force collect data on white supremacist groups and militias and promote the adoption and enforcement by states of antiparamilitary training laws. The center publishes numerous books and reports as well as the monthly *Klanwatch Intelligence Report*.

Washington Institute for Near East Policy
1828 L St. NW, Washington, DC 20036
(202) 452-0650 • fax: (202) 223-5364
e-mail: info@washingtoninstitute.org
Web site: www.washingtoninstitute.org

The institute is an independent nonprofit research organization that provides information and analysis on the Middle East and U.S. policy in that region. It publishes numerous books, monographs, and reports on regional politics, security, and economics, including *Vision of the West, Hamas: The Fundamentalist Challenge to the PLO, Democracy and Arab Political Culture, Iran's Challenge to the West, Radical Middle East States and U.S. Policy,* and *Democracy in the Middle East: Defining the Challenge.*

Bibliography of Books

Linda Jacobs Altman — *Hate and Racist Groups: A Hot Issue.* Berkeley Heights, NJ: Enslow Publishers, 2001.

Wayne Anderson — *The ETA: Spain's Basque Terrorists.* New York: Rosen Publishing Group, 2002.

Jillian Becker — *The PLO: The Rise and Fall of the Palestine Liberation Organization.* New York: St. Martin's Press, 2000.

Chip Berlet — *Right-Wing Populism in America: Too Close for Comfort.* New York: Guilford Press, 2000.

Kimberly Blaker, ed. — *The Fundamentals of Extremism: The Christian Right in America.* New Boston, MI: New Boston Books, 2003.

Kathleen Blee — *Inside Organized Racism: Women in the Hate Movement.* Berkeley and Los Angeles: University of California Press, 2002.

Ruth Murry Brown — *For a Christian America: A History of the Religious Right.* Amherst, NY: Prometheus Books, 2002.

Steven P. Brown — *Trumping Religion: The New Christian Right, the Free Speech Clause, and the Courts.* Tuscaloosa: University of Alabama Press, 2002.

Jason Burke — *Al-Qaeda: Casting a Shadow of Terror.* New York: I.B. Tauris, 2002.

Ann Burlein — *Lift High the Cross: Where White Supremacy and the Christian Right Converge.* Durham, NC: Duke University Press, 2002.

Jane Corbin — *The Base: In Search of the Terror Network That Shook the World.* New York: Simon and Schuster, 2002.

Jane Corbin — *Al-Qaeda: In Search of the Terror Network That Threatens the World.* New York: Thunder's Mouth Press/Nation Books, 2003.

Mark Gabriel — *Islam and Terrorism: What the Quran Really Teaches About Christianity, Violence, and the Goals of the Islamic Jihad.* Lake Mary, FL: Charisma House, 2002.

Ann Heinrichs — *The Ku Klux Klan: A Hooded Brotherhood.* Chanhassen, MN: Child's World, 2003.

Brian Innes — *International Terrorism.* Broomall, PA: Mason Crest, 2003.

Eric Katz et al., eds. — *Beneath the Surface: Critical Essays in the Philosophy of Deep Ecology.* Cambridge, MA: MIT Press, 2000.

Andrew Kimbrell

The Fatal Harvest Reader: The Tragedy of Industrial Agriculture. Washington, DC: Foundation for Deep Ecology/Island Press, 2002.

Elinor Langer

A Hundred Little Hitlers: The Death of a Black Man, the Trial of a White Racist, and the Rise of the Neo-Nazi Movement in America. New York: Metropolitan Books, 2003.

Wayne K. LaPierre

Guns, Freedom, and Terrorism. Nashville, TN: WND Books, 2003.

Seymour Martin Lipset

It Didn't Happen Here: Why Socialism Failed in the United States. New York: Norton, 2000.

Joshua Muravchik

Heaven on Earth: The Rise and Fall of Socialism. San Francisco: Encounter Books, 2002.

Simon Reeve

The New Jackals: Ramzi Yousef, Osama bin Laden, and the Future of Terrorism. Evanston, IL: Northwestern University Press, 1999.

Mark Rowlands

Animals Like Us. New York: Verso, 2002.

Matthew Scully

Dominion: The Power of Man, the Suffering of Animals, and the Call of Mercy. New York: St Martin's Press, 2002.

Kim Stallwood, ed.

A Primer on Animal Rights: Leading Experts Write About Cruelty and Exploitation. New York: Lantern Books, 2002.

Carol M. Swain

The New White Nationalism in America: Its Challenge to Integration. New York: Cambridge University Press, 2002.

Carol M. Swain and Russ Nieli, eds.

Contemporary Voices of White Nationalism. New York: Cambridge University Press, 2003.

Jerome Walters

One Aryan Nation Under God: How Religious Extremists Use the Bible to Justify Their Actions. Naperville, IL: Sourcebooks, 2001.

Stephen D. Wayne and Clyde Wilcox, eds.

The Election of the Century and What It Tells Us About the Future of American Politics. Armonk, NY: M.E. Sharpe, 2002.

James Weinstein

The Long Detour: The History and Future of the American Left. Boulder, CO: Westview Press, 2003.

David P. Workman

PETA Files: The Dark Side of Animal Rights. Bellevue, WA: Merril Press, 2003.

Index

THE CALIFORNIA SEA OTTER TRADE
1784–1848

THE CALIFORNIA SEA
OTTER TRADE · 1784-1848

By

ADELE OGDEN

UNIVERSITY OF CALIFORNIA PRESS

BERKELEY, LOS ANGELES, LONDON

UNIVERSITY OF CALIFORNIA PRESS

BERKELEY, CALIFORNIA

UNIVERSITY OF CALIFORNIA PRESS, LTD.

LONDON, ENGLAND

CALIFORNIA LIBRARY REPRINT SERIES EDITION, 1975

ISBN: 0-520-02806-6

PRINTED IN THE UNITED STATES OF AMERICA

PREFACE

THE SEARCH for furs along the coast of Upper and Lower California was a part of the great rush for the fur wealth of the North Pacific. At the opening of the nineteenth century enterprising Yankee merchants and Russian American Company hunters pushed southward from the Northwest Coast, where the rush began, into California waters. In the face of a strong local enforcement of Spain's mercantile order, the intruders smuggled and poached until the end of the Spanish period, but not without frequent losses of furs, ships, and lives. When the barrier of mercantilism was finally removed by independent Mexico, Yankee captains quickly sailed to the opened area, and, although somewhat limited by national protective policies, they developed an extensive trade in California, soon integrating it with their new intra-Pacific business. These phases of California's maritime history of the early nineteenth century were one with contemporary movements in the Pacific—the maintenance of closed areas, the intrusion of smugglers and poachers, the opening of closed regions as a result of new governmental policies, and the establishment of wider business connections in a period of comparative free trade. The present study, therefore, is a contribution to the history of the commercial opening of the Pacific world.

The sea otter fur trade of California likewise had great local significance. Of the many commercial enterprises which attracted United States merchants to the Pacific Coast, it was the first in time and one of the most profitable. American products and American citizens entering through the ocean portals of Upper California during the Spanish and Mexican periods spread over the land influences and interests which determined to a great extent the ultimate political destiny of that segment of the Pacific littoral. The sailing vessel, like the covered wagon which it preceded to California by four decades, served during the westward movement as a conveyor of United States interests to the Pacific Coast.

The present geographical distribution of the materials for California's maritime history corresponds to the extent of its significance. Bancroft Library's rich treasury of manuscripts is a start, and other public repositories in the state offer additional help. But, since actors on the sea stage usually represent private rather than

[v]

public agencies, their documentary materials are not always found in centralized files. All along the California coast, in homes both humble and luxurious, are housed rare and yellowed documents, precious for a maritime study. The owners may or may not be residing in places where one would expect to find such materials, but, whether in Salinas or San Francisco, Carpinteria or San Pedro, all are proud relatives of some sea captain or businessman active in early Pacific trade.

Only half—if it is half—of the materials for California's sea story is located within the state. The archives at Mexico City yield an apparently inexhaustible supply of information, especially for the official Spanish and Mexican activities in the commercial field. The official attitude of the United States is presented in consular letters found at the Congressional Library, Washington. Richest of all documentary centers outside of California is the New England homeland of the American merchants who did business in Spanish and Mexican California. Documents formerly in private hands—journals, logbooks, letters, account books—have found their way to public depositories. Trunks and files of letters in the Harvard Library, the Harvard School of Business Administration, the Massachusetts Historical Society, the Peabody Museum Library, and other museums furnish materials which complete the picture half painted by Spanish and American documents in California.

Some of the most delightful experiences associated with my research have come in the course of meeting the owners of private collections of documents. The hospitality accorded by Mrs. John M. Williamson of Carpinteria, owner of a large collection of Alpheus Basil Thompson papers, and by Miss Frances Molera of San Francisco, who owns the logbook of the *Rover* and other John Cooper documents, will never be forgotten. Mr. James Hunnewell of Boston, Mr. A. Porter Robinson of San Francisco, and Mr. Henry Wagner of San Marino were all most generous in giving me access to the collections in their possession. Others have likewise permitted me to peruse collections which, although more directly concerned with other phases of California's maritime history, form rich background for the sea otter trade.

The materials for any phase of Pacific maritime history are not only scattered but fragmentary. Only by piecing together sentences from dozens of manuscript letters, each located in a different collection or in a different part of the country, is the story of a single vessel unfolded. Consequently, the shipping data which may be found compiled in the Appendix of this work, under the title of "Identified Vessels Engaged in the California Sea Otter Trade, 1786–1848," should prove a material aid to research in the Pacific field.

ADELE OGDEN

Berkeley, California

CONTENTS

[ix]

CHAPTER I

THE PACIFIC FRONTIER

The Opening of the Pacific Ocean

A SAILLESS EXPANSE, rimmed by secluded cultural areas and by the homelands of unexploited native peoples living beyond the pale of civilization—such was the Pacific Ocean at the beginning of the eighteenth century. From Cape Horn to the "Rim of Christendom" on the Sonora-Arizona frontier, Spain was building her missions, ranches, and pueblos, all protected from any chance foreign intruder by a strong wall of mercantilism. Across the vast water spaces, the peoples of the Celestial Empire and the Flowery Kingdom safeguarded their exquisite ceramics, colorful silks and fragrant teas from the grasping fingers of western "barbarians" by a rigorous policy of exclusion. To the north, around the icy Sea of Okhotsk, a few lonely fur posts marked Russia's portion of the Pacific rim. On the islands within the "Great Ocean" and on the northern borders, dwelt numerous aborigines unmolested as yet by intrusive profit seekers. Once a year, only, the Manila galleon cut a path from East to West.

Several decades beyond the turn of the century, a slight stir of new economic activity appeared on the northern rim of the closed Pacific. Russians, after the expeditions of the intrepid Bering, were pushing eastward from their Siberian bases in search of an animal—the sea otter. From island to island along the Aleutian chain moved the *promishlennik,* or fur trader, constraining the native hunter to pursue ruthlessly a creature whose fur proved to be more valuable in the China market than the finest fox, sable, or marten skins of Siberia. Thousands of otter pelts began to move annually toward Kiakhta, sole trade door legally open to Russians on the Siberian-Chinese border.

Economic stirrings in the north by subjects of the Tsar were countered by action on the Pacific frontier of the Spanish empire. California was occupied by Spain, not for the purpose of racing Russia to the sea otter fields, the value of which Spain did not yet realize, but to protect and expand her northern frontier at a time when the Russians were believed by Spanish administrators to be a greater menace than they actually were.

[1]

Spain did more than extend her frontier northward. Trusted mariners ventured forth to the unknown North Pacific to explore and find out more concerning the Russians. Incidental to these voyages were small trade negotiations between the sailors and natives. Thus began the sea otter trade on the actual mainland of North America, the Russians having confined their hunting as yet to the Aleutian Islands. Spanish sailors aboard the *Santiago* in 1774 displayed some of the beautiful abalone shells which they had idly picked up on the California coast at Monterey and Carmel. They found that the natives offered their finest furs in exchange for the iridescent "cunchi." On the next two Spanish voyages to the North Pacific, in 1775 and 1779, crew members bartered for otter skins with beads, pieces of iron, knives, and old clothes.[1]

Spaniards in Upper and Lower California began to collect skins purposely from the natives. They had known for some time of the presence of sea otters in California. As early as 1733 Father Sigismundo Taraval had observed them on his trip to Cerros Island, on the west coast of Lower California. "They found such numbers of them together that the seamen killed about twenty of them by following them only with sticks. Some of the skins of these creatures the father sent to Mexico."[2] About 1780 missionaries and soldiers began to purchase skins from California Indians for as low a price as three or four reales each. Otter furs were finding their way to the Orient on the Manila galleons. In 1783, the *Princesa* left Acapulco with from seven hundred to eight hundred pelts.[3] However, the number to be obtained was not great. California Indians, unlike those in the North Pacific, had not developed a technique of hunting otters, probably because the heavy skins were not needed in the warmer climate. Some few natives caught enough to make otter doublets, but their hunting methods were crude.[4]

The year of the Liberty Bell, 1776, marked the beginning of an expedition which was to accelerate the new activity in the Pacific. Captain James Cook embarked upon a voyage of exploration for England. Greater than any of his contributions was his world advertising of the otter's economic value, discovered accidentally by some sailors on the expedition. The excited crew upon arriving home told of the skin which, obtained on the Northwest Coast for

---

[1] For notes to chap. i, see pp. 186–187.

almost nothing, sold for fabulous prices in the Orient. Through English deserters, when England was attacking the Philippines in 1779, Spanish officials heard the news.[5] John Ledyard, an American on the Cook expedition, urged capitalists in the United States to embark upon the new business. Finally, in 1784, the published account of the English voyage verified previous rumors and directly recommended the sea otter trade as a lucrative enterprise.

The commercial opening of the Pacific Ocean was begun because of man's desire for the fur of an animal. Ships from the United States, from England, and, to a lesser extent, French and Portuguese craft, drove into the Pacific after 1784. The Russians were stimulated to new activity and founded in 1783 their first permanent base in North America on Kodiak Island south of the Alaskan Peninsula. And, in the very year that Cook's book was published, before outside merchants had yet arrived in the Pacific fur fields, the Spanish government was preparing to enter the sea otter trade on an extensive and organized basis.

THE SEA OTTER AND EARLY HUNTING METHODS

Sea otters are unique among marine mammals. Floating upon their backs, with forepaws placed peacefully upon their breasts, and riding up and down with the ocean swells on billowy, buoyant kelp beds, they present a picture of complete tranquillity and contentment. Not a sign is there of fighting or quarreling among them as, side by side, they lie upon the deep in groups of about one hundred. Now one rolls over and over in the water, or partially raises his glistening body to look about. Now one dives for nourishment. Shortly he reappears, turns on his back, and with his forepaws calmly disposes of the contents of his shell find. Man's noisy presence immediately transforms this otter Elysium. Shy and sensitive, the animals abandon their natural serenity for nervous vigilance, and, if pursued, resort to swift motion and clever maneuvers to escape the enemy. If sufficiently disturbed, the group disperses, as if knowing that protection for the whole lies in separation.

In general appearance the sea otter resembles the seal, but it is an entirely different animal.[6] The adult male measures from four to five feet from nose to tip of tail, and weighs up to eighty pounds. Its round or blunt head, short, thick neck, its small, flat, and pointed ears, its short, white whiskers—similar to, but coarser and stiffer, than those of a cat—and its black eyes, which may be either calm or gleaming wildly and vindictively, are all peculiar to the sea otter.

The fore and hind limbs differ greatly. The former are very short and thick, with naked, black, and granulated palms, and with toes closely connected and terminating in short, arched claws. The hind legs, on the contrary, are much longer and flipperlike in form, and the toes of the foot are webbed by hair-covered membranes. The otter uses its forepaws freely in obtaining and holding food and in handling and playing with its young. The hind legs serve as paddles in the water, where the broad flippers can be extended backward until they are nearly even with the tail; on land, they are of little use since the toes lack muscular power and the feet cannot be placed flat upon the ground. In moving on beach or rock, the otter normally walks slowly and awkwardly. Doubling its hind legs simultaneously, it proceeds rapidly over the ground by a series of quick jumps, usually with the result of damaging its flippers. The tail of the sea otter is flattish, less than one inch thick, about two and one-half inches wide, and a foot or less in length. Stiff and incapable of being bent to any extent, it serves as a rudder.

The fur of the otter is more beautiful than that of any other marine animal. According to a veteran hunter, William Sturgis, there were only two objects in the world which could rival the sea otter in appearance—a beautiful lady and a lovely infant.[7] Its coat consists of an unusually fine, soft, and dense underfur of about three-fourths of an inch in length, and a few longer and slightly coarser overhairs. At the base or roots the fur is a lustrous white or silver color, darkening toward the ends to black in the finest skins and to various shades of brown in the more common pelts. The predominant shade is lustrous brown, brightened with silvery overhairs. The most valuable pelts are a brownish black, known in the trade as "black." The hair on the head is lighter in color. "The choicest sea otters have dense, brownish black fur of silky, shimmering gloss and extreme fineness, exhibiting a silver color when blown open and with a reasonable number of white hairs regularly distributed, too many white hairs depreciating the value of the pelt."[8] The skin of an otter is remarkably loose, like that on the neck of a young dog, and it therefore always stretches to several feet more than the length of the animal. The largest pelts measure as much as ninety inches long and thirty-six inches wide, the more common dimensions being about six feet by thirty inches.

The color and condition of the fur, and the size of the pelt vary according to the age of the animal and the locality. A skin is at its prime in the third or fourth year. The fur of the northern race of the sea otter species, called *Enhydra lutris lutris,* is different from that of the southern group, *Enhydra lutris nereis.* California skins were brown and generally inferior to those taken in the north, but Otto von Kotzebue, who was along the coast in 1816, stated that "the difference is not very great."[9] Apparently the quality of the pelage remains about the same throughout the year, although some hunters claimed that the winter catches were better in color. Hunting was done in California at all seasons.

The best description of the California sea otter (*Enhydra lutris nereis*) is that given in the recent excellent book, *Fur-Bearing Mammals of California,* by Joseph Grinnell, Joseph Dixon, and Jean Linsdale. The passage describing a young adult female taken on the coast of Monterey County in 1908 is quoted in full.

Body from shoulders back, mummy brown, with a "frosted" appearance caused by the lighter-colored tips of the scattered, long, coarse hairs which project through the fine dense cover of fur. These light tips are of various shades of olive buff, most of them falling between deep olive buff and dark olive buff. From the shoulders forward these buff tips are most numerous and give the neck a decidedly grayish brown cast. The buff color is most nearly pure on the top and lower sides of the head.

The entire coat contrasts with that of the river otter in being much softer and more dense, with longer hairs. The coloration is in general much darker. Most of the pelt is made up of the dense fine underfur, the slightly longer over-hairs being scattered and scarcely visible to gross inspection. Fur on the middle of the back averages 25 mm. in depth.

The front feet of the sea otter are remarkably small, and the limbs are small and weakly developed. The digits are all small and so closely connected as to be scarcely indicated externally except by the small, short, strongly arched claw on each. The naked palm is nearly circular in outline, with a small projection behind the bare area on the outer side. The hind feet are greatly flattened and expanded, forming paddles, and are haired on both the upper and the lower surfaces except for small naked pads, one at the base of each claw. The short, strongly arched claws are spaced evenly across the terminal margin of the foot.[10]

Of great warmth and exceeding beauty, the sea otter fur was sought by Orientals for both practical and ornamental purposes. It became the royal fur of China. Otter-skin robes were the style of the day for Chinese mandarins. Ladies in high social standing wore otter capes, and some made belts or sashes of the fur, over which pearls were arranged. Tails were much esteemed for caps, mittens, and small trimmings. As the price ascended, the fur was used more commonly to weigh down and border rich silk gowns. By 1790 a sea otter skin commanded in the Chinese market a price of from eighty to one hundred and twenty dollars.[11]

Along an arc formed by the shores and islands of the North Pacific Ocean the sea otter ranged. From Yezo in north Japan the grounds proceeded northeastward past the Kuril group and Kamchatka to the Aleutian chain. Following the curve of the Northwest Coast of America, the otter fields extended southward to about the middle of the Lower California littoral.

Apparently there was a partial break in the arc delineating the sea otter habitat between the Strait of Juan de Fuca and the northern California coast at about Trinidad. The marked geographical differences of that part of the coast could well explain the fewer numbers of otters. A straight shore of sand dunes and cliffs replaces the irregular, rocky stretches, such as are most frequented by sea otters; the rocky coasts are characteristic of the littoral north and south. This gap no doubt forms the geographical division between the two races of the otter species.

Such a geographical division in the otter habitat is indicated in the trade records. Although some sea otters were obtained along the Oregon and northern California coasts, even in the earliest hunting days they were found only in very few numbers.[12] The vessels which entered the Columbia River traded mostly for land otter and beaver skins. Factors to be considered are that the Indians along the more northern coasts were extremely hostile, thus making barter difficult. Also, some of the early merchants did not trade there because of the lack of good harbors. However, neither of these conditions explains why later the Russians and the Yankees, both of whom had expert Aleutian hunters aboard, came directly to California without hunting on the way. Trust the Aleut to go after otters if there were any to be had. In this connection, it is interesting to note that Henry Wood Elliott, reporting in 1875 on numbers of marine animals in the North Pacific, stated:

It is also noteworthy that all the sea otters taken below the Straits of Fuca are shot by the Indians and white hunters off the beach in the surf at Gray's

Harbor, a stretch of less than twenty miles; here from fifty to a hundred are taken every year, while not half that number can be obtained from all the rest of the Oregon and Washington coast-line.[13]

In the Californias the sea otter's habitat included the coastal stretch as far south as Morro Hermoso Point, located twenty miles south of Lower California's westernmost headland, which forms the southern shore of Sebastián Vizcaíno Bay. North of Point Reyes, one of the favorite retreats of the animal was in rocky Trinidad Harbor. San Francisco Bay abounded in otters. Apparently they not only swam around in the bay but frequented the numerous estuaries and even hauled up on the shore. The animals were found on Point San Quentin, around the mouths of Petaluma and Sonoma creeks, and in the estuaries of San Jose, San Mateo, and San Bruno.

On the coast between San Francisco and Monterey, Pillar Point, forming the northwest extremity of Half Moon Bay, and Point Año Nuevo eighteen miles north of Santa Cruz, as well as Santa Cruz Point and Bay, are mentioned frequently in the records. South of Monterey great numbers of otters stayed in the kelp off Point Sur and along the coast around Cooper's Point, where the mountains come down to meet surging, heavy seas. San Simeon, the coast opposite San Luis Obispo, and Point Conception also appear often in the records as otter habitats.

The southern coast of Upper California apparently was not much frequented by the sea otter. There were a few around Santa Barbara, San Pedro, and San Juan Capistrano. The great otter rendezvous in the south was around the kelp-bound islands of the Santa Barbara Channel and also to a lesser extent on Santa Catalina and San Clemente.

In the Lower California area sea otters abounded. Extant hunting records would indicate that they were even more numerous there than along the Upper California coast. Seven bays, and the headlands and islands around them, were main centers. Proceeding from north to south they were, Todos Santos Bay, upon which present-day Ensenada is located, and Todos Santos Island on the west, the anchorage of Santo Tomás, Colnett Bay, San Quintín Bay, Rosario Bay with San Gerónimo Island on its south, Santa Rosalía Bay, and the great Sebastián Vizcaíno Bay, with the islands Natividad, Cerros, and San Benito continuing the curving sweep of the bay's shore line to the west and north into the Pacific. Sea otter hunting was likewise carried on around Guadalupe Island, lying far off to the west. The southernmost hunting place mentioned in the records was Morro Hermoso, where the rocky bluffs and outlying rocks surrounded with kelp, generally characteristic of the northern coast of Lower California, merge into sand cliffs and beach.

The habits of the sea otter are interesting; they have, however, been the subject of many erroneous and purely imaginative accounts. Its food seems to consist principally of shellfish, especially crabs and other crustaceans. A favorite food along parts of the California coast is the abalone, which at high water loosens its shell from the rock and is easily taken. Diving down, the otter takes its catch between its forepaws and comes to the surface to devour it. An old hunter is recorded as saying, "Why, I really believe that them otters has human sense. I've seen 'em dive down, catch a crab, come up to the surface and fasten themselves to a piece of kelp, then take the crab in their paws and leisurely eat it, giving the best part to the pup."[14] All foraging seems to be done at sea and not on land.

Waters about rocky shores, reefs, islets, and thick kelp beds form its favorite habitat. There, in from ten to twenty-five fathoms of water, is the source of its food. In stormy weather, or when the animals are resting, kelp patches afford an ideal shelter. The otter rarely leaves the water; when it does so, it comes on shore only in secluded, isolated spots, most usually during stormy weather at sea. Preferably it hauls up on rocks and islets some distance from the mainland. The records indicate that in all localities the animals came ashore much more frequently in former days before extensive hunting was pursued. If awake, the otter stretches out at full length on the rocks; when sleeping, especially in cold weather, it curls up, placing its forepaws over its nose.

At sea, where the otter spends most of its time, it progresses by swimming on its back. If not disturbed by too frequent hunting, otters congregate in schools of one hundred or less. All hunters describe the playfulness of the animal. Some observers have seen it lying on its back and tossing "a piece of sea-weed up in the air from paw to paw, apparently taking great delight in catching it before it could fall into the water."[15] The adults play with their young for hours. Apparently they do not leap about in the water, however, as asserted by some. Only when pursued do they breach.

The otter is noted for its cunning when being hunted. A favorite trick is that of diving in the opposite direction to that from which it is being chased, thus passing under the hunters' boat and coming up behind. Apparently realizing that boats travel more slowly against the wind, the otter often swims to the windward. Sometimes it will try to find a tide rip or, if near the shore, the animal has been known to make straight for the breakers among jagged rocks. It also hides behind rocks. A very common trick is to make a series of short dives followed by a very long one, when the boats are quite close, which takes the animal completely out of range. Early accounts mention that otters often tore out the arrows from their bodies with their teeth.

No other marine creature is more alert to danger. The least sound or scent of man causes the animal to disappear and even to leave a locality. According to Elliott, "They will take alarm and leave from the effects of a small fire, four or five miles to the windward of them; and the footstep of man must be washed by many tides before its trace ceases to alarm the animal and drive it from landing there, should it approach for that purpose."[16] Apparently in early days, before the animal was pursued so relentlessly, its shyness was less pronounced. For example, John Jewitt wrote concerning those at Nootka Sound in 1803: "They are in general very tame, and will permit a canoe or boat to approach very near before they dive. I was told, however, that they are becoming much more shy since they have been accustomed to shoot them with muskets, than when they used only arrows."[17]

The species reproduces slowly. As a rule only one pup is born at a time. As true children of the deep, they are born at sea on a bed of kelp. According to Frank Stephens, who is corroborated by others, "The single young are brought forth at any season, the intervals apparently being more than a year. The young are said to suckle more than a year."[18] Full growth is not attained until about the fourth year. The mother otter is noted for her affection for her young. Swimming on her back, she carries her pup clasped in her forepaws. If chased, she seizes the young one in her teeth by the skin of the neck and dives. Rarely will she desert it. The cry of the animal, according to some, resembles that of a cat, and

ALEUTIAN SEA OTTER CANOE, OR BAIDARKA, AND HUNTERS

From Charles Melville Scammon, *The Marine Mammalia of the Northwestern Coast of North America*, New York, 1874

according to Chase Littlejohn, an old-time hunter, the cries of the young sound exactly like those of a human infant.[19] The young otter when alarmed invariably betrays its location.

The recent discovery, in the spring of 1938, of a herd of sea otters off the mouth of Bixby Creek, about fifteen miles south of Monterey, makes it possible to extend our present knowledge of the animal. It is to be hoped that government authorities and the public will coöperate to enforce not only the letter but the spirit of the law protecting a supposedly "vanishing species," so that it may in time be able to restore itself.

The Aleutian method of hunting otters was similar to that of all the Indians in the North Pacific and was the one used along the California coast in the Spanish period. Small canoes, called *baidarkas* by the Russians and *kayaks* by the natives, scoured the coast for miles. The frame of the tiny craft was lightly constructed of thin strips of wood, or whalebone if wood was not procurable, fastened together with whale or sea-lion sinews. Over the whole, top and bottom, seal or sea-lion skins were stretched. Every seam was carefully sewed, and the whole skin surface was thoroughly smeared with oil to make it completely waterproof. In the top of the structure were left from one to three openings, each just large enough for one rower. Long, narrow, shallow, and sharp at each end, the baidarka served its purpose well. It was from twelve to twenty feet long, depending upon the number of holes, was about twenty inches to two feet wide, and not more than twenty inches deep.

In the hands of the Aleut the baidarka was a most efficient craft. It was paddled over the water at what all European navigators later considered an astounding rate. According to Martin Sauer, in a moderately smooth sea the baidarka was rowed with ease at about ten miles an hour.[20] Paddles were usually double-bladed and eight or ten feet long, although single-bladed ones with crutch handles, shifted alternately to each side, were likewise used. No one but a skilled Aleut who had grown up in a baidarka could manage with any satisfaction the skin-covered shell. Disquieted by the uncertain sensations arising from his trip across the Russian River in one of them, Auguste Bernard du Hautcilly compared the baidarka to old Charon's craft.

Its lightness and little steadiness could make it be supposed that it was, indeed, appointed to transport only shades; and the sort of gutteral grumbling heard from the Kodiak, when he designated the person who was to enter with him in his baidarka, must have much resembled the hoarse voice of the pitiless boatman of Hades, chiding the souls on the banks of the Styx.[21]

An Aleut would venture forth in a baidarka in any kind of weather. Concerning its durability, Georg Heinrich von Langs- dorff stated:

A good new-made and well-oiled canoe in fair and calm weather, or with a moderate wind, may remain in the water twelve or fourteen days, with- out being injured, or if the weather be stormy, not more than six days at the most, as the seams of the leather are apt to give way, and let in the water. To keep the baidarkas in good condition, they should be drawn out of the water after every voyage, and laid to dry upon the shore.[22]

Each hunter was well equipped for the chase. Clothed in skin, he fitted himself into the hole of his canoe and securely fastened the lower edge of his jacket to a ring around the opening. Not a drop of water could enter the boat. Kneeling, or sitting with his feet extended, he would remain in his restricted quarters for hours, while he sped his boat through the water. For weapons he had lashed alongside his canoe a supply of arrows or darts. These bone- pointed and single-barbed instruments were fitted loosely into a wooden shaft, to which it was joined by a line of whale sinew. Thrown from a sort of fluted board sling, the arrow when lodged in the prey was drawn from the shaft which, as it was pulled under the water, greatly retarded the progress of the fleeing animal. According to John Meares, the line was several fathoms long and was used to drag the otter to the boat.[23] Some accounts state that attached to the arrow shaft was a bladder, which served the double purpose of making it possible to retrieve the spear when thrown and of marking the course of the submerged animal. Apparently the bladder was used by the Aleuts along the California coast, since both Juan Bautista Alvarado and Antonio María Osio mention it.[24] The manner in which the arrow was thrown from the board sling was described by Langsdorff.

The planks from which they are thrown are about eighteen inches long and two inches broad; and in order that the weapon may be held the faster, they have a sort of handle at the lower end, and an opening through which the forefinger is thrust. At the other end is a small channel, into which the javelin fits with a little knob, which serves to retain it. When the javelin is to be thrown, the plank is held horizontally, and the aim being taken, the weapon is directed with the middle finger and thumb; this is done with so much dexterity, and the motion given to it is so powerful and so rapid that the object at which it is aimed is rarely missed.[25]

In parties of varying size, usually from five to twenty baidarkas, the hunters searched for the otter. Keeping their canoes spread out in a long line, they paddled about, ever silent, muffling each dip of their oars, ever on the alert. The moment the nose or head of an otter appeared above the surface of the water, the experienced "marine Cossack," as the Aleut was called, would distinguish it. Trembling "like the eager dog at the sight of game," he who sighted the animal would lift his paddle high above his head as a signal to his comrades. Then, approaching from the leeward as much as possible, he and the others would row swiftly and silently toward it and endeavor to circle it with a cordon of baidarkas.

If the animal was sleeping on its back on the surface of the water, and if its pursuers could get near enough without awakening it, all was soon ended. Such an easy catch was exceedingly rare, however. The wary otter almost always scented or heard approaching enemies and usually "stood." Dropping its hindquarters and raising its head, the animal would take a quick view of the situation and then dive. Maneuvering their baidarkas in such a manner as to cover the area where the animal might be expected to reappear, the hunters waited for fifteen minutes or so until it must come up for air. The native nearest the spot where the otter arose gave a wild shout to force it into another dive before its breathing could be completed. At the same time, if not too far away, he threw with incredible accuracy his bone-pointed arrow at the disappearing animal. Taking up his position at the spot where the otter dived, he elevated his paddle as a signal to his comrades. A second circle was formed, and thus the chase continued until the exhausted and wounded creature was finally dispatched, or until it escaped, as frequently happened.

The prize captured, an inquiry followed as to whom it belonged. He who had first wounded the animal or the one whose arrow was nearest its head held highest claims. Urey Fedorovich Lisiansky explained more of the established rules of ownership:

... if several wounded it at the same time the right side has the preference over the left, and the nearer the wound is to the head, the more weight it has. When two or more arrows are struck into the same part of the animal, and the lines of the arrows are broken, the longest piece of line determines the preference.[26]

Cruder or simpler methods of hunting the otter were used by some of the Indian tribes along the Pacific coast. In California and in certain places in the North Pacific, nets spread out on the kelp beds, snares, and clubs were used. On the Northwest Coast during bad weather, when the animals sought shelter in large numbers among the rocks, natives would sometimes under cover of a howling gale dispatch them with heavy wooden clubs. Padre Luis Sales described an interesting method—which may have been used only by California Indians since no known voyager to the Northwest has mentioned it. When the parent otter left its young on the surface of the water, which it did only when it dived for food, the Indian hunter would slip up and tie a cord to the foot of the baby. Fastened to the cord, close to the body of the animal, would be placed a couple of fishhooks. Retiring in his canoe to a short distance, the Indian would pull his cord and thus hurt the small otter so that he would cry. The mother would rush to the rescue and could be easily approached, either because she was occupied in freeing her offspring or because she herself would become caught in the line and hooks.[27]

CHAPTER II

THE SPANISH SEA OTTER TRADE IN THE PACIFIC

Spain's Establishment of the Otter Trade, 1784–1790

BEFORE THE GREAT DRIVE for the fur wealth of the Pacific began, Spain initiated her first organized plan for the sea otter trade.[1] Two considerations led the government to approve the project. Both reasons were clearly and forcefully presented in September, 1784, to the viceroy of New Spain by Vicente Vasadre y Vega, the originator of the entire plan.

Government officials well knew, Vasadre stated, that miners in New Spain, or Mexico, were much handicapped by an insufficient and irregular supply of quicksilver. China had large quantities of this needed metal. New Spain, however, had in her possession a highly acceptable exchange medium, for California waters abounded with sea otters. Vasadre then pressed his second point. Russians and English in ever greater numbers were pushing into the otter fields of the North Pacific. Vasadre pointed out that both problems could be met by a California-China trade. The supply vessels, instead of returning empty to San Blas every year, could bring the valuable pelts to Acapulco for reshipment on the Manila galleons. In Canton special arrangements could be made for exchanging such skins for quicksilver. Vasadre offered to open transactions in both California and China.[2]

The outlook for Vasadre's project became promising when, on June 2, 1785, the king of Spain ordered that the plan be given careful consideration. Provincial mining directors regarded it with favor. Finally, on January 22, 1786, Viceroy Bernardo de Gálvez decreed that it be executed. He immediately notified Governor Pedro Fages and Father Fermín Francisco de Lasuén and asked for their coöperation.[3]

In the latter part of August, 1786, Vasadre arrived in California.[4] He did not lack official support for his undertaking. In addition to his own salary of four thousand dollars he had been allowed eight thousand dollars from which to begin purchases. He was backed by viceregal orders which virtually gave him a monopoly

---

[1] For notes to chap. ii, see pp. 188–191.

of the otter trade. Father Lasuén was willing to help him. Fages was likewise a zestful collaborator and helped the commissioner to draft a working plan.[5] Apparently the governor had great hopes for the new project if any credence may be given to what he told the French navigator, Comte de Lapérouse, who arrived just a month after Vasadre. Perhaps he was only putting on a bold front before the Frenchman. At any rate, Fages asserted that he could ship annually twenty thousand skins from California and that an additional ten thousand could be procured as soon as two or three settlements were founded to the north of San Francisco.[6]

Californians soon complied with all points of the new commercial program.[7] Vasadre was the ultimate recipient of all skins. No one could trade with any other person, Spaniard or foreigner. Christian Indians soon learned to bring the returns of their hunts to mission padres, and in exchange they were given cloth and other Mexican articles. If an avaricious soldier or mayordomo bargained secretly with mission Indians, he did so at the risk of losing all by confiscation. Soldiers and inhabitants of pueblos purchased skins from the unconverted natives, but immediately they turned over everything to a corporal or alcalde, who, upon the first occasion, remitted all to the commander of the nearest presidio. Padres and commanders carefully classified the skins brought to them according to size and color. Prices were set by a special schedule and ranged from ten pesos for first-class skins, those of at least one and one-fourth varas, black in color and cured, to two pesos for those of the third class, skins of three-fourths of a vara, brown and raw.[8]

Under the circumstances, Vasadre's first collection of otter skins was most creditable. His stay was short, only three months, but traveling on land and sea he visited in that time nine missions, four presidios, and two pueblos.[9] Furthermore, his plan was a new one; never before had Californians been stimulated to hunt for the otter. Nevertheless, when the commissioner left San Diego for San Blas on November 28 he had with him 1,060 skins. Missions Rosario and San Fernando in Lower California had sent to San Diego a consignment worth two thousand dollars according to the schedule rates. Missions in Upper California contributing the most were those of San Carlos, San Antonio, San Luis Obispo, San Buenaventura, and San Diego.[10]

Vasadre now prepared for his trip to China. Just before his departure he made some heavy demands upon the Mexican government. He must have between twelve and fifteen thousand pesos with which to curry favor with elusive and fastidious Chinese mandarins, and he must take silver presents to the emperor. Also, he should be allowed an increase in salary. His small annual allowance of four thousand pesos was not sufficient for traveling expenses abroad nor for living in the high splendor befitting a Spanish commissioner in brilliant Oriental courts.[11]

Both the audiencia and the viceroy regarded Vasadre's requests as excessive and savoring of self-interest. His salary was to remain the same. However, if the governor and intendant of the Philippines considered costly gifts necessary to open the gateway of China, Vasadre was to be supplied with sufficient funds, but only after "a judicious examination and feasible surety of his conduct, and in the clear event that it is determined indispensable for the felicitous outcome of the commission."[12] Not all of Vasadre's requests were denied. He took with him a letter written by José de Gálvez, minister of the Indies, to the governor of the Philippines. Therein it was expressly stated, as Vasadre had insisted, that officials at Manila were not to interfere with the operations of the commissioner, who was directly responsible only to the Mexican government.[13] Thus protected, although financially limited, Vasadre put to sea on the *San Andrés* in the spring of 1787.

While Vasadre was fulfilling his mission in China, his trade plan as it related to California was further developed and improved. During the first few months of otter collecting, grave weaknesses and omissions in the original scheme became manifest. The business was basically handicapped because of unskilled hunters. Realizing the difficulty of training California Indians, the *alférez* of San Francisco had suggested that skilled hunters be brought from Europe.[14] Otter-hunting activities had been further limited because of the lack of suitable exchange media. A scarcity of bright-colored articles such as would appeal to the California native was advanced as the reason for the small number of skins collected in 1786 and 1787.[15] Most certainly Indians would not take to otter hunting unless they were compensated for their labor. And, what was more important, it could not be expected that the padres would further a project unless they could see that it contributed to the welfare of their charges. Furthermore, certain abuses had crept into the system. An early complaint was that soldiers were leaving the service in order to get otter skins, and that in obtaining them they used violent and unfair methods with the Indians.[16]

Vasadre outlined sound solutions for these various problems before he sailed to the Orient.[17] He had the wholehearted approval of California mission authorities, whom he had consulted at every turn. Vasadre placed first among his suggestions that of an exclusive mission control of the California otter trade. Only with the understanding direction of experienced padres would the Indians learn other ways. Only through the mission would it be practical to supply the natives with better hunting equipment. In special conference with Viceroy Gálvez, Vasadre had urged this course even before he had gone to California, and upon his return to Mexico City he wrote, "With the practical knowledge which I have acquired and which I lacked before, I am of the same opinion."

To meet the problem of exchange media, the Spanish commissioner submitted a plan connected with the established supply trade. Special goods to be exchanged for otter skins should be sent on the regular San Blas vessels. Such merchandise should be delivered by the presidial *habilitados* to the mission padres in the same manner as the usual supplies. The system would necessitate keeping accurate accounts of the goods distributed and of the skins received. When collecting the regular supplies, the California factor in Mexico City could prepare the special *memorias,* or consignments, which were destined to be exchanged for otter skins. Vasadre suggested that there be sent ten *memorias* of one thousand pesos each, made up of the following articles : blue cloth, blue Mexican flannel, cheap, narrow blankets, large glass beads of all colors except black or white, and *fresadas* with red, yellow, or green stripes rather than blue or black, because, although the latter were worth the same, "in the opinion of the Indian they are considerably different." Although Vasadre had not heard from the Lower California missions, to which he had dispatched a special messenger, he was certain that San Vicente, Santo Domingo, Rosario, San Fernando, and San Francisco de Borja should be included in the plan because of the abundance of otters along the southern coast. Five *memorias* of two thousand pesos each could be distributed from San Diego to points on the peninsula.

Vasadre's suggestions for improving the otter trade met with the entire approval of Mexican authorities. Early in March, 1787, a copy of the new regulations was sent to Father Lasuén who was asked to circulate it and to give the provisions his entire support.[18] The revised plan was to be in operation until "experience furnishes new light with which to establish solidly a business of such consequence, as much for the development of the Californias as for the maintenance of the balance of our commerce with China."[19]

Californians again responded loyally. Upon the receipt of the new provisions in September, 1787, Fages published a proclamation on the subject, and Lasuén circulated the rules among his missions. Father Pedro Benito Cambón of San Francisco in a letter to Francisco Palóu, Superior of the College of San Fernando, Mexico, expressed the general wholehearted approval of California padres. "As soon as I read it and heard it published, I rejoiced greatly because of its being the first measure for the help and benefit of these neophytes which has been executed since the establishment of their missions."[20]

For the next two years, 1787–1789, the California otter trade proceeded according to Vasadre's revised plan with only slight variations. Special goods destined for Monterey and amounting to $1,170 were sent from Mexico City in April, 1787, just after the new provisions had been enacted.[21] In November the *Favorita* and the *San Carlos* took 1,750 skins to San Blas. Of these 1,133 were received at San Diego from the Lower California missions. Monterey with 220 skins and Santa Barbara with 166 were the largest contributors in Upper California.[22] From San Blas the California skins were sent overland to Mexico City to be dressed. Although some California pelts were dressed before leaving the province, all skins were carefully treated by experts at the capital, placed in pitch-covered boxes to preserve them from moths, and then transported again over the highlands to the waiting Manila galleon at Acapulco.[23] Because of the late arrival of the supply vessels from the north in 1787, it was necessary to detain the *San José* until March of the next year. This provoked a letter from the fiscal. Collections of skins should be continued throughout the year and the pelts should be ready for the galleons so that delays would not occur.[24] Skins obtained in 1788 were few. In October Father Lasuén delivered to the *habilitado* 76 pelts and received in exchange some of the $8,000 consignment of goods sent from Mexico. Father Cambón of San Francisco sent 116 furs. A year later between 200 and 300 were collected from the missions of San Carlos, Santa Barbara, La Purísima, and San Buenaventura.[25] Increasingly small shipments were due to a fast ebbing of the original enthusiasm for Vasadre's program.

Dissatisfaction with the new trade system in California had been growing apace. From the first, New Spain officials had criticized in one respect Vasadre's management of his project. The price schedule for the purchase of skins, as drawn up by the commissioner and Fages, was believed to be entirely too high. The business would be a losing proposition if from seven to ten pesos had to be paid for skins of the first class. Consequently, in March, 1787, the governor and mission fathers were asked to suggest such an adjustment that the Indians would not "stop applying themselves willingly to an industry which will bring them inexplicable benefit, the king at the same time receiving what belongs to him."[26]

The opinions of the head of the California missions with respect to this matter were very definite. Father Lasuén in September firmly disapproved of the proposed price reform. He believed that the schedule as established by Vasadre was fair for that time, and that as soon as the exchange of quicksilver in China was effected, it would be possible for the king to pay even more. He pointed out that one of the chief objects of promoting the otter trade was to further the development of the Californias. Furthermore, he drew attention to the expense of sending out Indian hunters. Food, canoes, and nets must be supplied, and a fair compensation must be allowed. The father president concluded by saying that, until a final decision was rendered, the missions would deliver skins without statement of their value but with careful account of their number, quality, and size.[27] When in March, 1788, Father Lasuén was instructed to determine, according to the schedule of Vasadre, the worth of those skins which he had sent the previous year, he again protested directly to the viceroy that values had risen because of the stimulation given to the otter trade.[28]

Further objections were advanced early in 1788 by California missionaries. Goods, which had been promised by Vasadre in return for the first skin collections, were very slow in arriving.[29] Also, it seemed that, in spite of the royal decree to the contrary, some skins were slipping off to San Blas on private account rather than being handled exclusively through the missions for the government.[30]

The cause of the greatest disapproval of the otter-trading system in California was an order issued in June, 1787, restricting mission control of trade. Thereafter, merchandise destined for the purchase of skins was to be committed to presidial *habilitados,* who would distribute goods just in proportion to the number of furs presented. Furthermore, soldiers were to be allowed to barter. By the first provision Mexican officials hoped to lessen the danger involved in keeping valuable goods in unprotected mission storehouses. Both measures had been suggested in all good faith by Father Palóu as a means of checking an existing evil. It was believed that such concessions would put a stop both to the complaints directed by the military populace against the missionaries and to the stealing and destruction of property commonly practiced by soldiers illegally engaged in the otter trade.[31]

The new provisions had unforeseen results, however. Indian villages more than ever became the scenes of undue liberties. Military men had no thought for the native. Presidial *habilitados* who handed out goods to those bringing in skins, as well as soldiers who directly bartered for furs, cared only for private gain. Father Cambón described the situation to Palóu. In speaking of the *habilitados* he said, "They will pay the soldier well, and always will retain a profit; but to the Indian they will give a vara of flannel and six threads or a few beads for a large and fine skin, worth eight pesos, which the king will give them, and which will remain in their pockets."[32] He further wrote of the *habilitado,* "It is natural that the latter wishes to pay little to the Indian and credit much to the *real hacienda.*" Cambón also pointed out that the childlike natives, not fully realizing the benefit of receiving through the padres clothes and shoes in return for their hunting, preferred to receive by direct bargaining the small trinkets offered by outsiders in exchange for otter skins. Consequently, a derangement of the mission system threatened as more and more Indians were drawn from their daily work to an independent and alluring enterprise. Cambón closed his letter to Palóu by appealing to him as an old friend to do all he could to have the new trade regulations repealed. A few months later Father Lasuén in a letter to

Viceroy Manuel Antonio Flórez set forth the dire effects of the existing law upon mission life.[33]

In 1790 definite legislative action was taken by the officials in Mexico City to place the California otter trade upon a firmer business foundation. Contrary to the advice of Father Lasuén, a lower price schedule was established. For example, whereas skins of the first class formerly were purchased for from seven to ten pesos, they now were listed at from five to seven pesos. Attached to the new price schedule were minute regulations. Soldiers and individuals obtaining skins from Indians must give them to the mission padres. Ship commanders were to be held responsible for all pelts until they were landed in San Blas. To the padres they must give exact receipts noting the color, size, and number of pelts delivered. Upon every box they must place the mark of the mission which had sent the contents. The act of 1790 finally provided for a separate branch of the treasury department to take charge of the financial management of the otter trade.[34]

These new regulations, arising from the growing desire to promote a maritime project of utmost interest to New Spain, were short-lived. Early in September, 1790, Governor Fages circulated the order in California.[35] However, months before, in fact even before the final passage of the new act, a decree of the Spanish king had nullified all. The Vasadre project was to be discontinued. The news reached Mexico City in July, although in California word was not received until December.[36] Vasadre's experiences in the Orient will explain the royal decision.

The odds were against Vasadre from the first. Self-interest moved both the Philippine Company and the principal government officials in Manila to oppose his plan. Two years before, the former powerful organization had been given the right to bring quicksilver from China. Representatives of the company in Madrid were negotiating in 1786 and 1787 for permission to exchange that metal for California otter skins. Besides, Intendant Ciriaco González de Carvajal had made a proposal, then under consideration, which would not involve the exchange of quicksilver, and which would bring the California otter trade more directly under the control of island authorities than would the Vasadre plan, directed from Mexico.[37]

Not making any headway at Manila, Vasadre proceeded to Canton in November, 1787. Through lavish spending in high society, he was enabled to conclude a contract for his California furs.[38] It was a commercial victory. In addition to facing the usual difficulties and embarrassments experienced by foreign merchants in Canton, the Spaniard had to push transactions at the time of a general price slump. Skins brought from the Northwest Coast by French and English expeditions in 1786 and 1787 had glutted the market. Vasadre succeeded in making as good a bargain as any of the others in spite of the fact that his California furs were inferior in quality to those from the more northern regions.[39]

The independent spirit of the Spanish commissioner exasperated Philippine officials. Not considering it necessary to inform them of every move, Vasadre had written nothing until April, 1788. His letter was not received until after the governor had given an order which served only to increase the growing feeling of antipathy. In June the *San José* had arrived at Manila from Acapulco with 1,750 skins consigned to Vasadre. The lack of news from the commissioner was an excellent excuse for officials to take matters into their own hands. The governor determined to remit the entire lot of furs to the factors of the Philippine Company residing at Canton, and Vasadre was advised that the sale of the new consignment was to be arranged jointly by the factors and himself, the proceeds remaining in the care of the former. Also, the Spanish agent was instructed to hand over to Philippine Company merchants the money or quicksilver received for the first lot of California skins.

This was more than Vasadre would abide. In September he wrote a terse reply. He directly denied the right of the Philippine governor to have anything to do with the first consignment of skins. He intended to push through his negotiations for quicksilver, which from his own investigations he had found to be abundant and easy to export, contrary to the reports which Intendant González had made in his own interest. To his enemies this audacious epistolary style seemed to prove him "to be one of those proud men foolishly pleased with their own judgment who aspire to independence."[40] Again Vasadre was warned to coöperate in all transactions with the agents of the company at Canton. The climax was reached in December, 1788. The factors asked him, in consideration of the governor's order, to hand over either the first consignment of skins or the equivalent value. Vasadre now saw that it was use-

less to oppose an organization determined to keep all royal transactions in its own hands. He abruptly turned over all his business
affairs to the factors and with little ceremony left for Spain.[41]

Vasadre had accomplished much. California skins had been a
means of obtaining quicksilver for New Spain. Jars of Chinese
quicksilver, obtained in exchange for otter skins, arrived on the
Manila galleons from 1789 to 1793.[42] Above all, Vasadre had opened
the California otter trade. Visionary and self-interested he may
have been, desiring, as his opponents wrote, "to figure in the world
in the protection of projects very easy to conceive on paper, but
difficult to put into execution."[43] Nevertheless, the natives of the
province had taken up otter hunting, and government regulations
had stabilized the trade. Between 1786 and 1790, there were sent
to Manila 9,729 otter and some seal skins, and these, according to
Vasadre, brought $3,120,000 to the treasury.[44]

Bulwarking Spanish Otter Fields, 1790–1794

As the fur rush to the Northwest Coast increased, the sea otter
trade of the Californias assumed a more important part in Spain's
Pacific program. English merchantmen began to appear in California ports after 1790. Spanish administrators expressed general
alarm as the foreign menace grew. Outsiders must not be allowed
to take away valuable pelts. They must not occupy areas dangerously near those held by Spain, and they must not cut in on the
two-century-old trade of the Manila galleon. A bold move was made
to control the activities of foreign vessels in the North Pacific by
occupying Nootka Sound in 1789. But, to many, the most direct
way to keep out the foreigner was for Spain herself to develop
the otter trade.[45] From such convictions were born a number of
plans and a positive program in the last decade of the eighteenth
century.

While the Vasadre plan was still operating, two proposals for
larger commercial ventures in the Pacific were outlined. Both originated in the hope of private financial returns, but both, as presented to His Majesty, assumed an imperial cast.

Ciriaco González de Carvajal, intendant of the Philippines, was
the originator of one plan. Zealous for the economic development
of his province, he bent every effort to the building up of Manila
as a Spanish supply base in the Pacific. According to his proposi-

tion, advanced first in February and again in June of 1786, merchandise appropriate to "satisfy the needs and rouse the curiosity or the pleasure of the natives" could be brought on the ships of the Philippine Company to Monterey, from which point it could be distributed to the Indian otter hunters from San Diego to the Gulf of Bucareli, in the Prince of Wales Archipelago on the Northwest Coast. Colonists could be sent from the Philippine Islands to establish presidios in the Northwest. To dispose the king favorably toward his plan, the intendant stressed the importance of staving off English and Russian advances in the North Pacific.

It is undeniable that by treating those miserable natives with gentleness and affability, and by having them know the advantages of clothing themselves and of living under a pious chief, who will direct and govern them, enjoying all the rights of humanity, we shall be able to hold fast by their help a rich and powerful commerce to which other strong nations now aspire, which perhaps, if we are negligent, will gain sole rights in it when we are purposing it.[46]

When the González proposal was finally referred to the directors of the Philippine Company in Madrid, that body already had under way another otter-trade project of its own.[47] In July, 1786, it had asked to be allowed to procure California otter skins through the House of Cosío at Vera Cruz and exchange them for Chinese quicksilver. The directors of the Philippine Company offered to conduct the Oriental end of this venture either according to the provisions of the royal decree of 1785, which had given the company permission to bring quicksilver from China, or upon an entirely new basis. Royal sanction was given to the petition. However, the Mexican fiscal in 1787 insisted that any organization taking over the otter-quicksilver trade must first reimburse the government for the amounts which had been spent already upon the project. This the company did not wish to do.[48] Finally, after special investigations in Mexico, the directors formed other conclusions unfavorable to the González proposal.

. . . the sending of vessels from San Blas to run along the coast in order to purchase skins in exchange for money or goods is expensive, risky, and of very doubtful result because of the great scarcity of skins, the lack of inclination in the natives and of subjects established in those places capable of directing the business of hunting, buying, and shipment.[49]

Another damper was turned upon the original plan of the company by the governor and intendant of the Philippines, who constantly exaggerated the difficulties of obtaining quicksilver in China. For all these reasons the Philippine Company in August, 1788, dropped its own plan for trading in California otter skins, and also at the same time it definitely refused to consider the González project.[50]

Alarm springing from the Nootka Sound controversy brought forth a half-dozen plans for the development of the otter trade. The most extensive project was conceived on the actual scene of the Anglo-Spanish conflict. Its originator was the man who in 1789 daringly seized four English craft operating in Nootka otter fields— Esteban José Martínez. In fact, his precipitate act was without doubt considerably prompted by his desire to develop the skin traffic.[51] While still in the north, this Spanish seaman began to formulate his ideas. Foreign traffic in otter skins should be stopped. He recorded his thought in his ship's book as follows:

It is evident that our Spain possesses more advantages for trade on this coast than the English nation which has none. We have easier navigation, we have provisions nearer at hand in our establishments of San Francisco and Monterey, the stores for our ships can be brought from Asia at less cost than from San Blas, and the collection of skins is abundant since the Californias produce many. With these we could initiate this trade in Canton, first preventing foreign nations from doing it, and, there being no one except ourselves to carry these skins to Asia, we could make better sales than can those nations who are engaged in it today.[52]

Martínez' first conception of developing the otter trade grew into a comprehensive and elaborate plan when he outlined it to the viceroy shortly after arriving in San Blas from the North Pacific in December, 1789.[53] A company of Mexican merchants should be formed to handle the otter traffic. Such an organization would first of all take over the skin trade between the established California missions and China. During the following fifty years, when no duties were to be paid, the company was to develop unoccupied northern areas by establishing four presidios of one hundred men each and seventeen missions. Twelve fast sloops were considered necessary, half of which were to guard the coast while the others were sailing to and from China. Otter skins could be exchanged in Canton for clothing for the Indians, soldiers, and crews.

A real desire to drive away the foreigner from the otter fields led Viceroy Revilla Gigedo to consider Martínez' plan. However, from the first he realized its visionary nature. When first forwarding the project to Spain in January, 1790, Revilla Gigedo added some constructive comments. The practical operation of Martínez' plan required that it be a coöperative undertaking of Mexican and Philippine merchants. Collection of skins and founding of colonies should be managed from Mexico City, whereas transpacific navigation and Asiatic exchanges should be directed by traders at Manila. However, it was a commerce "in which it seems that the Philippine Company should not take part." He further pointed out that "in Canton there are not the exchanges imagined by the author of the project for clothing the troops and colonists." Also, he stated that such a plan would be prejudicial to the Manila galleon trade.[54]

The promotion of the Spanish otter trade as a means of removing and controlling the foreigner became a definite part of Revilla Gigedo's program, but his estimation of Martínez' proposal rapidly diminished. In June, 1792, the viceroy expressed a desire to place the otter trade upon a solid foundation, with less risk than that involved in Vasadre's venture. However, he again stated that Martínez' plan was weak and that the recent Chinese prohibition of skin importations further lessened its chances of success.[55] In January, 1793, in response to an inquiry from Spain, where the matter in the meantime had been considered, the viceroy frankly restated his views concerning a project "inopportune, difficult, costly, badly conceived and worse assembled."[56] He pointed out the immense cost of such an enterprise and the practical impossibilities of supplying the proposed new establishments. These views were reiterated in Revilla Gigedo's "Informe" of April 12, 1793.[57] As a result of the viceroy's adverse criticism, Martínez' project was dropped.

Alejandro Malaspina, head of an exploring expedition to the Northwest Coast in 1791, also outlined a plan for promoting the Spanish otter trade. No doubt the commander was fully informed of the projects proposed by Vasadre and Martínez. At any rate, he became most enthusiastic over the possibilities and importance of the fur trade.

In his report to the government and in a special letter to Mexican merchants, Malaspina presented his ideas.[58] Spain held singular advantages over other nations engaged in the skin traffic. Her Pacific outposts, east, west, and north, could serve as near supply bases. In the Manila galleon and San Blas trade she had long-established commercial routes in the Pacific. Articles most valued as exchange media on the Northwest Coast were her exclusive possessions. Copper from Chilean mines, woolen and flannel cloths manufactured in Querétaro, Guadalajara, and Cholula, and, above all, abalone shells from California, could be offered to the northern Indians by none other than Spanish merchants. All of these commodities were much preferred in that region to the iron brought by Englishmen.

The gleaming iridescence of the green-blue abalone shells especially caught the eye of the native. For one or two he would give the finest skin. Not even the pearl shells of Panama, Realejo, Acapulco, or the Philippines did he value as much as the California abalone shell. He delighted in adorning himself with the beautiful "cunchi," and desired nothing better than to see before him at mealtime an array of colorful shell dishes. Abalones were piled up by the hundreds on the beaches around Monterey and would be gathered by the neophytes for a trifling compensation.

Malaspina's actual plan was practical. The otter trade, he believed, should be undertaken by a small number of merchants in Mexico City and Manila. Under no circumstances were government funds to be tied up in the enterprise until it was stabilized. Expeditions should be independent of each other. Vessels coming from the Philippines either were to stop at Monterey for cloth, copper, and shells, and then proceed north, or were to sail directly for the Northwest and go later to Monterey for supplies and such articles as could be used as exchange media in the north. Malaspina pointed out that it was preferable, because of the nature of the traffic, to keep vessels operating along the coast rather than to attempt to establish permanent factories. In this respect his plan materially differed from that of Martínez, being indeed more practical. Nevertheless, owing to the loss of political favor, Malaspina was unable to push through his ideas for organizing the Spanish fur trade.[59]

Another Spanish seaman realized through firsthand knowledge the importance of the otter trade as a means of ejecting the foreigner from the North Pacific. Juan Francisco de la Bodega y Cuadra, after completing his Nootka commission in 1792, outlined a course of procedure which was, however, exactly the same as that of Malaspina. Bodega well knew of the value of California abalone shells in the fur traffic, since he himself had made several trips to the Northwest, and he also knew of the experiences of others.[60] He urged that Mexican merchants enter the Northwest Coast trade and exchange cloth, copper, and abalone shells for otter skins. However, the proposition was disapproved by Viceroy Revilla Gigedo, who advanced the same arguments as he then was using against the Martínez plan. According to him, Mexican merchants would refuse to engage in a venture rendered risky by recent Chinese laws and by lower prices.[61]

In the meantime, Revilla Gigedo had built up an otter-trade program of his own. He was opposed to any expensive schemes of organized trade but directed every effort to cut off foreigners from the profits of the skin traffic. In those critical years during and following the Nootka controversy, he saw to it that copper, shells, and other commodities suitable as exchange media for furs were placed aboard all the vessels sent to the north.[62] California with its abalones and a few skin collections still continued to be a part of such trade.

On his 1789 voyage to the Northwest Coast, Martínez obtained a number of skins. On May 6, when in Nootka, he wrote:

> They also brought some sea-otter and bear skins to exchange for copper and large shells; and, although they were offered woolen and flannel cloth, beads, scissors, and other trifles, they placed no great value upon them, but, on the contrary, they valued the large shells as much as if they were gold or silver.

On June 6, Martínez wrote that some Indians brought otter skins but, "as they place value on copper and shells alone, they took no interest in the glass beads which I offered them."[63]

Revilla Gigedo's handling of the Nootka affair was much influenced by his desire to keep the otter trade for Spain. On May 1, 1790, he explained to royal officials that the reason for capturing the English was that they "had advanced to our coasts of California where they had no right either to establish themselves or to profit by our commerce in skins."[64] When James Colnett, one of the Englishmen seized in the Northwest, asked in Mexico City for a passport to proceed to his destination, the viceroy informed him that he might go directly to Macao but could not touch along the California coasts to trade.[65] After the treaty of 1790 with England, Revilla Gigedo at least had the satisfaction of knowing that the otter fields along Spain's occupied coasts would not be entered by English merchants.

Even though furs along California shores were secure legally from the English after 1790, Revilla Gigedo's interest in the otter trade did not languish. He desired to strengthen further the Californias and to clear northern waters of foreigners. Toward that end, he gave secret instructions to Bodega, before that mariner's voyage to the Northwest in 1790, to fortify Nootka and to "prevent the commerce which foreign nations have on the north coast of California." The viceroy added, ". . . you will collect all the skins which you find in exchange for the copper which is embarked for that purpose, and will keep an exact account of its distribution as well as of the skins which are exchanged, which you will send on the first boats which return to this port."[66] In 1791 Francisco de Eliza on the *Concepción* exchanged shells for skins. In the following year Jacinto Caamaño on the *Aranzazu* and Dionisio Alcalá Galiano and Cayetano Valdés y Bazan on the *Sutil* and *Mexicana* did much trading, abalone shells, as usual, serving as the exchange medium.[67] Observing that both these Spaniards were employed not only in "geographical researches, but in acquiring every possible information respecting the commerce of the country," Captain George Vancouver interpreted their actions as showing "the degree of jealousy with which the court of Spain regards the commercial intercourse that is likely to be established on this side of the world."[68] Revilla Gigedo's proposals in 1791, 1792, and 1793 for explorations between San Francisco and Nootka were all for the purpose of preventing foreigners from trading on the California and northern coasts.[69]

During these years small collections of otter furs were being made also in Upper California. Father Lasuén on July 22, 1791, in a special letter requested the mission padres not to stop getting skins because of the end of the Vasadre project, since Mexican merchants would no doubt pay at least as high a price as that which had been established formerly by law.[70]

A final step taken by Revilla Gigedo to promote the Spanish otter trade was that of urging the government to lower duties on skins. In 1793, after criticizing Martínez' project because of the great expense involved, he suggested that the otter traffic be opened to "the Spaniards who wish to do it voluntarily at their cost and risk, with exemption from export duties on skins."[71] In February, 1794, by a special decree duties were lifted from skin exports "in order that foreigners may not profit so easily from the otter trade, and that abundant exports may be obtained through the port of Acapulco directly to the Philippines."[72]

Little is known of the response to the new tariff law. Information is at hand for only two individual merchants who asked for permission to undertake California voyages. Ramón Pérez, two months after the decree was announced, petitioned for a two-year permit to trade Mexican manufactured goods for otter furs. In February, 1795, Pérez' request was granted.[73] Also, Nicolás Manzaneli of San Blas in April, 1794, asked to be allowed to take skins from the Californias to Canton where he would obtain Chinese goods for Upper and Lower California. He asserted that "by this means the profit which foreigners were drawing from this business would be diminished." Because of the monopoly held by the Philippine Company in the importation of Chinese goods to America, Manzaneli's petition was referred to Spain. In February, 1795, word was received in Mexico that His Majesty had approved the merchant's request.[74]

Spain had been alert to the significance of the sea otter trade. An active program had been promoted, and it had served to protect her northern coast. A more extensive trade without doubt would have been developed, had it not been for the tenacious hold of the Philippine Company on its monopoly rights. Specially organized trading firms were checked in their activities, and individuals, even when given free hunting rights in California, had little incentive to proceed, in consideration of the Philippine Company's exclusive privilege of selling Oriental goods in America. Nevertheless, Californians knew the value of sea otter pelts and had learned to send them to San Blas on the annual supply vessels. As a result, at the dawn of the nineteenth century, the Pacific frontier settlement of Spain was commercially braced to meet any foreigner who might venture into California hunting fields.

CHAPTER III

THE FIRST YANKEE TRADERS IN SPANISH CALIFORNIA, 1796–1805

ESSELS WERE SWARMING into the North Pacific by the close of
the eighteenth century. Most of these were Yankee craft,
bold representatives of the new era of free trade. Individual
English merchants, handicapped by the remnants of a mercantile
order in the same way that private Spanish enterprise was checked
in California otter grounds, had virtually withdrawn from the
fur trade, owing to the opposition of the East India Company.
The Russian American Company, however, basically a fur organization, was extending its activities, especially after the founding of Sitka in 1799. Greater numbers of both Americans and
Russians sharpened competition on the Northwest Coast. At the
same time, another situation unfavorable to the fur trade developed. Coastal Indian tribes were becoming more and more hostile, chiefly as a result of the fraudulent and violent dealings of
unscrupulous white men.

Adverse conditions in the Northwest caused enterprising Yankees to try the southern otter fields along the Spanish coast. There
they found the mercantile wall erected high against all foreign
traders; behind it lived a people who were interested in the same
object for which the New England traders had come. It was a situation to try the ingenuity of even a Yankee.

YANKEE TRADERS VERSUS THE SPANISH MERCANTILE SYSTEM

With the arrival in 1796 of the first Boston vessel, the contest
between the otter men and the upholders of the Spanish mercantile
system began. For several days in the latter part of October a
frigate was skirting the pine-edged shore of Monterey as if uncertain of its bearings in the heavy mists which enveloped sea and
land. Finally, on the twenty-seventh, the unknown craft anchored
just opposite Mission Carmel. Early the following day, a boat was
lowered. It approached the shore, and then suddenly it capsized.
Several Spanish onlookers rushed to the rescue and helped to pull
out the boat and its five American occupants.

While the newcomers were still drying out at Mission Carmel,

Sergeant Macario de Castro arrived from the presidio at Monterey where he had been notified by a watchful soldier. He glanced over the passports handed to him by the officer in charge. The showy seals of the Spanish consul at Charlestown and of General George Washington authenticated the documents. The stranger was then asked to state his business. He represented Captain Ebenezer Dorr of the Boston ship *Otter*. They were taking a thousand skins collected on the Northwest Coast to China via the Hawaiian Islands. Now, however, they were without meat and water. The only remaining supplies were fifty ship biscuits. They must have help.

This was a case for the governor. At Monterey, His Excellency, Diego de Borica, extended a most "gracious welcome" to the strangers and promised everything the vessel might need to continue its voyage. For two days the *Otter*, guided by cannon fire in the daytime and by a light shining from the battery at night, tried to head into port against contrary winds. Shortly after noon on October 30 seven shots from the vessel announced a safe entrance. In response a like salute boomed forth from the presidio.

Real Spanish hospitality was extended to Captain Dorr and his men. While he was waiting to have his first audience with the governor, chocolate was served to all. "For men who for such a long time had been reduced to ship biscuit and salt fish, a cup of chocolate was like a great fortune," remarked one of the guests.[1] The governor's reception was kindly. During the next few days Captain Dorr received supplies to the amount of $187—8 cows, 1,000 pounds of meal, rice, beans, butter, tallow, and vegetables.

But "Mr. Dorr did not return this kindness," one of the passengers later wrote.[2] Or, as Borica expressed it, "the captain, forgetting the hospitality which he was given,"[3] did the one and only thing which the governor had told him he could not do. At a safe distance from the presidio, and at the point of a gun, he forced ten of his crew, whose services he no longer needed and whom he did not wish to pay, and also a woman convict from Australia, to disembark. Borica's first experiences with an American otter-trading vessel had not been altogether pleasant.[4]

The first of the Boston firms engaged in the China trade to give definite directions for a combined Northwest Coast and California voyage was that of James and Thomas H. Perkins and Company.

---

[1] For notes to chap. iii, see pp. 192–194.

The letter of instructions written in August, 1798, to James Rowan, captain of the *Eliza*, read in part as follows:

> Our calculation is that you will arrive on the n. w. Coast by the middle of January, where you will carry on a brisk trade . . . that you will leave the Coast by say July and arrive by the 1 August at Mont Rea and remain on that Coast until the 1 November where we hope you will collect 40 or 50 m dollars with wh you will proceed to China. . . . Should y'r Collection of Furs be less than 2000 provided you meet with success in your Southern Trade, it will be best you sh'd go to China with the skins you have, and the Dollars; but should you not get any skins and fail in the Spanish trade also, it will be best to return to the n. w. coast.[5]

The Boston firm's "calculation" did not extend to the probable reception of a foreigner at "Mont Rea." Although Captain Rowan was very successful in collecting furs in the North Pacific, he was led by news of the coming of other merchants to turn his vessel toward California early in the spring of 1799. He hoped to exchange all remaining goods not only for dollars, as directed by his employers, but for skins enough to complete his cargo. Rowan's reasons for coming to California were expressed in very different terms to the Spanish authorities at San Francisco where the *Eliza* arrived on May 24. He needed wood and water, and desired a safe place to pass the stormy season. The excuse was too thin. Governor Borica surmised that contrabandism was the real purpose of the captain the moment he heard that the supercargo of the Boston ship was one John Kendrick, Jr., a former pilot on Spanish coastal vessels, who would be thoroughly familiar with the country. A few supplies could be purchased, but the vessel must sail immediately and must not touch elsewhere along Spain's Pacific shores.[6]

Documentary substantiation of what were thus far only unproved convictions that illegal trade was going on was given unintentionally to Spanish authorities by a Boston merchant himself. On August 25, 1800, Charles Winship entered San Diego Bay in the *Betsy*. The story which he told was one which port officials could not circumvent. He had been in the north and at the Hawaiian Islands. Now he was on his way to China, but he must have wood and water immediately. However, only a few hours after the captain had been granted permission to remain in port on the basis of the veracity of his statements, he was writing to his brother in Boston an entirely different account of affairs. He described the progress of his voyage and then made mention of trade he had carried on with California Indians. It was evident that, instead of having gone to the Hawaiian Islands, he had cruised along the Spanish coast. Two months later, after sailing from port to port in Lower California rather than to China as was the stated intention of the captain, the *Betsy* entered San Blas. This was now Winship's story: the main mast had been broken in a northern storm, he had made course for San Diego but, not having been able to find that harbor, he had gone on to San Blas. Only after the Boston ship had sailed did Mexican authorities have enough evidence to put two and two together. The captain's letter to his brother, which came into the possession of the commander at San Blas, and reports from San Diego made it clear, as the Mexican fiscal wrote, "that said captain hid the truth in his declaration."[7]

Spanish officials in California now learned to take precautionary measures when a strange vessel came into harbor. Help was often given, because both international maritime law and the Spaniard's inherent sense of hospitality required it. However, the foreigner was much limited in action. An example was the experience of the *Enterprise* of New York. In December, 1800, Captain Ezekiel Hubbell had been helped materially at San Blas on his way to the north. Six months later the captain entered San Diego with the usual necessity plea. He must have bread and other supplies before he could continue his voyage to China. The discreet Manuel Rodríguez, port commander, was determined that the Yankees would not slip aboard something in addition to "bread." The *Enterprise* must remain anchored one league from the harbor. An *alférez*, stationed at Ballast Point near the entrance to the bay, watched every movement. From June 28 to July 3 boats plied back and forth, each flying a flag as a signal that it was coming into port solely for supplies. They brought to the Boston ship six cattle, eighteen *arrobas* of flour, six *fanegas* of beans, four *fanegas* of corn, and some salt. From San Diego the *Enterprise* sailed southward to Lower California ports. One part of Spain's enforcement machinery was not yet operating in California—that of immediately passing on marine data. Consequently, the vessel put in successively at the bays of Todos Santos, San Quintín, and San José del Cabo, only to repeat at each place the demand for supplies.[8]

The year 1803 showed a high record in contraband activity. Boston traders were of necessity becoming bolder. On February 26, 1803, just as the sun was sinking behind Point Loma, an American frigate anchored in San Diego Bay. Upon coming ashore, Captain John Brown presented the papers of his vessel to Commander Rodríguez. The ship was the *Alexander,* owned by Henry Bass and Company and Joseph Taylor of Boston, and was sent out, according to the passport signed by the Spanish consul in New England, for the purpose of "discovery." Captain Brown stirred the sympathies of Rodríguez by describing the scurvy-stricken condition of his men. The commander permitted the vessel to remain in port and gave orders that the water, meat, and salt for which Brown asked be provided. His feelings did not run away with his sense of duty, however. He tried to find a guard to place on board, but at that time in the evening he could not find sufficient soldiers. The following day every precaution was taken to prevent illicit actions. Six soldiers were stationed on the vessel. The sick sailors permitted to go ashore were left to convalesce in an isolated spot far removed from the presidio. All rowboats were carefully watched.

Five days passed by, and then Rodríguez got wind of some smuggling. Immediately he and four other soldiers rowed out to the *Alexander* and began a thorough search. In the storeroom next to the main mast the men found what they sought. A sharp command was given by Rodríguez. Skins flew through the storeroom door onto the deck. Another order came, and the pelts were counted— four hundred and ninety-one. Without further ado all were taken ashore and stored in the presidial warehouse.[9]

Under what circumstances the otter skins were put on board the *Alexander* is a mystery. Rodríguez indirectly hinted that it must have been done the first night the vessel was in port. Richard Cleveland's statement that the commander himself was interested in trading suggests another line of thought but is not backed by the Spaniard's record of rigid law enforcement.[10] Two letters throw some light on the affair. In March a corporal at San Diego asked Governor José Joaquín Arrillaga to have returned to him 223 otter skins which he "pretended" to sell the last of February to the captain of an American frigate.[11] Also, a padre at San Luis Rey desired the return of 170 skins which mission Indians had sold to the Americans.[12]

Forced to leave San Diego before the expiration of the time first granted by Rodríguez, the *Alexander* pursued its contraband way. Just at nightfall on March 7, Captain Brown entered the bay of Todos Santos where, as the San Diego commander wrote Governor Arrillaga, "he pretended to need wood, which he did not in this port because he did not wish to, and beans, lambs, and chickens which he did not ask for here; therefore, I advised the corporal to order him to go to sea, as beans, lambs, and chickens could have been asked for here."[13]

Again San Diego was set astir by the actions of another Anglo-American vessel. At five o'clock on March 16, just two weeks after the *Alexander* affair, the *Lelia Byrd,* commanded by William Shaler and Richard Cleveland, anchored within the harbor. The pompous formality with which Rodríguez conducted proceedings the following morning seemed to the brusque, unceremonious Americans but the arrogant display of a coxcomb. Saluting as he stepped aboard, the commander paused a moment until his dragoons had drawn themselves up on the deck. Then, passing with all dignity between the two lines of soldiers who stood at attention with hats off and swords in hand, he proceeded aft. He listened to the same pleas for necessities which had been advanced only shortly before by Captain Brown and ceremoniously listed the supplies which were mentioned as sufficient to meet the great need of the seventeen men on board—four cattle, nine *arrobas* of flour, one and one-half *fanegas* of salt, and twenty-four chickens.

The Boston men were soon to find out the calibre of Manuel Rodríguez. They approached him on the subject of buying the recently seized otter skins stored in the warehouse. He refused to listen. According to Cleveland's account, although there was no doubt that Rodríguez "would have been as well pleased to sell as we should have been to purchase them, if the transaction had been practicable without being known to the people, yet, as this was out of the question, and they were all spies on each other, he dared not indulge his desire of selling them to us."[14] On March 21 Rodríguez visited the vessel and informed the captain that since supplies had been delivered, he expected him to leave the following day.

Now was the time for quick action if the object of the call in port was to be accomplished. Night came. A boat was lowered and paddled out into the silence of the bay. Why was it going? asked the young Joaquín Arce, heading the Spanish guards on board.

Only to search for one of the crew who had not returned from hunting that day, was the reply. A little later the enveloping stillness was again broken by the splash of the ship's launch as it pushed off landward. Again a query from the Spanish sergeant—Where? Why? And the answer this time was—the launch was being sent to look for the boat!

Rodríguez was ready for them. Although the boat returned in good time with a few skins, the launch met a different fate. Silently the ship's caulker and two cabin boys rowed across the bay. Silently they pushed the launch up on a secluded spot along the beach. Then, while the two boys remained on guard, the caulker walked a short distance away toward a waiting Spanish soldier and toward a small pile of otter skins. Just as he began to examine the pelts, sand-deadened thuds aroused everyone. In an instant the two on guard were surrounded by six horsemen, headed by the resolute Rodríguez. The astounded American lads were asked for an explanation of their presence. They had come for no reason whatsoever! Catching a glimpse of a movement in the direction of the two bargainers, Rodríguez quickly turned his horse that way. Already the soldier had fled, completely forgetting his otter skins. The caulker was found nearby, hidden in some brush. Leaving the three sailors closely guarded, Rodríguez sped off to the presidio. He was on the trail of any possible contraband hidden away in the soldiers' headquarters at the battery. Every corner was searched. In the trunk of the corporal himself he found recently purchased foreign goods, which were sent at once to the warehouse. Returning to the beach, the commander completed his night's work by ordering that the three captured Spaniards be tied and closely watched.

In the meantime, Cleveland was impatiently waiting for dawn that he might investigate the reason for the failure of the launch to return. An early morning reconnaissance revealed the situation. To the American merchants it seemed "that the choice presented us was that of submission, indignant treatment, and plunder, or resistance and hazarding the consequences." The Spanish guards on the *Lelia Byrd* were disarmed. Cleveland and four others immediately rowed to the shore. Covered by pistols, the Spaniards were forced to release the three prisoners lying bound on the sand.

Preparations were made on board the *Lelia Byrd* for an immediate departure. All ashore was likewise tense activity. With the first faint land breeze, the vessel slowly began to sail out of the harbor. Shots were fired by both sides.[15] A few hours later, at a safe distance to the south, the Americans stopped to plug up a hole in the side of their ship. The trembling Spanish guards were put ashore. Then the vessel sailed on to San Quintín where just two days before, on March 22, the *Alexander* had arrived, soliciting supplies as usual. The two captains in many a sympathetic gam fumed against the impossible Spaniards.

Other events of the year 1803 excited Spanish circles. The *Alexander* offended again; the *Hazard* also caused trouble.

Sailing north from San Quintín in April, the *Alexander* touched at San Juan Capistrano for supplies and water and then remained for several days during the month of May in the port of San Francisco. Macario de Castro, who was there at the time, reported that, although he had not seen any of the presidial commanders trading, he had heard rumors to that effect. He knew of certain soldiers who had gone away from the pueblo of San José with money and who had come back with merchandise, and he had seen many people on the beach. But, "Quién sabe?" "Who knows?"[16]

After cruising about in the North Pacific, the *Alexander* again entered San Francisco Harbor on August 11. Captain Brown's entreaty for help because of damages inflicted by barbarous Northwest Coast Indians was met with an immediate refusal. The commander of the presidio, José Darío Argüello, reminded him that only four months ago he had taken on sufficient supplies for more than eight months; Argüello ordered him to leave. In Monterey Captain Brown again tried his luck. He explained his departure from San Francisco by saying that facilities were lacking for both his vessel and the *Hazard*, which was also in that port, to take on water at the same time. The Spaniards listened to this story and, after serious conference, they decided to give him help if his vessel proved to be in the condition he had described. A thorough inspection of the ship followed. Captain Brown looked on resentfully, because, according to the summarized testimony of a member of his crew, "he did not like the overcareful investigation which was made on board in order to find out if his necessities were false or real."[17] Since the *Alexander* was found to be in a leaky condition and really low in supplies, it was permitted to remain in port. However, Captain Brown returned the favor by an action which, added to his earlier exploits in San Diego, made his name known to every Spanish official on the coast. On the night of August 17, when a thick fog hung over the bay, the *Alexander* slipped away without making the least compensation for the supplies provided during its three days' stay.[18]

Monterey was excited by the precipitate leave-taking of the *Alexander*. Perhaps the vessel was speeding to join the *Hazard* in San Francisco in order to plan a joint attack on the capital. The commander of the supply ship *Princesa,* then anchored at Monterey, pointed out that, if their fears were realized, the Spaniards would stand but little chance since "the *Hazard* has twenty-four cannon, four short guns of large calibre aft, and forty-six men, and it is very well provided with slingers, as is also the corvette with eight [cannon], two mortars, and four slingers."[19]

The *Hazard* had entered San Francisco on the same day as the *Alexander* and likewise had been ordered to leave. However, Captain James Rowan did not give up. He began a letter to Commander Argüello. "Although you gave us orders to leave this port immediately, I tell you that I find myself in such need that I will much appreciate it if you will come on board my frigate, and you can see that it is true that I find myself in need."[20] He described at some length harassing and damaging encounters with Northwest Coast Indians, and he ended his letter by a strong appeal to the goodwill of the Spanish nation. Argüello personally inspected the vessel and satisfied himself that repairs and supplies were really necessary. He then granted the captain permission to remain four days. Heavy fogs and contrary winds provided an excuse for extending the *Hazard*'s stay, during which the worried Argüello with only three other soldiers tried to prevent any undercover proceedings. Just when the commander was heaving a sigh of relief that his repeated orders to Captain Rowan finally had been obeyed, a special message arrived from Monterey urging him to do everything possible to detain the *Hazard* in order to prevent the feared union with the *Alexander*. It was too late.

Southward the *Hazard* sailed, only two days behind the *Alexander,* following what was becoming the regular winter course for the Boston traders. Arrived in front of Santa Barbara, Captain Rowan directed a letter to Raymundo Carrillo, commander of the presidio. It was of this general tenor : he had only two barrels of water and a small amount of wood; there was much sickness among his crew; his vessel, coming directly from the Northwest Coast where he had furious combats with the Indians, was leaking badly; and the ship had been sent out for the purpose of whaling, as his passports would show. Carrillo as yet knew little of storytelling contrabandists. He permitted anchorage on condition that no one come to land except those getting wood and water. Four days passed during which Captain Rowan made not a move to fill his water barrels. Then suddenly the sails of the *Hazard* were unfurled, and the vessel sped off toward the Santa Barbara Channel Islands. The captain sent word that he was leaving because he could not find a boat with which to carry wood and water to his ship.

The next stopping place was San Juan Capistrano. Not as the *Hazard* did the vessel enter, but under the name of the *Eliza*. The corporal stationed there faithfully reported the same Northwest Coast story to Rodríguez at San Diego and told him that Captain Rowan had offered some trivial excuse for not presenting his passports. Rodríguez had had too much experience not to see through the representations of the wily captain. He ordered that the ship leave immediately.[21]

NEW SPANISH RESTRICTIONS

A general rallying of all Spanish officials north of San Blas was the result of the happenings of 1803. Every report forwarded to Mexico of the irregular doings of foreign vessels in California ports was followed by severe reminders from the viceroy that Spanish laws must be enforced.[22] Officials were told that every detail concerning each foreign ship's arrival should be passed on immediately to all port commanders.[23] Other movements were begun in order to meet the maritime crisis. Viceroy José de Iturrigaray launched the idea of sending a warship to cruise regularly along the coast between San Francisco and Lower California.[24] It was also proposed that a mission and a military guard be established on one of the islands in the Santa Barbara Channel, in order to prevent contraband trade.[25] Governor Arrillaga took up the alarm. He relayed on to each presidial and port commander all viceregal messages. He was thoroughly convinced that the putting in of foreign ships for supplies was merely an excuse because, as he stated to the viceroy, not one of the vessels entering California ports within the last five years had ever asked for more than thirty to forty *arrobas* of flour, three or four cattle, a few *fanegas* of corn and beans, and a little wood and water. Such small amounts were not sufficient for a trip to Asia or for a cruise in the north, the avowed destinations of the ships.[26]

Warnings and orders were heeded. Boston traders along the coast in 1804 and 1805 encountered a new administrative attitude.

Following the trail of the sea otter hunters from Lower California to the Hawaiian Islands, and then back across the Pacific to the Northwest Coast, the *Hazard* again appeared on the Spanish coast in 1804. The vessel had touched at San Francisco in January on the way northward, and at that time, according to reports sent to the governor, it was really seriously damaged by a severe storm. In September, following almost to a day the same schedule as that of the previous year, the *Hazard* sailed southward to Ventura, San Juan Capistrano, and Colnett Bay. This time all doors were closed. Supplies, even water, were absolutely refused. An attempted landing was made in San Diego, but, just as some of the crew were about to run the launch to shore, soldiers warned them to come no farther. Carrying out instructions, Rodríguez immediately sent a full report to Lower California officials. As a result, few California otter skins could have been on the *Hazard* when she sailed for China in the latter part of 1804.[27]

The *Lelia Byrd* trafficked along the California coast in 1804 and 1805 only by avoiding the main ports. A high price received in Canton for the otter skins taken aboard the vessel in 1803 and an opportunity to purchase some European goods induced Shaler and Cleveland to make another voyage to California. After obtaining a number of furs at Trinidad, north of Cape Mendocino, the *Lelia Byrd* on May 18, 1804, sailed to the south where, according to Shaler, "I got abundant supplies of provisions and began trade with the missionaries and inhabitants for furs."[28] No legal entrance into a Spanish port was attempted, however.

After a cruise along Lower California and Central America, the *Lelia Byrd* returned to California in February of the next year. Shaler's description of his trading activities on the coast is brief: ". . . we got plentiful supplies of provisions as usual and were not unsuccessful in our collection of furs."[29] The Spanish records give a few more details. The padre of San Luis Obispo received Shaler *con poca amabilidad,* "with little amiability."[30] For a few days in the first part of March the *Lelia Byrd* lay opposite the Ortega Rancho at Refugio, west of Santa Barbara. It next touched at San Pedro. From there the vessel ran over to Santa Catalina Island, to which Shaler decided to return in order to careen his vessel. But first he was going to collect "all the skins on the coast." Slipping past San Diego, probably with vivid memories of the shooting episode of but two years before, Shaler brought his vessel to anchor in Todos Santos Bay on March 31. The corporal had just received a circular letter about the *Lelia Byrd* from the Santa Barbara commander. Consequently, he refused to give the captain water. Six days later Shaler sailed, saying, according to the report of Rodríguez, that the only reason he did not get water by use of force was because he did not wish to make a noise. A blanket entry in Shaler's journal records these movements and the activities of the next four weeks as follows: "After completing our business on the coast, we returned to Santa Catalina and anchored in the harbour on the first of May."[31] A month later the *Lelia Byrd* ran over to San Pedro, obtained apparently without any difficulty provisions sufficient to last twelve months, and then continued southward "collecting all the furs in our way."[32]

This was the last time the *Lelia Byrd* was to trouble the Spaniards. The aged vessel was exchanged at Honolulu for a small craft named *Tamana.* Shaler then instructed his agent, Mr. John T. Hudson, to proceed to California on this forty-ton ship and collect the money owed to him. However, according to Cleveland, Mr. Hudson lacked the daring now necessary for a successful contrabandist along the California coast. He avoided entering any of the large ports. Furthermore, he found that it was then impossible to do much in the more isolated places.[33] Spanish soldiers were beginning to spring up in even the most secluded spots.

The Boston men were in a predicament. Conditions in the north made it necessary to extend the field of otter-skin collections. However, southern coasts had become uninviting and even hazardous, for each year the Spanish commercial system was tightened. Furthermore, the number of otter skins which might be obtained by bartering were few. California Indians did not naturally take to hunting on a large scale, and the mission fathers, until about 1810, when conditions changed, did not especially encourage them to do so, both because the shipment of otter skins on the supply ships was not a paying proposition and because the natives were open to exploitation by soldiers and citizens as soon as they had a few skins in their possession.[34] Something would have to be done—or the Yankees would have to leave California to the Spaniards.

CHAPTER IV

RUSSIAN OTTER HUNTING IN SPANISH CALIFORNIA

THE YANKEE-RUSSIAN CONTRACT SYSTEM, 1803–1812

YANKEES could not be expected to withdraw from a desired commercial field without trying every expedient.[1] The man who originated a new way of doing business in the otter grounds held by Spain was Captain Joseph O'Cain. Irishman by birth, reared in the United States, trained for the sea aboard an English merchantman, and navigator by 1803 on four of the early Boston vessels on the California and Northwest Coast, O'Cain possessed a background highly qualifying him for a Pacific seaman.

From firsthand experience Captain O'Cain realized that the California fur trade could not be continued by the method of bartering. It was not only risky, but it was also not as profitable as it might have been, for he had seen many more otters in the southern fields than were procurable through the local Indians. The thought occurred to him that, if Boston men could hunt the sea otter themselves, they could obtain more and could keep clear of populated centers watched over by law-enforcing Spaniards. However, equipment and expert otter pursuers they did not possess. O'Cain conceived the idea of seeking assistance from the rulers of the North Pacific.

In October, 1803, on Kodiak Island, the otter hunters' rendezvous south of the Alaskan Peninsula, New Englander and Russian met in conference. Captain O'Cain's plan was simple, but he proceeded carefully in his explanation to Governor Alexander Baranov. He began by enthusiastically describing some recently discovered islands on the California coast which abounded in sea otters. If Baranov would supply Aleuts[2] and baidarkas, he would provide transportation with the *O'Cain,* the vessel of which he was captain and which had been sent out by the Winships of Boston. All skins would be divided equally, and large profits could most certainly be realized.[3]

Baranov considered carefully before he made his decision. Many worries pressed upon him.[4] Just the year before, the new settle-

---

[1] For notes to chap. iv, see pp. 195–199.

ment at Sitka had been wiped out by the hostile Kolosh. Hunting parties sent to the northern mainland had been set upon by other treacherous Indian tribes. Foreign encroachments were becoming more and more annoying. To climax all, one of those intruders came to tell him of the discovery of new hunting grounds. Baranov, the indomitable, recalled the secret orders which he had received from his company the year before to push settlements southward. Baranov, the dreamer, in thought linked the new proposition with his vision of a greater Russia on the Pacific coast. O'Cain's idea might be the means of making that dream come true. He would venture. The first contract was signed.

Preparations for the California hunting experiment occupied old and young during the next few weeks. Aleutian women made waterproofs for their husbands. Old men contentedly whittled away at canoe paddles and frames. Native boys helped their fathers by cutting sticks and beams, or by smearing whale oil in chinks and seams of completed baidarkas. Russian American Company agents collected provisions palatable to northern hunters—*youkala* or dried fish, whale meat, and plenty of whale oil. Hooks and lines were supplied for catching fish to supplement food stores. At last twenty baidarkas and twice as many hunters under the command of an able Russian, Shvetsov, were ready. As pledge of good faith, O'Cain left behind twelve thousand roubles worth of merchandise.[5]

The *O'Cain* arrived opposite San Diego early in December, 1803. It did not venture within the harbor. Three men came in a small boat as far as Ballast Point to ask for supplies but were refused. After four days the vessel continued southward to San Quintín on the Lower California coast. Commander José Manuel Ruiz arrived posthaste from Mission Santo Domingo. Captain O'Cain then began to resort to the usual subterfuges practiced by Yankees in attempting to circumvent Spanish law enforcement. He told how he had not been on land for eleven months and how a terrible storm in the northwest had damaged his vessel. He must have help. Convinced by O'Cain's good story-telling and by a trip aboard the ship that the "necessity was real," Ruiz permitted the Boston ship to remain in port for a few days.

The few days lengthened into three months while the *O'Cain* stayed on in the calm waters of San Quintín. On March 4, 1804, Governor Arrillaga reported to the viceroy that "there is not an otter left from Mission Rosario to Santo Domingo." He had given repeated orders to O'Cain, but excuses had been the only reply. The Spanish governor continued, "There is no other way to prevent them except to tell them not to hunt and to this they pay no attention."[6] It was impossible to seize any of the skins piled up on the beach since five cannons were trained on the spot. Furthermore, some of the forty Aleuts were always stationed close at hand. In the latter part of March O'Cain completed his hunt. When preparing for the return voyage, he was prevented from getting wood and water at present-day Ensenada in Lower California. Arrived at Kodiak in June, he turned over to Baranov the half of 1,100 furs. In addition, O'Cain had 700 skins which he had managed to purchase on his own account from Spanish officials and missionaries.[7]

The contract system proved satisfactory to both parties. The problem of obtaining furs along the California coast seemed to be solved for the Boston men. Baranov, likewise, wished to continue the plan. The *O'Cain's* voyage had been financially satisfactory. Furthermore, the decreasing number of otters and the continued intrusions of foreigners into northern waters strengthened his conviction, which was further confirmed by the views of Nikolai Rezanov, that two steps would have to be taken immediately in Russian America.[8] Hunting grounds must be extended, and the Anglo-American must be prevented from taking away the fur wealth of both the old and new fields. Baranov saw that the contract system was the means of accomplishing these ends.

In the fall of 1805 three ships left Boston, each bound for the Pacific Northwest with the specific object of contracting with the Russians for a California expedition. One, the *Peacock*, was commanded by O'Cain's brother-in-law, Oliver Kimball, who probably heard many tales of California adventures before he sailed. Young Jonathan Winship, who had been on the last Pacific cruise of the *O'Cain*, returned in the same vessel. No doubt it was Jonathan's enthusiasm which led his famous merchant family to finance another similar voyage. O'Cain also decided to launch forth again, this time on the *Eclipse*.

Kimball first surveyed the otter fields of California on his way to the North Pacific. The *Peacock* arrived off San Gabriel in March, 1806, putting in supposedly because of a broken mast and lack of water, wood, and meat, although supplies had been taken on only a few weeks before at the Hawaiian Islands. If the Boston captain really was in need of supplies, Spanish vigilance prevented him from obtaining them. The watchful Rodríguez sent soldiers from San Diego as far north as the Santa Ana River to look out for the ship. The commander at San Juan Capistrano was ready for the vessel when it anchored a half league off the coast. Two of the crew who were sent to the mission for supplies were imprisoned. A quick dash to the beach resulted in the seizure of a small boat and another sailor. On April 10 the *Peacock* anchored outside of San Diego Harbor at a safe distance from presidial cannon. A boat dared to come in as far as Ballast Point, but no landing was made. Someone threw a package on the beach, and then the boat was rowed back to the vessel's protecting side. In the parcel were two letters. One, afterwards translated by one of the captured sailors into French which was then read by the padre, was a petition to the governor for the return of the prisoners; the other, addressed to the imprisoned mate, told him to escape as soon as possible. Receiving no answer, Kimball sailed on to Todos Santos Bay and Point Santo Tomás. Just about that time Argüello was proudly telling Rezanov, then in San Francisco, about the *Peacock* affair as an example of how the Spaniards were driving off the Anglo-Americans. The Russian, not knowing at the time that the ship's captain was soon to form a contract with his compatriots, reported to his government, "I congratulated the governor on the success of his arrangements which pleased the good old man very much."⁹

In the meantime, Jonathan Winship, Jr., had made a contract with Baranov in the spring of 1806. The *O'Cain* was to be well equipped for the California voyage. Over a hundred veteran Kodiak otter hunters, commanded by the Russian, Slobodchikov, and fifty baidarkas were on board. In addition, there were twelve native women destined to toil for hunting gangs on distant rocky islands. Provisions included the staples of a northern diet —15,400 *youkala,* 1,000 pounds of whale meat, and a large quantity of the much-liked beverage, whale oil. Muskets and flints for hunting game were given to each of the hunters.¹⁰ After completing final arrangements amid scenes of banqueting and general hilarity, Winship persuaded his intoxicated visitors to leave his vessel, weighed anchor, "saluted them with five guns and three cheers, and heartily rejoiced at their departure."¹¹

Winship did everything possible on this trip to avoid trouble with the Spaniards. After trading and hunting at Trinidad, he sailed directly to the Lower California coast in June, 1806, only two months after the *Peacock*. Here, by stationing his one hundred men upon various islands and by keeping the *O'Cain* in the mainland ports of Todos Santos and San Quintín removed from the actual hunting scenes, he created a situation impossible for the authorities to handle. Leaving his hunting parties well supplied, Winship sailed away in August with otter and seal skins worth sixty thousand dollars in the Canton market.[12]

O'Cain, likewise, contracted with Baranov early in 1806. His vessel, the *Eclipse*, was cruising along the Californias at the same time as the *O'Cain*. Again Captain O'Cain experienced Spanish opposition. The *Eclipse* anchored just beyond range of the famous cannon at San Diego on June 25. Although a distressing tale was told of an immediate need for repairs and supplies, the alert Rodríguez as usual refused all requests. The vessel left on June 29, but Rodríguez dispatched Corporal Juan Osuna with four soldiers to Todos Santos Bay.

The bold Boston captain celebrated July 4 by a conflict with the Spaniard. Landing twenty of his crew, fifteen of whom were well armed, O'Cain beckoned to Osuna. Meeting him at a short distance from the others, he told the corporal that he must have water. The resolute Osuna refused. Thereupon, O'Cain gave a signal. At the point of the gun each Spaniard was forced to dismount and go as prisoner aboard the *Eclipse*. A few days later two soldiers were released and instructed by O'Cain to bear a challenging message to Rodríguez—the pilot of the *Peacock*, who had been taken at San Juan Capistrano, must be freed; if this were not done, O'Cain would return to San Diego, finish the battery and afterward the presidio. On the eighth, Osuna was left at San Quintín, and early the following morning Commander Ruiz found the thirsty and tired corporal some miles to the north.

O'Cain was making a name for himself. Osuna reported that the Boston crew always carried guns and the captain was ever watchful; each morning, noon, and evening, a sailor would climb the mast and closely scan the seas. Without making any move to execute his threat, O'Cain stayed on for a few weeks more. On July 18 five of the crew of his vessel were seized when their longboat was dashed to pieces upon making a landing in San José del Cabo Bay. O'Cain had much to relate to the Russian governor when he returned to Sitka in August.[13]

Three Boston vessels under Russian contracts were operating along the California coast in 1807, the *Derby, Peacock,* and *O'Cain.* Captain Benjamin Swift of the *Derby* obtained twenty-five baidarkas and fifty natives under the same terms as those given to Winship.[14] With spirits not at all dampened by his first California experiences, Kimball of the *Peacock* formed a contract with Baranov in October, 1806. The latter agreed to provide twelve baidarkas and some Aleuts under the command of the Russian, Vasilii Petrovich Tarakanov, who had carefully viewed California otter fields with Shvetsov on the *O'Cain*'s voyage in 1803. For several reasons Kimball in 1807 steered clear of California ports. He could profit by the knowledge of Tarakanov. The captain also had learned his lesson while attempting to obtain California skins entirely by the use of the barter system. Finally, before starting, he was expressly warned by Baranov not to go "too near the Spanish settlements."

The harbor of Bodega was chosen as the hiding place of the *Peacock* from March to May. Crude houses were quickly erected on the beach. Canoes were sent up and down the coast and even into San Francisco Bay. Here a great hunt was in store for them, since only the year before, according to Langsdorff, "the valuable sea-otter was swimming in numbers about the bay, nearly unheeded."[15] As the Aleutian hunters slipped in, they hugged the coast farthest away from presidial cannon. One day about the middle of March, when five baidarkas were leaving, a shot from the fort caused the Aleuts to abandon hastily two of them. Sailing from Bodega in May, Kimball apparently made a quick voyage to Lower California. In June, 1807, he was in the vicinity of San Quintín. In August the *Peacock* brought back to Sitka 753 prime otter skins, 258 yearlings, and 250 pups.[16]

After taking his fur cargo to the Russian north in August, 1806, Winship returned on the *O'Cain* early in 1807 with additional canoes and fifty more Kodiak hunters. At the Farallons the exciting discovery was made of "a vast number of fur and hair seals." The vessel then sailed on to Catalina. Around that and near-by islands, baidarkas were sent forth for the sea otter. Arriving off Lower California in March, the *O'Cain* cruised from island to island, leaving new hunters to join the gangs which had been at work since the previous year. An account of the 1807 voyage states that "the *O'Cain* had now from seventy to eighty canoes, carrying about a hundred and fifty Kodiak Indian hunters, fitted out and hunting sea otter among the Islands of Guadalupe, Natividad, Cerros and Redondo, while other gangs were stationed on some of the islands to take fur seal."[17] Russian references mention a quarrel between Winship and Slobodchikov. No doubt there was a conflict of authority. The angry Russian purchased, for one hundred and fifty otter skins, a small schooner, naming it the *Nicolai*, loaded it with furs, and sailed in 1807 for the Hawaiian Islands where some of the skins were exchanged for provisions for the Russian American Company.[18]

Yankee-Aleutian activities on the island retreats along Upper and Lower California in 1807 were not unobserved by Spanish officials. Governor Arrillaga was informed in February of the canoes lurking about near Santa Barbara. He immediately ordered the commander at San Francisco to be on the lookout for the main vessel and to inform him as soon as it was seen. A few days later, when the *O'Cain* was sighted off the coast between Los Angeles and Santa Barbara, four soldiers were sent to watch its movements. In March Indian fishers of Mission Santo Domingo reported having seen three large vessels at sea and men in a canoe hunting at night. These three ships were undoubtedly the *O'Cain, Peacock,* and *Mercury.* José Ignacio Arce the next day led some soldiers to San Quintín. Here it was learned that baidarkas had just left and that the Aleutian rowers had killed four cows. Not satisfied, Arce went farther south to Mission Rosario. In a small bay he found ten hunters who succeeded in communicating the name of their vessel—the *O'Cain.* The Spanish soldier changed his mind about capturing them when he observed that they were all well armed. All he could do was to order them to leave the coast, and he appointed a watchman. The hunters promised to row back to the island opposite, there to await the larger vessel.[19]

Winship's hunters continued to worry the Spaniards until June, 1807. Kodiak gangs were finally collected in April, and, according to the ship's journal, the return voyage was begun. But it took two months to sail from Cerros Island to the northern limits of Lower California. In May a ship, reported as the *"Litayre"* commanded by "Juan Quinship," arrived opposite Santo Domingo, supposedly to repair tattered rigging. A month later the vessel was still there, and hunters were reported at San Quintín.[20] In a clash at that place one Kodiak was killed, and others were captured. The *O'Cain* finally beat its way northward. On the way Kodiak natives delightfully entertained with "exhibitions of their national dances and singing of the songs of their country."[21] In September, when the vessel arrived at Sitka, the total result of the hunt was found to be 3,006 prime otter skins, 1,264 yearlings, and 549 pups.[22]

The Yankee-Russian otter trade in California was quiescent from 1808 to 1810 while the Winship vessels were voyaging homeward via China and making the return trip. Only one Boston merchant pursued business under the contract plan during these years— Captain George Washington Eayrs, who commanded the *Mercury*, owned partly by Benjamin Lamb of Boston.[23] Captain Eayrs was one of the most daring and enterprising of all the Anglo-American otter traders.

Before entering into contract engagements, Eayrs had bartered for skins along the coast in 1806 and 1807 when the *Mercury* was under Captain William Heath Davis. He had an astounding way of making friends with the Spaniards. In November and December, 1806, Eayrs obtained from Padre "Lewis" of Santa Barbara 197 large otter skins at from nine to ten dollars each and 402 smaller ones at prices ranging from one to six dollars each. In exchange the mission fathers received much-needed supplies—blue cloth, chintz, cotton hose, dishes, knives, and handsaws. At San Luis Obispo, San Buenaventura, San Gabriel, San Juan Capistrano, San Miguel, and Rosario, Eayrs continued to have the same success. As the *Mercury* went on its way down the coast, it also left behind colorful gift reminders of its visit—five yards of blue cloth to an Indian who had sped to Mission San Gabriel with the news of the ship's arrival, a piece of red beige to another Indian who had brought grapes for the dried-beef-fed crew, bright sashes to soldiers for carrying letters and to padres for bringing vegetables and other refreshments. By August, when the *Mercury* left the coast for China, 2,848 otter skins had been collected.[24]

Although he had succeeded in obtaining skins by bartering, Captain Eayrs decided the following year to try the contract plan. In May, 1808, he and Baranov made final arrangements for the treatment and payment of the Aleuts who with twenty-five bai-darkas, all under the command of Shvetsov, were placed aboard the *Mercury*. After touching at Trinidad and Bodega, the vessel, with its canoes hovering close about, remained during the month of December at safe distances from the coast between San Francisco and Monterey. All movements were closely watched by the Spaniards. In April, 1809, the *Mercury* was hunting with twenty-four canoes opposite San Juan Capistrano. The next month Eayrs received a very direct letter from Francisco Javier Alvarado, *co-misionado* of Los Angeles, "I ask that as soon as you see this, you retire from this coast with your frigate and people who accompany you."[25] Eayrs obeyed shortly afterward but not before obtaining a cargo of 2,117 skins.[26]

Captain Eayrs made a second otter-hunting contract in the fall of 1809. His chief purpose, however, was to trade covertly for supplies for the Russians. As a supplementary activity he obtained otter skins both by hunting and bartering. On this trip the Boston captain received "several letters from the head People and Padres of California intreating me to bring them many Articles that they were in distress for and could not obtain from the Continent."[27]

A new Yankee-Russian intrusion into Spanish otter fields occurred in the years 1810, 1811, and 1812. The *O'Cain*, sent back by the Winships under Captain Jonathan Winship, Jr., arrived first in the North Pacific to equip for a southern cruise. In December, 1809, Baranov agreed to supply fifty baidarkas and the necessary hunters.[28] Captain Davis of the *Isabella*, who was along the Lower California coast in the summer of the same year, formed a definite contract in June, 1810, for forty-eight baidarkas and Aleuts under the command of the experienced Tarakanov.[29] Captain Eayrs also negotiated with the Russians about the same time and returned the latter part of 1810 with more hunters and with farming implements and other articles to meet the distress call of the "head People and Padres" of California.[30] Lastly, the *Albatross* was again on the scene in 1810. In July and August, before proceeding to the Northwest, the vessel sailed along the California coast and left parties of sealers on the Farallons and Cerros Island. However, Captain Nathan Winship could not catch the numerous otters in the kelp and about the shores of Santa Barbara Island because he had no Aleuts.[31] By November Winship had obtained what he lacked from the Russians and was California bound with some fifty hunters.[32] Thus, four Boston vessels from the Russian north were assembled on the Spanish coast in the fall of 1810.

Hunting activities became bolder. The *O'Cain* cruised along the Lower California coast. The *Isabella* made Bodega its base during September and October. But while the American crew passed the time comfortably in three huts on the beach, Aleuts were doing the daring work. The coast between Bodega and San Francisco was the field of the first hunt. Then canoes entered the Golden Gate. In the middle of September over twenty baidarkas were seen going from San Mateo toward the estuaries of San Jose. A few days later three Russian otter hunters were seized in those same estuaries. On September 24 seven Aleuts were imprisoned in San Francisco presidio and were still there the last of December. In late September, when the *alférez*, Gabriel Moraga, journeyed to Bodega, two Aleuts who came to meet him complained that soldiers had killed nine of their companions when they had been hunting in San Francisco Bay. Early in October five more hunters were captured there.[33]

All four of the contract vessels were anchored in Drake's Bay the last of November, 1810. Just before the *Albatross* arrived on the twenty-ninth, the canoes of the *Isabella* and *O'Cain* were worrying the Spaniards. Mission Indians had reported the presence of two large vessels. A Spanish lieutenant told of seeing thirteen canoes in San Francisco Bay between the estuaries of San Mateo and San Bruno, and an Indian informed him that on that same morning twenty baidarkas had left the small island off Point San Mateo. On the afternoon of the twenty-fifth two lads who were fishing near San Francisco found a note on the end of a stick which was thrust into the sand. It was from a certain "Guillermo," no doubt William Davis of the *Isabella,* and was addressed to Commander Luis Antonio Argüello. That was the Boston man's method of meeting the Spaniard. "Guillermo" begged Argüello to return to him "the poor Indians" whom he held at the presidio, because they had entered the bay "without his knowledge."[34]

William Dane Phelps's account, based upon the journal of the *Albatross,* describes the general movements of all three vessels while they were engaged in seal and otter hunting in 1810 and 1811.

Dec. 4th, the ship being off the Farallones, they communicated with the party on the island and found they had obtained 30,000 fur seal skins since they had been left there, five months since. The gang was increased by six Sandwich Islanders, and the ship bore away for St. Louis Obispo, to wood and water and procure beef of the Spaniards. A party of hunters, with their canoes and women, were left at the island of Santa Barbara to take otter. During the three days they were left here the hunters took about sixty prime sea otter skins. The ship then proceeded to St. Quintin, where she again joined the O'Cain. The hunters of this ship during her absence, had taken 1,600 sea otter skins and were still doing well. It seems that the two captains Winship pursued their business of hunting and trading on joint account, in different directions, and with gangs on various Islands, the ships moving between the points of observation, supplying their wants and collecting the proceeds of the parties. Many furs were also obtained from the Spanish Missions in Lower California.[35]

In the spring the three Boston vessels again shifted hunting activities to the north. The *Albatross* was first to leave the Lower California coast on April 1, 1811. Proceeding directly to the Farallons, the Boston men found that the party left there had taken about four thousand seals. After taking aboard the furs and supplying the men on the island, they sailed to Drake's Bay. A few days later, on May 11, the *Albatross* was joined by the *O'Cain* and *Isabella*.[36]

For one month Drake's Bay was used again as the base of activities for the three vessels. Canoes took provisions to the sealers stationed on the Farallons and brought back furs. No otter had a chance along the coast from Bodega to Point Pillar, south of San Francisco. Besides the Aleutian hunters of the Boston men, there were those from the Russian vessel *Chirikov*, anchored at Bodega under the command of Ivan Kuskov. On May 30 Indian neophytes reported to Argüello that one hundred and thirty canoes were operating between Bodega and San Francisco. Also baidarkas were seen near the vicinity of Points San Pedro and Pillar. The commander immediately sent troops from the presidio with orders to march along the coast and, "if there were such canoes, to surprise them because just at nightfall they would come to land on those beaches."[37] However, after a few days the men returned without having seen any sign of canoes. Once again baidarkas slipped into and around the edges of San Francisco Bay. When Kuskov's hunters entered in May, sixty baidarkas from the *Albatross* and forty-eight from the *Isabella* were operating in the harbor.[38] Aleuts belonging to the *Isabella* encountered the Spaniards, face to face.

Davis, according to Antonio María Osio, offered three thousand pesos to Argüello for permission to bring his hunters into San Francisco Bay. The Spaniard emphatically refused. Thereupon, Davis ordered all his canoes inside. In spite of the shots fired from the presidio to frighten them, the canoes kept on. Osio continues the story.

> When it was known that the canoes were always constructed of sea-lion skins and that they had to be taken from the water to be dried and smeared with oil, a soldier was put on guard. At the end of a few days he came with the communication that at twilight, in one of the most sheltered coves below the hill of San Bruno, the hunters had landed with some canoes.
>
> Upon the continuation of the communication, Alférez Don José Sánchez later left with twenty men who, after having approximated where the Kodiaks were, landed and, without being heard and in spite of the watchfulness of the Indians, went hunting for them above the wall of the cove. When they were within gunshot, and although the night was dark, all fired at the most visible objects. This resulted in killing two Kodiaks, and it was not known how many fled wounded, because immediately they embarked and left the shore. Two canoes were left on land because of the load of skins which they had and which one man alone could not move upon the water.[39]

Phelps, who had at hand only the logs of the three vessels concerned when he was writing an account of their activities along the California coast, could not understand why they chose Drake's Bay as the base of their hunting rather than the much safer San Francisco. Because even the name of the latter was not mentioned in the journals, he concluded that "it could not have been entered by either the ships or their boats." He finally ventured an explanation: "The supposition is that our American ships in trading and hunting on the coast, were doing what the Spaniards might consider a contraband business, and, therefore, to avoid a controversy with them, it was best to always have plenty of sea room."[40] Baranov expressed high satisfaction at the returns of the contracts of 1811. A total of 8,118 otter skins, including prime, yearlings, and pups, besides some otter tails, were obtained from California.[41] However, in a letter to John Jacob Astor the Russian governor added the significant statement that the Boston men "did not return without a small loss of men."[42]

While the three Boston ships were sailing across to the Canton market in 1812, others, likewise under contracts, entered Spanish seas. Baranov made two arrangements for California hunting voyages the latter part of 1811, one with William Blanchard of the *Katherine,* who was given fifty baidarkas, and another with Thomas Meek of the *Amethyst,* who received fifty-two canoes. From June to August, 1812, both vessels were hunting along the Lower California coast.⁴³ In 1812 the *Charon,* also under a contract and commanded by Captain Isaac Whittemore, left a sealing party at the Farallon Islands and then cruised along the coast to San Quintín.⁴⁴ Each of the captains mentioned above shared with the Russians from fourteen hundred to eighteen hundred skins.⁴⁵

Both Boston man and Russian had profited from the contract system of trade. The Angloman, in the face of Spanish law enforcement and because of his own lack of hunting equipment, could not have remained at that time in the California otter fields. The Aleut made it possible for him to establish a line of hunting bases, all removed from Spanish population centers. Bodega Bay, Drake's Bay, the Farallon Islands, the Santa Barbara Channel Islands, the bay of San Quintín, Todos Santos Island, and Cerros Island were such points, where seals were killed or from which the coast was scoured in all directions for otters. The Boston vessels were safe, always endeavoring to keep plenty of sea room. The Aleutian hunter, the tool of the Angloman, paid the penalty by seizure, searching examination, imprisonment, and life itself.

For the Russians the contract system was the means of hunting along the California coast at a time when they lacked transportation and when the finding of new otter grounds was of utmost importance. "Thus," wrote Langsdorff, "did the Russians endeavour to supply their want of ships and men, and to extend, by new means, the circle of their valuable fishery for sea-otters."⁴⁶ Furthermore, considering the Russian desire to keep the fur wealth of the Pacific from the Angloman, the contract system was undoubtedly a means of preventing their rival from having the exclusive run of the new fields.

INDEPENDENT RUSSIAN OTTER HUNTING, 1809–1823

By the opening of the nineteenth century, Alexander Baranov, lord of the North Pacific, was rapidly realizing his vision of a Russian Pacific Empire. His bold seamen were pushing ever southward along the Alaskan coast "in search of many gilded hides," as Baranov himself wrote in his celebrated song paying tribute to the spirit of the Russian sea hunters.[47] Nine years before the founding of Fort Ross, they entered the distant waters of Spanish California. True, the Russians were helped at first in their southward drive by the American trader, but the far-visioned governor had been using the contract system only as a means to an end. Russia's program in the Pacific demanded independent action and the ultimate extrusion of foreigners from the fur fields.[48]

Carefully Baranov had prepared the way for independent otter hunting in California. He determined "not to divide the profits of this business with anybody"[49] and "waited only for a chance to go there in person on some sea-otter expedition."[50] Looking to the future, the governor had given specific instructions in 1803 to Shvetsov and in 1806 to Slobodchikov, Russian directors of the hunters sent on the *O'Cain,* to make detailed observations of the quantities and habitats of valuable marine animals. Further information concerning the wisdom of engaging in the California otter trade was obtained as a result of the Rezanov expedition. Langsdorff was of the opinion that "a very advantageous trade might be established" in otter skins, although it was "very questionable whether the Spaniards would ever be brought to consent to such trade."[51].Furthermore, five years before the establishment of Fort Ross, the Russians knew, through the experiences of Tarakanov on the *Peacock,* of the value of Bodega Bay as a base sufficiently removed from Spanish centers.

The first independent hunting expedition of the Russians to California arrived in 1809. Kuskov, Baranov's trusty "co-laborer," was in command. Two vessels started from Sitka in October, 1808, but one was shipwrecked near the Columbia. The *Kodiak,* Captain Petrov, touched at Trinidad to look for sea otters, but, finding none, it sailed on to Bodega Bay. Temporary buildings were erected. According to the Spanish record, one hundred and thirty hunters, twenty native women, and forty Russians came on the vessel.

A new and safer approach was found to the rich otter field of San Francisco Bay on this first expedition. Marin Peninsula became a portage. Landing near Point Bonita, north headland of the Golden Gate, the Aleuts shouldered their canoes and tramped across the country to the bay. In February, 1809, about fifty canoes were seen landing at the northern end of the harbor in order to make the portage west.[52] As soon as the forbidden waters were entered, troubles began. Early in February skin craft were moving around Angel Island. One Aleut who landed was seized by San Francisco neophytes and brought to the presidio. Baidarkas were skulking around the southern shores of the bay during the last of March. On the twenty-sixth twenty canoes came ashore and seventeen men landed. A Spanish sergeant and eight soldiers hurried to the spot. Firing occurred, and, as the hunters fled, four were killed and two wounded. Careful treatment was given the latter, but the troops were ordered to be in readiness in the event that the crew of the large Russian vessel should attempt to take any means of revenge. In April canoes were still in the bay near Yerba Buena. The *Kodiak* did not leave Bodega until August when it took back to Baranov over two thousand skins.

A second otter expedition was supervised by Kuskov in 1811. The hunters on the *Chirikov* found very few skins along the coast near Bodega. Consequently, in May, while Kuskov was making observations in connection with the future settlement, twenty-two baidarkas were sent to San Francisco. These canoes with those of the three Boston contract vessels then anchored at Drake's Bay made a total of about one hundred and forty canoes hunting in the port at one time. Spanish officials employed a most effective method of handling the situation. Sentries were stationed at all wells and springs where the Aleuts obtained water. As a result, "the party was compelled to go away."[53] Aleuts were sent to the Farallons for a supply of sea-lion meat, and then the *Chirikov* sailed for the north in June with 1,160 prime skins and 78 yearlings.[54]

The next step in the Russian advance into California otter fields was the establishment of a hunting base. Dependence upon foreign vessels had become undesirable and unnecessary. Hunting in or south of San Francisco Bay was both impossible and unpolitic. In the first place, Spanish tactics had put a stop to activities in the bay. Furthermore, the desire of the Russians for some commercial arrangement with Spanish Californians caused them to consider it best to avoid all occasion for offense.[55] As Lieutenant Kiril Khlebnikov, agent of the Russian American Company, explained, "At the harbor of San Francisco the Spaniards kept strict watch and allowed no hunters to enter, and in order to retain their friendship we had to abstain from all attempts to visit that place for the purpose of hunting."[56] The pursuit of the otter north of the Spanish settlements from a permanent California base was the only form of independent hunting which could continue.

Fort Ross, therefore, was a center for sea otter hunting as well as for supplies.[57] Shortly after the construction of the new establishment was begun in the spring of 1812, Kuskov sent out hunters in the forty baidarkas brought on the *Chirikov*. Whenever Aleuts could be spared, they left on hunting expeditions, going up the coast as far as Cape Mendocino but rarely farther south than Drake's Bay.[58] Apparently a few skins were obtained by bartering with California natives, because a Spanish soldier later testified that, after the founding of the Russian settlement, Indians no longer brought their skins to the presidio.[59] Also, there is little doubt that hunting was carried on in San Francisco Bay in 1813 and 1814 when boats were allowed to enter for supplies. Khlebnikov stated that, whenever the Russians went to trade, they always took Aleutian hunters and sometimes obtained a few skins.[60] In 1813 four Aleuts were detained at the presidio, according to Kuskov, "without the least cause."[61]

Although extremely successful in sealing on their lonely outpost at the Farallon Islands, the Russians found that otter hunting along the Spanish coast was not easy to continue upon an independent basis. After 1813 Russian otter hunters began to try to extend their activities farther from their California base. In 1814 the *Ilmen* came to Fort Ross with supplies and with fifty Aleuts under Tarakanov. A hunting trip to the north was unsuccessful because of hostile natives. The vessel then sailed down the coast. For two days Aleuts hunted around the Farallon Islands. Then the captain ordered them to slip into the bay at night. Tarakanov tells what happened.

> The Aleuts did so and hunted all day, killing about 100 sea otter, but when we went to the beach on the south side to camp for the night we found soldiers stationed at all the springs who would not allow any one to take any water. At this the Aleuts became frightened and started back toward the ship which had remained outside. It was dark and some wind was blowing and two bidarkas were capsized and the men, being tired with their days work, could not save themselves.[62]

The Aleuts who were capsized must have been seized by the Spaniards. In July, 1814, Kuskov was petitioning Argüello for hunters held at the presidio, explaining that "they [had] done no wrong but were only compelled to save themselves from the surf in the bay at the port of San Francisco where they were captured."[63] The *Ilmen* continued to hunt southward, but the crew had learned to be on the lookout for the Spaniards. One night some Aleuts who were sent ashore for water were frightened at the sight of some soldiers and returned with empty kegs. Around the Santa Barbara Channel Islands one hundred and fifty sea otter and some fur seals were taken.

The day of reckoning was coming. Some Russian sailors, eleven Aleuts, and Tarakanov were ordered ashore to get some fresh meat. Seeing cattle grazing in the hills near San Pedro, the men landed. Almost immediately they were surrounded by Spanish soldiers on horseback. The frightened sailors pushed off without waiting for Tarakanov or the Aleuts, who were tied together with ropes and taken on a two days' march to Santa Barbara. There they were destined to work for two years and more before being released. Proceeding on down the coast, the *Ilmen* traded and hunted, finally returning to Fort Ross with almost four hundred otter skins.[64]

The *Ilmen* in 1815 experienced the strict enforcement policy of the new governor, Pablo Vicente de Solá. Orders had come from Madrid to limit trade with the Russians to agricultural and manufactured products, thus implying that the chief concern of Spanish authorities was to keep the marine wealth of the coast from the hands of the northerner.[65] Solá was determined to enforce the law.

After taking on supplies in San Francisco in June, the *Ilmen* sailed southward to trade and hunt. In July the vessel was between San Luis Obispo and Santa Barbara. The next month eight canoes, commanded by Boris Tarasov of the *Ilmen*, came ashore in San Pedro. When questioned by the *comisionado*, Sergeant Guillermo Cota, the Russian made known by signs that he had been there before and that "his purpose was none other than that of hunting for otters."[66] Cota ordered him to leave and warned him not to return. At that time Spanish threats meant nothing to Boris Tarasov. On September 17 he again appeared at San Pedro and asked to speak to Cota. The sergeant made full preparations because, since the Russian's first visit, he had received orders from the Santa Barbara commander to seize any such intruders. Early the next day Cota ambushed his twenty-seven men. As Tarasov and his hunters approached, the Spaniard gave a signal. Almost instantly, the Aleuts made for their canoes. Blows followed, and several of the unyielding northerners were wounded and stunned before they submitted. Twenty-four of them and Tarasov himself were seized and taken to the prison at Los Angeles.[67]

At his trial Tarasov by signs disclosed further information concerning Russian hunting activities. He had been in charge of Aleuts left on the Santa Barbara Channel Islands by the *Ilmen*, apparently before it had gone to San Francisco. He and his men had been stationed on San Nicolas for seven months and during that time had obtained 955 skins. These skins were deposited on the islands where a number of hunters were still at work. He claimed that he had started to leave for Santa Catalina after he had been ordered away by Cota, but that contrary winds had prevented his departure. He had desired to talk with Cota concerning the return of his companions held at Los Angeles. Later he testified that he had come to San Pedro for supplies and to take shelter from the wind. He also stated that the goods found in the canoes at the time of the seizure were solely for the use of his men and were not for trading purposes. However, satin, coating, and rice were never known to be among the needs or wants of an Aleutian otter hunter.[68]

Others on the *Ilmen* had a similar experience in northern California in 1815. On the morning after the seizure at San Pedro the *Ilmen* put in at San Luis Obispo supposedly for water, but it was refused help. On September 21 a ship was seen off Refugio near Santa Barbara. The captain and the supercargo, John Elliot d'Castro, landed but left when threatened by Sergeant Juan Ortega. The commander at Santa Barbara, José de la Guerra y Noriega, the next day sent five soldiers to that part of the coast. When the men returned two days later and reported that the vessel had sailed, de la Guerra scraped together fourteen soldiers and again dispatched them up the coast. They were told to seize as many as they could and "even the boat if it could be done."[69]

Early the next morning the soldiers arrived at Refugio, where they saw the *Ilmen* anchored in the cove. They waited in ambush. Shortly twenty-two Russians and Aleuts came ashore with the object of killing some cattle. When the Spaniards sprang out, there was a run for the water. Seven were seized—Elliot, four Russians, one American, and one Aleut. The captain of the vessel escaped only by swimming; although fired upon, he was missed. Elliot tried to obtain his own release by bribery but to no avail. He and Tarasov were freed only after a trip to Mexico, and from two to three years passed by before the other captives were returned to their homes.[70]

Independent otter hunting along the occupied part of the Spanish coast suffered a check by the incidents of 1814 and 1815. Until 1823 activities were limited for the most part to the seas north of Bodega, in spite of the fact that otters steadily decreased with the constant hunting in that locality. Gervasio Argüello reported that most of the eighty Aleuts at the Russian establishment were out hunting at the time of his visit in October, 1816.[71] Ludovik Choris in 1816 claimed that Kuskov had been obtaining every year almost two thousand otters which were ordinarily sold to American ships.[72] In 1818 the *Okhotsk* brought fifty Aleuts and their baidarkas to California.[73] In the same year, according to Captain Golovnin, seventy-four Aleuts were sent to Cape Mendocino for otters "which are found between there and Trinity Bay [Trinidad] though not in great numbers."[74]

The few otters obtained south of the Russian settlement between 1815 and 1823 were hunted surreptitiously. While the *Kutusov* was at Santa Cruz purchasing supplies in 1818, four Aleuts in two canoes hunted "very cautiously in order not to be noticed by the Spaniards,"[75] and in two weeks they killed seventy-two sea otters, twenty of them in one night. In 1820 a Russian vessel, probably the *Ilmen* since it is described as an American bark chartered by the Russian American Company, cruised opposite San Francisco while baidarkas were sent into the bay to hunt. "The Aleuts remained away two days and then came back with only a few otters. They said the Spaniards would not even let them land to get fresh water."[76] The vessel sailed to the south and at one of the Channel Islands took on over one hundred otter skins. However, "Here our supply of fresh water ran short and as the Spaniards would not allow us to land anywhere we sailed northward again."

Realizing fully both the political and natural limitations of independent hunting from the Fort Ross base, Russian officials had begun, in the meantime, a movement for a legal entrance into Spanish otter fields. "If our American company had the right to hunt on the shores of California, it might obtain from there about twenty thousand sea otter yearly," stated Captain Golovnin after his inspection of 1817–1819.[77] The basis of all negotiations to obtain the "right to hunt" was a contract between Spaniards and Russians, whereby the latter through Aleuts would do all the work and give half the skins in return for hunting rights along Spanish territory.

The first proposition for hunting upon a share basis was presented to the Spanish governor by Lieutenant Yakov Padushkin in the spring of 1817. Solá received the Russian with all the fine courtesy of a Spanish gentleman but conceded nothing. He promised to use his influence in obtaining viceregal permission to break down some of the trade barriers against the Russians. However, Solá stated in a letter to Baranov that the Russians should first withdraw from California before he would feel justified in asking the viceroy for any concessions.[78]

In October of the same year Lieutenant Leontii Hagemeister while at San Francisco corresponded with Solá on the same subject and outlined definite terms for an otter-hunting contract. He explained that "desiring to show my gratitude, I take the liberty to offer . . . to furnish for the army at the very lowest prices such things for which they may have need,"[79] under the following conditions. Aleutian hunters were to be allowed to enter San Francisco Bay. All expenses of hunting would be borne by the Russian company. Skins were to be divided equally between the Russians and Spaniards. The Spanish share of furs was to be exchanged at contract prices for Russian goods. Hagemeister reminded Solá that California Indians were not skilled in sea otter hunting and that neither skins nor goods could ever be obtained by the Spaniards "with such convenience and with such small expense."[80] Again Solá refused to consider the proposition. Provisions were sold to Hagemeister, but the governor would not allow otter hunting. Permission for that would have to be obtained from the viceroy.

Semen Ivanovich Yanovski, who was appointed governor of Russian America in 1818, tried to break down the firmness of Solá. He sent him a watch and a large mirror "of Russian manufacture, which I sent for to St. Petersburg, expressly for you, to give you some opinion of the esteem and regard I have for you."[81] At the same time he sent his agent Khlebnikov with instructions to try to arrange a commercial agreement. The reply of Solá was typical. He was very appreciative of the gifts and begged Yanovski to receive in return some pheasants. However, it was not in his power to give permission for otter hunting.[82]

In the meantime, the subject of hunting otters in California upon a share basis had been taken to European courts. After his first trip to California, Hagemeister presented the situation to the Russian ambassador at Madrid: "We are desirous of obtaining permission from the high Court of Spain to hunt furs on the coast of California in company with His Catholic Majesty's subjects on equal shares."[83] In 1820 the Russian American Company asked Count Nesselrode, minister for foreign affairs, to procure for it the right from the Spanish government to hunt otters and to trade in California. In return for these privileges the company was even willing to abandon the Ross settlement if necessary.[84] Yanovski and Matvei Ivanovich Murav'ev, the next governor of Russian America, continued to solicit Spain for trading concessions but to no avail.

"The Spirit of the Russian Hunters" and the zeal of Russian officials had carried them far—farther than any other foreigners in penetrating the Spanish mercantile system. By their policy of independent hunting, they were getting otters, at least on the northern California coast, "without having to divide the profits with anybody," as Baranov had dreamed. Also, they were handicapping their American rivals, both by not providing them with Aleutian hunters, and by a supplementary policy after 1816 of not purchasing supplies from foreign merchants, who by this means had been obtaining skins indirectly from the great fur power of the Pacific.[85] However, to the end of the Spanish period, although the bars had been let down frequently to permit trading for supplies, the Russians were checked in their activities along the shores south of Point Reyes, and they never succeeded in obtaining the much desired concessions for otter hunting in California.

CHAPTER V

LATER YANKEE ENTERPRISE IN THE OTTER TRADE

From Russian Partners to Ocean Tramps, 1812–1816

NEW CONDITIONS in and around the Pacific faced the Yankee fur trader after 1812. First, his Russian partner of nine years' standing was beginning to launch forth on independent otter-hunting expeditions along the California coast. Furthermore, he heard of a sea war between the United States and Great Britain, of cruising English men-of-war, and of an enemy blockade off Canton. It would be risky to take precious Oriental and fur cargoes over the old routes. Clearly the time would not permit the continuation of business on the former contract basis. But the Yankee had a vessel which must be employed, and there were still valuable furs to be obtained.

Along the California coast conditions favored bartering more than they had for many a day. Before 1812 Californians as a whole had not coöperated with foreign otter traders. Since supplies came to them by the regular government ships from San Blas, there was no need for missionaries or civilians to encourage the Indians to hunt for skins. Furs could not be sold legally to outsiders, and moreover they brought very low prices when sold to the government or to national merchants, as might have been done after 1811.[1] However, irregular supplies following the outbreak of the Mexican Revolution caused the missionary, as well as all classes in California, to push an enterprise which was a sure means of bringing food and clothing. California was a product-hungry land, rich soil for a flourishing contrabandism. Most of the inhabitants practiced the philosophy followed by Governor José Darío Argüello, "Necessity makes licit what is not licit by the law."

The captain who first operated along the California coast in the new period, and upon a new basis, was one who was thoroughly familiar with the contract method of obtaining furs—George Eayrs. In 1811, instead of renewing his partnership, Eayrs arranged to continue in the fur trade as middleman for the Russians at Canton where the doors were commercially locked against them.

---

[1] For notes to chap. v, see pp. 200–205.

Under the new arrangement the *Mercury* carried a cargo of skins for Governor Baranov to the Orient and returned loaded with Chinese goods. At the request of Baranov, Eayrs brought a few of these goods to the new Fort Ross settlement. He was then free to dispose of what he could on his own account in Spanish California. Without Aleutian helpers he must exercise all his smuggling arts, but in those George Eayrs was not deficient. A tempting Oriental array he had—nankeens, silks, crepe, canvas, silk handkerchiefs, rose-colored mother-of-pearl, blankets, shawls, rice, and pepper. His presence on the coast was soon known, and people as far away as Cape San Lucas, entreated him to come because "they were naked and in great want."[2]

As he sailed southward, Eayrs took care to pilot the *Mercury* into quiet coves and roadsteads "where there were no presidios."[3] In February, 1812, the vessel anchored at San Luis Obispo where the mission padre purchased $1,384 worth of goods for his needy charges and in exchange sent aboard the *Mercury* fifty-eight otter skins, grain, and meat. The next stopping place was Refugio. José Bartolomé Tapia sent a pressing invitation to Eayrs to come to his ranch, because "I wish to talk to you."[4] A padre wrote that he was waiting at the rancho house where he wanted to dine with the Boston merchant and talk about "the news of Europe and of all the world, and we shall trade also."[5] One of the Ortegas purchased goods and wished "Don Jorge" a successful voyage and a quick return. The *Mercury* sailed on to San Pedro and then traded along Lower California. Eayrs was welcomed everywhere. In April the father of Mission San Vicente sent him dried fruit and a little coffee. From Padre José Caulas came vegetables and eggs, with a note: "Tomorrow I shall come to dine with you on your frigate."[6] Eayrs traded as far south as Cape San Lucas and sold the larger part of his cargo before he returned to Sitka in September, 1812.[7]

The next year Eayrs again agreed to take supplies to the Ross settlement and to proceed from there with Russian furs to Canton. California would be visited on the side. Leaving Sitka in April, 1813, Captain Eayrs first landed molasses, rice, and nankeens at Bodega and then continued southward to his old haunts. Shortly after the *Mercury* had anchored at San Luis Obispo in late May, an Indian brought a letter to Eayrs. Soon a padre, accompanied by some other men, came aboard. They entered the captain's cabin and later carried away about forty pieces of cloth and other Chinese articles. A few days later twenty-five skins, some hogs, calves, and vegetables were brought out to the ship.

In the early morning of June 2, 1813, the *Mercury* was riding at anchor a little to the south of Point Conception. Sailors were on shore filling up water casks, and the ship's carpenter was cutting down oak for topmast caps. Suddenly, a boat came alongside the *Mercury*. Fifteen armed men jumped out and quickly took possession of the anchored vessel. In a moment the surprised captain and his men were seized. Eayrs indignantly demanded to know the names of his captors and the reason for such untoward treatment. Captain Nicolás Noé, commander of the Spanish merchant vessel, the *Flora,* was the one responsible; in seizing the Boston merchant, he explained, he was merely exercising his rights as a privateer.[8] Later Noé testified that he had come out looking for smugglers after he had been unable to sell his own goods in Monterey, the inhabitants asserting that they could get commodities at lower prices from Anglo-Americans.[9]

California officials attended to the case immediately. Eayrs and the most suspected sailors were taken to Monterey to prevent any possible communication with Americans who were known to be on and around the Santa Barbara Channel Islands.[10] An inventory was taken of the *Mercury's* cargo, and detailed depositions were obtained from all parties concerned.[11] The wily Boston captain was very clearly on the defensive. His sole purpose in coming to California, he declared, was to get supplies before he proceeded to China with a cargo of furs for the Russians. He admitted that he had traded on the Northwest Coast for furs but "on these coasts he had landed only to provide himself with water and wood . . . and he had asked also for some meat and provisions."[12]

Contrary to this statement, one of the crew testified that it was the intention of his captain to run down the coast of California as far as Cape San Lucas "to see if he could sell other goods to the missions."[13] Captain Eayrs asserted that he had planned to put in for supplies at the legal port, Monterey, but that he could not on account of a heavy fog.[14] If Captain Eayrs had done so, it would have been the first time he ever had entered a main Spanish harbor. He declared that all his goods had been exchanged for money. Throughout, he loyally protected the many Californians with whom he had dined so often and who commonly addressed him as "Friend George." He emphatically declared that "he did not know the names of those with whom he traded."[15] One truth he did tell— he had never touched in any of the "ports."

Later, when fighting for his rights in Mexican courts, Eayrs changed his plea. He wrote to the viceroy in October, 1813: "It is true, I have made a little Traffic with the Californias, and have not the least wish to conceal my whole Trade in this six years, whatever damage it may lay me liable to."[16] He then proceeded to his new point.

From the highest to the lowest Officers on this Coast, has been the means of my makeing any Trade here, and have Intreated me to bring them things for the Cultivation, and other articles that they was nearly in distress for—I have supplyed the Clergy for the articles of Religion from their great intreaties, not being able on account of the Revolution on the Continent to obtain them—I have taken in pay Provisions and a few Furs, have covered many a naked one, and received the produce of his land in pay—I have no doubt but there is some in high Office here, should your Excellency request the truth of them, relate to You just the same facts.

In March, 1814, Eayrs gave the same explanation for his California activities to Benjamin Lamb, one of the owners of the *Mercury*.

The very Comedant of the place who seems the most devoted and has an active part is the very Government officer, who has not long since received pay to admit me to take on board Wheat, Beef and other Provisions, and did use his indeavours to get me at Monterey for the purpose of supplying the Coast.[17]

The captains of two Pacific Fur Company vessels were forced in 1814 by the conditions of the times to find some temporary employment for their ships. Both men were interested in and knew of the possibilities of the fur trade in the California field, for John Jacob Astor's vision of a new Pacific trade included the southern coast. In 1810 the great fur magnate had given to Captain John Ebbets of the *Enterprise* special instructions to make inquiry concerning the possibilities in Spanish America, and Ebbets had forwarded such information to his employer.[18] Later, when the Pacific Fur Company's vessel, the *Forester*, was being outfitted in London primarily to bring supplies to the Astoria settlement, Ebbets put on board articles considered suitable for the California market.

Early in 1814 the *Forester* put in at Bodega, where Captain William Pigot succeeded in purchasing 3,400 sealskins. Swinging to the southward according to the original plans, the *Forester* touched at various ports and easily disposed of many goods to a populace cut off from its regular supplies. However, Pigot was disappointed. He wrote, "I could have sold from fifty to sixty thousand dollars but unfortunately the very articles that was laid in for this Market does not suit at all." The Yankee bargain driver added, "What I have sold, I flatter myself, my friends will be satisfied with—and they may rest assur'd that I have shav'd the Padres well."[19] About sixteen hundred sealskins were part of the "shaving."[20]

With the sudden end of the Astoria settlement, the *Forester,* as well as the *Pedler* which had been at the Columbia, became a tramp by necessity. Pigot, determining "to spin this small Cargo to the best advantage,"[21] sailed to Sitka in March. At the same time the Pacific Fur Company's agent, Wilson Price Hunt, after concluding the Astoria affairs early in 1814, sailed northward, intending to make the voyage of the *Pedler* as profitable as possible under the circumstances. Without a doubt Pigot gave full information to Captain Samuel Northrop of the *Pedler* concerning the Spanish California fur market. All succeeding transactions would indicate that Northrop was directed to trade for furs along the southern coast and then was to proceed with them to the Canton market. Sealskins from the *Forester* and some of its fresh cargo were loaded on the *Pedler*.[22] At the same time Northrop made a contract with the Russian governor similar to that of George Eayrs. He was to sail to the Russian California settlement with supplies, which meant that seal and otter skins would be given in exchange.

After leaving goods at Bodega, the *Pedler* continued southward. On August 26 the vessel was off the cove at San Luis Obispo. Suddenly in the distance appeared a frigate flying the American flag. Both vessels sailed into the cove; then the strange frigate lowered its ensign, ran up the Spanish national flag, and fired a salute. The *Pedler* immediately hoisted sails, but two cannon balls stopped further attempt to escape. Shortly, twenty-five Spaniards came aboard and took possession of the American craft. The captor vessel proved to be the *Tagle,* owned by José Cavenecia, South American merchant.

According to the Americans testifying in the *Pedler* case at Santa Barbara, the vessel had come to California for two reasons— to get fresh beef and to meet a Russian ship cruising along the coast, to which it was to deliver the remaining goods on board— looking glasses, tea, sugar, coffee, glass beads, Russian canvas, cotton goods, colored thread, coating, blankets, sailcloth, trousers, shirts, jackets, flannel, velveteen, hats, and taffeta. The name of the Russian ship was given as the *"Mana,"* recently purchased from Americans, who called it the *"Lere."* This undoubtedly was the *Ilmen,* formerly the *Lydia,* which at that moment was engaged in illegal skin traffic with the Spaniards; it no doubt could make use of such goods as were aboard the *Pedler.* Whether the *Pedler* did intend to transfer its cargo or to trade on its own cannot be ascertained. In either event, skins were the objective. On September 9 Governor Argüello decided to release the *Pedler,* since it appeared that it had come only to deliver goods to a Russian vessel. Captain Northrop was notified "to set sail and to withdraw from these coasts."[23]

In the meantime, Pigot of the *Forester* was trying to make a paying voyage. After giving up his original idea of running the English blockade at Canton in order to obtain Oriental goods for Sitka and Spanish ports, he decided in the fall to take his rum and Irish linens to California. On the way to the south he "fully explor'd that coast," and bartered extensively in Lower California. After wintering at the Santa Barbara Channel Islands, Pigot left for Sitka in April, 1815, and from there wandered to Kamchatka with fur seals purchased from the Russians.[24] In December the *Forester,* under the command of Captain Alexander Adams, again appeared with a small cargo on the California coast. One incident of the voyage is recorded. On December 20, while waiting for the arrival of some beef previously ordered, the vessel was anchored at San Luis Obispo. At last on the distant mainland the crew saw several Spaniards, driving along a herd of cattle. Immediately, sailors rowed ashore, but "to our great chagrin we found it was merely a decoy, as directly the boat landed, twelve soldiers rode toward them, and had they not been very active in launching the boat, they would all have been taken prisoners; but fortunately they got safe on board."[25]

Several of the Winship vessels which had been engaged in the fur trade under the contract system returned to California as tramps during the war period. Until peace returned, when the Winships planned to resume the otter trade under the old contract system, the vessels were kept employed in various parts of the Pacific, with California and the Hawaiian Islands as main trading centers. Since none of the Winship vessels were seized or detained, references to their movements are few. The *Albatross,* which had been chartered to take goods to the new Astoria settlement, sailed south from the Columbia in August, 1813, "to run down the coast of California in the hope of meeting there some American vessels which frequently visit that coast to obtain provisions from the Spaniards."[26] One of the vessels which it expected to meet was no doubt its sister ship, the *O'Cain,* since the latter arrived at the Hawaiian Islands in November, "last from the coast of California."[27] In 1814 the *Albatross* and the *O'Cain* were trading again in California, as was also the *Charon,* under Captain Whittemore, brother-in-law of Jonathan Winship.[28]

Upon receiving news of peace in 1815 wandering American craft sped across to the Northwest fur fields. Some captains hoped to resume the contract method of obtaining furs in California. But the doors which had been partially opened to them as carriers throughout the war period were now suddenly closed altogether. The Russian American Company had decided that the exchange of furs for goods was disadvantageous, and it had issued strict orders to limit all intercourse with foreigners.[29] The new policy was in harmony with all Russian moves, which since 1812 were apparently directed toward the creation of a monopoly in the Northwest. Her practice of making a carrier of the Yankee, whether purposely or not it is difficult to determine, resulted in limiting foreign activity in the fur fields. That the founding of Fort Ross and the opening of trade relations with Spanish California contributed to that end may be deduced from a statement of Captain Pigot. According to him the new law of 1815, cutting off trade with foreigners, had been passed because "California supplies them with provisions."[30]

In 1816 Baranov bought very little from the fifteen vessels at Sitka and refused to have anything to do with most of them.[31] As a result, a few of the vessels in the Northwest turned to California as a provisioning base and as a supplementary fur field. Those who had hopes of becoming partners with the Russians were made tramps once again, forced to pick up furs as best they could by themselves.

Two captains sailed in company from Sitka on December 1, 1815. Captain Henry Gyzelaar of the *Lydia*—owned by Benjamin C. Wilcocks, American consul in Canton, and by his brother, James Smith Wilcocks—had just brought goods from China for the Russians but, except for delivering his cargo, he could do no business. The other, Captain William Smith of the *Albatross,* knew the California coast and without a doubt was instrumental in causing Gyzelaar to proceed southward. Also, Smith must have told his friend something about the great contraband center at Refugio. Both vessels, although separated by a severe storm, appeared off the Santa Barbara coast in January within a few days of each other. Gyzelaar, the stranger, was reported by the Spaniards as having landed in the Refugio cove "very confident."[32]

The *Albatross* was first seen through a heavy fog opposite the Ortega Rancho at Refugio on January 10, 1816. Immediately, de la Guerra at the Santa Barbara presidio was notified. With all haste seven men under Sergeant Carlos Carrillo came under orders to seize anyone who attempted to land. As the mists slowly lifted the following morning, the outlines of the three-masted vessel were revealed. In the afternoon the *Albatross* slowly proceeded in the direction of the presidio. Carrillo and his small squad followed on land. Some fishermen brought the news that the captain had told them that his name was Smith and that he was coming to the presidio to get provisions. Next morning the Spaniards were still waiting. The vessel began to move toward the anchoring place, when suddenly it veered about and went out to sea.[33]

In the early dawn on the fourteenth the *Albatross* appeared off Refugio once again. At eight o'clock a little pinnace, leaking very badly, pushed ashore with the captain and five others. Scarcely had they landed when four of the men were seized by the waiting Carrillo. That night at the Ortega ranch house Smith faced de la Guerra himself, and, with "some words and many signs," he signified that he had come to that coast only because of "extreme need, for meat and supplies," and that he had on board only about two hundred nankeens as an exchange medium. He explained then and later that he "was driven on the coast of California," and that because of the crippled condition of his vessel he had been afraid to anchor in Santa Barbara which he did not know. De la Guerra might have asked him why he chose to anchor in the unprotected cove at Refugio. When told by the commander that he should have gone to one of the legal ports of entry, the captain, who had been on the *Albatross* since 1809 and who already had been along the California coast six times, answered glibly that "he did not know that."[34] De la Guerra tried to make the captain surrender his vessel, but that he refused to do, declaring later to the governor that "I did not come here to smuggle, but, Sir, merely to get provisions."[35] It was finally arranged that Smith was to send his vessel to the Channel Islands but that it was to return in eight days to find out the governor's decision with respect to the seized Americans.

On the sixteenth, just four hours after de la Guerra had finished writing his report about Smith and the *Albatross,* another seizure was made at Refugio. Captain Gyzelaar of the *Lydia* landed in the cove. Met by the watchful Carrillo, he was asked if he had any goods to sell. No, the captain had none, but could he obtain provisions from the Spaniards? An affirmative answer served as a decoy. Conducted to the Ortega rancho, Gyzelaar found that, when he was ready to return to his vessel, he was held as "prisoner of the King." Although the captain swore that he came "only on account of the necessity of procuring meat and wood," and that his boat belonged to the American consul in Canton where he was going with great haste after hearing of the peace between his country and England, de la Guerra was not satisfied. "While the real cause which had brought them there was being investigated," he sent out a boat to the *Lydia* and had the entire crew arrested.[36]

Twenty-one Americans were in jail at Santa Barbara in the latter part of January, 1816—eight from the *Albatross* and thirteen from the *Lydia*.[37] Gyzelaar pleaded his case vehemently. It had been absolutely necessary to put in to repair after a "boisterous voyage" and to get provisions since he could get none in the Northwest. He was going to the Marquesas Islands before he returned to Canton and was "in a great hurry to get off" because "$90,000 are at stake."[38] Smith, too, petitioned the governor for release, by resorting to the old humanitarian appeal. "I assure you, Sir, that I have not bought or sold anything on the coast and have not invaded your laws, I hope, by stopping to get a little provisions to keep myself and people from starving."[39]

Spanish officials were active in investigating both cases. A detachment of soldiers remained at Refugio to watch for the *Albatross*. The *Lydia* was ordered from Refugio to Santa Barbara and then to Monterey. On the way north it was to look about in the Channel Islands, especially around Santa Rosa Island, for the missing *Albatross*.⁴⁰ Governor Solá rendered his final decision on March 9. Since the inventory of the cargo showed that there were only hatchets and adzes aboard, and since, according to all declarations, the crew had needed supplies, the governor considered the case similar to that of the *Pedler* and declared the *Lydia* free. His resolution was concluded by a repetition of former orders to all officials—to be very careful when ships arrived claiming to need provisions and to prevent any landing or trafficking in skins while such a vessel was in Spanish waters.⁴¹ The *Lydia* sailed immediately for Santa Barbara to pick up the American sailors left there.⁴² At about the same time, the *Albatross*, which apparently had sailed south to Cerros Island, arrived at the Hawaiian Islands where Captain Smith joined it a little later.⁴³

Two other American vessels came in 1816, supposedly for supplies. In July the *Sultan* appeared at San Luis Obispo. Needy Californians hoped that the governor would allow them to trade. De la Guerra wanted cloth for his soldiers "who are naked," while Padre Luis Martínez pointed out that the new arrival was a source of supply, if Solá only would permit it to come to Monterey. The governor consented and ordered the vessel north. However, the captain of the *Sultan* did not find the proffered bills of exchange sufficiently enticing. Although given a few supplies, he was told to leave and was warned not to go into any other port in the province.⁴⁴

On November 28 the Boston frigate *Atala* entered Santa Barbara from Sitka for supplies and repairs and was later sent to Monterey for examination. Necessity once again led to special concessions; Solá wrote to de la Guerra, "Supply yourself with all you need from the *Atala* but in a public way, so that it is not thought that it is being done in bad faith."⁴⁵

From 1812 to 1816, when a sea war and the end of the contract system had disrupted former business methods, Yankees had remained in the fur business as ocean tramps. By acting in the capacity of middlemen for the Russians, some found temporary and profitable employment for their vessels and were guaranteed a safe passage in time of war. Immediately after the conflict, when real efforts were made to resume former business relations, the American merchant was again made a tramp by an exclusive Russian policy.

On the California coast the merchant wanderer of the period had to turn smuggler. Since he did not bring Aleutian hunters to enable him to keep his distance, he was forced to make direct personal contacts ashore. Conditions both favored and hindered him. The lack of supplies during the Mexican independence movement disposed the California population to break the law. However, never had so many Yankees been locked in Spanish jails, appeared before Spanish courts, and encountered Spanish officials as in this period of California maritime history.

INDEPENDENT YANKEE TRADE UNDER DIFFICULTY, 1817–1822

Merchants hurried from the United States to the Pacific with fresh cargoes immediately after the conclusion of hostilities with Great Britain. The fur fields of California were the direct objective of a number of these fortune hunters. Knowing full well the outcome of previous trials at independent fur trading on Spanish territory, all of them anticipated difficulty. But, as always, the Yankee was willing to risk all for a possible gain, and California's reputation for furs had traveled far.

The *Bordeaux Packet,* Captain Andrew Blanchard, brought an excellent cargo from Boston in 1817. Sailing north from Lower California, the captain took the precaution to touch at only small ports. The vessel anchored on July 13 at San Juan Capistrano, where men from the mission promised to trade the following day. However, going ashore in the early morning, the Bostonians were detained by soldiers, "who were amusing us with a story of trade all the day." James Hunnewell in his journal of the voyage continues his account of their difficulties.

Finding they had a design to take me and the boat's crew, and afterwards the vessel, we put to sea the same night without any commerce with the mission. From St. John's we made the best of our way for St. Louis [San Luis Obispo] . . . where we anchored and the boat was sent on shore, but no human being was found. Next morning sent our interpreter to the mission of St. Louis, when he returned with the answer that we could have no commerce with the shore, nor any supply of provisions, and that if we remained on that part of the coast there would be danger of our being taken. . . . Our crew now being reduced nearly one-half, and no prospect of trade on the coast, it was deemed unsafe to remain there any longer. The same evening we got under way for the Sandwich Islands.[46]

Captain Blanchard had accomplished nothing by coming to Upper California.

One Yankee distributor of Oriental wares, James Smith Wilcocks, brother of the American consul at Canton, attempted to enter California markets by ingratiating himself with the authorities. Wilcocks' business dealings with Spaniards before he came to California had not been pleasant. In Peru his vessel, the *Traveller*, had been fired upon when he was attempting to dispose of a valuable cargo of Chinese goods. After having repaired his boat at the Hawaiian Islands, Wilcocks determined to "try his fortune" in California.[47] Riding in with a storm, the *Traveller* put in at Santa Barbara on January 8, 1817. The clever Wilcocks began by pleading scarcity of supplies for which he offered to pay in money. On his guard, de la Guerra gave him a few necessities but notified him that if he wanted any more, he must secure permission from the governor.

Wilcocks apparently obtained the favor of Solá, for the governor purchased seven hundred dollars' worth of cloth for Guadalajara bills of exchange and commissioned Wilcocks to distribute it to the four presidios. Armed with a general passport from Solá, the captain as he went south sold goods which were very much needed. Father Joaquín Pascual Nuez of Mission San Gabriel wrote on March 17 that waiting for Wilcocks was making him a Thomas à Kempis, and that if the merchant did not come, "the mayordomos of the missions will be minus their sombreros as those which came in the *memoria* were only ten and they were moth-eaten."[48]

After going as far south as Loreto, the captain returned to Monterey in June with the explanation that he could not go to China because of all the delays. Being refused supplies and allowed only a limited stay by Lieutenant José María Estudillo, Wilcocks appealed to Solá. He made bold to advance his main point—that he had returned to California "with the hope that you might give me permission to buy otter skins in consideration of the good services which I have done for the Church and the State of California."[49] Solá responded promptly; permission to purchase otter skins could not be given, but Wilcocks might obtain supplies if he needed them. During the next two months the *Traveller* was again doing government service. It took supplies from Santa Cruz to Monterey, loaded lumber to be used for the rebuilding of the presidio at Santa Barbara, and carried grain from San Diego to Loreto. But there the *Traveller*'s journeys came to an end; on October 30 it was seized by one Francisco Ramírez of Lima. The charge was apparently that of engaging in illegal trade. Clearly, Wilcocks had traded on his own in California. Private trade by the padres of San Luis Obispo with him caused difficulties between the former and Solá for over four years.[50] Otter and seal skins were aboard his vessel at the time of its seizure. Further evidence that he had obtained skins in California was the statement of Camille de Roquefeuil when he visited San Francisco in August, 1817: "There were but few furs in the country, an American, who left Monterey a fortnight before, having taken away the whole stock."[51]

Both Wilcocks' ship and cargo were confiscated, in spite of the influence of Solá, who stated: "I had great regard for his person and good qualities."[52] The captain presented an eloquent defense of his actions, as follows:

> It is true that I have sold my goods in California, but in no other part of the Spanish domains have I done it, and I am glad that the guilt for this is upon myself, if it is guilt to give something to eat to the hungry, and to clothe the naked soldiers of the King of Spain, for it is well known not only in California but here in Guadalajara and Mexico that there was not one grain in Loreto for supplies on the first occasion that I was there, and that in that presidio and all those of California most of the soldiers and other people could not go to Mass because of lack of clothes, and that also the most Reverend Fathers had neither vestments nor ornaments appropriate for the use of the churches, nor tools to till the fields. Finally, my venerable Sir, it seems to me that all that I have done is good, and if I have transgressed against the laws, the services done for the Crown of Spain at least can offset the crime.[53]

William Heath Davis brought the *Eagle* into the Pacific in 1817, and came to California in order to "secure as many sea otter skins as possible."[54] Although the exact date of its first arrival in California remains uncertain, the vessel sailed from the Hawaiian Islands for Chile on December 1, 1817, and left the California coast in August, 1818.[55] The first place of call in California was Refugio. Captain Davis was "very watchful and cautious" and did not know "how he would be received."[56] Venturing ashore, he was asked by some officials who were waiting on the beach what he wanted, and he replied that "he would like some beef for the ship's use."[57] Then Davis began playing his cards. Ortega was invited on board, was entertained royally, and given some choice presents, "which not only pleased him but had an excellent effect upon the Californians."[58] Likewise, Ignacio Martínez, commander at Santa Barbara, was graciously received on board and so highly feted that he was "overwhelmed by the kindness and entertainment."[59] One of the Estudillos purchased a number of articles including silks, satins, crepe shawls, fancy silk handkerchiefs, satin shoes, sewing silk of all colors, and beautiful objects of lacquer. Apparently Captain Davis scored for, according to the Pacific merchant John Meek, on this, as well as on each of the *Eagle*'s later voyages, "he realized about $25,000 profit in Spanish doubloons and sea-otter skins, from sales in California, aside from profits in the Russian settlements."[60]

A vessel on the same mission as the *Eagle* was the *Clarion*, sent out by Abiel Winship from Boston. Arriving at Santa Barbara on October 6, 1818, Captain Henry Gyzelaar, who retained vivid memories of his forced detention of two years before, assured de la Guerra that the main purpose of his voyage to California was to give notice of some insurgents (the Bouchard party) who were coming from the Hawaiian Islands to the coast. Also, the captain stated that he needed supplies before going on to the Galápagos. Gyzelaar's real object was not a philanthropic one, however; his true purpose is exposed in a note in one of William Phelps's log books. "Cruising on the coast of California they were able to purchase of the people on shore some furs very valuable in Canton, paying therefor everything they had on board, saving what was indispensable to the safe navigation of the vessel."[61]

Phantom vessels appeared and disappeared during the last five years of the Spanish regime in California. Vague presences slip into the records in the same way that they slipped elusively along the coast. In 1817, the *Avon*, Captain Isaac Whittemore, the *Cossack*, Captain Myrick, the *Enterprise*, John Ebbets, and an unnamed vessel came for otter skins. In 1818 the *Ship*, Judais Coffin, in 1819 two unnamed vessels, and in 1820 the *Arab* were on the coast for the same purpose. The Spaniards did what they could, the most severe punishment being meted out at Guaymas to Captain Myrick who "was captured ... for smuggling and thrown into prison, where he was confined until March 29, 1821."[62]

After dealing with numbers of "phantom ships," it is a great relief to find one whose name, purpose, and movements are definitely known. A rare logbook kept in detailed form by Captain Eliab Grimes for the voyage of the *Eagle* in 1821 gives firm substance to the incomplete Spanish records.[63] The experiences of Captain Grimes may be considered as typical of the many other Yankee captains engaged in the great fur game of hide-and-seek at the end of the Spanish period.

In method of outfitting the *Eagle* was a pioneer. It was the first United States vessel trading in California which is known to have been loaded by Boston agents at the Hawaiian Islands. Purchased from Davis and Thomas Meek by Josiah Marshall and Dixey Wildes, two outstanding Boston merchants associated in Pacific business, it had been intended for the Northwest Coast trade. However, both Captain Grimes and John Coffin Jones, a resident agent of the owners at the Islands, decided that the schooner was much better fitted for trade along the California coast. After much difficulty in finding suitable commodities for the California market, Jones and Grimes placed a $10,000 cargo aboard the *Eagle*. All concerned had high expectations. Jones expressed the "greatest confidence in the judgment, experience, and stability of Grimes," and was waiting for the day when he would "see him coming around Dimon [Diamond] Hill loaded with dollars and skins."[64]

After touching at Bodega for wood and water, the *Eagle*, on August 26, 1821, entered San Francisco Bay—not a common point of call for fur smugglers, at least not according to the records. Two officers came aboard and were saluted on leaving by seven guns, a courtesy which was returned. Several days of sociability followed. Luis Argüello sent a bullock with his compliments to the ship. Captain Grimes then paid his respects to the commander who "appears a fine looking middle-aged man, of easy and agreeable manner." The next day Argüello called on board and was likewise saluted on his arrival and departure. At another time he and several officers had tea aboard. Again, he and his family and one of the padres came for a visit, "but owing to sea sickness the ladies had to retire shortly." The bay must have been rough.

Grimes concluded by September 1 that, despite all his social efforts, there was no prospect of doing any business at San Francisco. He recorded several reasons in his log. A Russian ship had just collected about fifteen hundred dollars in money and furs, there was no money in circulation because "the troops have not been paid off for the last ten or twelve years," and, lastly, "there having been but few traders here for several years back, they have neglected the taking of sea otters as the skins frequently have spoiled on their hands."

The information that a Spanish letter of marque was on the coast haunted Grimes as he went southward. On September 5 he ran close in to San Luis Obispo but, seeing a large ship at anchor, he bore away. The incident found its way into the Spanish records. Solá on the seventh notified the commanders at Santa Barbara and San Diego that "a boat" had been seen off San Luis Obispo but that it had left as soon as it saw the frigate *La Reyna de los Angeles*. The governor asked for alertness, and in a circular letter he requested the mission fathers to have horses ready for any emergency.[65]

On the very same day that Solá addressed his letter of warning to Commander de la Guerra of Santa Barbara, the latter was royally entertaining Captain Grimes who had just anchored his vessel. On the ninth he again invited the captain to dine with him. Goodfellowship preceded any mention of business among Spaniards. And the Yankee conformed to California custom. It was only "after dinner" that he "sent for the invoices and some samples of goods and sold him to a considerable amount."

Once sales were made to de la Guerra, the way was opened for trade with others; a stamp of legality had been placed upon it. One of the padres bought goods in exchange for skins, and then other people came on board to make purchases. On September 11, under the heading of "Remarks on Santa Barbara," Grimes slipped some advice into his log. "It would be advisable at this place to always deal with the Comdt. in the first instance as in that case he will lay no obstacle in the way of trading with others although he requires a duty of 12½ p Cent on all goods not sold to himself. These are free." He added, "At this place I sold more goods than I had any reason to calculate on and should no doubt have sold considerable more had I had the articles suited for this market, as many were wanted."

The Spanish war vessel still haunted Grimes. Finding that he needed water and "not knowing what reception we may get at St Diego," the captain directed the schooner to Catalina. Just after a launch had put off toward the island, a gun fired from the schooner caused Grimes to hasten back on board. There to the windward was a strange sail. "Supposing it must be the Spanish ship in pursuit of us," the captain gave orders to leave immediately. The next day they cautiously ventured back. Daylight revealed to them the same ship. It was "in the same place and she was certainly fixed there for ages past for it proved a large Pinacle Rock a considerable distance from the shore and when the Sun reflected on it, it had the appearance of a ship under full sail."

Throughout the rest of September the *Eagle* sought trade in southern California roadsteads and bays. On September 20 José María Estudillo at San Diego refused to be stirred by the old plea of need for supplies. After looking at the ship's papers, he informed the captain that, since the vessel had been at other places, "he was sorry to say he could not allow us to procure any." At least one Spanish official obeyed Solá's orders. On the twenty-third they "traded considerable" for skins at San Pedro but were "informed that it would not be safe to remain all night as the Spanish ship was expected that evening." An attempt was made to do business at San Juan Capistrano on the twenty-fifth, but the boat which had been sent out "returned with information that we could not be permitted to anchor at the present time."

Trade was continued with difficulty throughout October. At San Luis Obispo on the twelfth the padres declined to make any purchases because of continued difficulties between themselves and Solá due to their trade with Wilcocks four years before.[66] After the *Eagle* had traded "considerable" at San Pedro with "a prospect of doing more," a sergeant with thirty soldiers took possession of a certain bridge over which all traffic from the inland came. When bribes would not work, the *Eagle* again got under way, "leaving two persons on the beach, one with cash and one with skins."

On October 19 the dreaded Spanish ship was seen inshore. At the fateful moment the *Eagle* was becalmed while a light land breeze was taking the enemy ship along at a good rate. But "to our surprise it appeared to take no notice of us but stood along down the land without altering her course."

Pacific Ocean breakers checked trade with San Luis Rey. A messenger from the mission had traveled as far as San Pedro to tell Grimes that they "wished to purchase considerable goods." On October 20 the *Eagle* anchored in an open roadstead at Las Flores Creek, to which goods could be brought from San Luis Rey. A boat was sent shoreward and reported that someone was on the beach waiting for them, "but the surf was so high and broke so far from the shore they could neither hear him nor land." Two other trials at landing were made. The third time the boat was sent with "a hedge and warp to haul off." It had no sooner reached the first line of breakers, however, than it upset. All reached shore safely. With the aid of tackles fitted on another boat, three of the Yankees were pulled back through the surf. But two "could not be prevailed to venture," although some of the Kanakas which were aboard "were swimming to and fro continually." Rather than brave the breakers, the two preferred to go the twenty miles north to San Juan Capistrano in order to meet the *Eagle*.

At San Juan a little business was done with the same official who had refused to trade when the *Eagle* was there before. About one thousand dollars' worth of goods, among them many church ornaments, were purchased by the agent of San Luis Rey. After a day of trading, they "received a polite intimation from the officer on shore that it would be necessary for us to leave that place for the present as it would not answer for him to permit any further trade." The coast must be clear by the time any chance investigator arrived from San Diego, he could have added. Grimes obligingly left, although within a week, after a short visit at San Pedro, he returned. He had no luck at either place.

What would be the story of the *Eagle*'s activities from August to the last of October if based solely upon the Spanish documents? The mere presence of the *"Sigloe"* at Santa Barbara was reported by de la Guerra who had traded so freely. At San Luis Obispo the vessel was seen running away from the *Reyna*. Estudillo gave full details of his refusal of supplies when the *"Eglioe"* entered San Diego and also reported that it had been seen several days before off San Juan Capistrano and behind the islands off the coast.[67] Not one word appears concerning specific commercial operations.

Something happened at the very end of the *Eagle*'s stay on the coast to produce several lengthy Spanish reports on the subject, although there is no mention of the vessel's name. On October 30 the vessel anchored off Point Dume in Santa Monica Bay in response to a previous call for goods from Mission San Fernando. While waiting for the padres who were said to be on their way, Grimes transacted business with someone who had come all the way from San Diego with a bundle of skins.

On the night of November 5 a fire signal was lit on the beach, whereupon one of the boats put out from the vessel. It returned with the information that "the friar's man" reported that the padres had decided they could not trade since they could not offer sufficient skins and cash in payment for all the things they wanted. The strange man informed them that he had some money and was ready to do business.

The next morning "the friar's man and two or three others" were still waiting on the beach to trade. They sent a list of goods to Grimes. The Spanish records throw more light on the situation. A soldier, Antonio Briones by name, and some accomplices had decided to enter upon a venture of their own. Filling a large sack to bulging with stones, they put in a top layer of some one hundred pesos. This, according to them, was the bait used to bring the Yankees ashore to trade.[68] Six men, including the clerk and interpreter, were sent out with goods from the *Eagle*. Suddenly, when the money was being counted at the conclusion of the bargaining, "fifteen or eighteen persons who were concealed" rushed out. Four of the Yankees by some lively moving reached the water's edge and swam out to the schooner. However, the interpreter and clerk were seized and bound, and all the goods were taken.

After safely hiding their booty, the Spaniards appeared on top of a high cliff with the prisoners. From their safety zone they began bidding for a ransom. From three thousand dollars the figure was finally reduced to one thousand, to be paid half in goods and half in cash. Immediately Grimes acted. The whaleboat was manned, muskets and cutlasses were put in the bottom and concealed by cotton goods.

At this point the Spanish account and Grimes's log differ. According to the former, the prisoners were untied by one of the party who was drunk and were taken down to the beach. While the Spaniards were engaged in a great argument among themselves, "ten to twelve men armed with guns" came upon them.[69] Grimes wrote that the crew with guns rushed for the hill. In any event, the Spaniards, who were unarmed, fled to their horses. They reported that some guns were fired at them, but Grimes recorded that they went in great haste, "not even allowing us a shot at them" and leaving behind "three saddle housings, a quantity of potatoes and some trifles."

The aftermath of this incident is worth mentioning. The wetting which Grimes received in rushing to rescue the captives brought on an attack of rheumatism from which he suffered severely throughout his next voyage.[70] The implicated Spaniards were severely punished. Although they tried to keep the affair quiet, it came to the notice of the authorities a few days afterward. All the goods which had not been sold were confiscated. The sales value of the other articles plus a duty double the ordinary amount was to be paid by the offenders, who were to contribute the total amount toward the construction of the Los Angeles chapel. Finally, the two leaders were condemned to work in chains for six months "on the public works of Santa Barbara," and all the others involved were to be imprisoned one month.[71]

Financially, the returns of the *Eagle's* voyage were "as well as might have been expected," as Jones stated to the home firm. Grimes had sold only $1,938 worth of his cargo, which had not been suited for the California market. However, in return for that amount sold he received $4,292 in cash and $656 in skins. "This will give you an idea what may be done on the coast with a good selection of goods," wrote Grimes to Marshall and Wildes.[72]

Yankee traders had made some headway by daring to revert to the pre-contract method of obtaining skins by smuggling. Conditions were all in their favor since the local population, in the face of continued need because of the irregular arrival of the supply ships, was sorely tempted to disregard regulations. When Americans gave thirty pesos in exchange value for each otter pelt, instead of the usual five to nine pesos offered by the Spanish government or by private national merchants, business transactions took only one direction, regardless of the law.

Consequently, contrabandism was very prevalent during the last decade of the Spanish period in California. One smuggling center, the Ortega ranch at Refugio, was brought to light at the time of the Bouchard raids in 1818. Quantities of contraband were found—trunks full of silks, boxes with fine cloth, fancy handker-chiefs, and piles of silver and gold jewelry.[73] Padres, contrary to their early policy, were urging both Indians and Spaniards to hunt the otter, as a means of getting needed goods. They taught the natives how to build better boats and also "how to shoot and cap-ture otters in the best manner."[74]

Conditions at the time were favorable, but the way of business for Yankee traders was by no means easy. Enforcement of the law was continued by a number of officials, although it was not done consistently. Yankees had to know how to entertain royally and how to elude certain authorities. They had to run the risk of con-fiscation of cargo, and perhaps they would even have to take a ducking, as did Captain Grimes, in order to take on goods at se-cluded roadsteads.

As it was in the beginning, so it was to the very end of Spain's political control of California—foreigners driving into the south-ern otter fields were greatly checked in their business.

THE NEW CHINA TRADE, 1822–1835

Independent Mexico cast off Spain's mercantile system for a lib-eral commercial policy. For the first time foreign vessels could trade legally in California for otter skins. Contemporary with the commercial opening of the Spanish Americas, other conditions developed in the Pacific. A new trade order was inevitable.

Merchants who had been following the Northwest Coast–Canton path to fortune were faced by an especially critical situation after 1820. The North Pacific was becoming an inferno. Russians enforc-ing the ukase of 1821, angry Kolosh, and sharp competitors—one or all three beset the fur trader on every voyage. Also, the rapid decrease in sea otter numbers was diminishing the profits of north-ern expeditions. By 1830 it was reported that the Northwest Coast was nearly abandoned by Americans.[75] At the same time, in the Hawaiian Islands the decline of the sandalwood trade and a grad-ual glutting of the market with importations from the United States created a business crisis.[76]

The west coast of the Americas, under the circumstances, became a commercial objective. A gradual shift from the old Northwest field to the unbarred regions was inevitable. The newly opened markets from Cape Horn to the Golden Gate created a trade vacuum for Yankees in the Pacific. For the Russians on the Northwest Coast, the Fort Ross base served as an indirect means of continuing to obtain needed supplies from American ships banned in the north.[77] The California sea otter trade was affected by the new commercial movements.

The first move for readjustment of business to fit the changing times came from Marshall and Wildes, an important Boston-Hawaiian firm engaged in the Northwest-Canton trade. It was Eliab Grimes, seasoned captain and capable master of one of their vessels, who visioned the new system. He knew the Pacific and he knew California. He continually stressed to his home firm the increasing danger of the Northwest Coast. In spite of the difficulties encountered on his 1821 voyage for otter skins, Grimes became a California enthusiast. He explained to his employers that because of his knowledge of that field he had an advantage over their Pacific competitors. In order to keep secret some information concerning the California market "worth something handsome,"[78] he increased the pay of his clerk who had been formerly employed on one of Astor's vessels.

Marshall and Wildes apparently began to share Grimes's opinion of California. A letter which he received in the latter part of 1821 stated that they thought "something might be done on that coast."[79] However, they made the mistake, to be persisted in by many Boston firms, of not sending suitable goods. It was difficult for easterners to realize, in spite of repeated representations from their agents, that California had special needs—that it was not a land of savage Indians. An excellent cargo for the Northwest Coast came on the *Owhyhee,* which arrived at the Islands in December, 1821, but Grimes was "sorry to find none for California."[80] He was supported in his attitude by Thomas Brown, another employee of Marshall and Wildes, who wrote home that with a California cargo they "might have embraced that business to a great advantage and kept others out."[81]

Captain Grimes prepared to do the best he could. He decided to take the *Owhyhee* first to the Northwest field and then in the winter season to the south. In the meantime, in order to be "well provided for both coasts next season,"[82] he ordered from Canton about four thousand dollars' worth of goods—articles which "are wanted very much and may be got cheaper there than any where else."

After trading on the Northwest Coast from March to October, the *Owhyhee* turned toward California and entered San Francisco on November 1, 1822. Its purpose in coming was both to trade and to increase its meat supply. About twenty-five barrels of beef were put up during its stay in port. Also cloth, rice, silk, and other articles to the amount of $319 were sold to the mission and presidio, a few otter skins and bar silver being received in exchange. At Santa Barbara Grimes first encountered a difficulty with which all the merchants trading via the Hawaiian Islands had to reckon. Their hide-and-tallow compatriots were flooding the market with goods. Some of the very articles which Grimes had ordered specially from the United States, such as damasks and satins, had already been supplied. However, he saw that he had one advantage. Since his competitors were not connected with the China trade and came only for cow hides, he could trade with those who had otter and seal skins to sell. Grimes could not do much because of the nature of his cargo and the condition of the market. He brought to the Islands one hundred and fifty sea otter skins, only a few of which were obtained in California.[83]

Bryant, Sturgis, and Company, a competitor of Marshall and Wildes, now tried the California field. One of its vessels, the *Mentor*, after having difficulties in the Northwest, left the Hawaiian Islands for California in September, 1823. Most of its blankets and other leftover Northwest goods were delivered at Bodega to a Russian frigate. Almost $14,000 worth of goods were sold, and $2,995 worth of fur-seal skins received in partial payment. What the Russians refused to take from foreigners in the northern center of their colonial empire, they obtained indirectly via their distant border post. On November 1 the *Mentor* anchored at San Francisco, where it exchanged $568 worth of goods—hatchets, powder, wine, cloth, and rice—for money and four otter skins valued at ninety dollars.[84]

Well-satisfied with his California voyage, Captain George Newell determined to use the *Mentor* in the kind of business which had been begun by Marshall and Wildes. He would bring China goods to the "Spanish Main." He wasted no time. Arriving at Canton in March, 1824, he loaded and had returned to Monterey by June 15. Some $1,800 worth of goods were purchased by the mission, presidio, and individuals in exchange for $251 in otter skins and silver bars. Before proceeding on to Mazatlan, Newell both at Bodega and Monterey again did good business with Russian vessels.[85]

The agents of Marshall and Wildes continued to depend wholly or partly upon California and Mexico, "the Spanish Main," in place of former fields. In February, 1824, Jones urged Marshall to develop the trade further, because in case of failure elsewhere "an excellent business can be done on the coast of California and up the Gulph."[86] He added, "I shall be mortified myself to have Sturgis carry the day in the Pacific, which he will do if you retire from the ground."

For some months Grimes was unable to make any move because of lack of goods. Finally, in March, 1824, Captain Wildes brought a cargo from Boston. An invoice of $16,000 was placed on the brig *Owhyhee,* which Captain John Kelly was directed to take to the California coast and then northward if the voyage seemed feasible after he had obtained the latest reports at Bodega. From the Russians Kelly learned that, although American vessels were not being captured, they were still limited in their trade. He decided to turn southward and entered San Francisco on May 4. After collecting $13,000 in furs, silver bars, and dollars in various California ports, Kelly sailed to Mazatlan.[87]

By that time, news had reached the Hawaiian Islands that the difficulties with the Russians had cleared. Jones and Wildes decided to send the schooner *Washington* after the brig with all the goods—principally blankets and muskets—which they could scrape together suitable for the Northwest. Arriving on the California coast in August when the *Owhyhee* was in Mazatlan, the *Washington* traded on its own until September when the two vessels met at San Luis Obispo. The schooner transferred its Northwest cargo and received the funds collected by Captain Kelly from the Spanish Main "together with the small remains of his California cargo."[88] Then the two vessels parted. The *Washington* arrived at the Islands on October 29 with the total proceeds from both voyages to the Spanish Main. For the brig she had $5,000 worth of bar silver, $8,000 in specie, 110 California sea otter skins, and 4 mink furs. For herself the *Washington* brought $642 in cash, 500 sealskins obtained from the Russians, and 18 California sea otter skins.[89]

The plan of taking to the Spanish Main combined cargoes of

Chinese and Atlantic Coast goods to be exchanged for as many California furs as possible was perfected by Marshall and Wildes from 1825 to 1829. Each year from one to three of the company's vessels followed the new China trade route.[90] A regular system for obtaining Oriental goods was organized. About the same time that one of their vessels left the Hawaiian Islands for California, the first of every year, one sailed to the Orient for goods for the Spanish Main.[91] Special attention was paid to the peculiar needs of California trade. Chinese goods suitable for Hawaiians did not do for Spaniards and therefore had to be selected with care.[92] Vessels of small tonnage carrying small amounts of goods which could be quickly disposed of were preferable to larger craft.[93] Masters apparently had to possess certain temperaments and characteristics to qualify for the Spanish trade. For example, one captain, employed by Marshall and Wildes in the Northwest Pacific, was not considered satisfactory for the southern coast.[94]

Besides the two main firms of Marshall and Wildes, and Bryant, Sturgis, and Company, other merchant venturers saw possibilities in the Oriental-Spanish trade of this period. After the last of the Astor vessels, the *Tamaahmaah,* had made a most unprofitable trip in 1824 and 1825 on the old Northwest-California route, Ebbets and John Meek in January, 1826, decided to take the brig to China for a special cargo suited to the Hawaiian and California markets. In June, 1827, the vessel was in San Francisco.[95]

The *Nile,* of Perkins and Company at Canton, in 1825 brought Oriental goods to the Islands and then came on to the American coast. Bodega was its first objective, but supercargo George Newell was disappointed "in not finding the regular vessel there from the n.w. coast which comes down annually with Seal Skins."[96] The vessel entered the principal California ports, but sales were small although they "nett a very good profit."[97]

Several American merchants established in the Hawaiian Islands brought mixed cargoes of Chinese and United States goods to California and took in exchange as many furs as possible. William Goodwin Dana, with others, in 1827 and again in 1828, chartered the *Waverly,* but owing to the competition of the hide-and-tallow vessels he had difficulty in selling even the great variety of articles which he had to offer. In order to make a paying voyage in 1828, Dana bought "everything that came along." Only a few casks of otter skins found a place in the hold, which was finally filled by taking on thirty-five horses.[98] Another Hawaiian merchant engaging in the same business was William French. Encouraged by his 1827 voyage on the *Kamehameha,* French purchased the *Diana* and brought a Chinese cargo to California in 1829. The same year the *Tamaahmaah,* chartered by French and John Meek, appeared at San Francisco with an assorted cargo.[99]

By the end of the decade a new commercial development in California somewhat modified the new China trade. Prior to 1828 exchange media in Mexican California had been limited in variety. Otter skins continued to be the chief objective as they had been in Spanish days, but owing to the increased numbers of vessels, as well as to the fact that until 1830 otter hunting was at a low ebb, the number of skins taken away per ship was very small. Specie or horses made up the balance of most cargoes to the Hawaiian Islands. After 1828, when the mission contract of the pioneer hide-and-tallow firm, McCulloch, Hartnell, and Company, expired, the multiform products of Mexican ranches—hides, tallow, soap, horns, and dried beef—awaited universal exploitation.

A great sailing-vessel rush to the California coast followed. The stream from the Hawaiian entrepôt to the Spanish Main continued and increased. Another line pushed up the Pacific Coast from the young Hispanic American countries. Around the Horn from distant Boston came others, bound directly for the California market. Considering the expanding field of exports and the great influx of vessels, what would become of the otter trade to China? Would the fine marine fur take second place to cow hides? And what vessels would get them if they were wanted, for very apparently even the hunting impetus of the 'thirties would not bring in enough spoils for all of this gathering of foreign craft.

The business intentions of the merchants who had been following the Hawaiian-Spanish Main route were soon revealed. Before leaving California for Mexico in May, 1830, Jones, owner and supercargo of the *Volunteer,* left instructions for the disposal of his cargo. He wanted John Rogers Cooper, chief exporter, wholesaler, and retailer in northern California, to collect both hides and sea otter skins in return for the goods left with him for sale, but he expressly stated that he preferred otter skins to hides and that he would pay thirty dollars each for them.[100] Later in the year, when the *Volunteer*, following the circle route, appeared again, Cooper received the same orders not only from those interested in the vessel but also from James Hunnewell, Hawaiian agent of Bryant, Sturgis, and Company, who on his own account sent a consignment of *aguardiente*, the proceeds of which he wanted if possible in otter skins.[101] Whether the *Volunteer* had any otter furs among the hides which it took to South America is not known. Three years later, however, Cooper reported that the net returns of $379 from Hunnewell's *aguardiente* would be remitted mostly in otter skins to Henry Peirce, new agent for Bryant, Sturgis, and Company at Honolulu, who would in turn transship them to James Perkins Sturgis, the company's Canton agent.[102]

Special requests from Hawaiian merchants for otter skins continued to come. In contrast to the full correspondence giving orders for furs is the provoking lack of data concerning return shipments. Four who sent invoices on the *Convoy* in 1831, French, Grimes, Jones, and Alpheus Basil Thompson, all specified furs as a remittance along with hides.[103] Jones stated directly his preference for the former. The only documentary trace of any otter transaction on this voyage is a brief entry in Thompson's commercial account with Cooper on October 12—"4 sea otter skins, $120."[104] The *Victoria*, belonging to the same group, returned the next year with 106 skins valued at $3,436, part proceeds of goods consigned to merchants at Monterey. Jones had instructed his consignees to exchange their hides for as many otters as possible.[105] In 1831 French, acting in his capacity as agent for the Boston firm of William Baker and Company, asked Cooper to collect hides and furs for the *Louisa* when it touched California on its way from Sitka. The vessel took back, along with hides and horses, four hundred otter skins, only part of which probably came from California.[106]

Several vessels of the Jones-Thompson-French group were on the coast in 1833. The *Volunteer* is known to have obtained from Mission Dolores between eighty and one hundred skins which may have been transferred before the vessel proceeded to Lima with its tallow. The *Loriot* was taking on "furs" and other produce immediately before its seizure at San Francisco in September. Earlier in the month Thompson, the supercargo, is known to have purchased five skins from Nathan Spear, merchant at Monterey. When the schooner *Harriet Blanchard* sailed in November, it had "a number of fine otter skins." Before leaving, Jones agreed to receive otters at forty dollars each from Cooper on account of money owed. Prices were going up, forty dollars being the highest recorded price offered up to that time. Twice the next year Jones urged Cooper to collect as many skins as possible for him.[107]

William Sturgis Hinckley, rising Hawaiian merchant, picked up as many otter furs as he could on various voyages to the coast. In 1832 Spear, with whom he did most of his business, consigned to him on the *Crusader* the skins of 93 grown otters and 3 pups, worth altogether $3,065. In 1833 Hinckley, purchased $429 worth of otter skins from Spear. The next year the *Don Quixote,* owned by Hinckley, Peirce, John and Thomas Meek, and others, was on the lookout for otter pelts; it picked up five at San Francisco to add to its hide-and-tallow cargo. Hinckley is recorded as purchasing six otter skins from Spear and thirteen more from another merchant when he was on the coast in 1835, both lots being shipped along with hides and horses on one or both of his two vessels, the *Clementine* and *Avon.*[108]

Others besides Hawaiian merchants sought to collect otter furs in the course of their trade for rancho products. Bryant, Sturgis, and Company after 1824 had ceased to send vessels to the coast exclusively for otter skins. One of their fur ships, the *Griffon,* came to California as a matter of chance in 1828.[109] However, the firm in the course of its hide-and-tallow trade with California continued to deal in otter skins.

Shortly after the arrival in 1829 of the *Brookline,* a vessel sent by Bryant and Sturgis for hides, the supercargo wrote Cooper that he wanted otters at twenty-five dollars each.[110] A few skins were picked up by the *Brookline* before it sailed homeward. Alfred Robinson, the company's California agent, slowly added to the collection until by July, 1831, he had enough to make up a consignment to Russell and Company, Canton agents for Bryant and Sturgis. Four hundred and seventy-eight skins, well packed in nine casks and carefully assorted according to size, were freighted at the rate of ten dollars per cask on the Hawaiian sloop, *William Little,* and from the Islands they were reshipped by Peirce to Canton.[111]

While managing the hide business of Bryant, Sturgis, and Company, Robinson succeeded for a while in collecting enough otter furs to make annual consignments to the Orient. In October, 1832, the *Plant* took 316 skins to the Hawaiian Islands for transshipment before it sailed on to Boston with hides.[112] Late the following year 114 prime otter skins packed in two casks and valued at $3,420 were freighted aboard the Hawaiian cutter *Maraquita*.[113]

As a result of the commercial opening of the Spanish Americas and contemporary difficulties on the Northwest Coast, a new foreign movement for California otters had been set in force. The great trade circle of the Pacific, rather than passing to northern waters, swung from the Hawaiian Islands toward and down the Pacific Coast of Spanish America and back to the mid-ocean entrepôt. Combined Oriental and United States cargoes, made up at the Hawaiian center, were exchanged in California, both at Spanish centers and at the Russian base, for as many furs as possible.

When rancho products took first place among exports, the new China trade continued but was changed. Vessels of Hawaiian merchants with the same mixed cargoes followed the same circular route, but because of the increased competition they came no longer exclusively for otter skins. Nevertheless, California furs continued to go to China. Hawaiian merchants stowed with their hide cargoes as many furs as they could get and transshipped them at the Islands as before. By making use of the same Hawaiian stream of vessels, the first Boston hide-and-tallow firm had also continued in the fur business.

CHAPTER VI

OTTER HUNTING UNDER THE MEXICAN REGIME

THE EVOLUTION OF A HUNTING POLICY IN MEXICAN CALIFORNIA, 1823–1831

ALTHOUGH sea otter traders benefited from Mexico's commercial policy, foreign otter hunters did not experience so revolutionary a change. Until the central government determined upon a definite national program, local officials handled the situation themselves, for the most part continuing to carry out the spirit of Spanish laws, while at the same time taking care of momentary exigencies.

The semblance of a guide to a national policy appeared at the very beginning of the Mexican period. It was the consummation of a move begun in the latter part of the Spanish regime. Fulfilling his promise to the Russians, Solá had presented the question of contract hunting to the central government. In December, 1821, Agustín de Iturbide referred Solá's letter concerning the matter to competent Mexican officials. By January a report was submitted. Beginning with a frank recognition of the fact that the Mexican government did not have sufficient ships to prevent clandestine otter hunting, it recommended that an agreement be made with the Russians for one year only, on the conditions that no settlement be established on the coast and that none of the mission Indians be employed in Russian canoes.[1] Although there is no record that the 1822 report was forwarded to California, apparently it was, since the idea behind it formed the basis of the actions of the first California governor.

Luis Antonio Argüello, acting governor of Mexican California, 1822–1825, entered into the otter business in a big way. Beset by financial difficulties and receiving little help from Mexico,[2] he entertained the possibility of supplying and paying California troops by bringing goods directly from China in a government vessel. It would seem that the idea first came to him in the course of talking to Captain John Rogers Cooper, who arrived on the coast in May, 1823, for the purpose of selling the remainder of his Boston cargo

---

[1] For notes to chap. vi, see pp. 206–210.

and also his eighty-three-ton schooner, the *Rover*, owned by Cooper with Nathaniel Dorr and William Blanchard, Massachusetts merchants.[3] On June 24 Argüello agreed to purchase Cooper's vessel for $9,000.[4]

In looking around for the necessary skin cargo for his vessel, Argüello apparently tried first to negotiate with the prefect of the missions, José Señan, for furs amounting to the purchase price. On August 5 Señan wrote that, although he "would get ready the $9,000 of goods" which Cooper had asked for the *Rover*, he did not believe the missionaries would see any benefit in the purchase of a vessel which "will be a source of continual expense."[5] Therefore, he could not comply with Argüello's request.

Argüello finally seized upon the plan of a Russian contract as the means of obtaining otter skins. According to the Russian sources, Khlebnikov was able to make the arrangement by "profiting by the confused condition of the California government."[6] Argüello's stated motive was first of all to supply the troops and next to prevent all the profits of hunting from going to foreigners whom they had no means of controlling.[7] In December, 1823, Argüello completed final arrangements both with the Russians and with Captain Cooper.

On December 1 the first Mexican-Russian contract for otter hunting was signed at Monterey. For four months the Russians were permitted to hunt otters and other marine animals anywhere from San Francisco to San Diego. Skins were to be divided into two equal parts. The Russians were to sell their share to the Mexican government at forty-five pesos for each skin and were to receive in return wheat at three pesos per *fanega*. The Russians also agreed to pay the Aleuts and to keep their baidarkas in repair. Provisions for the hunters were to be supplied by the California government, although the expenses were to be borne equally by both parties. If the contract was renewed, Californians were to pay the Aleuts at the rate of two piastres for large skins and one piastre for small ones.[8]

Only the general provisions of the final agreement concluded the same month between Cooper and Argüello are known. On December 29 Cooper by bill of sale acknowledged receipt of $9,000 for the *Rover*, and according to a letter of December 24 he had "at last received the pay of the schooner in seal skins," which apparently were taken from a Russian brig. Cooper agreed to remain on the vessel for the Oriental voyage, and some arrangement was made for giving him a regular salary or commission. The entire transaction had the approval of the provincial deputation.[9]

The Russians wasted no time in taking advantage of their otter-hunting permit. One group of canoes came down from Fort Ross about the middle of December, and these were joined the latter part of the month by others, making a total of twenty-five in San Francisco Bay. By January 4, 1824, only one month after the contract was signed, 455 skins had been taken in the bay. About that time, all the baidarkas returned to Fort Ross to be repaired.[10]

The returns of the first hunt were taken on board the *Rover* in San Francisco Bay the latter part of January. On the twenty-second Cooper received 100 skins from the Russian brig *Rurick*, and six days later 203 more were brought down from Mission San Rafael. The latter number was the exact quantity of skins due the Mexican government as its portion under the contract and may have been sent to the mission for stretching and drying. The 100 taken from the *Rurick* may have been some of the Russian portion which, according to the contract, they were supposed to sell to the Mexican government. When the *Rover* finally sailed from Monterey on February 7, it had besides the 303 otter skins, 300 tails, and 1,310 sealskins. While at sea, especially after leaving the Hawaiian Islands, the crew spent much of the time overhauling, stretching, and packing skins. A tedious job it was, for only seven skins were taken off the frames a day.[11]

While the *Rover* was sailing to the Orient, the Mexican-Russian contract plan continued to function in California. In February, 1824, eleven baidarkas arrived at San Francisco, and eight more were expected. All were sent immediately to San Pablo Bay "in order not to miss the calm days."[12] At the same time, Aleuts were hunting in Monterey Bay where 429 skins were obtained by March.[13]

Other contracts were made by Argüello with the Russians in 1824. Canoes were hunting in June, and a new contract was definitely made in August. Shortly afterward, Aleutian hunters went as far south as San Pedro. Twenty canoes entered San Francisco Bay from Fort Ross in November, and twenty came down in the middle of December. The total returns from the various hunts in

1824, not including those taken by the *Rover*, seem to have been 1,053 skins.[14]

In the meantime, Captain Cooper was trying to sell the fur property of the Mexican government in the Orient. At Manila, on April 26, 1824, he took on shore as samples four otter skins, four sealskins, and ten sticks of sandalwood which he had taken on at Honolulu in connection with his own business. A few days later some Chinamen came on board to look at and later to count and take off the otter skins. In return Cooper received among other things bags of sugar, baskets of panocha, bales of cloth, rice, and straw hats. Proceeding across to Canton, Cooper discharged his sealskins and took on other goods.[15] The otter skins and tails, at an average price of $24.50 each, brought $7,419, and the sealskins, $2,449, both together netting $9,299. The invoice of the return cargo of Chinese goods was evaluated in California at $12,781.[16]

Soon after his arrival at Monterey on September 13, 1824, Cooper prepared for a second trip to China. For over a month the *Rover* remained at Bodega to repair and to receive the skins taken in the vicinity of San Francisco. Only 112 were finally sent down to the schooner, however. Cooper promptly asked Khlebnikov for an explanation. The captain had been inquiring about the activities of the Russians, and although, as he stated to the Russian commissioner, he did not "pretend to understand the contract between you and Don Lewis," nevertheless, " . . . it is a plain and evident fact too notorious to be contradicted that there was taken by this expedition upwards of 700 otter skins in and about St. Fran. . . . the last information was that there was about 600 dried and on the stretch. It appears very mysterious to me that Don Lewis' part is but 112 out of upwards of 700."[17] Cooper explained that, unless 600 or more skins were obtained, he could not make the China voyage for the governor, and he concluded, "I have no doubt but you will come forward and divide the skins equally between yourself and Don Lewis."

The fur cargo of the *Rover* when it left for the Orient on March 23, 1825, was not as large as Cooper had wished. At Monterey he had taken on 265 additional skins and 263 tails, which probably had been stored in the government warehouse. The total was 100 skins less than what should have been the Mexican government's quota according to the hunting returns since the *Rover's* first trip.

At the Hawaiian Islands Cooper transshipped his otter skins to a Canton-bound vessel which was taking a few other furs and some sandalwood on his private account. For the purpose apparently of increasing the profits of the voyage, Cooper then made a side trip to the South Pacific to freight some bêche-de-mer from Fanning Island to Manila. Proceeding on to Canton, he obtained a price of $18.75 each for the Mexican government's otter skins, which yielded net proceeds of $6,677. Besides concluding his government business by purchasing blue and white nankeens, chintz, long cloth, and other merchandise, Cooper received a number of personal consignments from individuals and companies in both Manila and Canton.[18]

The second voyage of the *Rover* to the Orient did not prove a happy one for Cooper. When he arrived in Monterey on April 23, 1826, another governor, José María Echeandía, was in charge. Difficulty arose over finding proper papers to show that the vessel had been nationalized and properly sold, since for business reasons it was still flying the American flag. Echeandía insisted upon a series of judicial inquiries on the case. Furthermore, Argüello entered numerous complaints concerning the manner in which the voyage had been handled and made unexpected financial demands upon Cooper. Depositions, lawsuits, and letters heaped up before the matter was settled. Cooper's attitude toward his personal obligations in the Orient, insofar as they were involved in the case, was expressed in a letter of July 30, 1829. He would pay all his debts honorably "if I have to sell everything I have on earth but my wife."[19]

Direct participation by the Mexican government in the otter trade ended with the experiment of the *Rover*. Thereafter, also, a stronger policy with respect to otter hunting gradually appeared. Even before the *Rover* had returned from its second voyage to the Orient, the new governor had occasion to make a stand on the question. While Echeandía was establishing himself at his chosen headquarters in San Diego, José María Herrera, Mexican fiscal agent for California, concluded at Monterey some arrangement on account of the government with Captain Christopher Beuseman of the *Baikal*. The Russian, with his vessel fully equipped for hunting, proceeded to San Diego in November to take on grain, and he fully expected his Aleuts to pursue otters from that point. At the southern port the captain and governor met on board the *Baikal* and drank together a toast to the young Mexican Republic. However, upon learning of the nature of the arrangement under which the Russian was doing business along the coast, Echeandía was highly incensed at the man with whom he was to quarrel throughout his administration. He immediately canceled all agreements. In commenting at the time on the relations between Herrera and Echeandía, William Hartnell wrote, " . . . it seems that these two gentlemen do not like each other very much, for, as I see it, everything that the former does, the latter undoes."[20]

Echeandía took charge of the otter-hunting situation himself. He concluded a new arrangement with Beuseman "in order," as he explained to the minister of war, "not to rebuff completely foreigners who, trusting in the authority of the commissary, went to all the expense necessary to complete their bargain."[21] The terms of the agreement were much limited in scope. While the Russian was taking on cargo at San Diego and San Pedro, he might for that once hunt in the port of San Diego and its environs, meaning more specifically, according to the Russian record, between the coast · opposite San Luis Rey Mission and Todos Santos. One half of the skins obtained were to be delivered "under the good faith of the captain" to the Mexican government. Between November 26 and February 14, 1826, Aleuts from the *Baikal* in twenty canoes collected 468 furs. "The good faith of the captain" caused him to take into consideration the additional expense arising from the delay of his expedition, and on that basis Beuseman estimated that only 322 skins came under the contract and "of these he gave 161 to the government, leaving 307 as Company's share."[22]

The succeeding acts of Echeandía pointed to stricter otter-hunting legislation. Commenting on his agreement with Beuseman, the governor drew attention to the fact that a continuation of the contract system might be compromising, since both Mexican citizens and some foreigners were hunting along the Californias without any sort of license. Therefore, he recommended "an ordinance on the matter and some boat to cruise these seas."[23]

Apparently about the same time that Echeandía made his special arrangement with Beuseman, he also outlined and presented to Khlebnikov the conditions upon which he would grant another special contract to the Russians at Fort Ross. The time limit of the contract was four months, or until the superior government might resolve on the subject. In size the expedition was restricted to one brigantine and twenty-five canoes, and hunting was to be confined to the coast and islands between Santa Cruz and San Diego. Included in their crew must be ten California Indians, "so that they may learn to hunt," and also a Mexican officer. One-third of the skins were to be delivered to the Mexican government. It was understood that no pups were to be killed. Lastly, the Russian commissioner himself must remain on Mexican territory until the conclusion of the hunt and "answer for whatever abuse is committed."[24] Khlebnikov does not seem to have agreed to any such terms, probably owing both to their severity and to the fact that he was considering other plans at the time.

Not having made much progress in dealing with the Mexican governor, Khlebnikov had conceived what might be a way out of the difficulty. After the contract negotiated by Herrera had been canceled, Santiago Argüello, *alférez* at San Francisco, had presented some proposition whereby hunting was to be done under his citizenship rights by canoes and men furnished by the Russians. According to William Hartnell the contract was "conceived in such absurd terms that as I understand he [Khlebnikov] will not wish to accept it."[25]

However, the idea of using the license of a Mexican citizen to get California otters was later seized upon by Khlebnikov. In February, 1829, he approached Herrera with an offer. He would gladly supply him with all the baidarkas he might want if the commissary would take up otter hunting. He gave him a letter directing the commander of Fort Ross to deliver the needed equipment if the Mexican decided to try the proposition.

Herrera took steps to accept Khlebnikov's offer. He asked Hartnell and José de la Guerra to join with him for the purpose of financing a hunting project. It was suggested that the license be asked for in the name of José Antonio Argüello because he was "a Californian and more of a man than Santiago."[26] The proposition was still being considered in April, 1826,[27] but after that the records are silent. Probably the affair was dropped in the course of Echeandía's investigation in 1827 of Herrera's administration.

Not until 1828 did any Russian again solicit the Mexican government for hunting privileges. Captain Adolf Karlovich Etolin brought the Baikal in that year, principally to load with salt at San Quintín. He was fully commissioned by the governor of the Russian American establishments to make some permanent agreement for the extraction of salt from Lower California and also "an arrangement for the hunting of otter according to the mutual contract of 1826."[28] Etolin bore strict orders not to make use of the Aleuts on board "without obtaining permission."

On December 10 Echeandía conceded only temporary permission, "for this one time," to the Baikal. Etolin was to hunt with two canoes, "no more," and was to limit himself to the coast from San Diego to San Quintín, "without touching at the islands." The arrangement was to hold only "during the time the ship is taking on salt which will be from one to two months." One half of the skins were to be given to the Mexican government. Echeandía also appointed a special agent to watch over the activities of the Russian ship and to receive from it the specified legal dues.[29] An extract from the log of the Baikal indicates that the contract was kept by the Russians. On December 23, when the vessel was anchored at San Quintín, "the two baidarkas went to the point of San Martín to kill otters or to Todos Santos."[30] However, four Aleuts in two canoes could spear but few otters—only sixty-three up to February, 1829, while the larger vessel was taking on salt.[31]

Direct interest of the Mexican government in California sea otter hunting began in 1828 when a provisional hunting license was issued in Mexico City to two Englishmen. On April 28 Richard Exter and Julian Wilson were permitted to hunt for otters, beavers, and other fur animals in New Mexico and both Californias. Although the exclusive privilege for which the men asked was not granted, it was stated that Congress intended to consider the question. The giving of the temporary license was justified for several reasons, some of which indicate a close knowledge by federal authorities of hunting conditions along the California coast, contrary to the impression given by later correspondence. Such a license would serve to develop the industry in California and would be a means of bringing in revenue and of preventing clandestine hunting. In return for their privilege, the two Englishmen were required to obey the recent law providing that at least two-thirds of the crew on all coastal trips be composed of Mexican citizens; also they were to pay the legal duties on all skins.[32]

For some reason the Exter-Wilson concession created a great stir in Mexico and eventually led the central government to give more serious attention to California otter hunting. Newspapers in the capital city criticized the authorities for granting to foreigners what they understood to be a monopoly. In August, 1828, the president of the Republic found it necessary to explain to the California governor that the license was not, and never would be, exclusive to the detriment of Mexican citizens, "who do not need a special concession to hunt."[33] About the same time, in the course of the current discussion on the subject, Enrique Eduardo Virmond, outstanding Mexican merchant who traded to California, mentioned to the authorities that the ex-governor, Argüello, had made a hunting contract with the Russians as a result of which the otter wealth of California was almost depleted.

The possibility of an end to California's fur supply because of foreign contracts aroused the authorities to action. Although the secretary of the treasury recognized the fact that the report might have had its origin in opposition to the Exter-Wilson concession, he urged that an investigation be made and, if the statement should be found to be true, he believed that not only should the permit be withdrawn but also that a general prohibition should be placed upon all otter hunting for at least five years.[34] Apparently ignorant of what had been going on in California, the authorities ordered that the governor incumbent render a report on the otter negotiations of his predecessor, Argüello, and on "the measures which may have been taken to check this abuse."[35]

Before Echeandía received notice of the central government's new interest in otter hunting, he not only had concluded his special, limited arrangement of 1828–1829 with Beuseman, but also had made a definite stand with respect to the Exter-Wilson concession. Early in May, 1829, the agents of the two Englishmen arrived in California. However, they made little progress in their project since, according to Mariano Guadalupe Vallejo, "the coarse and rude manner which characterized them, and the arrogant and haughty tone with which they discussed the affair with the Californians drew upon them the hate of all of us."[36] Echeandía also showed his disapproval, so that the men were forced to leave the territory precipitately.

In his 1829 report to Mexican officials Echeandía reviewed

clearly the territorial policy of the last five years and repeated his opinion on the necessity of strong central measures to regulate otter hunting. Coming to the defense of Argüello, he explained that his predecessor had contracted with the Russians as a means of getting supplies for the troops, as Argüello himself had informed the Mexican government in two letters. Also, he, Echeandía, had permitted limited hunting to a Russian captain in 1826, and that fact likewise had been reported in a letter written that same year. On the whole, the Russians always conducted themselves "with the greatest delicacy and honesty," whereas the Americans hunted without ever asking for a license. Concerning the possibility of exhausting the otter supply by the contract system, Echeandía stated that marine animals of all kinds abounded in California in spite of hunting by the Russians, Americans, California Indians, and Mexican citizens. The solution of the whole question, as he saw it, was the establishment of a strict license system, which he had been endeavoring to introduce. Each permit should designate a time limit, a specified place, the amount to be paid to the government, and should contain an express statement that young otters were not to be killed.[37]

A number of factors combined about the year 1830 to contribute to the formation of what might be called a national policy in otter hunting. Echeandía's report was referred for careful consideration to Mexican officials, although apparently none of the former correspondence from California on the subject could be found. Also, definite laws concerning the coastal trade, which would naturally include marine hunting, had been passed between 1825 and 1830. Foreigners were excluded from all coastal trade, this being restricted to national boats with two-thirds of the crews composed of Mexican citizens.[38] To climax all, came the victory of the conservative party in Mexico in 1830 and the appointment as California governor of Lieutenant-Colonel Manuel Victoria, stern believer in strict enforcement of the laws.[39]

Victoria did not delay in announcing what the law of the land was to be in otter hunting. Only a little over a month after the new governor arrived in California, Virmond stated, in connection with some difficulty over a foreigner obtaining a license, that he was certain Victoria would not grant it as "I know from himself that he will allow the hunting of sea otters only to the inhabitants of the territory and not to foreigners."[40] Victoria's first occasion to make a stand was in the spring of 1831 when dealing with a new request of the Russians. Baron Ferdinand Petrovich von Wrangel, governor of Russian America, in October, 1830, sent out an expedition for the specific purpose of reëstablishing commercial relations with California. So confident was he of success in his overtures that he wrote to the Mexican governor, "The certainty which I have that you . . . will not hesitate in permitting us to hunt otters on the coasts of California . . . has made me give before hand to Mr. Khlebnikov the order to take aboard the frigate *Baikal* a certain number of Aleuts with their baidarkas."[41]

Victoria's reply on March 5, 1831, was a direct refusal. He could not "permit the taking of otters, this being prohibited in the terms asked for by a law with whose execution I am charged."[42] The law to which he referred was no doubt that reserving the coastal trade to nationals, for orders sent from Mexico on July 1 and July 23, 1830, had reminded all officials to observe it carefully.[43] As a result of Victoria's response to the Russians, Khlebnikov with his Aleuts and baidarkas left San Francisco. However, when reporting on his decision, the governor insisted that the Russians "are good people," very different from those of the United States who were operating without a license.[44]

While attempting to control the otter-hunting situation in the early days of Mexican California, local officials began to urge a stricter national regulation. Their feeling about the matter had concurred with the entrance of a conservative regime in Mexico. After 1831, according to Victoria, the otter fields were to be reserved for *hijos del país*, or citizens.

HUNTING IN MEXICAN RESERVES, 1830–1836

Governor Victoria's positive renunciation of the Russian contract system had legally cleared the hunting ground of foreigners. But could those fields be kept clear? Furthermore, would land-loving *hijos del país* venture along a surf-pounded coast and through heaving, choppy seas to extract the fur wealth which was exclusively theirs by law?

Even before Victoria's pronouncement a few resident Mexicans had begun to move seaward. It did not seem as if they could be longer accused of laziness and indifference to the natural riches about them. Luis Bringas was licensed to hunt in June and again in December, 1826. Echeandía in his 1829 report mentioned that Mexican citizens were engaging in the enterprise. In 1830 J. B. López, Eugenio Morillo, "two inhabitants of Santa Barbara," and one naturalized citizen, John Cooper, went hunting under licenses granted by Echeandía.[45] William Goodwin Dana also succeeded in obtaining a license probably on the basis of his first naturalization papers, which he received in 1828. An employer rather than a hunter, Dana hired the expert marksman, Isaac Galbraith, of giant strength, and two Kanakas to hunt upon a share basis. Transported to Santa Rosa, the most livable of the Santa Barbara Channel Islands, Galbraith had remarkable success even without canoes. Otters were abundant. From the shore he shot into their midst, his Kanaka swimmers bringing in the slaughtered game. In this fashion he obtained as many as thirty a week. By 1831 Dana had invested in "otter boats" which returned in the spring to Santa Barbara from a hunting expedition.[46]

To keep this new activity of Californians within the bounds of the law was a constant aim. Uncertain about the rules, the commander of Santa Barbara in December, 1830, asked the governor whether two local hunters had to pay duties and was told that, since they were Mexicans, they were exempt.[47] In April of the next year Lieutenant Romualdo Pacheco found himself embarrassed when it was rumored that he had assumed gubernatorial prerogatives in allowing Dana and Carlos Carrillo to launch a boat to hunt otters. It took a letter of his own and the certification of a witness to clear him.[48]

By 1831 prominent Mexicans were availing themselves of their hunting reserves. But even though they were citizens, they raised difficult problems for those charged with the enforcement of the law. In that year, Juan Bautista Alvarado and José Castro joined in the otter business. As neither of them knew anything about hunting, they petitioned for permission to hire Kodiak natives. Even though their government had broken off hunting relations with the Russians, they must get skilled hunters some way or other. With careful thought to his announced policy and to the laws of the land, Victoria drew up a special license for these leading *hijos del país*. In accordance with Mexican regulations applying to nationals engaged in the coastal trade, only one-third of those employed might be Kodiaks, the remainder must be natives. On the portion of the skins assigned to the Northwest hunters for their work, the petitioners must pay a duty. A limited time, April to May, and a definite place, "from the presidio of San Francisco to the north," were designated.[49]

Alvarado and Castro lost no time in making arrangements with the manager of Fort Ross, Peter Kostromitinov. For the Russians this was a means of getting a few skins from the forbidden fields. According to Salvador Vallejo a contract was made for enough Kodiak hunters to man eighteen canoes. A Russian commissioner was to head them, and it was agreed that he alone should have the right to direct all hunting operations. Included in the bargain was a provision looking to the day when outsiders would not be necessary in the Mexican reserves—free lessons in the art of otter hunting were to be given by the Kodiaks to the native Indians on the expedition.

In order to obtain their two-thirds quota of Indian hunters, Alvarado and Castro appealed to the president of the missions. Because of past experiences Father Narciso Durán expressed himself as opposed to contracting neophytes but, in deference to Father Tomás Esténega, who had recommended the two petitioners, he finally consented to the hiring of thirty Indians for a moderate price.

By April 3, 1831, eleven canoes had arrived from Fort Ross. José Joaquín Ortega also associated himself with the other Mexican citizens. Restricting the field of their hunting to the area stipulated, the company encamped at San Francisco arroyo and on an island in "the center" of the bay. When otters began to be scarce at the mouth of the harbor, the hunters went to the estuary of Mission Dolores. While they were there, the contract expired, and according to Alvarado the Russians refused to renew it because orders came from Sitka not to hire out Kodiak hunters.[50]

Just as resident Californians were beginning to get used to the water, another type of landsman decided that the Mexican hunting reserves offered a quick way to fortune. American beaver trappers, left to their own devices after their parties had broken up on the Pacific coast, were lured by reports of the fur wealth of the sea. But could buckskin-clad men readily turn from tramping through the wilds to riding ocean swells, from propelling "bull boats" on inland streams to paddling light craft of sea-elephant skin or pine board through Pacific waters? And how could foreigners enter grounds reserved exclusively for citizens?

With the overland party of Jedediah Smith in 1826 came the first of the beaver trappers to try his fortune in sea otters—Isaac Galbraith. The giant marksman found Dana's license a means of engaging in otter hunting in 1830, but he chafed at doing all the work and getting only half the spoils.[51] The leader of another band, James Ohio Pattie, while waiting in the spring of 1830 for a boat to take him to San Blas, took rifle in hand and "joined a Portuguese in the attempt to kill otters."[52] Along a forty-mile coastal stretch near Monterey they took in ten days sixteen otters, yielding Pattie three hundred dollars as his share.

In the William Wolfskill party there were several who turned to the sea. George Yount had not much more than seen the ocean for the first time in his life when he took to chasing otters. Since it was February, 1831, when his party arrived and too late in the season to trap on the San Joaquin, the restless huntsman left the hospitality of San Gabriel Mission and explored about the seashore of southern California. The reputation of the queerly garbed "Captain Buckskin" soon traveled far. On the lookout for expert marksmen, Dana of Santa Barbara sought him out by special messenger. Satisfactory terms were arranged—Dana for one-half the proceeds would furnish provisions, canoes, and transportation to the islands or coast, and Yount and his helpers would receive the other half.

While waiting for the return of Dana's boats from a hunting trip, Yount proved that in spite of his acknowledged ignorance of the sea he could learn to be as good a sailor as he was a trapper. On a pleasure cruise off Santa Barbara, although having difficulty in standing on deck, he of all the guests "was able to enjoy his dinner."

The boats finally arrived, and the hunt was on. With Galbraith, two Kanakas, and a mulatto, Yount made "Galbraith's Point" on one of the Channel Islands, probably Santa Rosa where the Point's namesake had been before. With combined astonishment and admiration he saw otters in groups of several hundreds lying upon the surface of the water near the land. Eagerly he lifted his rifle. Fifteen times he fired but not an otter did he hit. Was his reputation as a perfect shot to be lost on an otter? Chagrined and confused, Yount put ashore. Great was his relief to find that it was not his eye nor his hand which had failed him but his gun, for the sight of his rifle had been appreciably disturbed.

In the following days Yount completely retrieved himself. On calm mornings his Kanaka helpers were kept constantly employed plunging into the water and swimming back with game. Galbraith, "ill-natured and uncomfortable" because of the loss of his boat, left the party much to the satisfaction of Yount. Shortly afterward, a poisonous herb made Yount violently ill. His Kanakas became greatly excited. Loss of boat, illness of the chief—the Devil was on that side of the island sure enough! Nothing would do but they must move the camp. No sooner had they settled down again than a large vessel, one of the illegal hunters along the coast, appeared in the offing. Six canoes were lowered into the water and began to approach rapidly. That was too much for the poor Kanakas, who could be quieted only with much difficulty. Yount's first hunt was limited to only one island and to only a few weeks. But those few weeks brought him "the snug sum of $2,000," proceeds of seventy-five skins.

The sport was exciting and the returns profitable. Yount immediately set forth on his second hunt, this time among the other Channel Islands. On Santa Barbara "he took ten sea elephants and otter in great abundance."[53] On San Clemente he added to his hunting equipment by building a boat of sea-elephant skins.

In the meantime, Wolfskill himself was preparing in a big way to go ottering. Application was made to hunt, but, even though a naturalized Mexican citizen, he had some difficulties. According to Jonathan Trumbull Warner, Wolfskill sought to hunt under his New Mexican license, which permitted him to obtain "nutrias" anywhere in the Mexican Republic. Although the word "nutria" as used provincially meant "beaver" to the governor of New Mexico, it conveyed only one meaning to Californians—otter.[54] Also, California was clearly within the area designated in the license. But apparently local authorities intended that the otter fields be reserved for *hijos del país* as interpreted in the strictest sense—resident citizens. Certainly, it was the custom for licenses to be limited to the state or territory in which they were issued. Victoria on February 19, 1831, stated emphatically to the alcalde of Los Angeles that "William Wolfskill should not hunt in California but in

Sonora where he obtained his license."[55] After demurring at the broad powers assumed by the governor of the adjoining Mexican state, Victoria finally decided that the object and place of the license could not be disputed.[56]

In the summer of 1831 Wolfskill set himself to building his own boat for the proposed expedition. Associated with him in the undertaking were Samuel Prentice, an expert boatsman, Richard Laughlin, carpenter, and Nathaniel Pryor, and encouraging him and backing him materially was Father José Bernardo Sánchez of San Gabriel. Wolfskill with "some of his associates" climbed into the San Bernardino mountains and with ax and saw made ready piles of rough lumber. Down the long trail to San Pedro it was carted and there made into a thirty-ton schooner, the *Refugio*.

In January, 1832, the Wolfskill band set sail. Ewing Young was probably with them, and Sam Prentice added to the party the strong assets of "a capital shot and patient hunter." Southward as far as Cerros Island the *Refugio* proceeded. But the expedition was not very successful owing, according to one authority, to "some misunderstanding." By the following summer they had returned. Almost immediately they again pushed out to sea, up the coast to San Luis Obispo and to the Channel Islands. Wolfskill's last ottering was done a year later under a license granted by Governor José Figueroa for six months beginning in October.[57]

Another beaver trapper and leader of an overland party, Ewing Young, also tried his hand at ottering. As soon as Young had helped his partner, David Jackson, across the Colorado with his mules and horses, he returned to Los Angeles in June, 1832, with the purpose of spending the summer shooting otters. The problem of how to enter the otter reserves was solved when he made arrangements to hunt for Mission San Gabriel. Father Sánchez agreed to furnish the mission's vessel, the *Guadalupe*, commanded by Captain William Richardson, to transport Young and his party to some hunting ground. On the shore of San Pedro the ship's carpenter helped them build two pine-board canoes.

While waiting there, some of the hunters displayed their qualifications for an ocean-going voyage. One of them—who, judging from later actions, may have been Young himself—had never before seen salt water. With some distrust he stepped aboard the anchored *Guadalupe*, but, according to Robinson, "the smell of the

sea and the boat's motion had probably made him sick. Stepping
upon deck, he staggered against the main-mast. 'Gory! how she
totters!' said he, 'if it hadn't been for that are post, I should have
fell down.' "[58]

Before the end of July all was ready. Young and six others, including Warner and two Kanakas, with canoes and stores, were
taken by Captain Richardson to Point Conception. Before sailing
northward, the captain left the brig's yawl as a welcome addition
to their hunting equipment. Robinson reports that the man who
had been seasick on a rocking boat anchored at San Pedro had
sufficient nerve to brave the roughest weather in one of the pine-
board canoes to do his share.

However, the leader of the band did not take readily to the business he had chosen. His sea legs were not very well developed, and
he did not relish the frequent duckings he received when "spilled
out of a canoe into the surf." Having enough of it after a few
days, Young abruptly left for Monterey. The others hunted on
around Point Conception. Then, tying their canoes on behind the
old yawl, they hoisted sail and proceeded southward across the
Channel to San Miguel, then around the two larger islands to the
east, Santa Rosa and Santa Cruz. It was September when the
hunters reached San Pedro with their spoils.[59]

Although neither Wolfskill nor Young pursued the otter business for long, members of their parties continued in it for a number of years. "To hunt sea otters" was Job Dye's purpose in coming
to California. He purchased a whaleboat shortly after his arrival
with Young in March, 1832. His first two expeditions were not
very successful. But the third time, the outlook was much more
hopeful. He contracted with Father Luis Gil y Taboada of San
Luis Obispo to hunt for the mission on equal shares, the padre
furnishing the full equipment—provisions, three Indians, and one
canoe. Good luck was his, for by November he had secured about
two thousand dollars' worth of otter skins. In the spring of 1833
Dye and Edward McIntosh, who had just been naturalized and
was therefore entitled to a license, started down the coast together.
"I killed eighteen otter," says Dye, "and McIntosh one, and the
profits were equally divided between us."[60]

None of the hunters worked from the bottom up more truly than
Isaac J. Sparks of Young's party. When he began in 1832, his

rifle was his only capital. Shooting from the shore, he himself would swim out to secure the prize. Soon he was able to hire a swimmer. In a year or so he built himself a small light boat. Some time in 1832 or 1833 he was hunting on Santa Rosa Island with eleven others. Early in 1834 Sparks and John Burton of the Wolfskill band worked together under Dana's license around the Channel Islands. Job Dye, "who had been trying to go on an otter voyage for eight months,"[61] became the third interested party on the next hunt. The three chartered the newly built, twenty-ton schooner *Peor es Nada* for a trip to Lower California, but, "having made a very poor hunt owing to their failure to agree among themselves,"[62] they returned some time the next year with only twenty-five skins. The latter may have been the lot of twenty-nine which Sparks in September, 1835, was offering for sale at thirty dollars each.[63]

An outstanding hunter of the period was George Nidever who arrived at Monterey with Joseph Walker in November, 1833. His first experiences with ottering were at the invitation of Yount. In June of that year Yount had gone to Monterey where he built another boat, but in his hunting he "met with poor success."[64] Thereupon, he had decided to try his luck at San Francisco, and, shipping his boats on a northward-bound Russian vessel, he had started overland. In November he was again in Monterey and suggested to Nidever that they make "an otter and beaver hunt around the bay and up the San Joaquin River."[65] Nidever sent his baggage in a Russian brig, probably the *Polifemia,* which left Monterey for San Francisco in January, 1834, while he went with Yount in his canoe. The two men hired hunters from Bodega, who paddled half a dozen skin boats about the Petaluma side of the bay and "around Suisun and other places." According to Charles Brown, boat-tender of the party, "our hunt was very successful."[66]

His first sample of marine life was to Nidever's liking. The offer from Yount of a steady job making shingles was refused—he "was not in the habit of working for wages."[67] The matching of skill and brawn against nature for the spoils of the chase was the only life for a red-blooded man. Sailing to Santa Barbara in April, 1834, Nidever met a kindred spirit in Daniel Sills. The two made arrangements with Dana for the use of his license and shortly afterward were taken to Santa Rosa Island. Not having any boats, they hunted from the land and employed a Kanaka at sixteen dollars a month to swim out for all the otters they killed. At the end of about two weeks Sills was taken sick and had to return. Nidever "remained about six weeks longer and killed in all eight or ten otters, Sills having got none."[68]

The next year Nidever met another good hunter, Allen Light, a negro and deserter from the *Pilgrim,* which arrived at Santa Barbara in January, 1835. His name did not seem fitting to his realistic companions, who dubbed him "Black Steward." Nidever and Black Steward, each with a boat and one Kanaka, went up the coast as far as Point Conception. The trip was short, but they brought back twenty-one skins. A second hunt followed almost immediately. Dana supplied the license and provisions and paid the wages of one man for each of the two hunters. In return he was to receive 40 per cent of the skins. Going no farther north than San Luis Obispo, the party in three or four months shot fifty otters.[69] For the next year Nidever and Black Steward, with the help of Sparks, continued to organize hunting parties to the Channel Islands and up the coast. From fifty to sixty skins were the usual returns for a trip of three or more months.[70]

The fall expedition of 1836 "was the last trip we made under Captain Denny's license," wrote Nidever.[71] As long as they were foreigners, there was no hunting except under a citizen's permit. But no one lived and did business in California very long before becoming a Mexican. In 1837 Nidever was naturalized. His friend Sparks asked for his first papers the same year, and Black Steward became a Mexican in 1839.

The coming of the American trapper had raised new problems. To draw the line between hunting under a permit which had been illegally sublet and working for someone else who was legally licensed was almost an impossibility for law enforcers. Also, some mainland foreigners were hunting without the protection of a citizen's license, especially when engaged in small trips of their own.[72] It was apparent, too, that in many instances the regulation requiring two-thirds of the crew to be natives was not observed. Dana's parties were never known to fulfill the law in this respect.

Another easy way of evading the law was to make use of one's Mexican wife. As a resident citizen, she could not be denied a license. In October, 1831, María Josefa Boronda and Eduarda Osuna both became bona fide hunters. Victoria was not deceived, for to Eduarda he wrote, "Although the one who undertakes this will be your husband, a foreigner, nevertheless I grant the right to hunt otters for six months, he subjecting himself to the law."[73]

Nevertheless, the foreign rush to the otter fields had been controlled and used. Victoria restrained foreigners who were hunting under the license of a citizen, unless they were acting within the legal one-third allotment. On February 1, 1831, he rescinded the license of Joaquín Ortega because he had been allowing aliens to hunt. Alcalde Vicente Sánchez of Los Angeles, however, was commended on March 6 for not permitting foreigners to shoot otters.[74] As foreigners came in greater numbers, it became a common practice for licensed citizens to hire them. With the help of expert riflemen the Mexican could get the most from his hunting fields. But the foreigner was far from being a free agent, for not more than half the returns were ever his.

The license system was fairly easy to enforce as far as resident hunters were concerned. Not having ocean-going vessels to carry their skins away to distant markets, they must sell to retail merchants on the mainland. If hunting on any large scale was attempted without a license, it was very apt to be discovered. Such was the case when four Americans, Milton White, Thomas Lewis, Nathaniel Pryor, and Samuel Prentice, called "accomplices" of Thompson, were operating without permission in 1833. On September 2 a boat, which had run aground at the time two of the men leaped out to escape the authorities, and some goods belonging to all four offenders were confiscated by court order.[75]

A general tendency to increase the conditions attached to licenses indicated an attempt to control the hunting situation. By Figueroa's time a set form for licenses had evolved which included all pertinent legal points. For a definite time and usually in a limited area the petitioner might hunt with a stated number of canoes, in order that he might benefit from the privilege given by the old Spanish decree of April 16, 1811, which had ended the government monopoly and opened hunting to individuals. In addition to the ruling that two-thirds of the crew must be natives, other conditions were set down. "In order to conserve the species," pups were not to be killed, and the individual must show his license to the mission padres along whose coast he passed so that they might know that all was being done legally."[76]

In the matter of duties the Mexican government further carried out its general policy. In conformity with Spanish and early Mexican laws providing for no imposts on skins of marine animals, native hunters in California were at first exempt. In 1832, in order to check the incoming American element, the law was modified to apply only to those who fulfilled the requirement concerning the employment of a two-thirds native crew. As Mexicans became more active in otter hunting, Victoria proposed that the government obtain some benefit from the developing industry. According to the ultimate decision, which came only after long debate by both central and local authorities, an export duty of twelve reales for large skins and four reales for small was charged; a four-real tax for each skin was also exacted of hunters.[77]

Resident Mexicans were otter hunting fully as much as Americans in the early 'thirties. The movement was no doubt partly stimulated by the foreign influx, but much of it was a continuation of a lucrative activity which had been begun before the Americans arrived, and much was also due to direct encouragement by Victoria. True, some who took out licenses sent others to sea rather than go themselves. The only ones doing this of whom we find record, however, were the two naturalized citizens Dana and Cooper, Roberto Pardo, and Missions San Gabriel and San Luis Obispo. Also, some who had licenses hired foreigners but headed the expedition themselves and engaged in the hunt just as actively as their employees. Such were McIntosh, Castro, Alvarado, Ortega, and José Ramón Estrada. And a number of Mexicans engaged in ottering solely on their own behalf.

Castro and his associates continued to hunt in the same manner as they had before Americans entered the California fields. In March, 1832, they hired James William Weeks and George Brown, deserters from an American whaler, for an ottering expedition. Weeks complained bitterly that, because they were sailors, "they treated us like Indians" and that they never received a dollar for their labors. He and his partner asked for blankets to cover their tired bodies on chilly nights, but they did not receive them, so that "we were pulling about those estuaries chasing otters, shivering at night with cold as if we had the palsy." Another hunt was on in July when six canoes arrived from Fort Ross. Castro and Estrada were limited by their license in time to one month and in place to the waters outside of the port. The commander at San Francisco raised the question of duties. A late reply came from Governor Agustín Zamorano, who reviewed the legal requirements, stating that hunting was free to nationals if at least two-thirds of the crew were natives; otherwise they must report on the number and quality of skins taken and pay the corresponding duties.[78]

Castro and Estrada next ventured to ask for an exception to the rule. On January 24, 1833, they explained to the new governor, Figueroa, that they were in a predicament. The previous December Zamorano had granted a license to them on the usual terms. They had tried their best to obtain the necessary two-thirds of native hunters but could not find them. Under the circumstances they asked if they might proceed with ten canoes of Northwest Coast hunters, "for which we have already contracted."[79] Figueroa replied the next day—Castro and Estrada might complete their crews with foreigners "for this once."[80]

Two other Mexicans who were known to employ others to hunt were John Cooper, naturalized citizen, and José Joaquín Ortega, who apparently was not associated with Castro and Alvarado for long. Whether these men themselves actually hunted is not clear. During most of 1833 Cooper had twelve baidarkas with Kodiaks operating along the coast. Again in January, 1834, he was given permission to hunt for seven months from San Luis Obispo to Bodega.[81] Ortega received licenses in December, 1833, in January, 1834—for a six months' hunt with ten canoes from Point Conception to San Diego—and in August, 1834, for a like period.[82]

A list of the names of other Mexicans who are recorded as hunting under licenses from 1831 to 1835 can serve only to indicate the extent of native activity—Teodoro González, Angel Castro, Juan Bandini, José Joaquín Carrillo, Ignacio Leonardo, Antonio Buelna, José Joaquín Gómez, Vicente Cané, and Juan Machado. Also, McIntosh and Pardo received licenses to hunt in other years than those in which they were known to be hiring foreigners.[83] Machado was authorized to operate in the region around Rosario Bay, Lower California. Only a few of the other licenses, as recorded, indicate the area of the hunt, which in all instances was the coast of Alta California, no mention being made of the Channel Islands. Few of the many Mexican hunters of the period left journals or reminiscences relating their experiences, but this omission does not make them less important than those usually considered the chief actors on the stage.

The Russians in this decade had not forgotten the California hunting fields. They were being good. The Russian American Company was only waiting for an opportune moment to propose the revival of the old contract scheme, and consequently it desired to keep on satisfactory terms with territorial officials and with the Mexican government. Also, since the only means of getting furs from Mexican waters was through the hiring out of Northwest Coast hunters, the company wished to retain the good will of individual Californians.

Governor Wrangel was especially eager to improve trade relations with California. In April, 1833, he succeeded in obtaining Figueroa's consent to a conference to consider the problem.[84] However, Wrangel could not accept the Mexican invitation at the time since he was apparently waiting for instructions from his home office.

When a situation arose in 1833 which Wrangel felt would interfere with the realization of his company's objectives, he aroused himself immediately. The narrative of Captain Frederick William Beechey's voyage in the Pacific in 1826 and 1827 had just been published. According to Wrangel, the Englishman had accused the Russians of illegal hunting operations along the California coast. On July 24, 1833, Wrangel addressed to Governor Figueroa a long refutation in which his motives were very clearly stated. He feared that Beechey's "false assertions" might "very likely have prejudiced the mind of some of your subjects against the Russians, especially the inhabitants of San Francisco and Monterey," meaning thereby such citizens as Castro, Estrada, and Cooper, who had been hiring Indians from Fort Ross. In conclusion, Wrangel wrote, "I prize the opinion of the Mexican government and the California authorities of the Russians in regard to their activities on the coast."[85]

Wrangel's reason for prizing opinions was revealed in 1836. He had finally heard from his home government. Emperor Nicholas I still refused to recognize the young country which had won its political station by a revolution. However, Wrangel was authorized to negotiate a commercial treaty, among the terms of which was to be an article permitting otter hunting on a share basis. Although much disappointed in his instructions, the governor sailed for Mexico to see what he could do.

On February 28, 1836, Wrangel explained to the Mexican secretary of foreign relations the object of his visit. He stated that the former governor, Figueroa, had expressed himself in favor of concluding a commercial understanding with the Russians, but that before he could see him the Californian had died. He was now asking the secretary to make arrangements for a commercial treaty, the main provisions of which he listed as they had been outlined in his instructions.

The Mexican's reception of the Russian was cool. An unaccredited agent of a power which had steadily refused to extend its recognition could scarcely expect anything else. On March 12, 1836, the secretary sent his answer. Without commenting on any of the specific terms mentioned by Wrangel, he stated that Mexico also desired to establish commercial relations between California and Russian America by means of a treaty. He would inform the Mexican minister at London "to make the necessary steps."[86] In a few words the secretary had closed the door, which only proper diplomatic keys could open.

The Russian American Company was soon to retire altogether from the Mexican otter grounds. Legal restrictions by both the Spanish and the Mexican governments, and the rapid extermination of sea animals around the Fort Ross area, had resulted in the steady decline of the Russian otter industry in California. An important means of support was ended, and furthermore one of the chief reasons for the founding and maintenance of the colony, its advantage as a hunting base, no longer existed. The decline of the sea otter business was consequently an important reason for the abandonment of Fort Ross in 1841. Sir George Simpson reported to the Hudson's Bay Company in 1842 that, "after the loss of that profitable branch of trade . . . the Russian American Company withdrew."[87]

During a critical half-decade Mexicans had worked consistently to maintain their hunting reserves. Resident citizens had for the first time taken up ottering. The overland movement of fur traders had tested to the utmost the Mexican policy. By special laws the American was controlled as he first rushed into the Mexican otter reserves, although by becoming a naturalized citizen he continued to benefit from a lucrative enterprise. The Russian, although proceeding through legal channels, had again been refused entrance into the forbidden grounds.

However, another type of foreigner—one coming from the Hawaiian entrepôt—was not so easy to handle.

CHAPTER VII

CONTRABANDIST AND CAPITALIST IN SEA OTTER FIELDS

War on the Contrabandista, 1831–1842

WHILE CANOE FLOTILLAS were pushing out from the land in a new burst of marine activity in the early 'thirties, another hunter lurked on the edges of the Mexican hunting reserves. He had a man-of-war appearance—a vessel with several guns on a side, hammock nettings, and a large crew. He slipped stealthily around the islands or stayed far offshore; he sent forth canoes filled with Indians of the northland. He was a *contrabandista.*

Foreign merchants, most of them American residents in the Hawaiian Islands, fitted out large vessels purposely to engage in illegal hunting along the California coast. To pay from 40 to 50 per cent of the proceeds of a hunt for the privilege of operating under another's license was not necessary in the order of contrabandism. Northwest Coast Indians could be hired at much less expense, and hunting could proceed on a much larger scale.

The first hunter *contrabandista* of the decade was a vessel owned by a foreign company in China. It was the *Griffon,* formerly belonging to Bryant, Sturgis, and Company, and was outfitted by Mr. Cole, Hawaiian agent of the Oriental firm. Following the old North Pacific–California circuit of business, the brig *Griffon,* Captain Charles Taylor, collected furs on the Northwest Coast in the early months of 1831 and then proceeded southward with thirty Indians and their canoes. Protected by eight cannon and a crew of twenty-four, they pursued the hunt for two months, July to September, from the Channel Islands to San Quintín. Luck was unusual, for "after *two months* [they] obtained 300 Sea Otter Skins!!"[1] According to the testimony of one of the three who deserted the ship when it was at San Quintín, 150 of these skins were taken during the first six days.

Such a fur harvest was worth going for again. As soon as the *Griffon* could be fitted out, she sailed back to the California coast. The first returns were again encouraging. Captain Taylor wrote on

---

[1] For notes to chap. vii, see pp. 211–214.

March 2, 1832, that within the short space of twelve days they had obtained eighty skins. But very suddenly otters became scarce. Little wonder it was, considering all the rifles which had been aimed at them for the past year. When the *Griffon* returned to the Hawaiian Islands in September, it brought only 100 sea otter skins and 700 land furs. Peirce expressed the opinion that "the owners will not lose or gain anything by the voyage."[2]

Jones and Thompson, who had become business partners, attempted in the early 'thirties to make an arrangement for hunting which would have some measure of legality to it. If the vessel bringing Indians from the north could be nationalized, all would be well. The law could be met on this point if a small portion of the boat could be sold to a Mexican.

An agreement to this end was signed by Jones and Cooper on April 23, 1830. Jones was to send a vessel of from 100 to 150 tons which was "to be employed on the coast of California and Mexico in coasting, collecting furs, hunting otter or in any manner or way thought most advisable for the owners of said vessel."[3] Cooper was to buy a proportion of the ship not to exceed one-half and was to place it under Mexican colors. To prepare further the way for the coming venture, Cooper made arrangements at Bodega for hunters.

Jones finally found a vessel suited to his purpose—the brig *Convoy* of 135 tons. Three others, Thompson, French, and Grimes, joined with him in purchasing it and in sending invoices of goods. On March 1, 1831, a few days before the vessel left Honolulu, Jones wrote to Cooper, "The *Convoy* is intended if possible to be put under Mexican colours and remain on the coast of California to hunt according to the plan we talked of when I was in Monterey."[4] He wanted a portion of it to be sold to a Mexican citizen, to Cooper if he wished it. He hoped it was not too late to procure the hunters from Bodega, but, if there should be any difficulty, the brig could proceed to the Northwest Coast for the purpose. Jones concluded his letter by asking Cooper to help Captain Thompson in every way and warned that "secrecy and caution will be necessary in every proceeding."

On May 30 Thompson and Cooper took another step toward completing the transaction. Thompson contracted to sell to Cooper one-fifth part of the *Convoy* for twelve hundred dollars, provided Cooper could put the brig under Mexican colors.[5] But changes involving foreigners could not be effected overnight in the Mexican Republic, especially when Victoria was at the helm. Also, a new law of the previous August had outlined exacting rules for nationalizing vessels.⁶ Those interested in the *Convoy* experienced a delay, as might have been expected. What the nature of it was is not clear. Apparently permission to put the brig under Mexican colors was received by August. On the twenty-second of that month Jones asked Cooper to consult with Thompson "on further proceedings." He feared, however, that it would be "too late to do anything this season," but "I hope she will take the colors immediately as something may be done in another way."⁷ Again secrecy was in the air, for Cooper was advised to "keep a good lookout to windward and work and say nothing." A month later, October 28, Jones at Honolulu expressed the hope that the *Convoy* was then under the colors, and that it "will ere long be getting the nuckies."⁸ The only "nuckies" which the *Convoy* obtained on this trip, however, were by means of barter.

Thompson and Jones did not give up their original idea. They wanted to obtain legal sanction for hunting with Northwest Coast Indians. On September 22, 1831, a unique agreement was entered into between Thompson, for himself and his partner, and Abel Stearns, leading San Pedro merchant. The latter, being discredited in the eyes of Victoria, could not have obtained a hunting license even though entitled to one by his naturalization. Accordingly, it was agreed that Stearns was to go to Mexico for a special license "to hunt and take the Sea Otters and Fur Seals that may be found in the waters on the Coast of Upper and Lower California including the Islands adjacent to said Coasts."⁹ If, as a condition of granting the permit, the Mexican government demanded that the vessel be nationalized, Stearns agreed to make necessary arrangements. Thompson on his part would provide the vessel and obtain thirty hunters. The percentages of the proceeds to be distributed were stipulated—10 per cent to the Mexican government, 5 per cent to an agent appointed to look after the government's proportion, 20 per cent to the hunters, 50 per cent to the owners of the vessel, and 15 per cent to Stearns.

Thompson had high hopes for the proposed venture. He wished Stearns to notify him as soon as possible of the outcome. No time should be lost since "a fortune can soon be acquired with good luck and good management."[10] Curiously enough the agreement was signed just the day before Stearns received the passport which banished him from California. Whether the contract was made in anticipation of his forced trip to Mexico is an interesting supposition. But Stearns went only as far as the frontier and then became embroiled in the revolution which broke out against Victoria in November. He was in no position to carry out the contract.

Jones and Thompson did not wait to hear from Stearns. If legal hunting was made impossible, it would be done illegally. Chartering the brig *Crusader*, the two merchants together with Grimes and French and Company dispatched her on March 21, 1832, to Norfolk Sound. There Thompson, supercargo, discharged her, took on thirty-five Kaigani hunters, and proceeded southward. The vessel was cruising along the California coast by July 4, for an unnamed resident dined aboard her on that day. A month's hunt yielded 160 skins.[11]

In November, 1832, Thompson was preparing at Honolulu for another otter trip on the *Convoy*. For eight months the hunt went on along the California coast, and between 300 and 400 skins were the spoils. Apparently the vessel made another trip in the last months of 1833, for in January, 1834, Peirce reported that it had lately arrived from a hunting voyage with "about 170 Black Sea Otters."[12]

Mexican officials were not unaware of these forays after otters, but as usual they were handicapped by the lack of boats. As early as June, 1831, Victoria explained that, although by putting a stop to the Russian contract system he had checked the practice of foreigners carrying off Mexico's sea wealth, still he could not prevent it because he had no national vessel. He added that the problem was becoming more serious since extermination of the otter was threatened by the indiscriminate killing of pups.[13] A later governor, Figueroa, on July 30, 1833, reminded the receptor that, if vessels were seized, he should see that confiscation proceedings were taken before the proper judge.[14]

Even without ships Figueroa found a way of punishing Jones and Thompson. The *Crusader* and *Convoy*, true to *contrabandista* type, had not put in their appearance at any port. But judicial ears are long. In 1833 the judge of Los Angeles heard that the *Convoy*, supercargo Thompson, was "clandestinely engaged in otter hunting in the very waters of this coast."[15] With the additional evidence, obtained from earlier reports, of illegal hunting by the *Crusader*, the court and Figueroa decided to act.

On September 26, 1833, the *Loriot* belonging to Thompson and Jones was suddenly seized while anchored at San Francisco. The cargo was disembarked and Thompson himself arrested. Although attachment on vessel and cargo was lifted through the influence of Jones, who also furnished a bond for his partner's release, the case was suddenly revived three years later upon the unexpected appearance of Commodore Edmund P. Kennedy, who was making his official rounds of "protecting" American citizens in the Pacific. To Kennedy's strong demand that Thompson be released from his bond, Governor Nicolás Gutiérrez in clear-cut words presented the Mexican view of the affair. Thompson's case had been handled according to Mexican legal procedure, "because the fact that he is a foreigner does not authorize him to violate with impunity the laws of the country that gives him hospitality, nor could the Mexican authorities have tolerated that Mr. Thompson should hold himself superior to the laws and should flout their provisions as it happened at Santa Barbara in the year 1832.[16]

Others besides Mexican officials were annoyed by the elusive presence of armed hunting vessels and their canoe satellites. The huntsman from the mainland considered the *contrabandista* his greatest rival. Cooper was incensed by the "piratical manner" in which hunting was done by those "sent out from the Sandwich Isles," who not only took all the otters they could get but "stole cattle and wantonly killed horses belonging to the missions."[17] In 1833 he decided to wage a little war of his own against the *contrabandista*. He was going to keep his twelve boats hunting "till there is not an otter left on California." This would not take long, he thought, considering the recent slaughterings. "Where there was taken 700 a few years ago I took but 32 from San Francisco to Monterey, and actually as things appear [I] do not think we shall get 600 skins in all on the coast."[18]

The American hunter out on the Channel Islands hated the sight of a Northwest Coast Indian. Although the employers of the detested northerners were usually fellow-Americans, still the chance meeting of Indians with another hunting group meant trouble. The Northwesterner was aggressive, would fight fiercely for the full possession of his hunting grounds, and would strip the seas of all the otters in his path. He would not hesitate to steal the supplies and furs of smaller parties. And at all times he was protected by a floating fort.

The rival hunters encountered each other soon after the hunting movement of the 'thirties began. Yount had met Northwest Indians, who probably came from the *Griffon,* on his first trip to the islands in 1831. When Sparks and his company were on Santa Rosa in 1832 and in the early part of 1833, an American brig, which was very likely the *Convoy,* anchored offshore. Knowing that Indians were aboard, Sparks's group decided to capture the intruder. In the dead of night the daring huntsmen approached the brig. They reached its side. All were ready to board her, when there was a noise. We are discovered, said one Thompson, they will overpower us. The majority of the party agreed, and the plan was given up much to the disgust of some of the more venturesome.[19]

On one occasion Sparks and Black Steward were driven into the highlands of Santa Rosa Island by Northwest Coast hunters who stole their supplies.[20] The Channel Islands were so often visited by northern Indians in the early part of the decade that many hunters considered Lower California a more profitable field, since few Indians had been seen in the southern hunting grounds for some years, although they "did hunt along that coast afterward."[21]

Contrabandists continued to come regardless of the opposition of the Mexican government and of mainland huntsmen. In August, 1834, Captain John Dominis with twenty Indians from Tongass, Alaska, left Fort Simpson on the *Bolivar,* a Salem-owned vessel managed by agents in the Hawaiian Islands, to hunt "between the Columbia and the Spanish settlements." Another ship, armed and flagless, dared to send forth its canoes within sight of San Pedro in January, 1835. Four or five men were stationed to watch that no goods were disembarked—that was all that could be done about it. The latter part of the same year the *Bolivar,* after trading for furs in the Northwest, was again cruising along the southern coast. It arrived at Honolulu on January 14, 1836, with "400 Black skins," only a part of which could have come from California. The *Joseph Peabody* was probaby hunting in June, 1836, on Catalina, where she touched on her way from the Northwest Coast to the Hawaiian Islands. The *Loriot* hunted around Cerros Island in

July. The same month Governor Mariano Chico reported from Monterey that two brigs and one frigate were hunting "in sight of all the world."[22]

Only one Russian contrabandist is known to have been on the coast during these years. Its hunting operations were more incidental than intentional. In 1835, when Alexander Markov was returning from a trip to the salt mines near Mazatlan, a few of his crew, as a side line, killed nearly fifty sea otters. The news of the illegal act sped ahead of him. No sooner had the Russian vessel put in at San Francisco than a Spanish official came out in a boat to see the captain. Markov was told "that it had been reported that we had been killing sea otters along the coast and that we would not be permitted to enter the harbor again."[23] Only by making a side trip of some two thousand miles across to the Hawaiian Islands could the Russian get the supplies he needed.

Governor Wrangel's contention in 1833 that the Russians did not engage in illicit hunting on the Mexican coast was, in the main, true. This abstention was part of their program of being good in the hope of renewing the contract system. Whether or not the Russians rejected offers of foreigners to hunt along California on a share basis when they learned that the business was to be done illegally, as Wrangel asserted, is not known.

Figueroa was likewise sincere in agreeing with Wrangel that, although there had been a time when "such enterprises were countenanced by the Russian establishment of the Northwest," the Mexican authorities were very well satisfied with their present conduct. He did not forbear criticizing the real offenders. "It is true," he said, "that other foreigners . . . have constantly violated the law of nations by hunting copiously the marine animals on our coasts." From out of the midst of Figueroa's polite expressions to Wrangel, however, came this warning: "I take the liberty of recommending to you that you never permit this traffic."[24]

Continued efforts were made to control the hunting situation. In December, 1834, Figueroa again asked for one or two warships to go against "the enemy" who were benefiting from the natural products of the country.[25] On July 22, 1836, Chico wrote that foreigners were hunting otters almost to the extermination of the species. Since he had no national vessel to prevent illegal activities, he decided to commission "an active, bold foreigner" to patrol the coast in one of his vessels. This foreigner was secretly to get a sufficient crew and "by some strategy, such as that of pretending to contract to deliver some cattle, surprise the boat and bring it as a prize to some port."[28]

Huntsmen from the mainland also continued to fight the intruders. A real battle occurred on Santa Rosa Island in 1836 between Northwest Indians and the hunters of Nidever's party. About January 1 some of his men sighted a brig far out at sea. Since nothing happened, they supposed that it was a passing merchant vessel and dismissed the thought that it might be bringing the dread enemy. On a foggy morning a few days later the party pushed out in their canoes in spite of the bad hunting weather. About seven o'clock an otter was spied. Maintaining the usual triangular formation, Black Steward, Nidever, and Sparks started to run the animal toward the northern head of the island. Suddenly Black Steward called out a word of warning—"Northwest Indians!"

Charging through the fog curtain came five or six canoes, each with from two to three men. Directing their course by the shots of the hunters, the attackers were pushing ahead with all speed in an attempt to cut off the party from shore. The Americans pulled for all they were worth and finally made the beach amid a shower of buckshot. Not waiting even to haul up their boats, the scared Kanakas in Nidever's party took to the hills in order to escape the bullets which they swore passed them when they were a mile away from the beach. The three leaders and one O'Brien remained to face the enemy.

Black Steward, who was the first to land, fired, but "the powder having partly escaped from his gun the ball fell short." A shot from Sparks's gun, followed by one of Nidever's, finished an Indian. The oncoming canoes halted and, in the face of continued firing from the four who had taken to the bushes, drew back beyond gun range. Three of the Northwesterners had been killed in the conflict, and four or five were wounded. Shortly, they pulled away to the brig, which stood revealed by the lifting fog.

All night long those on land kept watch. The next morning they saw canoes lowered from the brig. Back and forth the Indian rowers paddled, maneuvering about as if they were hunting. Closer and closer they approached and passed once, twice, the vital spot of the encamped hunters' existence—their provision storehouse, a cave with a small entrance but "so large inside that a hundred persons could occupy it with ease." Time passed, and then came the cry that the Indians were landing near the cave. Shots were exchanged, and one Northwesterner was killed, whereupon again they put off to their brig.

For two days the vessel lay becalmed, but not an Indian came forth. With the first breeze on the third day the brig lifted anchor. As its sails disappeared, the Kanakas and "the valiant Portuguese, Manuel" came forth half-starved from their hiding places in full expectation of finding their comrades slaughtered in cold blood. "This defeat," says Nidever, "was a severe blow to the Northwest Indians, who for several years had been the terror of the coast. This was the first reverse they had met with."[27]

The brig which harbored these fighting Northwesterners was the *Convoy*, Captain John Bancroft. It was owned by Grimes and outfitted by the same merchant group, Thompson, Jones, Grimes, and French, which had sent it out in 1832–1833. Richard Henry Dana met it off Point Conception on January 8, 1836. The vessel arrived at the Hawaiian Islands with its sea otter cargo on March 27 and set out a month later for the Northwest, no doubt to return its Indian hunters.[28]

The battle at Santa Rosa did not disconcert Captain Bancroft. It was a mere incident in the pursuance of a profitable voyage. Two years later he directed a similar expedition in the *Lama*, owned by Grimes. The vessel, last from Cerros Island, arrived at the Hawaiian Islands on January 23, 1838, with a cargo of furs. In July of the same year the ship reëntered Honolulu from California with twenty-seven Northwest Coast Indians and furs.[29]

In the autumn Bancroft again sailed down the coast in the *Lama*, bringing twenty-five fierce Kaigani Indians, canoes, and provisions of dried fish and fish oil. Apparently trouble was brewing from the outset for a number of reasons. On the one hand, a captain addicted to drinking and using harsh treatment, and his amorous Kanaka lady, harboring a strong racial antagonism toward the wild Kaiganies; on the other hand, quarrelsome Indian hunters, who liked to work when and where they pleased and who were incensed by the slim rations handed out to them as a matter of discipline when the hunt was unsuccessful—all this was bound to cause friction.[30]

Exactly what happened on the coast of California is best described by one of the officers of the *Lama,* who reported to Mr. Grimes upon his return to the Hawaiian Islands. On November 16, when the vessel arrived at San Miguel Island, the canoes were sent out to hunt. On the eighteenth two came back with only three skins. Upon questioning the Indians, Bancroft made out that they had not been hunting at all on the day before. "He had a few words with them and sent them away again."[31] But one of the Indian leaders, Yeltenow, left with the sulks and began to spread his dissatisfaction.

On the twentieth two more canoes came from Santa Rosa with eight skins, and a little later a Mr. Robinson, their white leader, arrived with four more. Robinson reported that the Indians had been quarreling over the skins and had not been hunting well. When Bancroft signaled by gunfire for them all to come back to the boat, none obeyed. Robinson returned to the island with orders to hunt around it thoroughly before going to Santa Cruz. On the fatal day of the twenty-third Bancroft saw canoes coming from the direction of Santa Cruz. Thinking they were strangers, he had the guns made ready, but he soon discovered they were his own canoes.

At 11 A.M. they were all on board, and Captain Bancroft began to find fault with them, and they came to very high words, all in the N.W. language, so that we could not understand what was said. At last it appeared to be all settled, and the Captain went down to dinner, all the Indians remaining on the forecastle talking together. When he came up the row began again, and by what we could understand, very bad language passed between them.

On a sudden the Indians began to pass their muskets up out of their canoes, and had got them nearly all up before any notice was taken of it. When Captain B. saw it, he told Mr. Robinson not to let any more come up, and he stopped them. Captain Bancroft then went on the forecastle amongst them, but Yeltenow shoved him away, and he ran aft and jumped up on the rail, saying something which we supposed to be, "Fire if you dare," for they immediately fired, and he fell down in the waist.[32]

At the first musket reports the other three white men on board, a few Kanakas, and the captain's wife jumped up from their dinners and rushed to the deck. Running to her husband, Mrs. Bancroft interposed her body and begged for his life, but she was herself terribly wounded. One of the white crew was shot in the head. Armed with knives and boarding pikes, the Indians demanded all the ammunition and the keys of the arms chest. In possession of the ship, they forced Robinson to take them back to their northland. There on December 26 the Indians disembarked, stripping the brig of many of its effects, and keeping most of the furs, but "leaving 5 skins and 21 tails as a present for Mr. Robinson."[33]

The voyage of the *Lama* in 1838 had important effects in the war against the *contrabandista*. Just after the vessel had dragged itself back to Honolulu on January 13, 1839, it was reported that resident merchants, alarmed at the news of the mutiny, had abandoned all idea of fitting out such an expedition again.[34] Also, Mexicans were aroused to action. Two local hunting groups had been on the Channel Islands and up the coast in 1838. When they returned, the hunters talked. Governor Alvarado heard rumors that some vessel along the coast and in the Santa Barbara Channel had been hunting seals and "a great number of otters without the necessary license" and had been "destroying even the pups of both species."[35] On January 25, 1839, he ordered the alcalde of Santa Barbara, Antonio Rodríguez, to conduct a special judicial inquiry.

One by one the hunters gave their testimony. Allen Light declared that almost two years ago he had seen a brig, "Captain Bancrof," hunting. Sparks had been twice on a vessel by the name of *"Lima"* of about 200 tons, equipped with four or six cannon, twenty or twenty-five muskets, and some lances for hunting. He had observed the Indians paddling about in their canoes and had seen skins on board the vessel. George Hewitt knew that the *"Lima"* had been hunting because its officers had sold him some furs. Stephen Simmonds had been on board the vessel and had seen a number of skins stretched out to dry on deck and had noticed six mounted guns. Two years ago he saw some twenty armed Indians land on the coast of San Pedro and had observed the same thing at San Juan Capistrano at another time. From another source it was learned that these armed men were killing cattle without compensating the owners. Luis Carrillo declared that the preceding November, the very month when Bancroft was killed, a ship had anchored off Point Conception, while twenty-two Northwest Coast Indians took on wood for three days. Carrillo and Francisco Ortega had gone on board and had found out from the captain that they had been hunting all along the coast, but that he had not gone into any port for fear of being captured.[36]

The inquiry had not been concluded before Alvarado acted. He entrusted a special commission to Allen Light, alias Black Steward, who because of his long hunting career on the coast was addressed by the governor as "the principal representative of the national armada employed in this branch of otter hunting."[37] Complimentary titles indeed these were for both negro hunter and the privately owned canoe flotillas engaging in the business. Light was to prevent illegal hunting by "using the methods which you think best and using force in case of resistance even to the point of placing the mentioned vessel and crew at the disposition of the governor." The wording of the document indicates that Light's commission was special, not general, in nature. He was to seek the *Lama* with his small ottering force and do what he could. But the *Lama* was far away by the time Light received his orders and the ship was never to reappear on the same mission.

Some efforts were made to correct the greatest weakness in the Mexican enforcement system—lack of government patrol boats. In 1837 an eighty-three-ton schooner, the *California,* had been purchased to "prevent scandalous contraband and hunting for otters and seals in the refuges furnished by solitary places."[38] However, according to Davis, "she was not fitted for revenue-cutter service, having only one or two small guns," and was consequently used mostly for a mail boat.[39] In September, 1840, a privately owned Mexican vessel, the *Catalina,* was sent with the *California* to look for contrabandists, apparently with no success.[40]

Another means of checking contrabandism was tried in 1840. On February 27 Alvarado received an order from Mexico authorizing him to grant the Channel Islands to some responsible citizens in order "to prevent foreign adventurers from benefiting from them to the great prejudice of our fishery."[41] Antonio and Carlos Carrillo were recommended "because of their useful and patriotic services."

The day of the *contrabandista* was rapidly passing. Only a few were reported in the next two years. According to Eugène Duflot de Mofras a vessel from the Hawaiian Islands was hunting otters around Cerros in 1839. There was a rumor that in December, 1840, a ship had anchored in the roadstead of San Juan Capistrano "with the object of hunting otters." In December, 1841, the brig *Clementine* left the Hawaiian Islands for the Northwest Coast to get Indians for hunting in California. Just about the time the *Clementine* should have arrived there, in February of the next year, it was reported at Fort Simpson that an American vessel bound for California with hunters aboard had been forced by the weather to return to her anchorage, and that before setting forth again it had been pillaged and "the crew left with little more than the bare ship to pursue fortune as best they might."[42]

The Northwest Coast Indian, the Mexican government, and the mainland huntsmen had all fought the *contrabandista*. Quite as important as any of these factors accounting for its disappearance was the rapid decrease in sea otter numbers. Large vessels sent from afar no longer paid. With the hunting smuggler out of the way, the Mexican reserves, although much less rich in fur wealth, were no longer legally menaced. Truly by 1840, just as a Hawaiian merchant had predicted, Sparks—and all his fellow hunters, whether Mexican by birth or by naturalization—could have "the range of the whole coast without interruption."[43]

OUTFITTING BY MERCHANT EMPRESARIOS, 1840–1848

Sea otter hunting continued until the gold rush, but a continued decrease in otter numbers caused a change in the method of organizing hunting parties. In order to get to the less ravaged and therefore more distant otter grounds, it was necessary to have a large boat and more equipment. For this, as for many another enterprise, the business *empresario*, resident American merchant who had become a Mexican citizen, provided the requisite capital.

The change in hunting organization was very gradual. In the late 'thirties and early 'forties, small groups of hunters continued to make short trips both to the Channel Islands and along the coast between Santa Barbara and Monterey. Known returns per hunt compare favorably with those at the beginning of the local hunting movement although there are a few indications that otters were decreasing in number along the upper coast. Nidever with two companions made one or more trips every year. In 1837 a hunt of two and one-half months between Santa Barbara and Monterey brought fifty skins; the next year a short trip of about two months to the islands resulted in twenty-five or thirty skins; in five months in 1838 sixty pelts were found between Santa Barbara and Monterey; in 1839 two months in the Channel Islands brought thirty otters;

and in 1841 Nidever and Sparks found twenty to thirty pelts in a two months' hunt on the islands. Black Steward hunted on his own along the coast in 1839, and two years later he and a few companions were shooting otters around San Juan Capistrano. The *Alert* landed an ottering party and equipment on Santa Rosa Island in 1840. The veteran hunter Sparks came in from the chase in July, 1841, but brought only nine skins.[44]

More than the north coast and islands, the Lower California fields seemed to attract the otter men. In the spring of 1839 Sparks, Nidever, and Hewitt with a schooner-rigged whaleboat of four tons and three canoes sailed as far south as "Redondo Island." One hundred and nine skins, which sold in San Diego for thirty-seven dollars each, were the spoils of their five months' hunt.[45]

The next year the trio and a crew of eight others, including four mission Indians, again put forth in their whaleboat going as far as Cerros Island. After returning to San Diego at the end of six months for supplies, the party continued the hunt off Lower California. At San Quintín Bay nine others from Los Angeles and San Diego were already operating in nine canoes. But Nidever was not particularly disturbed since his rivals were very poorly equipped and, with the exception of Black Steward and a few others, were little skilled in the hunting art. Both parties headed for a distant field to the south known to abound in otters but not hunted for some time.

Eager to be the first to arrive at the rich hunting grounds, the two groups raced through the coastal mists. As a dense fog descended, the whereabouts of each party became unknown to the other. Elated to find the field unoccupied when they finally arrived, Nidever's men immediately fell to hunting. By the time their competitors appeared on the scene, they had already killed seventeen otters and had the skins staked out on the shore to dry. Chagrined and swearing that they would beat the others yet, the latecomers rowed on southward but went "beyond the otter grounds entirely." When Nidever returned to Santa Barbara, he brought one hundred and fifty-three skins as the total yield of his seven months' hunt.[46]

In 1842 Sparks, Nidever, and Black Steward were again on the southern coast. Sparks left Santa Barbara in April with three canoes and nine men bound for San Quintín. In October he entered San Diego from Lower California with five canoes, and a party "composed of the most noted hunters on the coast," including Nidever and Black Steward. Excited by the war rumors following the Commodore Jones incident, the ottering party accepted the invitation of the captain of the *Alert* to place their furs valued at four thousand dollars on board his vessel until the scare was over.[47]

The Lower California field seemed to be yielding richer returns in numbers and quality of skins than the northern coast. But the more distant southern grounds required larger equipment and more men. Nidever's and Sparks's investment in a four-ton whaleboat for their southern expeditions was indicative of the trend.

Other larger hunting enterprises began to be organized. In 1841 Captain John Wilson, naturalized Mexican who was employed with his partner James Scott in a profitable trade with Mexico, obtained the financial help of another prosperous merchant, Lewis Burton, to outfit an expedition. Supplies, canoes, and men were put aboard a brigantine belonging to Scott and Wilson for an extended trip along both the upper and lower coasts. Nidever, James William Breck, Hewitt, and Burton himself, all of whom for a number of years had hunted on their own in small groups of two or three canoes, found themselves serving as employees of large outfitters. Although several, "because of closeness of Wilson and Burton," left the expedition after a two and one-half months' trip to the north, the brigantine continued southward to Cerros Island.

Apparently the returns were gratifying. Burton paid duties on otter skins in San Diego in October, and in the following two months Burton and Wilson were reported to be holding for sale at Santa Barbara 105 otter pelts in addition to about 200 fur-seal skins. All described the otter furs as superior in quality, "good black ones, indeed the best lot that has been got this long time in California."[48] But the price of thirty-seven dollars, increased soon to thirty-eight dollars, was considered "outrageous."

The outfitting of otter expeditions was undertaken by other merchant *empresarios*. In 1843 Thompson and Jones sent forth to the hunt their brig, the *Bolivar*, renamed the *Oajaca*. Jones reported that, when the vessel left on the last day of August, she had "everything I could possibly obtain for her,"[49] including the valued services of Sparks, Nidever, and other skilled hunters. However, Jones predicted that, if rich finds kept the *Oajaca* out at sea for four months or so, "she will be short of bread and flour, fat and cocoa."[50]

Rough weather chopped the waters of the Channel when the *Oajaca* reached the field of its first hunt. Undaunted, the men set to work around the islands San Nicolas and San Clemente, and within a few days they took twenty-one skins, principally prime. Pleased with their spirit, Captain Stevens reported that the "hunters and their men behave uncommon well and vie with each other who can do the best."[51] Arrived off the Lower California coast, the canoes pushed out for the chase while the big ship sailed on to Todos Santos Bay. In about half the time estimated by Jones, provisions ran low. Rations were doled out, then all activities had to come to a halt in November when the *Oajaca* turned back to Santa Barbara.[52]

Immediately Thompson planned another expedition for his brig. He sent the vessel under Captain John Roderick to San Diego for provisions and repairs.[53] Roderick wrote his friend Talbot H. Green about the middle of January, 1844, that he had almost finished fitting the ship "from stem to stern" and that "she looks as blooming as the Mrs. Green, which will be, going to church on a Sunday."[54] From San Diego the *Oajaca* proceeded to Guadalupe Island, the main field of its hunt, and from thence to Mazatlan.

Over a year passed by before Thompson and Jones again financed an ottering party. It was, Thompson declared, the "best fitted . . . that has ever left the coast."[55] Twelve hunters headed by Sparks and including four Kanakas and three mission Indians, with canoes, supplies, and lumber for building a large boat, were taken down the coast in April, 1845, on the *Oajaca* and landed on Cerros Island. After the party had fixed up a suitable camp, eight men shoved off for a hunt on the west side of the island, the others remaining to construct the boat.

For twenty days wind and seas conspired against the light canoes. Then the men put back to camp with only six or seven otters. Deciding to make another try farther away, two of the group daringly rowed thirty miles southward to Morro Hermoso on the mainland. Luck was better, for within a week the hunters took twenty-seven skins, but they had to bring them back in a green condition, the barren cliffs about Morro Hermoso not yielding enough sticks even to stake out a few pelts to dry.

Within a short time the new boat, a four-ton, schooner-rigged craft without keel, was completed. Hiding some of their supplies, the entire party sailed across to Morro Hermoso. Several times the boat ran north to Cerros to get fresh water for the huntsmen. Once the finding of a large school of otters lifted their hopes for a successful trip. About fifty-eight of the animals were shot by the end of a month's hunt. Returning to Cerros for their cached supplies, the Jones-Thompson group hunted their way northward. In August they delivered to their outfitters about one hundred and five skins.[56]

Occupying a mercantile position similar to that of Thompson in the north, Henry Fitch in southern California outfitted otter expeditions in the 'forties. First entering the fur business as retail agent for sellers and hunters in Lower California, Fitch soon financed hunts of his own. In 1841, 1843, and 1844 he is known to have sent out expeditions. In 1847 and 1848 he was still receiving skins from Lower California hunters.[57]

A rival outfitter of Fitch, one who likewise operated from San Diego along the Lower California coast, was the old-time hunter, Black Steward. The negro had risen from the position of employee to that of employer. In 1843 Fitch apparently agreed to purchase, at the rate of thirty-seven dollars a skin, all the otters obtained by Steward's party.[58] The next year a friend, in advising Fitch of the activities of his otter hunters, urged that he "had better push them before the Black Steward comes, for after they arrive the San Diego Hunters may go to sleep."[59]

The coast of Upper California was not entirely abandoned for the Lower California field, but returns apparently were decreasing. Lewis Burton left Santa Barbara in 1842 with two canoes and seven men, Warner applied and received a license to hunt in the Channel Islands in 1843, and Francis Day was given a license at Monterey the same year.[60] In 1845 Marcelino Escobar of Monterey financed an expedition of two canoes and six men, including two hunters, two steersmen, and two mission Indians. Proceeding southward along the coast, they obtained nothing until they reached Point San Luis Obispo. There, after four or five days of hunting, someone shot an otter. For three months they hunted around Piedras Blancas, San Simeon, and San Luis Obispo, but only one more otter was added to their catch.[61]

A larger expedition had better success the next year. Four experienced hunters and a crew of mission Indians, all headed by

Nidever, were sent forth by Thompson in the spring of 1846 with a few supplies loaded in a large surfboat. They carried instructions to stop at Monterey to purchase additional equipment, but for some reason they could get nothing on Thompson's credit. Paying for the rest of their supplies on their own account, the hunters went on up the coast, entered San Francisco Bay, where they shot twenty or so otters around the mouth of either Petaluma or Sonoma creeks, and then proceeded as far north as Fort Ross. In November they returned with ninety skins.[62]

The *empresario* movement did not alter the Mexican policy of protecting the otter reserves. The fact that both outfitters and hunters were either native Mexicans or naturalized made the task comparatively easy. But authorities were ever alert to enforce the law and to prepare for new contingencies.

Central control of license issuing was put to the test by the new developments in otter hunting. As Santa Barbara increased in importance as an outfitting center, most petitions for licenses passed through the hands of the commander of that port. Very soon, well-known outfitters could easily persuade the Santa Barbara official to grant the license himself without referring it to the governor. Alvarado in May, 1841, made a very definite stand with respect to the matter. The port commander was told that "it is a power of the governor to concede these licenses,"[63] and that it was the duty of the official at Santa Barbara to prevent any person from going hunting until "the superior document" was received. Those who had gone out without the proper license were ordered to return. The following year it was again decreed that no one was to leave Santa Barbara to hunt otters without presenting a license.[64]

Some difficulties arose in enforcing the government's policy with respect to duties on skins. A new clause appeared in hunting licenses—the hunter must return to the port from which he had embarked, render an exact account of the skins obtained, and pay the legal duties. But when hunts were conducted in the more distant fields, complications ensued. Skins were sometimes brought to San Diego in the middle of a hunt. This was done by Burton in 1841 when he paid his duties at San Diego. In 1842 Sparks received a certificate for paying duties on ninety-five skins at San Vicente, on the Lower California coast, although his license stipulated that all imposts were to be met at Santa Barbara. Sparks took some of the same lot of skins to San Diego for sale. In 1844 duties were paid at San Diego in two instances. Apparently the accepted system was to pay the legal impost at the port of outfitting unless receipts or certificates were presented showing payment at other points.[65]

Both on the northern and southern coasts sea otters lived in comparative peace for a year or two after 1846 while men fought each other on land. Just as Nidever and Sparks joined Fremont's band, so did other otter hunters participate in the hostilities of the Mexican War. Probably, too, they were unwilling to risk having valuable furs seized.

Only two expeditions are known to have hunted along the upper coast after the outbreak of war, and none seems to have gone to the Lower California field. In the spring of 1847 Carl Dittmann, Redding McCoy, William Fife, and crew pushed up the coast from San Francisco to Point Reyes in three boats specially built for the trip. They shot only about a dozen otters in Bolinas Bay. Refitting at San Francisco, the trio hunted down the coast until they reached Santa Barbara. Most of the same group and Nidever immediately set out again for a hunt to the Channel Islands.[66]

By 1848 sea otters were again being hunted but not many were obtained. The loss of one hundred of them by the capsizing of a boat caused such a scarcity that Henry Mellus could find none to put aboard the *Barnstable* sailing that May.[67] A good-sized expedition was organized that same month by Nidever, Sparks, McCoy, and Fife. With their canoes and a five-ton boat built at San Francisco for the purpose, they hunted as far north as Cape Mendocino. A "few otters" were found twelve miles above San Francisco and "a few more" in Drake's Bay, but no more than twenty were the total returns of their labor.[68]

In August of the same year Dittmann and a friend started on foot up the coast from Santa Barbara. "We killed one, but the beach being rocky and the surf bad at that point, we did not dare to swim out for it, and so it was floated away and lost."[69] Weary and discouraged at losing their one single prey, Dittmann and his companion turned back toward Santa Barbara. A nugget of gold in the hand of a passing miner infused new life into them. They were off to try their fortunes in a new kind of hunt on land.

At about the same time, Nidever's party, on the way back from their northern expedition, put in at Fort Ross and heard of the gold diggings. "The prospect of getting $16 a day when their monthly wages barely amounted to that was too great a temptation for our men, who insisted on leaving us at San Francisco."[70] The large boat carried Nidever and his party up the Sacramento River as far as the Yuba, from which point the light canoes took them to the mining area. Otter-hunting craft became conveyances for a new chase—to the mines. The search for Pacific gold was abandoned for the El Dorado of the hinterland.

CHAPTER VIII

A GENERAL SURVEY OF THE SEA OTTER TRADE

SEA OTTER NUMBERS AND LATER HUNTING METHODS

T O OBTAIN even a general estimate of the numbers of sea otters along the California coast is very difficult. In the first place, hunting records are extremely incomplete. Furthermore, one has to consider the fact that hunting returns in no way correspond to the existing numbers owing to various political or economic conditions which either facilitated or restricted coastal activities. Holding these main factors in mind, one may make an analysis of known figures for a general appreciation only.[1]

California sea otters seem to have been most numerous until about the year 1815. The highest specific figure for any one year is that for 1811 when 9,356 skins are known to have been obtained. However, several facts must be considered. This figure does not represent all the furs taken that year, since mission Indians, as always, were hunting on a small scale and the *Mercury* was also operating along the coast. However, the time was the height of the great hunting days under the contract system when Yankees and Russians by combining forces were enabled to operate more easily. This figure represents the catch of four vessels with a total of about one hundred and fifty canoes and twice as many men. Also, one must remember that hunting figures are much more complete for the period of the contract system than for any other time, since the source of information is Russian American Company accounts. Another important consideration, especially if comparison is made of numbers obtained in the Spanish and Mexican periods, is that all totals for the early days of hunting include not only prime skins, but also yearlings and pups, the latter two classes together equaling from one-third to more than one-half of the entire catch.

The number of skins obtained by individual vessels varied. The *O'Cain* on its 1803 voyage, in five months, with twenty canoes, procured 1,800 furs. On the next trip of the *O'Cain* in 1806–1807, Aleuts in some fifty canoes, supplemented later by twenty-five more, killed 4,819 otters. The same vessel in 1810–1811 with fifty

---

[1] For notes to chap. viii, see pp. 215–217.

baidarkas obtained in California 3,952 skins, while the *Isabella* that year with forty-eight canoes took 2,976.

For about two decades after the end of the contract system the greatest hunting was done in the Russian area, between Point Reyes and Trinidad Bay. In 1816 Choris gave the conservative estimate that Russians at Fort Ross were getting every year about two thousand otters.[2] Except for those few obtained by clandestine hunting, these would have been taken in the region north of the Golden Gate. Very early, however, the animals were becoming exceedingly scarce along that part of the coast, one report in 1817 even stating that they were entirely exterminated.[3] The animals in San Francisco Bay were molested now and then during the same period. In 1814 Indians from the *Ilmen* killed 100 in that port in one day. Under the Russian-Mexican contract of 1823–1824 about 1,200 were obtained from the bay, 455 of these being taken within about two weeks' time.

The leaders of maritime expeditions touching at California in the early part of the Mexican period all remarked upon the scarcity of the otters. However, their observations were made at a time when very little hunting was being done, between the time of the Russian-Mexican contracts and the 1830 hunting rush. Kotzebue in 1824 stated that although the animals were scarce, more were caught in California south of Fort Ross than in any other place in the Pacific.[4] Beechey two years later estimated that about two thousand a year were taken.[5] Bernard du Hautcilly, who was able to purchase only one hundred and fifty for himself, stated that otters were "very few" in California and of an inferior quality.[6]

At the very beginning of the impetus given about 1830 to otter hunting, sea otters south of Point Reyes seem to have been almost as numerous as in the first decade of the nineteenth century. This statement holds especially for those areas where very little hunting had been done for ten or more years, namely the Santa Barbara Channel Islands and Lower California. All hunters to the Channel Islands in the early 'thirties commented on the abundance of otters. Yount described them as "lying upon the surface of the water, near the land, in groups of several hundreds together."[7] Returns, considering the number of hunters and the length of time of hunts, support these observations. In 1830 one gunman, with two helpers but no canoes, obtained by shooting from land on Santa Rosa

Island thirty otters a week. In 1831 a party of four in "a few weeks" on Santa Rosa Island shot seventy-five. The *Griffon* the same year with thirty Indians in a two months' cruise from the Channel Islands to San Quintín took three hundred. Even in San Francisco Bay the hunting of the early 'twenties could not have reduced the numbers very much. About the time of the first Mexican-Russian contract, Alvarado stated that otters entered the port in great shoals, and José Fernández wrote that in the bay from San Francisco to the estuary of Santa Clara, "the ground appeared covered with black sheets due to the great quantity of otters which were there."[8] Also, Phelps was told by José María Amador, the mayordomo of Mission San José, that in 1830 he and three or four Indians caught by lassoing thirty sea otters out of about a hundred which were on the shore at Point San Quentin.[9]

For the Mexican period it is impossible to form any accurate opinion of numbers from the known quantities exported or hunted. The only records of the catches made by the many small groups of men who were working on their own in the period after 1830 are one or two reminiscences and a few scattered official entries. Also, the exact figures for vessels' cargoes are not often recorded.

An important factor which should be taken into consideration in analyzing all figures for the Mexican period is the conservation policy of the Mexican government. Echeandía on his own initiative introduced into all the licenses which he issued the qualifying clause that pups were not to be killed. He, as well as Victoria, in their official reports called the matter to the attention of the central government. The regular form of licenses issued in the early 'thirties included a provision prohibiting the shooting of young otters. Since all furs, except those of the *contrabandista*, were sold to local retail merchants, it can be assumed that hunting returns in the Mexican period include only prime skins and not the 30 to 50 or more per cent of young ones, composing catches in Spanish days.

Very soon after the hunting rush of the 'thirties began, a change in otter numbers may be discerned. The most direct statement to that effect was made by Cooper, who resented the indiscriminate slaughtering being done by the *contrabandista*. In 1833 he wrote that between San Francisco and Monterey, where a few years before he had taken 700 skins, he had been able to obtain only thirty-two and he predicted that "I do not think we shall get 600 in all

on the coast."[10] In 1841 Charles Wilkes, United States naval commander, estimated that from 400 to 500 sea otter skins were brought
in each year.[11]

After 1840 the largest kills were made on the edges of the otter
grounds and in secluded places not recently hunted. An example
was the trip of Nidever's party to a distant field along Lower
California in 1840. Five years later at Morro Hermoso, on the very
limits of the otter grounds, Nidever and his men found "a large
school of otter," and killed about eighty-five of them.[12] In 1846 a
party found "on the right of the Petaluma Creek," or, according
to another, "about the entrance of Sonoma Creek," a number of
otters which had not been disturbed for years owing to Vallejo's
protection of them. "Not having the fear of the General before
their eyes," the Santa Barbara hunters shot between twenty and
forty of these animals.[13]

All evidence points to a great decrease in otters during the decade before California became the property of the United States.
Hunting parties, although they were small in size in comparison
with the earlier groups of Aleuts, had been numerous and persist-
ent in their methods. Also, it may be assumed that the disappearance of the animal in California was due to a great extent, as
reports indicate have been true elsewhere, to the new method of
hunting with guns instead of spears.

Exactly when guns began to be used for hunting sea otters in
California is not certain. The overland trapper introduced the
fashion for local hunters. About the same time, the Northwest
Coast Indians who came on the *contrabandistas* began to use firearms. The first specific reference to this method of hunting is a
statement by Nidever in 1836 : "They generally used buckshot, their
arms being the old English musket." He added, "The range of these
guns is something incredible. Our men assured us that the bullets
from the Indians' guns passed them when they were fully a mile
from the beach."[14] According to Davis, the northern Indians used
"Russian rifles,"[15] which probably described their source of purchase rather than place of manufacture. Spears were apparently
not entirely abandoned since they formed part of the hunting
equipment, along with muskets, of one of the *contrabandistas*
in 1839.

Hunting methods of the American gunman differed from the

mass methods used by the Aleut with his spear. Although some shooting was done from the land, most hunting was pursued at sea by small groups of from three to twelve men. For long hunts the party always included a cook and camp keeper. Kanakas, or Hawaiian Islanders, were taken along to paddle the boats and also to swim out for the game. Gradually California Indians were employed more frequently, and, according to Nidever, in paddling "they soon superseded the Kanakas."[16] The men composing the party, except one or two leaders, worked not on a share basis but for definite wages, from ten to twenty dollars a month.

The party set forth to sea in light wooden boats and was usually accompanied by a larger craft to carry provisions, especially when hunts became more distant and more extended in time. If a launch or whaleboat could not be had for the trip, some vessel on its passage north or south would leave the party and provisions on a designated island or point on the coast. Often parties on coastal hunts would set forth only in rowboats, with the intention of putting into ports along the way for anything needed. In spite of careful preparations, many distant hunts were ended prematurely because of exhaustion of supplies. The provision boats were usually schooner-rigged, of four or five tons, and often with no keel. A typical sea otter hunting shallop was described as follows. "The boat was about twenty-eight feet long and eight feet broad, clinker built, and sharp at both ends like a whale-boat, which she may in fact have originally been, rigged with two lug sails, and looked like a fast craft."[17] Sometimes shooting was done from these small sailers although, on account of maneuvering, the small rowboat was the more common hunting craft.

If a coastal trip was made, the party progressed steadily forward, getting into action whenever they happened upon their marine game, and lying by in rough weather. At night they put ashore, hauled their boat clear of the water, and either turned it over for a shelter or pitched tent. Then, "a fire is made of driftwood, or, if this fail, the dry stalks of the cactus, or a bunch of dead chaparral, serves them, and, if the provisions should be getting short, an excursion is made up some one of the many ravines or intervals—perhaps to a stagnant water-pool, where the deer and antelope in that arid region resort to quench their parching thirst."[18] If hunting was to be confined to one general locality, such as the

Channel Islands or Lower California coast, one island was chosen as a base. Camp was established, and the canoes scoured the waters in all directions from that point. If the hunters were to be absent for some days, they cached their main store of provisions on the island base. Parties operating for long periods of time off Lower California often returned to San Diego for provisions. One of the most difficult problems of the otter hunter was to keep a sufficient water supply. On the Lower California coast hunters made a special point to learn the location of dependable watering places and to fill barrels whenever they were within the near vicinity. Even so, long trips often had to be made specially for water; the party hunting in 1845 at Morro Hermoso went several times for that purpose thirty miles north to Cerros Island.

When putting out to sea, the gunman took his position at the prow of the boat. Near at hand were two or three favorite rifles, with perhaps a musket or two, and a plentiful supply of ammunition. The equipment of a typical hunter is described by Yount.

Each hunter was armed with two Rifles, with every possible convenience for charging very quickly. His powder was carried in a horn by his side, with small bits of cotton or linen strung upon his vest conveniently, one of which was hastily laid over the muzzle after the powder had been poured into the Rifle, a bullet placed upon it from the mouth of the hunter, which was kept always full, and all hastily rammed down. They used flint locks, and their pieces were self-priming.[19]

The common way to hunt was in groups of three canoes, in each of which were three men, a gunman, and two rowers. At sea a triangular formation was kept. One canoe pulled in advance with the others following in place on each quarter stern. As soon as an otter was seen within rifle shot—which, according to Phelps, was from seventy-five to one hundred yards—the hunter immediately fired. The nearest boat followed in the wake of the fleeing animal, the others falling into proper position with the object of keeping the animal inside the triangle. Standing in the bow of his boat, with his rifle to his shoulder, the hunter fired every time the otter rose to the surface or breached. It was not work for a novice. But Snow explains that "when a hunter gets used to standing in his boat, he can keep perfectly steady, and shoot as well as on land, no matter how violent the motion of the boat. His ankles, knees, and hips, act like gimbals, and take up all the motion of the boat, and his rifle, when pointed at an object, can be kept on it with ease."[20] If by chance a herd was discovered, the method pursued is described as follows:

... The fastest canoe pulls through the shoal without attempting to shoot; the other two come up, one on each side, and as it were corral the otter, and then shoot among them, right and left. When the shoal scatters, which it will in a short time, they attack them singly, taking care to select a large one. The boats form a triangle around the spot where he dives, and as soon as he again rises to the surface of the water, they shoot. They then form another triangle around him and as often as he appears he is greeted by musket balls, so that, if not killed, he is again obliged to dive. In this way he soon becomes exhausted, for want of air, and rises within gunshot, when he falls an easy victim to his pursuers.[21]

An environment of cracking gun reports and showers of musket balls is not conducive to the preservation of the otter species and accounted for their rapid decrease in California after the 1830's. The extinction of the species along the California coast was considered inevitable until a short time ago. In the 1890's and early in the twentieth century until 1917, occasional otters were seen and shot between San Luis Obispo and Monterey and around the islands opposite Upper and Lower California.[22] Fortunately, some of the long, lonely stretches of the California coast have served as quiet havens where a few of this rare species have been able to live their natural life, undisturbed by man.

Californians have in the sea otters recently discovered near Monterey living monuments of a great period in local and Pacific Coast history. Furthermore, they have a unique animal species of great interest to the entire scientific world. If the public demands and supports the strict enforcement of the present state law protecting this animal, the sea otter may again become the prized possession of California.

NEW MARKETS FOR THE LAST OF THE OTTER SKINS, 1835–1848

By 1835 the exportation of otter skins by way of the new China trade route was on the ebb. Transpacific shipments of otter furs began to feel the pinch of price changes. In the face of increased competition and an ever-decreasing supply of skins, retail prices in California climbed from thirty to thirty-five dollars per pelt and even to forty dollars when furs were offered as debt payments. However, although California skins brought fifty-five dollars in

China in 1831, Canton sales for 1834 were reported by Jones as being only thirty dollars. He added that "the Chinese are getting quite out of the use of them and probably they will never command the price they have formerly."[23] Two years later Stephen Reynolds reported that "nukies sold very low this year in Canton."[24]

Fur shipments to the Orient dwindled. Bryant, Sturgis, and Company discontinued consignments from California after 1833. The firm wrote in 1838 that "Sea Otter skins are too high on the Coast."[25] Hawaiian merchants were interested in otters only insofar as they formed a negotiable product from California debtors. For example, in 1836 several of the Honolulu merchants with whom Hinckley did business expressed their interest in sea otters. Reynolds desired remittance in furs, McIntosh and Company preferred cowhides but would take the otter, whereas French merely gave otter skins equal weight with other California produce. However, he wrote Thompson in February, 1837, when sending an invoice on the *Bolivar,* that "I should prefer good sea otters to any other remittance if you can get them at forty dollars each."[26] Hinckley's accounts for 1836 show that he purchased a few otter skins, but records do not indicate upon which of his two ships they were sent.[27]

Reynolds was one of the most pressing of Hinckley's creditors. Several times he urged Spear, his collector in California, to exert himself to obtain beaver and otter fur, the most merchantable articles, for which Hinckley would be answerable. The price he set at forty dollars for average skins and from forty-three to forty-five dollars for first-class fur. Otter values were still going up in California. Spear accepted the proposition. By June, 1836, he had purchased at Santa Barbara thirty skins which he intended to ship to Reynolds. But otter remittances to the Hawaiian Islands were very small. One single skin went to Reynolds in January, 1837. Five very inferior ones left on the *Don Quixote* early the same year. A few, also of poor quality, were sent by Spear on the *Clementine.*[28]

Continued low prices in the Orient worked against the transpacific fur trade. "You will perceive the state of the market to be against California prices," wrote Reynolds in the fall of 1837 when he was reporting results of sales in Canton the previous year.[29] Superior skins sent by Thompson to Peirce and Brewer in May, 1837, and offered on the Hawaiian market at forty dollars, remained on hand until September.[30] "A small lot" remitted by Thompson to Reynolds in 1838 could be sold for no more than thirty-five dollars per skin.[31]

However, the Oriental situation did not end the California otter trade. Other competitors were in the field. New fur markets opened.

In 1837 Nidever readily disposed of fifty skins at thirty-five dollars each to a German, John Daniel Meyer, who traded between California and Mexico. The next year a prominent hide-and-tallow merchant from Mexico, José Antonio Aguirre, was buying otter skins from Fitch at forty dollars. In October, 1840, Thompson was complaining that "all furs were bought up at a great price for the Mexican market," and stated that forty-seven and one-half dollars "were paid for each of a lot of 109 skins a short time since in Cash."[32]

By 1840 Mexico apparently had become one of the new markets for California otters. Unfortunately, data for exports to Mexico are scarce. In December, 1840, skins were sent there on the *Nymph*. Robert Dare and James McKinlay, merchants who had traded along the Pacific coast for some years, consigned one box of twenty-five skins to Machado, Yeoward and Company, while Meyer embarked 130 pelts to San Blas. On the second expedition of the *Nymph* late the next year a profit of $159 was made from otter skins sent to Mexico. In December John Wilson was considering sending some 200 fur-seal skins to Mazatlan. In 1842 Fitch delivered eleven otter skins at forty-five dollars each in connection with his business with the Mexican brig *Trinidad*. Two years later Henry Dalton wrote from Mazatlan that a prime lot of otters had been sold there at thirty dollars each. Dalton in 1846 was still collecting skins for the Mexican market.[33]

Another line of shipment took the place of the old China route after 1840. California otter skins began to go around the Horn to New England from where many of them were sent to north Europe.[34] Eight years after discontinuing transpacific shipments, the agents of Bryant, Sturgis, and Company added to the hide cargo of one of its last vessels several casks of otter skins, consigned directly to the home firm. While the *Alert* sailed down the coast from Santa Barbara in April, 1841, the "watch was employed in overhauling otter skins and packing them in casks."[35] At San Diego the furs were transshipped to the *Monsoon*, which was nearly loaded for Boston.

The mercantile successor of Bryant, Sturgis, and Company, William Appleton and Company, early expressed its interest in sea otters as a profitable supplement to hide shipments. On August 27, 1843, the firm's California agent, Henry Mellus, was instructed "to procure as many Sea Otter skins as possible, they will sell now at a price that would make them as favorable a remittance as hides if well selected."[36] Since furs occupied a comparatively small space and were extremely valuable, it was very desirable to include them, as well as gold, in every shipment of hides since it was "important to send home as large amount of value in a cargo as possible."[37] Furthermore, it was pointed out that the two Boston firms competing with William Appleton and Company lacked sufficient funds to speculate in furs along with hides.

In response to his company's instructions, Mellus the next April wrote that he was very "glad that other articles can be shipped from California. I shall always obtain a small quantity of Sea Otter skins."[38] He proceeded immediately to make collections. By June, 1844, fifty skins were on the *Barnstable*.[39] In December, just before the vessel sailed for Boston, thirty more were purchased from Fitch and packed with the others in a large cask. Mellus wrote from San Diego, "The otter skins now sent are, as a lot, very superior in quality having been selected from one hundred and fifty and cost high,"[40] as high as forty-five dollars. He stated that "the demand here is great for them, and we have been rather fortunate in obtaining so many." He added, "I have understood only the best are saleable in the U. S. and I wish you would inform me if inferior skins can be advantageously sent."

The *Barnstable*'s otter skins sold almost immediately after the ship's arrival at Boston in April, 1845. William Appleton and Company was delighted with the sales price, fifty-six dollars each, and expressed the hope that Mellus would "send a quantity of gold and Sea Otter skins in addition to the hides"[41] on the *Admittance* which was then on the California coast. Again in October the firm repeated that they wanted Mellus to ship "any sea otter you can procure."[42] A few weeks later a stronger statement went by the *Barnstable*. It would help the voyages of their ships "very much if you can send out in addition to full cargoes of hides as many Sea Otter skins and gold as came in the *Barnstable* this year."[43] An explanatory statement followed. "As good a load of Sea Otter skins as you sent last time costing twenty-five to forty dollars would at any time pay better than hides; but it is necessary to be very particular in selecting them." However, "Otter skins of less value we have no doubt would pay a proportionate profit, and we advise you to send any you can get at about the usual prices even if you have to send fewer hides."

In the meantime, Appleton's agent was finding it difficult to do the bidding of his employers. Whereas the first cargo sent from Boston on the *Barnstable* amounted to almost $40,000, those of the next two vessels, the *Admittance* and the *Tasso*, were evaluated at only a little over $21,000 and $27,000 respectively. Mellus complained in October, 1845, that "it requires all of so small an invoice to procure a return cargo of hides leaving nothing for Sea Otter and gold."[44]

Nevertheless, Mellus in 1845 and 1846 picked up a few furs. The accounts of the *Admittance* and *Tasso* showed a total number of one hundred and nine skins, most of them obtained at San Diego, probably from Fitch. Fifty-five skins, purchased for $1,953 at prices ranging from thirty-four to forty dollars each, were sent by the *Admittance* early in 1846. The entire consignment was sold at fifty dollars each within a month after the vessel arrived.[45]

The Boston competitors of William Appleton and Company shipped practically no otters around the Horn. Some went by the *California* of Benjamin T. Reed in 1843, and again in 1846. The ones sent the latter year apparently had been purchased from Fitch, for Captain James Arther reported to him that he had sold "the otter skins of yours on two months' credit. I smuggled them on shore. They did not pay duties," but even so, because of the temporary lowness of the fur market, "we scarcely got our own for the skins."[46]

The collection of otter skins by Boston hide vessels was considerably impeded after 1846. Apprehensive of the effect of the Mexican War upon business conditions, Atlantic coast merchants sent fewer ships to the California coast, and those craft which did arrive came with the specific purpose of collecting debts, paid most commonly in cowhides. The *Loo Choo* of William Appleton and Company in 1847 took back one cask of forty sea otter skins purchased for thirty-five dollars each and sold at a little over fifty dollars, less 4 per cent for cash. Davis reported that in 1847 the *Vandalia* belonging to Reed took away "otter skins," but the few extant accounts indicate that they were land otter. Only two sea otter pelts at twenty dollars each appeared on the 1847 invoices of the *Sterling* belonging to Joseph B. Eaton and Company.[47]

During the few years before the fur business was cut short by the Mexican War and by the gold rush, both otter hunting and the otter trade were almost entirely in the hands of Americans. Hunting, which then necessitated larger financing, could be managed on a profitable basis only by established merchants, and the latter at that time were Americans who had become naturalized Mexicans. Likewise, the exportation of otter skins, even though markets had changed, continued for the most part to be done by American firms.

THE SEA ROUTE IN NATIONAL EXPANSION

The sea otter trade was one of several major maritime enterprises forming the economic basis for the acquisition of California by the United States. It brought the first New Englanders into the Pacific and to California. For a quarter of a century Yankee free traders drove against the mercantile wall of Spain's northern outpost. Along with valuable skins, they picked up important information, the full significance of which was realized at the time only by Spanish officials whose worried reports to superiors repeatedly warned of the serious results of the marine invasion.

For a decade after the opening of California ports in the Mexican period, sea otters continued to be the chief economic incentive for the many Americans in the Hawaiian Islands who included California in the new China trade route. Toward the end of the decade the mountain men, engaging in a land drive for furs contemporary with the great sea drive, pushed westward beyond the bounds of their country into Mexican California. Many of them were prompted to remain by the possibilities of a fortune from otter skins. By the 'forties the hide-and-tallow and whaling industries exceeded the sea otter business in importance, but the latter continued to engage a number of resident and nonresident Americans until the outbreak of the Mexican War.

The otter trade furthered the progress of United States expansion. It contributed greatly to the rise of a resident American population in northwestern Mexico. Many of the United States citizens who as naturalized Mexicans established themselves permanently in Mexican California either came or were induced to remain because of the sea otter business, as for example, Francis Branch, Lewis Burton, John Cooper, Job Dye, William Dana, Robert Elwell, Eliab Grimes, William Hinckley, George Nidever, Nathan Spear, Samuel Prentice, Isaac Sparks, Alpheus Basil Thompson, and Jonathan Warner. The first call for a United States warship "to afford protection to our commerce and citizens" came from one of the leading American merchants in the Hawaiian Islands who had vessels engaging in the otter trade.[48] The first United States warship to arrive on the coast, although it came ostensibly because "of many serious outrages and unjust acts . . . committed . . . upon American vessels and seamen," in reality appeared as the result of difficulties arising from clandestine otter hunting.[49] The first known petition for a United States consul was respectfully solicited "with others, my fellow citizens, resident merchants in California," by Jonathan Warner who established himself financially on the coast through otter hunting.[50]

The government reached out to support its real and erstwhile citizens. How United States diplomacy prior to the Mexican War was rooted in a realization of commercial values on the Pacific coast has been set forth at length by several outstanding historians.[51] With victory came an expanded United States—culmination of a movement begun and greatly furthered by the American drive around the Horn into the North Pacific for sea otters.

APPENDIX

IDENTIFIED VESSELS ENGAGED IN THE CALIFORNIA SEA OTTER TRADE
1786–1848

THE FOLLOWING CONTRIBUTION was prompted both by frequent inquiries for shipping data from historians working in the Pacific field and by the excellent work of Judge Frederick William Howay in listing vessels engaged in the fur traffic on the Northwest Coast. The present list includes only identified vessels which are known to have been engaged in the California sea otter trade. It by no means includes either all the ships touching on the California coast in the period designated or, owing to the illegal nature of the business and to incomplete records, all the sea otter traders. In some instances, especially during the latter part of the Mexican period, vessels listed were concerned only incidentally with the otter trade.

Vessels are classified according to the year of each trip to California, although usually complete data for every voyage are given, from the time of the ship's departure from home port to either its return, disposal, or reappearance in California. In citations of uncertain or approximate time data, parentheses are used. The item "otter skins" refers only to furs known to have been obtained in California. Place entries in California are limited to ten for each vessel.

Princesa (or *Nuestra Señora del Rosario*), 1786

Frigate, 189 tons; captain, Estevan José Martínez; on board, Vicente Vasadre y Vega; owner, Spanish government; otter skins, 1,060; sailing schedule: June 8, left San Blas; August 27, at Monterey; October 8, left Monterey; October 19, arrived Santa Barbara; November 28, left San Diego; December 18, arrived San Blas.

Favorita (or *Nuestra Señora de los Remedios*), 1787

Frigate; captain, José de Cañizares; owner, Spanish government; otter skins, 1,750 (joint cargo of *Favorita* and *San Carlos*); sailing schedule: ——, San Blas; October 6, at Monterey; October 23, arrived Santa Barbara; November 25, at San Diego; ——, San Blas.

San Carlos (or *Filipino*), 1787

Packetboat or snow, 196 tons; owner, Spanish government; otter skins, 1,750 (joint cargo of *San Carlos* and *Favorita*); sailing schedule: ——, San Blas; October 6, at Monterey; ——, San Blas.

Aranzazu (or Nuestra Señora de Aranzazu), 1788

Frigate; captain, José de Cañizares; owner, Spanish government; otter skins, 116 at San Francisco; sailing schedule: July 8, left San Blas; September 18, arrived San Francisco; October 4, arrived Monterey; October 26—November 15, Santa Barbara; December 7, at San Diego; ——, San Blas.

Aranzazu (or Nuestra Señora de Aranzazu), 1789

(See *Aranzazu*, 1788); otter skins, 234 at Santa Barbara; sailing schedule: ——, San Blas; October 21, arrived Santa Barbara; November 9, at Santa Barbara; ——, San Blas.

San Carlos (or Filipino), 1790

Packetboat or snow, 196 tons; captain, Salvador Fidalgo; owner, Spanish government; otter skins, 656; sailing schedule: February 3, left San Blas; April 5—May 4, Nootka; May 23, arrived Prince William's Sound; September 15—October 24, Monterey; November 14, arrived San Blas.

Butterworth, 1793

Ship, 392 tons; captain, William Brown; owners, Alderman Curtis and others, London; sailing schedule: 1792, Northwest Coast; February, 1793, Hawaiian Islands; ——, Santa Cruz; March 13–15, off San Francisco; ——, Northwest Coast; ——, Hawaiian Islands. (Continued, *Butterworth*, 1794.)

Jackal, 1793

Schooner or cutter; captain, Alexander Stewart, William Brown after vessel left Hawaiian Islands, fall of 1793; owners, Alderman Curtis and others, London; sailing schedule: 1792, Northwest Coast; February, 1793, Hawaiian Islands; ——, Monterey; March 15, at Bodega Bay; ——, Northwest Coast; ——, Hawaiian Islands; February 24, 1794, left Canton; June 20, at Yakutat Bay; January 1, 1795, at Hawaiian Islands (William Brown killed); ——, Canton.

Prince Lee Boo, 1793

Sloop, 30–40 tons; captain, —— Sharp, —— Gordon after vessel left Hawaiian Islands, fall of 1793; owners, Alderman Curtis and others, London; sailing schedule: 1792, Northwest Coast; January, 1793—March, Bodega Bay; March, Monterey; ——, Bodega Bay; ——, San Francisco; ——, Northwest Coast; ——, Hawaiian Islands; February 24, 1794, left Canton; August, October 5, at Nootka Sound; January 1, 1795, at Hawaiian Islands (Gordon killed); ——, Canton.

Butterworth, 1794

Ship, 392 tons; captain, —— Sharp; owners, Alderman Curtis and others, London; sailing schedule: ——, California Coast; April, Galápagos Islands; ——, England.

Jenny, 1794

Ship, 78 tons; captain, John William Adamson; owner, Sidenham Teast, Bristol; sailing schedule: October, 1793, left Bristol; April, 1794, California; May—September, Northwest Coast; ——, Hawaiian Islands; December 25, arrived Canton; July 25, 1795, arrived Bristol.

Phoenix, 1795

Bark; captain, Hugh Moore; on board, Joseph O'Cain, from Northwest Coast to Santa Barbara; owners, at Bengal; sailing schedule: ——, Bengal; July, 1794, Northwest Coast; March, 1795, Northwest Coast; August 28—September 5, Santa Barbara; ——, Hawaiian Islands; ——, Canton.

Otter, 1796

Ship, 14–31 crew, 6 guns; captain, Ebenezer Dorr; on board, —— Péron, Thomas Muir; owners, Dorr & Sons, Boston; sailing schedule: August 20, 1795, left Boston; February 18, 1796, left Sydney; April 29—October, Northwest Coast; October 23, arrived Santa Cruz; October 27, off Carmel; October 30—November 6, Monterey; December 9—January 1, 1797, Hawaiian Islands; February 13—March 27, Canton; January 27, 1798, arrived Portland, Maine.

Garland, 1798

Brig, 21 crew, 6 guns; captain, Bazilla Worth; owners, at Boston; sailing schedule: March, 1797, left Boston; ——, Northwest Coast; ——, Hawaiian Islands; March 24, 1798, left Valparaiso (detained by governor); April, Juan Fernández Island; August 21, arrived Hawaiian Islands; November 6, California, 40°30'; November 16, off Todos Santos Bay; December 4–11, Santo Tomás; January 8, 1799—March 6, Acapulco (detained by authorities, ship sold).

Eliza, 1799

Ship, 159 tons, 24–36 crew, 12 guns; captain, James Rowan; supercargo, John Kendrick, Jr.; third mate, William Sturgis; owners, J. & T. H. Perkins, S. G. Perkins, Stephen Higginson, George Higginson, Boston; sailing schedule: (August 15), 1798, left Boston; January, 1799, arrived Hawaiian Islands; February 13, arrived Sitka; May, left Northwest Coast; May 24, arrived San Francisco; June 15, arrived San Blas; October—December, Canton; May, 1800, arrived Boston.

Betsy, 1800

Brigantine, 104 tons, 19 crew, 10 guns; captain, Charles Winship (left at San Blas, died December 4, 1800), —— Brown, from San Blas to Canton; supercargo, Joseph O'Cain (left at San Blas); second mate, —— Brown; on board, Nathaniel Winship; owners, Abiel Winship and Joseph O'Cain, Boston; sailing schedule: August 3, 1799, left Boston; ——, off Chile, 56° (seized); April, 1800, Valparaiso (released); ——, Northwest Coast; August 25—September 4, San Diego; ——, Todos Santos Bay; ——, Colnett Bay; ——, San Quintín Bay; October, San Blas; ——, Cape San Lucas; 1801, Canton; October, arrived Boston.

Enterprise, 1801

Ship, 240 tons, 21 crew, 10 guns; captain, Ezekiel Hubbell; supercargo or mate, Joseph O'Cain (apparently after ship touched at San Blas in December, 1800); owner, Hay & Thorn, New York; sailing schedule: February 28, 1800, left New York; ——, Valparaiso; December 23—January 8, 1801, San Blas;

February 5, arrived San José del Cabo; ——, Northwest Coast; June 28—July 3, San Diego; July 5–13, Todos Santos Bay; July 13–27, San Quintín Bay; August 13–19, San José del Cabo; November 20—January 31, 1802, Canton.

Alexander, 1803, first trip

Ship, 180 tons, 19 crew, 14 guns; captain, John Brown; pilot, George Eayrs (left at Monterey, August 17); owners, Henry Bass & Company and Joseph Taylor, Boston; otter skins, 491 skins found on board at San Diego; sailing schedule: July 19, 1802, left Boston; ——, Valparaiso; February 26, 1803, arrived San Diego; March 7–17, Todos Santos Bay; March 22—April 4, San Quintín Bay; ——, San Juan Capistrano; May, San Francisco; ——, Northwest Coast. (Continued, *Alexander*, 1803, second trip.)

Alexander, 1803, second trip

(See Alexander, 1803, first trip); sailing schedule: August 11–12, San Francisco; August 14–17, Monterey; ——, San Juan Capistrano; August, San Quintín Bay; January 20, 1804, left Canton; June 5, arrived Boston.

Hazard, 1803

Ship, 350 tons, 50–60 crew, 26 guns; captain, James Rowan; owners, John Curtis, William F. Magee, and Benjamin Page, Providence, Rhode Island; sailing schedule: September (10), 1801, left Liverpool; February 4, at Masafuera Island; March 31, 1802, left Valparaiso (detained by authorities); ——, Hawaiian Islands; November, Canton; ——, Northwest Coast; August 11–19, 1803, San Francisco; August 23–27, Santa Barbara; September 1–2, San Juan Capistrano; September 2, off San Diego; September 18, off Monterey; December 1, at Hawaiian Islands. (Continued, *Hazard*, 1804.)

Lelia Byrd, 1803

Brig, 175 tons, 17–24 crew, 24 guns; captain, William Shaler; second in command, Richard J. Cleveland; owners, William Shaler, Richard J. Cleveland, Count de Rouissellon; otter skins, 1,600 California skins purchased at San Blas, January, 1803; sailing schedule: November 8, 1801, left Hamburg; January 2–9, 1802, Rio de Janeiro; February 24—May 7, Valparaiso (difficulties with authorities); July 11—August 1, October 20—January 25, 1803, San Blas; March 16–22, San Diego; March 24—May 3, San Quintín Bay; May 25–30, San José del Cabo; June 21—July 7, Hawaiian Islands; August 26—February 8, 1804, Canton. (Continued *Lelia Byrd*, 1804.)

O'Cain, 1803–1804

Ship, 280 tons, 18 guns, 40 Aleuts, 20 baidarkas; captain, Joseph O'Cain; commander of Aleuts, —— Shvetsov; on board, Jonathan Winship, Jr., Vasilii Petrovich Tarakanov; owners, Abiel Winship, Benjamin P. Homer, Jonathan Winship, Jr., and others, Boston; otter skins, 1,800; sailing schedule: January 23, 1803, left Boston; October 26, left Kodiak Island; December 4–8, San Diego; December 13—March 26, 1804, San Quintín Bay; April 15–19, Todos Santos Bay; June, arrived Kodiak Island; September 8, left Northwest Coast; January 2, 1805, at Canton; July 1, arrived Boston.

Hazard, 1804, first trip

(See *Hazard*, 1803); sailing schedule: January 30, arrived San Francisco; February 21, at Queen Charlotte Islands. (Continued, *Hazard*, 1804, second trip.)

Hazard, 1804, second trip

(See *Hazard*, 1803); sailing schedule: ——, Ventura; September 3–5, San Juan Capistrano; September 7, off San Diego; September 8, off San Miguel; September 11, at Colnett Bay; December—February, 1805, Canton.

Lelia Byrd, 1804

(See *Lelia Byrd*, 1803); sailing schedule: February 8, left Canton; May 1, off Columbia River; May 11–18, Trinidad; ——, San Francisco; July 5, arrived Ventura; July 13, off Cerros Island; July 22, at Cape San Lucas; August 2–18, Guaymas; August 19—October 1, Lower California, Gulf coast; October 18, left Mazatlan; December 24—January 14, 1805, Guatemala. (Continued, *Lelia Byrd*, 1805.)

Activo, 1805

Brig, 6 guns; captain, Francisco Baridon; owner, Spanish government; otter skins, 292; sailing schedule: ——, San Blas; August 30, arrived Monterey; ——, San Francisco; November 21, arrived San Blas.

Lelia Byrd, 1805

(See *Lelia Byrd*, 1803); sailing schedule: February 24, arrived California; March 1, arrived San Luis Obispo; March 7, arrived Santa Barbara; March 14, arrived Santa Catalina Island; ——, San Pedro; March 27, off San Diego; March 28, arrived San Miguel; March 31—April 6, Todos Santos Bay; May 1 —June 9, Santa Catalina Island; ——, San Pedro; June 3, off Santa Barbara; June 26, off San Diego; June 29—July 3, Colnett Bay; July 28–30, Cape San Lucas; August 22, arrived Hawaiian Islands (sold to Kamehameha I in exchange for the *Tamana*).

Princesa, 1805

Frigate, 189 tons; captain, Juan José Martínez; owner, Spanish government; sailing schedule: ——, San Blas; August 30, arrived Monterey; ——, San Francisco; November 21, arrived San Blas.

Eclipse, 1806

Ship, 343 tons, 35 crew, 18 guns; captain, Joseph O'Cain; owners, J. & T. H. Perkins, James Lloyd, and others, Boston; sailing schedule: January 26, left Boston; ——, Hawaiian Islands; June 22, off San Juan Capistrano; June 25–29, San Diego; June 30—July 8, Todos Santos Bay; July 8–10, San Quintín Bay; July 18–21, Cape San Lucas; August, Sitka; March—May 8, 1807, Canton; ——, Kamchatka; September, Northwest Coast (wrecked).

O'Cain, 1806

Ship, 280 tons, 16–30 crew, 18 guns, 100 Kodiak hunters, 12 Kodiak women, Kanakas, 50 baidarkas; captain, Jonathan Winship, Jr.; mate, Nathan Winship; commander of hunters, —— Slobodchikov; on board, Samuel Patterson, from Hawaiian Islands, October, 1806; owners, Abiel Winship, Benjamin P. Homer, Jonathan Winship, Jr., and others, Boston; otter skins, 17 at Trinidad; sailing schedule: October, 1805, left Boston; March, 1806, Hawaiian Islands; April 1, arrived Sitka; May, Norfolk Sound; June 11–25, Trinidad; June 29, arrived Cerros Island; ——, Todos Santos Bay; ——, San Quintín Bay; July 31—August 12, off San Borja; August 13, at Cerros Island; October 12, left Hawaiian Islands; ——, Sitka; November 9—January 16, 1807, Kodiak Island. (Continued, *O'Cain*, 1807.)

Peacock, 1806

Brig, 108 tons, 14–18 crew, 8 guns; captain, Oliver Kimball; sailing schedule: September 14, 1805, left Boston; February 12, 1806, arrived Hawaiian Islands; March 19, off San Gabriel; March 25, off River Santa Ana; April 3–9, off San Juan Capistrano; April 10–13, off San Diego; April 19, left Todos Santos Bay; April 20, arrived Carmen; April 21, left Santo Tomás; July 19, in Hecate Strait; October 25, at Kodiak Island. (Continued, *Peacock*, 1807.)

Tamana, 1806

Schooner, 45 tons; captain, John T. Hudson; owners, William Shaler, Richard J. Cleveland (purchased vessel from Kamehameha I); sailing schedule: ——, Honolulu; February 4–7, San Luis Obispo; February 11–12, Ventura; ——, San Pedro; ——, Todos Santos Bay; February 23–27, Carmen; March 10, at Carmen. (Continued, *Tamana*, 1807.)

Maryland, 1806–1807

Ship; captain, Jonathan Perry; owner, at New York; sailing schedule: 1805, left New York; ——, Peru; fall, 1806, on Lower California coast; January 15, 1807—February (5), San José del Cabo.

Mercury, 1806–1807

Ship, 145 tons; captain, William Heath Davis; on board, George Washington Eayrs; owners, Benjamin Lamb and others, Boston; otter skins, 2,848 (1,772 large, 1,076 small); sailing schedule: January, left Boston; July 19, arrived Hecate Strait; November 24, at San Luis Obispo; December 12, at Santa Barbara; December 22–23, off Los Angeles; December 24, at Santa Barbara; January 1–5, 1807, Todos Santos Bay; January 28, at Rosario Bay; April 4, off Los Angeles; ——, San Juan Capistrano; August 9, off Santa Barbara; August 21, at Santo Tomás; October 10, at Hawaiian Islands; December—January, 1808, Canton. (Continued, *Mercury*, 1808.)

Activo, 1807

Brig, 6 guns; owner, Spanish government; otter skins, 273 (joint cargo of *Activo* and *Princesa*); sailing schedule: March 18, left San Blas; May 2, arrived Monterey; ——, San Francisco; June 16—July 1, Santa Barbara; July 20, at San Diego; December 10, arrived San Blas.

Derby, 1807

Ship, 300 tons, 50 Kodiak hunters, 25 baidarkas; captain, Benjamin Swift; owners, J. & T. H. Perkins, George Lyman, and William Sturgis, Boston; sailing schedule: September (5), 1806, left Boston; September 10, 1807, on Northwest Coast; ——, California; March 23, 1809, left Canton; August 18, arrived Boston.

Nicholai (probably formerly the *Tamana*), 1807

Schooner; owner, Slobodchikov (purchased vessel at Cerros Island from an American for 150 sea otter skins); sailing schedule: ——, California; ——, Hawaiian Islands; August 22, arrived Sitka.

O'Cain, 1807

(See *O'Cain*, 1806); additional party on board, 50 Kodiak hunters, 7 Kodiak girls, 2 Kodiak boys, 1 Russian; otter skins, 4,819 (3,006 grown, 1,264 yearlings, 549 pups); sailing schedule: January 16, left Kodiak Island; February 15, arrived Farallon Islands; ——, San Pedro; ——, Santa Catalina Island; March 6, arrived Todos Santos Bay; March 7, arrived San Quintín Bay; May 4, arrived Santo Domingo; May 31, at San Quintín Bay; September 8—October 9, Sitka; ——, Hawaiian Islands; December 31—February 14, 1808, Canton; June 15, arrived Boston.

Peacock, 1807

Brig, 108 tons, 14–18 crew, 8 guns, 12 baidarkas; captain, Oliver Kimball; commander of hunters, Vasilii Petrovich Tarakanov; otter skins, 1,231 (753 grown, 228 yearlings, 250 pups); sailing schedule: (March 5—May 15), at Bodega Bay and along coast; May 31, arrived San Quintín Bay; August 3, arrived Sitka; ——, Hawaiian Islands; January 24, 1808, at Canton; March, Batavia (sold).

Princesa (or *Nuestra Señora del Rosario*), 1807

Frigate, 189 tons, 30 guns; captain, Ramón de Saavedra; owner, Spanish government; otter skins, 273 (joint cargo of *Princesa* and *Activo*); sailing schedule: March 18, left San Blas; May 2, arrived Monterey; June 16—July 1, Santa Barbara; July 20, at San Diego; September 20, arrived Monterey; October 21, at Monterey; December 10, arrived San Blas.

Tamana, 1807

(See *Tamana*, 1806); on board, Samuel Patterson (from California to Hawaiian Islands); sailing schedule: ——, Honolulu; February, Santa Catalina Island; May 2, between Santa Monica and Ventura. (See *Nicholai*, 1807.)

Kodiak, 1808–1809

Forty crew, 130 Northwest Coast hunters, 20 Northwest Coast women; captain, —— Petrov; commander of expedition, Ivan Kuskov; owners, Russian American Company, Sitka; otter skins, 2,350 (1,453 grown, 406 yearlings, 491 pups); sailing schedule: October 15, left Sitka; ——, Trinidad; December 28—August 18, 1809, Bodega Bay; October 4, arrived Sitka.

Mercury, 1808–1809

Ship, 145 tons, 18 crew, 25 baidarkas; captain, George Washington Eayrs; commander of hunters, —— Shvetsov; owners, Benjamin Lamb and others, Boston; otter skins, 2,117 (1,688 grown, 256 yearlings, 136 pups, 37 others); sailing schedule: January, left Canton; May, Northwest Coast; June 17 or 26, left Kodiak Island; ——, Queen Charlotte Islands; ——, Columbia River; ——, Trinidad; ——, Bodega Bay; December 1–12, San Francisco; December 17–21, Todos Santos Bay; ——, San Diego; 1809, San Pedro; April 26, at

San Juan Capistrano; May 14, off Los Angeles; June, Northwest Coast; ——, Columbia River. (Continued, *Mercury*, 1809–1810.)

Dromo, 1809

Ship, 492 or 600 tons, 100 or 108 crew, 26 guns; captain, —— Woodward; owners, Andrew Cabot, James Lee, Jr., and Henry Lee, Boston; otter skins, 1,700; sailing schedule: December 6, 1807, left Boston; March 16–24, 1808, Concepción; April 2–15, Coquimbo; August 24—September 5, Realejo; November 22—December 25, Guaymas; January 4, 1809—February 6, Todos Santos Bay; February 24—March 15, Hawaiian Islands; May 10—September 29 or December 11, Canton; May 6 or July 7, 1810, arrived Boston.

Isabella, 1809

Ship, 209 tons; captain, William Heath Davis; owner, Boardman & Pope, Boston; sailing schedule: 1809, left Boston; August, off Santo Domingo. (Continued, *Isabella*, 1810–1811.)

Mercury, 1809–1810

Ship, 145 tons; captain, George Washington Eayrs; owners, Benjamin Lamb and others, Boston; otter skins, 96 at Santa Barbara; sailing schedule: 1809, San Luis Obispo; ——, Santa Barbara Channel Islands; December 4, off Refugio; ——, Santa Barbara; 1810, San Quintín Bay; June 17, on Columbia River; July 19, left Columbia River; July 27, arrived Sitka. (Continued, *Mercury*, 1810.)

Albatross, 1810

Ship, 165 tons, 22 crew, 25 Kanakas; captain, Nathan Winship; assistant, William Alden Gale; chief mate, William Smith; owners, Abiel Winship, Jonathan Winship, Jr., Nathan Winship, Benjamin P. Homer, and others, Boston; sailing schedule: July 6, 1809, left Boston; February 23, 1810, arrived Nukuhiva Island; March 30—April 13, Hawaiian Islands; May 26, arrived Columbia River; June 17, arrived Gray's Harbor; July 19, left Columbia River; ——, Trinidad; July 30, arrived Farallon Islands; ——, Santa Barbara Island; ——, Cerros Island; October 22—November 16, Sitka. (Continued, *Albatross*, 1810–1811.)

Mercury, 1810

(See *Mercury*, 1809–1810); otter skins, 20 at Santa Barbara; sailing schedule: November 29, at Drake's Bay; ——, San Quintín Bay; December, Santa Barbara; September, 1811, left Canton. (Continued, *Mercury*, 1812.)

Albatross, 1810–1811

Ship, 165 tons, 22 crew, 25 Kanakas, 50 Kodiak hunters, 30 baidarkas; captain, Nathan Winship; assistant, William Alden Gale; chief mate, William Smith; commander of hunters, —— Lasseff; owners, Abiel Winship, Jonathan Winship, Jr., Nathan Winship, Benjamin P. Homer, and others, Boston; otter skins, 1,190 (778 grown, 140 yearlings, 202 pups, 70 others), 1,220 tails; sailing schedule: November 29, arrived Drake's Bay; December 4, arrived Farallon Islands; ——, San Luis Obispo; December 21, arrived San Quintín Bay; January 24, 1811—March 3, Drake's Bay; April 1, left Lower California; May 4, arrived Farallon Islands; May 24—June 3, Farallon Islands; June 15, arrived San Benito Island; June 19, left Lower California; August 8, arrived Sitka; August 19–23, Point Woodhouse; September 11, left Northwest Coast. (Continued, *Albatross*, 1811.)

Isabella, 1810–1811

Ship, 209 tons, 48 baidarkas; captain, William Heath Davis; commander of hunters, Vasilii Petrovich Tarakanov; owner, Boardman & Pope, Boston; otter skins, 2,976 (1,987 grown, 432 yearlings, 566 pups); sailing schedule: June 28, at Sitka; July 30, gang of *Isabella's* sealers found on Farallon Islands; September, Bodega Bay; November 29, at Drake's Bay; February, 1811, hunters of *Isabella* in San Francisco Bay; May 11, arrived Drake's Bay; November—January 1, 1812, Hawaiian Islands; February 26—April 24, Canton; June 15, arrived Hawaiian Islands; February 15, 1813, Canton; June 29, arrived Hawaiian Islands; November 7, at Honolulu. (Continued, *Isabella*, 1814.)

O'Cain, 1810–1811

Ship, 280 tons, 50 baidarkas; captain, Jonathan Winship, Jr.; owners, Abiel Winship, Jonathan Winship, Jr., and others, Boston; otter skins, 3,952; sailing schedule: May, 1809, left Boston; ——, Hawaiian Islands; December, Sitka; ——, Queen Charlotte Islands; August 26, 1810, arrived Sitka; November 29, at Drake's Bay; December 21, at San Quintín Bay; April 1, 1811, on Lower California coast; May 11, arrived Drake's Bay; November 20—January 1, 1812, Hawaiian Islands; February 26—April 24, Canton; June 15, arrived Hawaiian Islands; October, at Hawaiian Islands. (Continued, *O'Cain*, 1813.)

Albatross, 1811

(See *Albatross*, 1810); sailing schedule: September 27—October 2, Farallon Islands; (November 1)—January 1, 1812, Hawaiian Islands. (Continued, *Albatross*, 1812.)

Chirikov, 1811

Schooner; captain, Ivan Kuskov; owner, Russian American Company, Sitka; otter skins, 1,238 (1,160 grown, 78 yearlings); sailing schedule: January 22, left Sitka; February 21—June 20, Bodega Bay; ——, Farallon Islands; July 28, arrived Sitka.

Chirikov, 1811–1812

Schooner, 40 baidarkas, 86 Kodiak hunters; captain, Ivan Kuskov; owner, Russian American Company, Sitka; sailing schedule: November, 1811, left Sitka; ——, Bodega Bay.

Albatross, 1812

Ship, 165 tons; captain, Nathan Winship to Hawaiian Islands, William Smith after July; sailing schedule: January 1, left Hawaiian Islands; February 26—April 24, Canton; June 15—July 10, Hawaiian Islands; August 13 or 15, arrived Farallon Islands; ——, Drake's Bay; October 25, arrived Hawaiian Islands. (Continued, *Albatross*, 1813.)

Amethyst, 1812

Ship, 270 tons, 52 baidarkas; captain, Thomas Meek; owners, John Dorr, George Washington Eayrs, and owners of *Mercury*, Boston; otter skins, 1,442 (655 grown, 49 yearlings, 17 pups); sailing schedule: September, 1811, left Canton; November, Sitka; January, 1812, left Sitka; June, August, San Quintín Bay; ——, Sitka (sold to Russians).

Charon, 1812

Brig, 283 tons; captain, Isaac Whittemore; owner, P. T. Jackson, Boston; otter skins, 1,792 (1,596 grown, 136 yearlings, 60 pups); sailing schedule: November, 1811, left Boston; 1812, Sitka; ——, San Quintín Bay; August, sealing party on Farallon Islands; September, Northwest Coast; July, 1813, Hawaiian Islands. (Continued, *Charon*, 1814.)

Katherine, 1812

Ship, 287 tons, 50 baidarkas; captain, William Blanchard; owner, at Boston; otter skins, 1,516 (1,252 grown, 186 yearlings, 78 pups); sailing schedule: April, 1809, left Boston; ——, Hawaiian Islands; April 12, 1810, in Hecate Strait; September, 1811, Kaigani; November, Sitka; January, 1812, left Sitka; June, August, San Quintín Bay; August–September, Sitka; November 10, arrived Honolulu; ——, Canton; ——, Boston.

Mercury, 1812

Ship, 145 tons; captain, George Washington Eayrs; on board, Antipatro (*sic*), son of Alexander Baranov; owners, Benjamin Lamb and others, Boston; otter skins, 500; sailing schedule: January, left Sitka; ——, Bodega Bay; February, San Luis Obispo; February 26, March 21, off Refugio; ——, off Los Angeles; April 7, April 19, at San Quintín Bay; April 21, at Santo Tomás; May 7, June, at San Quintín Bay; August 16, at Refugio; ——, Cape San Lucas; September 27, arrived Sitka. (Continued, *Mercury*, 1813.)

Albatross, 1813

(See *Albatross*, 1812); sailing schedule: ——, Canton; July, Hawaiian Islands; August 20, arrived Columbia River; ——, California; November 15–24, Marquesas Islands; December 20, arrived Hawaiian Islands. (Continued, *Albatross*, 1814.)

Mercury, 1813

Ship, 145 tons; captain, George Washington Eayrs; owners, Benjamin Lamb and others, Boston; otter skins, 1,603 skins, 947 tails; sailing schedule: April 28, left Sitka; ——, Bodega Bay; May 25–31, San Luis Obispo; June 1, arrived Point Conception (seized by Noé of the *Flora*); June 2, Santa Barbara.

O'Cain, 1813

Ship, 280 tons; captain, Jonathan Winship, Jr.; owners, Abiel Winship, Jonathan Winship, Jr., and others, Boston; sailing schedule: April, Canton; June 30, arrived Hawaiian Islands; ——, California; November 10, arrived Hawaiian Islands. (Continued, *O'Cain*, 1814.)

Albatross, 1814

Ship, 165 tons; captain, Nathan Winship in March, William Smith in September; sailing schedule: March, Hawaiian Islands; June 26, left California; July 9, arrived Hawaiian Islands; September, Hawaiian Islands; April, 1815, Hawaiian Islands; May, September—December 1, Sitka. (Continued, *Albatross,* 1816.)

Charon, 1814

(See *Charon,* 1812); sailing schedule: ——, California; February 9, arrived Hawaiian Islands; June 18, at Hawaiian Islands (captured by English ship, the *Cherub*).

Forester, 1814

Brig, 10 guns; captain, John Jennings to Hawaiian Islands, William J. Pigot after November; clerk, Richard Ebbets; mate, Alexander Adams; owner, Pacific Fur Company, New York; sailing schedule: ——, New Holland; November 9, 1813, arrived Hawaiian Islands; ——, Bodega Bay; January 14, 1814, at San Luis Obispo; March, left California; April, Washington coast; June 25, arrived Sitka. (Continued, *Forester,* 1814–1815.)

Ilmen (formerly *Lydia*), 1814

Brig, 50 Aleuts and creoles, 25 baidarkas; captain, —— Wadsworth; supercargo and pilot, John Elliot d'Castro; commander of hunters, Vasilii Petrovich Tarakanov; on board, Antipatro (*sic*), son of Alexander Baranov; owner, Russian American Company, Sitka; sea otter skins, 392 (322 grown, 50 yearlings, 20 pups); sailing schedule: January, left Sitka; ——, Bodega Bay; (before August 26), Farallon Islands; ——, San Francisco; ——, Santa Barbara Channel Islands; ——, San Pedro (Tarakanov and 11 men seized). (Continued, *Ilmen,* 1815.)

Isabella, 1814

Ship, 209 tons; captain, William Heath Davis, —— Tyler in 1815; owner, Boardman & Pope, Boston; sailing schedule: ——, California; March, Hawaiian Islands; June 9, left Sitka; July 10, September, Hawaiian Islands; September, 1815—October 17, Sitka; December 24, at Hawaiian Islands; February 26, 1816, arrived Canton.

O'Cain, 1814

Ship, 280 tons; captain, Jonathan Winship, Jr., Robert McNeil in February, 1814, and May, 1815; owners, Abiel Winship, Jonathan Winship, Jr., and others, Boston; sailing schedule: ——, California; February, Hawaiian Islands; July 15, left Hawaiian Islands for "the Main"; May, 1815, September, Norfolk Sound. (Continued, *O'Cain,* 1816.)

Pedler, 1814

Brig, 225 tons; captain, Samuel H. Northrop; on board, Wilson Price Hunt; owner, Pacific Fur Company; sailing schedule: January 8, at Hawaiian Islands; January 22, left Hawaiian Islands; February 28—April 2, Columbia River; June, Sitka; ——, Bodega Bay; August 26, at San Luis Obispo (seized by the *Tagle,* released September 9); May 25, 1815, September, at Sitka; December 27—January 9, 1816, Hawaiian Islands; February, Canton; October, arrived New York.

Forester, 1814–1815

Brig, 10 guns; captain, William J. Pigot, Richard Ebbets after Kamchatka; clerk, Alexander Adams; owner, Pacific Fur Company, New York; sailing schedule: ——, California; November, near Loreto; 1815, islands off California; March 24, off San Diego; April, left Point Conception; June 4, left Bodega Bay; June 18—July, Sitka; November 4, left Kamchatka. (Continued, *Forester*, 1815.)

Forester, 1815

Brig, 10 guns; captain, Richard Ebbets; clerk, Alexander Adams; owner, Pacific Fur Company, New York; sailing schedule: December 20, arrived San Luis Obispo; January, 1816, Hawaiian Islands; ——, South America; April 6, arrived Honolulu (sold to Kamehameha I and renamed *Kaahumanu*).

Ilmen, 1815

(See *Ilmen*, 1814); commander of hunters, Boris Tarasov; otter skins, 955 obtained around Santa Barbara Channel Islands; sailing schedule: June, San Francisco; July, between San Luis Obispo and Santa Barbara; August, off San Pedro; September 18, off San Pedro (Tarasov and 24 Aleuts seized at San Pedro); September 19, arrived San Luis Obispo; September 21–25, off Refugio (seven, including Elliot, seized); ——, Bodega Bay; ——, Hawaiian Islands; ——, Sitka; 1816, Hawaiian Islands.

Albatross, 1816

Ship, 165 tons, 6 guns; captain, William Smith to Refugio, Nathan Winship from Cerros Island; sailing schedule: January 10–11, off Santa Barbara; January 14, near Refugio (Smith and 5 others seized); ——, Cerros Island; March 8, arrived Honolulu; October 16, at Honolulu (vessel sold to Kamehameha I).

Atala, 1816

Ship, 260 tons; captain, —— Winship, —— Kelly when vessel in California; on board, Captain William Blanchard and Captain —— Brown from Hawaiian Islands, 1817; owners, in Boston; sailing schedule: September, 1815, left Boston; ——, St. Catherines; ——, Galápagos Islands; July 12, 1816, arrived Honolulu; November, left Sitka; November 28, arrived Santa Barbara; ——, Monterey; August, 1817, Peru; November 6, at Hawaiian Islands; December 9, left Honolulu; May, 1818, Canton (vessel condemned).

Lydia, 1816

Schooner; captain, Henry Gyzelaar; on board, William Smith from Santa Barbara to Hawaiian Islands; owners, B. C. Wilcocks, American consul at Canton, and James Smith Wilcocks; sailing schedule: July 12, 1815, left Canton; September 27—December 1, Sitka; ——, Fort Ross; January 16, 1816, arrived Refugio (vessel seized); January 20—February 2, Santa Barbara; March 9, at Monterey (vessel released); March 15, arrived Santa Barbara; September, Hawaiian Islands (vessel sold to Kamehameha I).

O'Cain, 1816

Ship, 280 tons; captain, Robert McNeil; on board, William Smith, from Honolulu to Canton; sailing schedule: May, left Galápagos Islands; ——, Cerros Island; July, Honolulu; January 7, 1817, left Canton; June 8, arrived Cowes, England; October 15, arrived Boston.

Sultan, 1816

Ship, 274 tons; captain, —— Reynolds; owner, Boardman & Pope, Boston; sailing schedule: August, 1815, left Boston; November 25, left St. Catherines; April–May (26), Sitka; ——, San Luis Obispo; July 22, arrived Monterey; ——, Columbia River; ——, Northwest Coast; 1817, Hawaiian Islands; ——, Marquesas Islands; ——, Chile; 1818, Marquesas Islands; September 20, at Honolulu; ——, Canton.

Traveller, 1816–1817

Schooner, (89 tons); captain, James Smith Wilcocks; owner, James Smith Wilcocks; sailing schedule: December, 1815, left Canton; 1816, Sydney; ——, Coquimbo; ——, Galápagos Islands; ——, Peru; November 25—December 7, Honolulu; December 25, arrived Bodega Bay; January 8, 1817, arrived Santa Barbara; March 3–16, Santa Barbara; March, San Diego; ——, San Quintín Bay; April 27, arrived Loreto; June, Monterey; July 27–28, San Luis Obispo; July 29, arrived Santa Barbara; September 2, left Santa Barbara; October 30, Loreto (vessel seized by Francisco Ramírez and confiscated, January 7, 1818).

Avon, 1817

Ship; captain, Isaac Whittemore; sailing schedule: 1815, left Boston; October, Galápagos Islands; November, 1816, Sitka; January, 1817, "St. Stephens," California coast; January 20, at San Pedro; February, Santa Barbara Channel Islands; November 6—December 1, Honolulu; ——, "Spanish Main"; April, 1818, Coquimbo (vessel sold).

Bordeaux Packet, 1817

Hermaphrodite brig, 180 tons; captain, Andrew Blanchard; on board, James Hunnewell, —— Dorr; sailing schedule: November 16, 1816, left Boston; March 26, 1817—April 22, Hawaiian Islands; ——, Lower California, latitude 27°; ——, Cerros Islands; May 18, off Cape San Lucas; ——, Gulf of Lower California; May 25, off Loreto; July 6, arrived Todos Santos Bay; July 13–14, San Juan Capistrano; July 26–27, San Luis Obispo; August 12, arrived Honolulu; September 17, at Honolulu (vessel sold in December to Kalaimoku, renamed Kalaimoku).

Bordelais, 1817, first trip

Ship, 200 tons, 8 guns, 34 crew; captain, Camille de Roquefeuil; owner, —— Balguerie, Jr., Bordeaux, France; sailing schedule: October 19, 1816, left Bordeaux; January 1, 1817, off Falkland Islands; February 5–14, Valparaíso; February 26—May 29, Callao; August 5–14, San Francisco; September 1–18, Nootka Sound. (Continued, Bordelais, 1817, second trip.)

Bordelais, 1817, second trip

(See Bordelais, 1817, first trip); sailing schedule: October 13–15, Bodega

Bay; October 13—November 20, San Francisco; December 22—February 28, 1818, Marquesas Islands. (Continued, *Bordelais*, 1818.)

Chirikov, 1817

Schooner; captain, Christopher Martinevich Beuseman; commander of expedition, Lieutenant Yakov Padushkin; owner, Russian American Company, Sitka; sailing schedule: February, left Sitka; ——, Bodega Bay; March, arrived San Francisco; May 12, at Monterey; ——, Santa Barbara; June, arrived Sitka.

Columbia, 1817

Brig, 185 tons, 25 crew, 10 guns; captain, John Jennings; chief officer, Peter Corney; owner, Northwest Company; sailing schedule: January 10, left Columbia River; January 27—April 16, Hawaiian Islands; May 10, arrived Sitka; June 12—July 12, Columbia River; July 24, arrived Trinidad; July 28 —August 8, Bodega Bay; August 9, at Farallon Islands; August 10, at Drake's Bay; August 20–22, Trinidad; August 23, arrived Point St. George; October 10—November 14, Columbia River; December 6, arrived Hawaiian Islands (vessel sold May 2, 1818, to Kamehameha I).

Cossack, 1817

Brig; captain, J. Brown when left Boston, —— Myrick after October, 1817; probably on board, Vasilii Petrovich Tarakanov and Aleuts, from Honolulu to California; owner, John Jacob Astor, New York; sailing schedule: (May), 1815, left Boston; November 4—December 10, Hawaiian Islands; September, 1816, Northwest Coast; November, left Sitka; ——, Hawaiian Islands; February 20, 1817, arrived Canton; May 7, arrived Honolulu; October 19, left Honolulu; ——, California; December, Guaymas (vessel seized and renamed *San Francisco de Paula*).

Kutusov, 1817

Captain, Leontii Hagemeister; on board, Ivan Kuskov; owner, Russian American Company, Sitka; sailing schedule: ——, Sitka; ——, Bodega Bay; October 16, 29, at San Francisco; November 11, left San Francisco; November 20, arrived Sitka.

Bordelais, 1818

(See *Bordelais*, 1817, first trip); sailing schedule: April 5—May 1, Sitka; May 12—June 1, Kodiak Island; June 26—July 6, Sitka; September 5–10, Nootka; September 20—October 20, San Francisco; November 9—December 13, Sitka; January 12, 1819—January 26, Honolulu; March 13—April 23, Canton; November 21, arrived Bordeaux.

Clarion, 1818

Brig, 149 tons, 17 crew, 6 guns; captain, Henry Gyzelaar; on board, William Alden Gale; owner, Abiel Winship, Boston; sailing schedule: September 1, 1817, left Boston; ——, Cape of Good Hope; 1818, Tasmania; August 22—September 10, Honolulu; October 6–11, Santa Barbara; October 14, off San Diego; November 1, at Honolulu; 1819, Sitka; July 23, 1820, at Honolulu; November 28, at Canton; March, 1821, left Canton; ——, Boston.

Eagle, 1818

Schooner; captain, William Heath Davis, Thomas Meek after arrival at Chile, 1818; on board, William Smith, from Sitka, 1819, to Canton; owners, Boardman & Pope, William Heath Davis, and others, Boston; sailing schedule: December 2, 1816, left Boston; January, 1817, Rio de Janeiro; May, Hawaiian Islands; ——, Sitka; August, October, Hawaiian Islands; December 1, left Honolulu; ——, "Spanish Main"; February, 1818, Coquimbo; August, California coast; September 13–19, Honolulu; ——, Sitka; January, 1819, Hawaiian Islands; June, Sitka; August 27, December, at Hawaiian Islands; March 25, 1820, left Canton; July 25, arrived Boston.

Kutusov, 1818

Captain, Leontii Hagemeister; owner, Russian American Company, Sitka; otter skins, 72 at Santa Cruz; sailing schedule: July 2, left Sitka; August 1, arrived Monterey; ——, Santa Cruz; September, left Monterey; October 3, arrived Sitka.

Okhotsk, 1818

Fifty Aleuts; owner, Russian American Company, Sitka; sailing schedule: spring, left Sitka; ——, Bodega Bay.

Ship, 1818

Two hundred and twenty tons, 20 crew; captain, Judais Coffin (*sic*); owner, "Governor of Philadelphia"; sailing schedule: July 10, arrived San Pedro.

Ilmen, 1820

Brig; captain, Kiril Khlebnikov; supercargo, Adolf Yenlen (*sic*); owner, Russian American Company, Sitka; sailing schedule: June 13, at Sitka; August 2, at Monterey; ——, Sitka.

San Francisco de Paula (or *Dos Hermanos*, formerly *Cossack*), 1820

Brig; owner, Spanish government; captain, Blas Cosio; sailing schedule: ——, Mazatlan; May 25, arrived Santa Barbara; May 29, at San Francisco; June 25, at Monterey; July 9, left Ventura; ——, Mazatlan; ——, Acapulco.

Eagle, 1821

Schooner; captain, Eliab Grimes; on board, —— Dominis and —— Rogers (after December, 1821); owner, Marshall & Wildes, Boston; sailing schedule: May—July 19, Hawaiian Islands; August 23–25, Bodega Bay; August 26—September 3, San Francisco; September 7–12, Santa Barbara; September 16–18, Santa Catalina Island; September 20, arrived San Diego; September 30—October 4, Santa Monica Bay; October 10–13, San Luis Obispo; October 15–18, San Pedro; October 29—November 6, Santa Monica Bay; November 7–8, San Juan Capistrano; November 27—January, 1822, Hawaiian Islands. (Continued, *Eagle*, 1822.)

Eagle, 1822

Schooner; captain, —— Rogers; owner, Marshall & Wildes, Boston; sailing schedule: July 11, at Hawaiian Islands; ——, Monterey; September 13, at Santa Barbara (attempted to seize *San Francisco de Paula*, was stuck in kelp, was sold to Padre Antonio and renamed *Santa Polonia*).

Owhyhee, 1822

Brig, 166 tons; captain, William Henry, Boston to Hawaiian Islands, Eliab Grimes, after Hawaiian Islands; owner, Marshall & Wildes, Boston; otter skins, 150, number collected after July 8; sailing schedule: July 9, 1821, left Boston; December 12—February 2, 1822, Hawaiian Islands; July 8, August, Northwest Coast; November 1–19, San Francisco; November 30, at Santa Barbara; December 22, arrived Honolulu; November, 1823, Hawaiian Islands. (Continued, *Owhyhee*, 1824.)

Volga, 1822

Brig, 23 crew; captain, Prokop Tamanin (*sic*); owner, Russian American Company, Sitka; otter skins, 15 (10 grown, 5 yearlings); sailing schedule: ——, Sitka; December 3, arrived San Francisco; December 31, at Monterey; ——, Sitka.

Sachem, 1822–1823

Ship; captain, Henry Gyzelaar; supercargo, William Alden Gale; owners, Bryant & Sturgis, and others, Boston; sailing schedule: ——, Boston; June, arrived Monterey; July 31, at San Diego; October 1, arrived San Diego; April 15, 1823, arrived San Francisco; July 20, at San Francisco; August 18, at Monterey; October, left California; ——, Boston.

Ann, 1823

Schooner, (204 tons); captain, —— .Hersey; owner, Bryant & Sturgis, Boston; sailing schedule: July, 1822, left Boston; January 14, 1823, at Honolulu; September 6, left Honolulu; October 11, arrived Monterey; November 20, at Monterey; ——, San Luis Obispo; January, 1824, San Blas; April, Northwest Coast.

Buldakov, 1823

Brig; captain, Cristof Vickilman (*sic*); owner, Russian American Company, Sitka; otter skins, 46 (44 grown, 2 yearlings); sailing schedule: ——, Sitka; August 28, arrived San Francisco; ——, Santa Cruz; September 22, left San Francisco; ——, Sitka.

Mentor, 1823

Ship; captain, George Newell; owner, Bryant & Sturgis, Boston; sailing schedule: June 31, 1822, left Boston; November 16—February 7, 1823, Hawaiian Islands; ——, Northwest Coast; July 19, arrived Hawaiian Islands; September 6, left Honolulu; ——, Bodega Bay; October 11, arrived Monterey; November 1, arrived San Francisco; November 19, arrived Monterey. (Continued, *Mentor*, 1824.)

Rover, 1823

Schooner, 83 tons; captain, John Rogers Cooper; first officer, Thomas M. Robbins; owners, John Rogers Cooper, Nathaniel Dorr, William Blanchard, Roxbury, Government of California after July, 1823; sailing schedule: June 5, 1822, left Boston; December 23, arrived Honolulu; February 27, 1823— March 9, Fanning Island; March 19, arrived Honolulu; May 9, left Honolulu;

May 28—June 11, San Francisco; June 12, at Santa Cruz; June 13—July 19, Monterey; August 5–17, Honolulu. (Continued, *Rover*, 1823–1824.)

Rover, 1823–1824

Schooner, 83 tons; captain, John Rogers Cooper; first officer, Thomas M. Robbins; owner, Government of California; otter skins, 303 skins, 300 tails; sailing schedule: September 17—January 18, 1824, Monterey; January 20–29, San Francisco; February 7, left Monterey; February 29—March 15, Honolulu; April 25—May 20, Manila; June 8—July 1, Canton. (Continued, *Rover*, 1824–1825.)

Becket, 1824

Brig, 130 tons; captain, Abraham Hall; owner, Kaumaulii, King of Kauai; sailing schedule: November, 1823, at Hawaiian Islands; April 10, 1824, left Honolulu; July 20, arrived San Pedro; ——, Guadalupe Island; August 8, arrived Honolulu; January, 1825, Hawaiian Islands.

Mentor, 1824

(See *Mentor*, 1823); otter skins, 18 at San Francisco; sailing schedule: ——, Hawaiian Islands; March 13—April 2, Canton; ——, Bodega Bay; June 15, arrived Monterey; July 7, at San Francisco; ——, Santa Barbara; September, San Diego; ——, Mazatlan; February, 1825, Canton; ——, Boston.

Owhyhee, 1824, first trip

Brig, 166 tons, 22 crew; captain, John Kelly; owner, Marshall & Wildes, Boston; otter skins, 110; sailing schedule: April 1, left Honolulu; May 2, arrived Bodega Bay; May 4, arrived San Francisco; July, San Pedro; July 17, at Mazatlan. (Continued, *Owhyhee*, 1824, second trip.)

Owhyhee, 1824, second trip

(See *Owhyhee*, 1824, first trip); sailing schedule: September 12, left San Luis Obispo; September 13, left Monterey; ——, Northwest Coast; July 26, 1825, left Queen Charlotte Islands. (Continued, *Owhyhee*, 1826.)

Sultan, 1824

Ship, 274 tons; captain, George Clark; owner, Boardman & Pope, Boston; sailing schedule: 1823, Northwest Coast; October 17, arrived Honolulu; 1824, California; ——, Mexico; June 22, arrived Honolulu; ——, Canton; July, 1825, arrived Boston.

Washington, 1824

Schooner, 45 or 52 tons; captain, —— Stevens; supercargo, Robert Elwell; owner, Marshall & Wildes, Boston; otter skins, 18; sailing schedule: July 21, left Honolulu; ——, Bodega Bay; ——, San Francisco; September 3, arrived Monterey; September 12, at San Luis Obispo; October 10, left San Diego; October 29, arrived Honolulu. (Continued, *Washington*, 1825.)

Rover, 1824–1825

Schooner, 83 tons; captain, John Rogers Cooper; owner, Government of California; otter skins, 444 skins, 263 tails; sailing schedule: September 13—

October 17, Monterey; October 23—December 1, Bodega Bay; December 2—
January 5, 1825, San Francisco; January 7—March 23, Monterey; April 16
—May 20, Honolulu; June 7–21, Fanning Island; August 24—September 14,
Manila; September 26—October 25, Canton. (Continued, *Rover*, 1826.)

Nile, 1825

Brig, 15 crew; captain, Robert Bennet Forbes; supercargo, George Newell;
owner, Perkins & Company, Canton; sailing schedule: ——, Hawaiian Islands;
September 16, arrived Bodega Bay; September 19, arrived San Francisco;
October, Santa Barbara; November 7, arrived Mazatlan; January 20, 1826,
at Sonsonate; June, Guayaquil.

Tamaahmaah, 1825

Brig, 180 tons; captain, John Meek; on board, Captain John Ebbets, Honolulu to Canton, 1826; owners, John Jacob Astor, W. Roberts, John Ebbets;
sailing schedule: April 9, 1824, left New York; August 9—November 13,
Honolulu; ——, Sitka; January 15, 1825, arrived San Francisco; February
23—March 27, Honolulu; August 24, left Lima; September 7, at Galápagos
Islands; October, December 23, at Honolulu; January 18, 1826, left Honolulu; ——, Canton; December 9, at Honolulu. (Continued, *Tamaahmaah*,
1827.)

Washington, 1825

Schooner, 45 or 52 tons, 9 crew; captain, Robert Elwell; owner, Marshall &
Wildes, Boston; sailing schedule: January 6, at Honolulu; February 23, ar-
rived San Francisco; March 9–23, Monterey; October, at Hawaiian Islands;
December 22, left Honolulu. (Continued, *Washington*, 1826.)

Baikal (formerly *Arab*), 1825–1826

Brig, 180 or 203 tons, 20 baidarkas; captain, Christoper Beuseman; owner,
Russian American Company, Sitka; otter skins, 468; sailing schedule: ——,
Sitka; November 17–26, San Diego; January 4, 1826, arrived Monterey;
February 14–16, San Diego.

Convoy, 1826

Brig, 135 tons; captain, William H. McNeil; owner, Josiah Marshall, Boston; sailing schedule: October, 1824, left Boston; March 16, 1825, arrived
Honolulu; April, Northwest Coast; November 2, arrived Honolulu; 1826,
Northwest Coast; November 6, at Hawaiian Islands; ——, California; January 6, 1827, left Honolulu; ——, Tahiti; ——, Valparaiso.

Harbinger, 1826

Brig, 180 tons; captain, Joseph Steele; supercargo, Thomas B. Park; sailing schedule: January 12, at Honolulu; March 1, at San Diego; ——, San
Pedro; ——, Guaymas. (Continued, *Harbinger*, 1826–1827.)

Owhyhee, 1826

Brig, 166 tons, 30–40 crew; captain, Eliab Grimes; owner, Marshall &
Wildes, Boston; sailing schedule: January 10, at Honolulu; February 1, left
Honolulu; March 1, arrived San Diego; April 29, at Las Tres Marías Islands.

Rover (renamed San Rafael), 1826

Schooner, 83 tons; captain, John Rogers Cooper, José Cardenas after December; owner, Government of California; sailing schedule: January 28—March 3, Guam; April 23—July 16, Monterey; July 19, arrived Santa Barbara; July 25—August 15, San Diego; October 15–22, Santa Barbara; November 6—December 17, Monterey; June 15, 1827, at Monterey.

Washington, 1826

Schooner, 45 or 52 tons; captain, —— Little; supercargo, Alpheus Basil Thompson; owner, Marshall & Wildes, Boston; sailing schedule: January 20, at San Francisco; February 4, at Santa Barbara; ——, San José del Cabo; ——, Mazatlan; May 25, at Honolulu.

Waverly, 1826

Brig, 142 tons, 9 crew, 40 Kanakas; captain, William Goodwin Dana; owner, Government of the Hawaiian Islands; otter skins, 138; sailing schedule: ——, Honolulu; June, arrived San Francisco; September 7, arrived San Diego; September 26–30, San Diego; ——, Guadalupe Island; October 11–22, Santa Barbara; November 18–26, Santa Barbara; November 29, arrived San Diego; ——, Honolulu. (Continued, Waverly, 1827–1828.)

Harbinger, 1826–1827

(See Harbinger, 1826); sailing schedule: November 20–30, San Diego; January 11, 1827, at Monterey; ——, Honolulu.

Harbinger, 1827

(See Harbinger, 1826); sailing schedule: February 28, left Honolulu; April 18, at San Francisco; May 24, at Santa Barbara; June 6, at San Diego; June 28, at San Pedro; July 12, at Santa Barbara; July 20, at San Juan Capistrano; ——, San Diego; November 12, at Monterey; November 20, at San Pedro; ——, San Luis Rey; ——, Honolulu.

Kamehameha, 1827

Brig; captain, William French; sailing schedule: February 18, March 6, at Honolulu; July 6, at Monterey; ——, Honolulu.

Karimoku (formerly Becket), 1827

Brig, 130 tons; captain, John Lawlar; owner, at Hawaiian Islands, chartered by John Coffin Jones, Jr., agent of Marshall & Wildes, Boston; sailing schedule: March, left Honolulu; May 9, at Santa Barbara; ——, Honolulu.

Tamaahmaah, 1827

Brig, 180 tons; captain, John Ebbets; owners, John Jacob Astor, W. Roberts, John Ebbets; sailing schedule: March 2, at Honolulu; June 20, at San Francisco; June 26, left San Francisco; December, left Honolulu; ——, Manila; February 19, 1828, at Hawaiian Islands (vessel sold to Kaahumanu).

Waverly, 1827–1828

Brig, 142 tons; captain, William Goodwin Dana, Thomas M. Robbins part of time in California; on board, John Temple, Honolulu to California; owner, Government of the Hawaiian Islands; sailing schedule: May 20, left Honolulu; July 2, at Monterey; September 15, at Santa Barbara; October 5–21, San Diego; November 6, at San Pedro; ——, Santa Barbara; November 10, December 10, March 11, 1828, at Monterey; March 25, May 12, at Santa Barbara; ——, San José del Cabo. (Continued, *Waverly*, 1828–1829.)

Griffon, 1828

Brig, 180 tons; captain, Marcus Tullius Peirce; clerk, Henry Augustus Peirce; owners, Bryant & Sturgis, Boardman & Pope, Boston; otter skins, 40 at San Francisco; sailing schedule: October 24, 1824, left Boston; March 25, 1825, arrived Honolulu; ——, Northwest Coast; September, 1828, left Tongass; October, arrived San Francisco; February, 1829, left Honolulu; ——, Northwest Coast; November 7, 1829, at Honolulu; ——, Canton.

Héros, 1828

Ship, 370 tons, 32 crew, 12 guns; captain, Auguste Bernard du Hautcilly; owners, —— Javal, Martin Lafitte, Jacques Lafitte, Havre, France; otter skins, 150; sailing schedule: February 28, left Callao; May 3, arrived Monterey; July 3—August 27, San Diego; September 17—November 15, Hawaiian Islands; March 26, 1829, left Canton; July 19, arrived Havre.

Karimoku, 1828, first trip

Brig, 130 tons; captain, John Lawlar; owner, at Hawaiian Islands; sailing schedule: ——, Hawaiian Islands; April, arrived San Pedro; June 3, at San Pedro; July, Honolulu.

Karimoku, 1828, second trip

(See *Karimoku*, first trip); sailing schedule: September 17, at San Francisco; September 22, at Monterey; October, San Pedro; ——, San Diego; ——, Guadalupe Island; October 28, arrived San Diego; February, 1829, arrived Honolulu.

Baikal, 1828–1829

Brig, 180 or 203 tons, 12 Aleuts, 6 baidarkas; captain, Adolphus Etolin; owner, Russian American Company, Sitka; otter skins, 63; sailing schedule: ——, Sitka; December 10, at San Diego; December 17, left San Diego; December 19, arrived San Quintín Bay; February 12, 1829, at San Diego.

Washington, 1828–1829

Schooner, 45 or 52 tons; captain, Alpheus Basil Thompson; on board, Luis M. Bringas and Charles Lang (from California to Mazatlan); owner, Marshall & Wildes, Boston; sailing schedule: September 8, at Honolulu; October 7, left Honolulu; November 18, arrived San Francisco; December 3, arrived Monterey; January 13–21, 1829, Santa Barbara; ——, San Diego; ——, Mazatlan; ——, Acapulco. (Continued, *Washington*, 1829.)

Waverly, 1828–1829

(See *Waverly*, 1827–1828); sailing schedule: August 23, arrived San Diego; October, Bodega Bay; ——, Santa Barbara; November (7)—December 21, Monterey; December 25—January 30, 1829, Santa Barbara; February, Honolulu.

Dhualle, 1829

Brig, 182 tons; captain, William Warden; owner, at Hawaiian Islands; otter skins, 40 at Monterey; sailing schedule: July 1, at Honolulu; August 19, at Monterey; September 1, at Santa Barbara; September 11–17, San Pedro; October 3, left Santa Barbara; October 17, arrived Honolulu.

Diana, 1829

Brig, 199 tons; captain, William C. Little; on board, George Rice; owner, William French, Honolulu; sailing schedule: 1828, Canton; November 29, December 11, at Honolulu; January 4, 1829, at Monterey; February, Cape San Lucas.

Volunteer, 1829

Ship; captain, Charles Taylor; on board, Reverend Jonathan S. Green; owner, Bryant & Sturgis, Boston; chartered by Charles Taylor; sailing schedule: February 13, left Honolulu; March 11, arrived Sitka; ——, Northwest Coast; August 31, at Sitka; September 30, arrived San Francisco; October 18, left Monterey.

Washington, 1829

Schooner, 45 or 52 tons; captain, Alpheus Basil Thompson; on board, Charles Rand Smith; owner, Marshall & Wildes, Boston; sailing schedule: September 3, at San Diego; September 12, at Santa Barbara; October 1, at Monterey; October 24, arrived Honolulu.

Brookline, 1829–1830

Ship, 375 or 417 tons, 10 crew; captain, James O. Locke; supercargo, William Alden Gale; clerk, Alfred Robinson; owners, Bryant & Sturgis, and others, Boston; sailing schedule: 1828, Boston; February 15, 1829—March 17, Monterey; March 26—April 29, San Diego; May 18—June 3, Santa Barbara; June 26, left San Diego; July 18, arrived San Francisco; September 1–13, Santa Barbara; February 4, 1830, at San Diego; April 24—May 9, Monterey; June 8, left Santa Barbara; August 17, at Santa Barbara; ——, Boston.

Volunteer, 1830

Bark, 126 tons, 15 crew; captain and supercargo, John Coffin Jones, Jr.; on board, James Ohio Pattie, William Sturgis Hinckley, and political prisoners, from California to San Blas; owner, John Coffin Jones, Jr., Honolulu; sailing schedule: February 12, 1830, at Honolulu; March 29, arrived Monterey; April 20—May 8, Monterey; May 19, arrived San Blas; ——, Mazatlan; June 18, left San Blas; July 19, arrived Honolulu.

Convoy, 1831

Brig, 135 tons, 13 crew; captain, Benjamin Pickens; supercargo, Alpheus Basil Thompson; owners, William French, Eliab Grimes, John Coffin Jones, Jr., and Alpheus Basil Thompson, Honolulu; otter skins, 4 at Monterey; sailing schedule: March 6, left Honolulu; April 7–14, Monterey; ——, San Francisco; June 15–18, Monterey; ——, Santa Barbara; August 7, at San Pedro; August 22, at San Diego; September 22, at Monterey; October 21, at Santa

Barbara; November 8, at San Pedro; before March, 1832, at Honolulu; ——, Lima; July, arrived Honolulu.

Griffon, 1831

Brig, 180 tons, 24 crew, 8 guns, 30 Northwest Coast Indians, 18 canoes; captain, Charles Taylor; otter skins, 300; sailing schedule: September 3, 1830, on Northwest Coast; November 5, at Honolulu; 1831, Northwest Coast; July—August, California; ——, San Quintín Bay; September 10, arrived Honolulu.

Louisa, 1831

Bark, 174 tons, 16 crew; captain, George Wood; supercargo, John Coffin Jones, Jr.; assistant supercargo, Charles Rand Smith; on board, William Heath Davis, Jr.; owner, John Coffin Jones, Jr., Honolulu; otter skins, 400 (only part from California); sailing schedule: April 14, at Honolulu; ——, Sitka; June 26, arrived Monterey; ——, Santa Barbara; July 30—August 22, San Diego; September 14–24, Honolulu; ——, New York.

William Little, 1831

Sloop, 36 tons, 7 crew; captain, Henry Carter; owner, Henry Carter, Honolulu; otter skins, 478; sailing schedule: ——, Santa Barbara; July 6, arrived Monterey; July 31, August 12, at Santa Barbara; September 19, arrived Honolulu.

Crusader, 1832

Brig, 110 tons, 35 Kaigani hunters, 60 canoes; captain, Benjamin Pickens; supercargo, Alpheus Basil Thompson; owner, Eliab Grimes, agent; chartered by John Coffin Jones, Jr., Alpheus Basil Thompson, Eliab Grimes, and French & Company; otter skins, 160; sailing schedule: March 21, left Honolulu; ——, Northwest Coast; July 4, on California coast; ——, Cerros Island; September, at Honolulu.

Griffon, 1832

Brig, 180 tons; captain, Charles Taylor; otter skins, 100; sailing schedule: March 2, on California coast; September, arrived Honolulu; October 18, 1833, at Honolulu (vessel sold to Eliab Grimes, French & Company, and Stephen Reynolds).

Plant, 1832

Brig, 208 tons; captain, —— Rutter; owner, Bryant & Sturgis, Boston; otter skins, 316; sailing schedule: June, 1831, left Boston; February, 1832, arrived Santa Barbara; October 31, left Santa Barbara; ——, Honolulu; ——, Boston.

Victoria, 1832

Schooner; captain, Charles Brewer; on board, Nathan Spear; owner, William French, Honolulu; otter skins, 106; sailing schedule: December 10, 1831, left Honolulu; ——, Northwest Coast; August 14, 1832, at Monterey.

Crusader, 1832–1833

Brig, 110 tons; captain, Thomas Sturgis; supercargo, William Sturgis Hinckley; owner, William Sturgis Hinckley, Honolulu; otter skins, 96 (93 grown, 3 pups); sailing schedule:. October 17, at Honolulu; November 18, at Monterey; January, 1833, California coast; March 11, at Honolulu.

Convoy, 1833, first trip

Brig, 135 tons; supercargo, Alpheus Basil Thompson; owners, outfitted by Alpheus Basil Thompson, John Coffin Jones, Jr., Eliab Grimes, and William French; otter skins, 300–400; sailing schedule: November 13, 1832, at Honolulu; 1833, California coast; August 19, at Honolulu.

Convoy, 1833, second trip

(See *Convoy*, 1833, first trip); otter skins, 170; sailing schedule: November 28, at Santa Barbara; ——, San Pedro; January, 1834, arrived Honolulu.

Harriet Blanchard, 1833

Schooner, 62 tons, 10 crew; captain, Levi Young to November, Thomas Shaw of *Volunteer* after November; supercargo, John Ebbets, Jr., until November; on board, John Coffin Jones, Jr., and William Heath Davis, Jr., from California to the Hawaiian Islands; owner, John Coffin Jones, Jr., Honolulu; otter skins, 10 at San Pedro; sailing schedule: January 9, arrived Honolulu; April 1, at San Francisco; April 25, left Santa Barbara; May 19, left Todos Santos Bay; May 22, arrived San Diego; June 18, at Santa Barbara; August 1, left San Diego; August 26, at San Pedro; September 30, at Monterey; October 17, left San Pedro; November 11, left San Diego; December 3, arrived Honolulu.

Maraquita, 1833

Cutter; captain, Sherman Peck; owner, John Coffin Jones, Jr. (vessel chartered from Mexican captain, Agustín Poncabaré); otter skins, 114; sailing schedule: October 17, at Santa Barbara; October 30, at San Pedro; December 20, at Santa Barbara; ——, Honolulu.

Loriot, 1833–1834

Brig, 90 tons; captain, Gorham H. Nye; supercargo, Alpheus Basil Thompson; owner, at Hawaiian Islands; otter skins, 5 at Monterey; sailing schedule: July, left Honolulu; August 23—September 5, Monterey; September 14, arrived San Francisco; September 26, at San Francisco (vessel seized); October 16, at San Francisco (vessel released); November 13, left San Francisco; November 28, at Santa Barbara; January 4, 1834, at San Pedro; January 13, at Santa Barbara; February 18–20, Santa Barbara; ——, Honolulu.

Volunteer, 1833–1834

Bark, 126 tons; captain, Thomas Shaw to November, Levi Young of *Harriet Blanchard* after November; supercargo, John Coffin Jones, Jr. until November, John Ebbets, Jr. after November; assistant supercargo, Sherman Peck until about October; on board, William Heath Davis, Jr., Honolulu to California; owner, John Coffin Jones, Jr.; otter skins, 80–100 at San Francisco; sailing schedule: April 8, at Honolulu; May 10, arrived Monterey; June 18, at Santa Barbara; July 19, at San Pedro; August 1, left San Diego; August 23—September 17, San Francisco; October 17, at Santa Barbara; October 23, November 15, at San Diego; January 3, 1834, at San Barbara; ——, Lima; April 4, at Honolulu.

Bolivar Liberator, 1834

Brig, 212 or 224 tons, 20 Tongass Indians; captain, John Dominis; owners, at Salem; sailing schedule: August 8, left Columbia River; ——, coast between Columbia River and Spanish settlements.

Don Quixote, 1834

Bark, 260 tons; captain, John Meek; owners, William Sturgis Hinckley, Henry Augustus Peirce, and others, Honolulu; otter skins, 5 at San Francisco; sailing schedule: April 30, left Honolulu; May 25, at Monterey; June 21—July 22, San Francisco; August 6, at Monterey; August 22, at Santa Barbara; August 29, at San Pedro; September 8, at San Diego; October 14, at Santa Barbara; November 2, at San Pedro; December 23, at Honolulu.

Avon, 1835

Hermaphrodite brig, 120 tons; captain, William Sturgis Hinckley; owner, John Coffin Jones, Jr., Honolulu; otter skins, 6 at Monterey; sailing schedule: June 24, at Honolulu; October 22, left Monterey; October 29—November 7, Santa Barbara; ——, San Pedro; November 25, at Santa Barbara; January 10, 1836, at Honolulu.

Bolivar Liberator, 1835

Brig, 212 or 224 tons; captain, John Dominis; otter skins, 400; sailing schedule: June 12, near Columbia River; December 25, left California; January 14, 1836, arrived Hawaiian Islands.

Convoy, 1836

Brig, 135 tons; captain, John Bancroft; owner, Eliab Grimes; outfitted by Alpheus Basil Thompson, John Coffin Jones, Jr., Eliab Grimes, and William French; sailing schedule: ——, Santa Rosa Island; January 8, off Point Conception; March 13, left California; March 27—April 23, Honolulu; ——, Northwest Coast.

Diana, 1836

Brig, 199 tons; captain, Joseph O. Carter; owner, French & Company, Honolulu; sailing schedule: 1835, Canton; ——, Honolulu; ——, Sitka; December 29—January 6, 1836, Monterey; February 4—March 20, Honolulu; ——, Canton.

Don Quixote, 1836

Bark, 260 tons; captain, John Meek; supercargo, Stephen D. MacKintosh; on board, William Sturgis Hinckley; owners, William Sturgis Hinckley and others, Honolulu; sailing schedule: September 9, 1835, left Boston; February 18, 1836—May 14, Honolulu; June 14, arrived Monterey; June 30—July 9, San Francisco; July 18, left Monterey; July 24, at Santa Cruz; August 11, at San Diego; October 11, at San Francisco; December 25, left Santa Barbara; January 13, 1837, arrived Honolulu; February, at Honolulu (vessel purchased by Kamehameha III).

Joseph Peabody, 1836

Brig, 225 tons; captain, —— Moore; owner, at Salem; sailing schedule: September 6, 1835, left New York; February 3–19, 1836, Honolulu; April,

Northwest Coast; July 15, left Santa Catalina Island; July 29, arrived Honolulu; November 24, left Honolulu; ——, New York.

Loriot, 1836

Brig, 90 tons; captain, —— Blinn; owner, at Hawaiian Islands; otter skins, 68 (57 grown, 11 pups), 78 tails; sailing schedule: December 27, 1835, arrived Honolulu; July 14, 1836, left Cerros Island; August 1–21, Honolulu; September 30, left Northwest Coast; November 1–24, Honolulu.

Clementine, 1837

Brig, 95 tons; captain, William Sturgis Hinckley; supercargo, John Coffin Jones, Jr.; clerk, Joseph Mellish; owner, Jules Dudoit, Honolulu; chartered by William Sturgis Hinckley; sailing schedule: April 17, arrived Honolulu; May 10, at Honolulu; October 18, at Monterey; ——, San Francisco; December 5, left Honolulu.

Lama, 1837–1838

Brig, 145 tons, 6 guns; captain, John Bancroft; owner, Eliab Grimes, Honolulu; sailing schedule: August 6, left Honolulu; September 9, on Northwest Coast; January 1, 1838, left Cerros Island; January 23, arrived Honolulu.

Rasselas, 1837–1838

Ship, 307 tons; captain, Joseph O. Carter; supercargo, John Coffin Jones, Jr.; owner, Eliab Grimes & Company, Honolulu; sailing schedule: February 3, left Honolulu; ——, Canton; September 30, at Honolulu; October 29, at Santa Barbara; November 15, at Monterey; January 12, 1838, left San Francisco; January 13, at Monterey; March 27, left San Francisco; April 23, arrived Honolulu; ——, Canton.

Lama, 1838, first trip

Brig, 145 tons, 6 guns; captain, John Bancroft; owner, Eliab Grimes, Honolulu; sailing schedule: January 23—February 19, Honolulu; ——, Northwest Coast; July 12, left California; July 30—August 30, Honolulu; ——, Northwest Coast.

Lama, 1838, second trip

Brig, 145 tons, 6 guns, 25 Kaigani Indians; captain, John Bancroft; mate, —— Robinson; officer, J. Molteno; owner, Eliab Grimes, Honolulu; sailing schedule: November 15, left Point Conception; November 16–21, San Miguel Island; November 22–23, Santa Rosa Island; November 28, left Point Conception; December 26, arrived Kaigani; January 13, 1839, arrived Honolulu.

Morse, 1839–1840

Schooner, 98 tons; captain, Henry Paty; owners, Henry Augustus Peirce, Charles Brewer, and Henry Paty, Honolulu; sailing schedule: April 21, left Boston; August 31—September 5, Valparaiso; October 19—December 1, Honolulu; December 20, arrived Monterey; January 21—February, 1840, San Pedro; February 12, at Monterey; ——, Mazatlan; April, arrived Honolulu (vessel sold to Henry Delano Fitch and renamed *Nymph*).

Monsoon, 1839–1841

Ship, 327 tons; captain, George W. Vincent; supercargo, Thomas Shaw; owners, Bryant, Sturgis, & Company, and others; sailing schedule: November

19, 1838, left Boston; April 17, 1839, arrived Santa Barbara; June 16, left Monterey; July 4, at San Francisco; January 21, 1840, at San Pedro; May 5, at San Francisco; June 30, left San Diego; October 26, left San Francisco; November 14, left Monterey; December 16, arrived San Diego; April 26, 1841, left San Diego; September 24, arrived Boston.

Alciope, 1840

Ship; captain, Curtis Clapp; on board, Benjamin W. Parker; owners, at Boston; consigned to Peirce & Brewer, Honolulu, and chartered by Alpheus Basil Thompson; sailing schedule: February 22, left Honolulu; ——, Northwest Coast; April 20—May 27, Monterey; May 29—June 2, Santa Cruz; July 19, at San Francisco; September 4, left Monterey; September 6—October 2, Santa Barbara; October 2, at San Pedro; November 7—December 8, Honolulu; February 3, left Tahiti; —— Boston.

California, 1840

Schooner, 86 tons, 10 crew; captain, John Rogers Cooper; supercargo, Henry Delano Fitch, from California to the Hawaiian Islands; owner, Mexican government; otter, 16 belonging to Henry Delano Fitch; sailing schedule: January, at San Francisco; February 21, at San Diego; March 16, left San Diego; April 16, at Honolulu; June 10, left Honolulu; July 2, arrived San Francisco.

Nymph (formerly Morse), 1840

Schooner, 98 tons; captain, Henry Delano Fitch; owners, Henry Delano Fitch, John Temple, and James McKinlay, California; otter skins, 155; sailing schedule: June 15, arrived Monterey; July 6, at Santa Barbara; July 25, left San Pedro; August 30—September 5, San Pedro; September 12, left Santa Barbara; October 31, at Monterey; November 28, arrived San Diego; December 16, at San Diego; March 24, 1841, at Mazatlan; April 22, at San Diego.

Fama, 1841–1842

Ship, 362 or 397 tons; captain, Cornelius Hoyer; owner, Alpheus Basil Thompson, Santa Barbara; sailing schedule: November 6, at Honolulu; January 4, 1842, at San Pedro; January 19, left Monterey; January 29, at San Francisco; March 24, left Monterey; April 10, at Santa Barbara; April 14, at San Pedro; May 7, at Santa Barbara; June, at Honolulu.

Maryland, 1841–1842

Brig, 128 tons; captain, Henry Augustus Peirce; owner, Peirce & Brewer, Honolulu; sea otter, 47 at San Diego; sailing schedule: November 4, left Honolulu; November 23—January 3, 1842, Monterey; January 5, arrived Santa Barbara; January 18-27, San Diego; February 4-7, Mazatlan; ——, Honolulu; April 31, left Mazatlan; May 24, arrived Honolulu.

Trinidad (formerly Avon), 1842

Brig, 120 tons; captain, Ramón Menchaca; owners, under Mexican colors; goods shipped by John Temple and Henry Delano Fitch; skins, (11); sailing schedule: April 15, at San Blas; June 9, at San Pedro; September 17, at San Francisco; November 20, left Monterey; ——, San Blas.

Barnstable, 1842–1844

Ship, 373 tons, 18 crew; captain, James B. Hatch; supercargo, Henry Mellus; clerk, Henry Frederick Teschemacher; owner, William Appleton & Company, Boston; otter skins, 80; sailing schedule: February 9, left Boston; July 7, arrived Monterey; September 20, at San Francisco; October 2, at Santa Barbara; November 9, at San Pedro; December 15–29, San Diego; January 7, 1843, at San Pedro; August 27, at San Francisco; October 20, at San Pedro; June 25, 1844, at San Francisco; December 17, left San Diego; April 5, 1845, arrived Boston.

California, 1842–1844

Ship, 369 tons, 20 crew; captain, James P. Arther; supercargoes, William Davis Merry Howard and Curtis Clapp; owner, Benjamin T. Reed, Boston; sailing schedule: July 16, 1841, left Boston; November 28—January 18, 1842, Honolulu; February 3, arrived Monterey; April 12, at San Diego; May 29, at Monterey; August 30, arrived Santa Barbara; November 4, at San Francisco; November 20, arrived San Pedro; December 24, arrived San Diego; April 25, 1843, at San Pedro; December 7, at San Francisco; March 8, 1844, left San Diego; July 2, arrived Boston.

Bolivar Liberator, 1843–1844

Brig, 212 or 224 tons; captain, John Coffin Jones, Jr. from Honolulu to California, —— Stevens on sea otter hunt, John Roderick after December; on board, Alpheus Basil Thompson and John Coffin Jones, Jr., from San Diego to Mazatlan; owners, Alpheus Basil Thompson and John Coffin Jones, Jr., Santa Barbara; otter skins, 21 around San Nicolas and San Clemente islands; sailing schedule: May 4, at Honolulu; June 20, at Monterey; August 31, left Santa Barbara; ——, San Nicolas Island; ——, San Clemente Island; September 9, off San Diego; December 25, at San Pedro; January 17, 1844, at Santa Barbara; ——, Guadalupe Island; January 30, at San Pedro; March, Mazatlan (vessel placed under Mexican colors, renamed *Oajaca*).

Admittance, 1843–1846

Ship, 420 tons; captain, Peter Peterson; supercargo, Henry Mellus; clerk, George Cushing, Jr.; owner, William Appleton & Company, Boston; otter skins, 55; sailing schedule: October 26, 1842, left Boston; March 2, 1843, arrived Monterey; October 31, at Santa Barbara; December 22, at San Pedro; June 13, 1844, left San Francisco; August 10, at Monterey; December 17, left San Diego; March 10, 1845, at San Francisco; March 18, at San Pedro; May 2, arrived Monterey; October 1, at San Francisco; January 26, 1846, left San Diego; May 15, arrived Boston.

Oajaca (formerly Bolivar Liberator), 1845

Brig, 212 or 224 tons; captain, John Roderick; owners, Alpheus Basil Thompson and others, Santa Barbara; sailing schedule: March 26, arrived San Pedro; April 3, left Santa Barbara; April 12, left San Pedro; ——, Cerros Island; May 2, at Mazatlan.

California, 1845–1846

Ship, 369 tons; captain, James P. Arther; supercargo, William Davis Merry Howard; owner, Benjamin T. Reed, Boston; otter skins, (10); sailing schedule: December 4, 1844, left Boston; March 16, 1845, arrived Monterey; June 14, July 30, at Monterey; ——, San Francisco; August 26, at San Pedro; September 23, left San Diego; September 30, at Monterey; December 16, at San Pedro; January 1—February 4, 1846, at San Diego; June 24, arrived Boston.

Tasso, 1845–1848

Bark, 286 tons, 21 crew; captain, Elliot Libbey, —— Lindsey in 1848; supercargo, Henry Mellus; owner, William Appleton & Company, Boston; sailing schedule: August 13, 1844, left Boston; February 12, 1845, arrived San Diego; May 6, at San Francisco; August 26, at San Pedro; January 22, 1846, at San Diego; March 8, left Monterey; November 4, at San Francisco; January 22, 1847, left San Diego; September 10, at San Francisco; June 5, 1848, at San Diego; August 27, at San Francisco (vessel sold).

Loo Choo, 1847

Ship, 639 tons; captain, James B. Hatch; owner, William Appleton & Company, Boston; otter skins, 40; sailing schedule: September 26, 1846, left New York; January 23, 1847, left Valparaiso; March 26, arrived San Francisco; April 25, at San Francisco; May 21, at San Pedro; June 21, at San Diego; July, left California; November 8, arrived Boston.

NOTES

NOTES

Owing to the nature of the materials, the process of selecting references has been difficult. In the notes the key documents have been cited, although in no instance has a complete documentary picture of any voyage been given. When the reference is first cited, the depository and classification (originals or transcripts) are indicated in parentheses for all single, bound manuscripts and for all collections of manuscripts. For individual manuscripts which are unbound or not in collections the depository and classification follow each citation. For the place of deposit of the originals of transcripts, see the bibliography. Most of the transcripts which appear in the references are those made by Hubert Howe Bancroft from documents in local archives or in the Archivo de California, destroyed by the San Francisco fire of 1906. If the original was used, no copies, either in the bound collections of Bancroft or elsewhere, are cited.

The following abbreviations indicate the depositories of the materials used:

A.G.P.M.	Archivo General y Público de la Nación, Mexico City.
B.L.	Bancroft Library, University of California, Berkeley.
B.N.M.	Biblioteca Nacional, Mexico City.
C.H.S.	California Historical Society, San Francisco.
H.L.	Huntington Library, San Marino.
H.S.B.A.	Harvard School of Business Administration, Boston.
H.U.L.	Harvard University Library, Cambridge.
L.C.	Library of Congress, Washington.
L.P.L.	Los Angeles Public Library.
M.H.S.	Massachusetts Historical Society, Boston.
M.N.M.	Museo Nacional, Mexico City.
S.G.	Secretaría de Gobernación, Mexico City.
S.G.M.	Secretaría de Guerra y Marina, Mexico City.
S.R.E.	Secretaría de Relaciones Exteriores, Mexico City.
U.C.L.	University of California Library, Berkeley.
W.M.L.	Widener Memorial Library, Harvard University, Cambridge.

NOTES TO CHAPTER I

THE PACIFIC FRONTIER

[1] The otterskin traffic of Spanish crews on the Northwest Coast expeditions of 1774, 1775, and 1779 is described in the following logbooks, transcripts, B.L.: Esteban José Martínez, *Santiago*, 1774; Fray Tomás de la Peña, *Santiago*, 1774; Juan Crespi, *Santiago*, 1774; Miguel de la Campa, *Santiago*, 1775; Juan Francisco de la Bodega y Cuadra, *Sonora*, 1775; Francisco Antonio Mourelle, *Favorita*, 1779; Juan Pantoja y Arriaga, *Princesa*, 1779.

[2] Miguel Venegas, *A Natural and Civil History of California* (London, 1759), I, 38.

[3] References to shipments of otter skins on the Manila galleon prior to 1786 are as follows: Ciriaco González de Carvajal to José de Gálvez, Manila, June 20, 1786, transcript, L.C.; Manuel de Barrionuevo to the *contadores mayores*, Mexico, December 10, 1787, transcript, L.C. References to collections of otter skins in California before the Vasadre project are as follows: Vicente Vasadre y Vega to Matías de Gálvez, Mexico, September 26, 1784, transcript, L.C.; José Francisco de Ortega to Pedro Fages, Rosario, June 8, 1786, Provincial State Papers (transcripts, B.L.), VI, 168.

[4] See p. 14.

[5] Vasadre to Matías de Gálvez, Mexico, September 26, 1784, transcript, L.C.

[6] The best account of the sea otter is that by Joseph Grinnell and others, *Fur-Bearing Mammals of California* (Berkeley, 1937), I, 286–92. An authentic work, based on personal experience, is that of Henry James Snow, *In Forbidden Seas* (London, 1910). For important references in addition to those cited above and in chapter proper, see note 27 below.

[7] Elliott C. Cowdin, "The Northwest Fur Trade," *The Merchants' Magazine*, XIV (June, 1846), 534.

[8] Charles H. Stevenson, "Utilization of the Skins of Aquatic Animals," U. S. Bureau of Fisheries, *Report of the Commissioner for the Year Ending June 30, 1902* (Washington, 1904), p. 321.

[9] Otto von Kotzebue, *A Voyage of Discovery* (London, 1821), III, 42.

[10] Grinnell, *op. cit.*, pp. 286–87.

[11] Two especially detailed accounts of the use by the Chinese of the otter fur are in the following: Luis Sales, *Noticias de la provincia de Californias* (Valencia, 1794), p. 28; Georg Wilhelm Steller, "The Early History of the Northern Fur Seals," U. S. Treasury Department, *The Fur Seals and Fur Seal Islands of the North Pacific Ocean* (Washington, 1898–1899), III, 211–12.

[12] The *Columbia* in 1788 obtained "several" sea otter at Cascade Head, Oregon, "a number" at Tillamook Bay, just south of the Columbia River, and "several" north of Gray's Harbor. Vancouver in 1792 found "none" at Orford, near Cape Blanco, and only "a few" at the Columbia River. On its 1792 trip the *Columbia* obtained "many fine otter skins" north of Cape Blanco—whether sea or land otter is not clear; "furs" in general were found north of the Columbia River, whereas those obtained at the river seem to have been entirely land otter and beaver. The *Jenny* in 1791 acquired "a few" after ten days' trade north of Cape Blanco. The *Ruby* in 1795 purchased as many as one hundred sea otter at the Columbia, but the log stated that they were "not in abundance" at that place. When two of the animals were seen north of Cape Blanco, the fact was entered in the log.

[13] Henry Wood Elliott, *A Report upon the Condition of Affairs in the Territory of Alaska* (Washington, 1875), p. 56.

[14] A. W. Chase, "The Sea Lion at Home," *Overland Monthly*, III (October, 1869), 353.

[15] Elliott, *op. cit.*, p. 60.

[16] *Loc. cit.*

[17] John R. Jewitt, *A Narrative of the Adventures and Sufferings of John R. Jewitt* (New York, 1816), p. 87.

[18] Frank Stephens, *California Mammals* (San Diego, 1906), p. 233.

[19] Grinnell, *op. cit.*, p. 292.

[20] Martin Sauer, *An Account of a Geographical and Astronomical Expedition* (London, 1802), p. 159.

[21] Bernard du Hautcilly, *Voyage autour du monde* (Paris, 1834–35), II, 216.

[22] Georg Heinrich von Langsdorff, *Voyages and Travels in Various Parts of the World* (London, 1813–14), II, 42–43.

[23] John Meares, *Voyages Made in the Years 1788 and 1789* (London, 1791), II, 54.

[24] Juan Bautista Alvarado, "Historia de California" (original, B.L.), II, 7–10; Antonio María Osio, "Historia de California" (original, B.L.), pp. 25–27.

[25] Langsdorff, *op. cit.*, p. 44.

[26] Urey Federovich Lisiansky, *A Voyage round the World, in the Years 1803, 4, 5, & 6* (London, 1814), p. 204.

[27] Sales, *op. cit.*, pp. 30–31. Methods of hunting by California Indians are also mentioned in the following: Comte de Lapérouse, *A Voyage round the World* (London, 1798), II, 228; Alvarado, "Historia," II, 7–9; Lasuén to the Audencia, Mission San Carlos, September 24, 1787, Archivo de la misión de Santa Barbara (transcripts, B.L.), X, 3–7.

The complete accounts of the sea otter and the methods of hunting as given by the authorities already cited are as follows: Steller, pp. 210–18; Elliott, pp. 56–62; Jewitt, pp. 86–88; Sauer, pp. 157–59, 180–81; Langsdorff, pp. 41–45; Meares, I, xvii–xviii, II, 23–28, 54–56; Lisiansky, pp. 203–6, 211–12. In addition, the following accounts have been most used: Elliott Coues, *Fur-Bearing Animals* (Washington, 1877), pp. 325–48; Charles Pierre Claret de Fleurieu, *A Voyage round the World* (London, 1801), I, 307–13; Vasilii Golovnin, "Extracts from a Description of a Voyage round the World," Russian America (transcripts, B.L.), Vol. III, Pt. 4, pp. 70–71, 155–56; Otto von Kotzebue, *A New Voyage round the World* (London, 1830), II, 39–40, 46–48; Stepan Petrovich Krasheninnikov, *The History of Kamtschatka* (Glocester, 1764), pp. 130–31; Alexander Markov, "Journey," Russian America, Vol. VII, Pt. 1, pp. 63–66; Thomas Pennant, *Arctic Zoölogy* (London, 1784–85), II, 88–91; Charles Melville Scammon, *The Marine Mammals of the Northwestern Coast of North America* (San Francisco, 1874), pp. 168–75; Leonard H. Stejneger, *Georg Wilhelm Steller* (Cambridge, 1936), Index; P. Tikhmenev, "Historical Review of the Origin of the Russian American Company," Russian America, Vol. I, Pt. 1, pp. 135–38; Vol. II, pp. 259–64; Salvador Vallejo, "Notas históricas sobre California" (original, B.L.), pp. 36–37.

NOTES TO CHAPTER II

THE SPANISH SEA OTTER TRADE IN THE PACIFIC

[1] The main body of this chapter has been published under title of "The Californias in Spain's Pacific Otter Trade," *The Pacific Historical Review*, I (December, 1932), 444–69.

[2] Vasadre to Matías de Gálvez, Mexico, September 26, 1784, transcript, L.C.

[3] Bernardo de Gálvez to Pedro Fages, Mexico, January 23, 1786, Provincial State Papers (transcripts, B.L.), VI, 205–7; Gálvez to Fermín Francisco de Lasuén, Mexico, March 1, 1786, Archivo de la misión de Santa Barbara (transcripts, B.L.), I, 283–84.

[4] *Gazetas de México*, II (1786–87), 162.

[5] Fages, Proclamation, Monterey, August 29, 1786, Provincial State Papers, VI, 140–44; Lasuén to Bernardo de Gálvez, Monterey, September 8, 1786, Archivo de la misión de Santa Barbara, X, 10.

[6] Jean François Lapérouse, *A Voyage round the World* (London, 1798), II, 227.

[7] Fages, Proclamation, Provincial State Papers, VI, 140–44.

[8] Fages, list of prices, Monterey, August 31, 1786, *ibid.*, p. 145.

[9] Council of the Indies, "Consulta sobre proyecto de Vicente Basadre para comerciar pieles de nutria," Madrid, June 22, 1791, transcript, B.L.

[10] José de Zuñiga to Fages, San Diego, October 7, 1786, Provincial State Papers, VI, 37; Zuñiga to Vasadre, San Diego, October 7, 1786, *ibid.*, p. 38; Barrionuevo to the *contadores mayores*, Mexico, December 10, 1787, transcript, L.C.

[11] Eusebio Sánchez Pareja to Pedro Sarrio and González, Mexico, March 8, 1787, transcript, L.C.; the Audiencia to José de Gálvez, Mexico, March 26, 1787, Correspondencia de los virreyes (originals, A.G.P.M.), Vol. CXLI.

[12] *Ibid.*

[13] *Ibid.;* Vasadre y Vega, "Informe sobre perjuicios en la comisión que se le dió de conducir á la China pieles de nutria," Madrid, April 11, 1791, transcript, B.L.

[14] Hermengildo Sal to the *subdelegado* of the *real hacienda*, Monterey, February 12, 1787, transcript, L.C.

[15] José Francisco de Ortega to Fages, Mission Rosario, September 13, 1786, Provincial State Papers, VI, 180; Vasadre to Ramón de Posada, Mexico, January 14, 1787, transcript, L.C.

[16] Ortega to Fages, Mission Rosario, September 13, 1786, Provincial State Papers, VI, 179.

[17] Vasadre to Posada, Mexico, January 14, 1787, transcript, L.C. For relations between missionaries and Indians in the otter-skin traffic, see Fabián de Fonseca and Carlos de Urrutia, *Historia general de real hacienda* (Mexico, 1845), I, 374.

[18] The Audiencia to Lasuén, Mexico, March 8, 1787, Archivo de la misión de Santa Barbara, X, 8.

[19] The Audiencia to José de Gálvez, Mexico, March 26, 1787, Correspondencia de los virreyes, Vol. CXLI.

[20] Pedro Benito Cambón to Francisco Palóu, San Francisco, February 29, 1788, Documentos relativos á las misiones de California (originals, M.N.M.), III, 99–100.

The most important references on the execution of the 1787 regulations follow: Fages, Proclamation, Monterey, September 15, 1787, Provincial Records (transcripts, B.L.), I, 35; Fages to Ortega, Monterey, September 15, 1787, Provincial State Papers, VII, 158; Lasuén to Fernando José Mangino, San Carlos, November 8, 1787, transcript, L.C.

[21] José de Arvide to Lasuén, Mexico, April 14, 1787, Archivo de Santa Barbara, XII, 5; Fages to Mangino, Monterey, November 6, 1787, transcript, L.C.; Lasuén to Mangino, San Carlos, November 8, 1787, transcript, L.C.

[22] José de Cañizares, bill of lading, Monterey, October 6, 1787, Provincial State Papers, Benicia, Military (transcripts, B.L.), IX, 14; Cañizares, bill of lading, Santa Barbara, November 4, 1787, transcript, L.C.; Cañizares, note of skins, San Diego, November 25, 1787, transcript, L.C.

[23] Francisco Hijosa to Mangino, San Blas, December 24, 1787, transcript, L.C.; Posada to ———, Mexico, March 4, 1788, transcript, L.C.

[24] Posada to ———, Mexico, April 11, 1788, transcript, L.C.

[25] Accounts of skin collections and shipments of goods in 1788 and 1789 are numerous. The most important follow: Cambón to Palóu, San Francisco, October 9, 1788, Documentos relativos á las misiones, III, 105–8; Lasuén to Arvide, San Carlos, September 30, 1789, Archivo de la misión de Santa Barbara, XII, 7–8; Felipe de Goycoechea to Fages, Santa Barbara, November 9, 1789, Provincial State Papers, IX, 146.

[26] The Audiencia to Lasuén, Mexico, March 8, 1787, Archivo de la misión de Santa Barbara, X, 1–2; the Audiencia to José de Gálvez, Mexico, March 26, 1787, Correspondencia de los virreyes, Vol. CXLI.

[27] Lasuén to the Audiencia, Monterey, September 24, 1787, Archivo de la misión de Santa Barbara, X, 3–7.

[28] Manuel Antonio Flórez to Lasuén, Mexico, March 4, 1787, ibid., XII, 4; Lasuén to Flórez, Monterey, July 30, 1788, ibid., I, 289–92.

[29] Lasuén to the Audiencia, Monterey, September 24, 1787, ibid., X, 3–7; Lasuén to Flórez, Monterey, July 30, 1788, ibid., I, 289–92.

[30] Cambón to Palóu, San Francisco, October 9, 1788, Documentos relativos á las misiones, III, 105–8.

[31] Mangino to José de Gálvez, Mexico, July 26, 1787, Correspondencia de los virreyes, Vol. CXLIII; Fages to Mangino, Monterey, November 6, 1787, transcript, L.C.; Junta Superior, Mexico, July 11, 1788, transcript, L.C.

[32] Cambón to Palóu, San Francisco, February 29, 1788, Documentos relativos á las misiones, III, 99–100.

[33] Lasuén to Flórez, Monterey, July 30, 1788, Archivo de la misión de Santa Barbara, I, 289–92.

[34] List of prices, Mexico, May 18, 1790, Documentos relativos á las misiones, IV, 35–38.

[35] Fages to Lasuén, Monterey, September 7, 1790, Archivo de la misión de Santa Barbara, II, 1.

[36] Conde de Revilla Gigedo to Pedro de Lerena, Mexico, July 27, 1790, Correspondencia de los virreyes, Vol. CLVIII; Fages to Ortega, Monterey, December —, 1790, Provincial State Papers, IX, 144.

[37] For the plans of the Philippine Co. and of González, see pp. 24–26.

[38] Juan Gutiérrez de Piñeres to Pedro Aparici, Madrid, December 5, 1790, transcript, L.C.; Council of the Indies, "Consulta."

[39] Vasadre received about fourteen dollars each for his first skins and eighteen dollars for his second consignment. Dixon sold his cargo of Northwest Coast skins in 1787 for only seventeen dollars a pelt. Vasadre, "Informe"; Council of the Indies, "Consulta"; Lapérouse, *op. cit.*, p. 287; William Beresford, *A Voyage round the World* (London, 1789), pp. 300–303, 320.

[40] Gutiérrez to Aparici, Madrid, December 5, 1790, transcript, L.C.

[41] Additional correspondence concerning Vasadre's management of affairs in China is as follows: Vasadre, "Informe"; Council of the Indies, "Consulta"; Gutiérrez to Lerena, Madrid, July 16, 1791, transcript, L.C.

[42] Fonseca and Urrutia, *op. cit.*, p. 380; Revilla Gigedo to Antonio Valdés, Mexico, January 20, 1790, Correspondencia de los virreyes, Vol. CLIV; Revilla Gigedo to Valdés, Mexico, May 27, 1790, *ibid.*, Vol. CLVII; Revilla Gigedo to Gardoqui, Mexico, November 30, 1792, *ibid.*, Vol. CLXVI.

[43] Gutiérrez to Aparici, Madrid, December 5, 1790, transcript, L.C.

[44] Vasadre to Príncipe de la Paz, Vera Cruz, May 1, 1796, transcript, L.C.; Fonseca and Urrutia, *op. cit.*, p. 377.

[45] The desire to keep foreigners from the otter trade is expressed in the correspondence of many Spanish officials and seamen during the last decade of the eighteenth century.

[46] González to José de Gálvez, Manila, June 20, 1786, transcript, B.L.; González to José de Gálvez, Manila, February 3, 1786, transcript, B.L.

[47] Valdés to the Directors of the Philippine Co., San Ildefonso, September 28, 1787, July 17, 1788, transcript, B.L.; Directors of the Philippine Co. to Valdés, Madrid, August 13, 1788, transcript, B.L.

[48] The Audiencia to José de Gálvez, Mexico, March 26, 1787, Correspondencia de los virreyes, Vol. CXLI; Directors of the Philippine Co. to Valdés, Madrid, August 13, 1788, transcript, B.L.; Fonseca and Urrutia, *op. cit.*, p. 374.

[49] Directors of the Philippine Co. to Valdés, Madrid, August 13, 1788, transcript, B.L.

[50] The Audiencia to José de Gálvez, Mexico, March 26, 1787, Correspondencia de los virreyes, Vol. CXLI; Council of the Indies, "Consulta."

[51] For a full discussion of this subject, see Charles L. Stewart, "Martínez and López de Haro on the Northwest Coast, 1788–1789," Ph.D. dissertation, University of California, 1936.

[52] Martínez, Logbook of the *Princesa*, 1789, transcript, B.L., passage between entries for September 30 and October 1.

[53] Revilla Gigedo to Valdés, Mexico, December 27, 1789, January 12, 1790, January 31, 1793, transcripts, B.L.; Revilla Gigedo, "Informe," April 12, 1793, in Carlos María de Bustamente, *Suplemento á la historia de los tres siglos de México ... por el padre Andrés Cavo* (Mexico, 1836), III, 150.

[54] Revilla Gigedo to Valdés, Mexico, January 12, 1790, transcript, B.L.

[55] Revilla Gigedo to Gardoqui, Mexico, June 30, 1792, Correspondencia de los virreyes, Vol. CLXV.

[56] Revilla Gigedo to Valdés, Mexico, January 31, 1793, transcript, B.L.

[57] Revilla Gigedo, "Informe," pp. 150, 160.

[58] Alejandro Malaspina to the Comercio of Mexico, Mexico, 1791, transcript, B.L..; Malaspina, "Examen político de las costas del NO. de la América," transcript, B.L. Although no author of the "Examen" is indicated, it is evident from the description and names mentioned that it is part of the report submitted by Malaspina to the Spanish government. This report is described in

Martín Fernández de Navarrete, *Examen histórico-crítico de los viajes y descubrimientos apócrifos* (Madrid, 1849), pp. 96–98.

[59] Malaspina's plan, although never published as such, appears in the introduction to Navarrete, *Relación del viage hecho por las goletas "Sutil" y "Mexicana" en el año de 1792* (Madrid, 1802), p. cxlix. The name of the real author is not mentioned, however.

[60] *Ibid.*, p. 31; Navarrete, *Examen*, pp. 116–17, 330.

[61] Revilla Gigedo to Conde de Aranda, Mexico, November 30, 1792, transcript, B.L.

[62] Revilla Gigedo to Lerena, Mexico, November 26, 1790, transcript, B.L.

[63] Martínez, Logbook of the *Princesa*, 1789, transcript, B.L.

[64] Revilla Gigedo to Valdés, Mexico, May 1, 1790, transcript, B.L.

[65] Revilla Gigedo to Valdés, Mexico, May 27, 1790, transcript, B.L.

[66] Revilla Gigedo to Francisco de la Bodega y Cuadra, San Blas, February 4, 1790, transcript, B.L.

[67] Jacinto Caamaño, Logbook of the *Aranzazu*, 1792, transcript, B.L.; Navarrete, *Examen*, pp. 116–17, 330; Navarrete, *Relación*, pp. 31, 58. For Spanish voyages to the Northwest Coast, see Henry Raup Wagner, *Spanish Explorations in the Strait of Juan de Fuca* (Santa Ana, 1933).

[68] George Vancouver, *A Voyage of Discovery to the North Pacific Ocean* (London, 1798), I, 408–9.

[69] Revilla Gigedo to José Monino Floridablanca, Mexico, March 27, and September 1, 1791, transcripts, B.L.; Revilla Gigedo, "Informe," pp. 130–50.

[70] Lasuén to the mission fathers, San Carlos, July 22, 1791, Archivo de la misión de Santa Barbara, IX, 314.

[71] Revilla Gigedo, "Informe," pp. 150–51.

[72] Revilla Gigedo to Gardoqui, Mexico, April 30, 1794, Correspondencia de los virreyes, Vol. CLXXIV.

[73] Ramón Pérez to Revilla Gigedo, San Blas, April 24, 1794, Provincias Internas (originals, A.G.P.M.), Vol. CLXV; Beltrán to the *real tribunal*, Mexico, November 6, 1794, *ibid.*

[74] Revilla Gigedo to Gardoqui, Mexico, April 30, 1794, Correspondencia de los virreyes, Vol. CLXXIV; Miguel de la Grua Talamanca y Branciforte to Diego de Borica, Mexico, February 28, 1795, Provincial State Papers, XIII, 12; Borica to the commanders of presidios, Monterey, June 8, 1795, Provincial Records, IV, 134.

NOTES TO CHAPTER III

THE FIRST YANKEE TRADERS IN SPANISH CALIFORNIA, 1796–1805

1 —— Péron, *Mémoires du capitaine Péron* (Paris, 1824), II, 126.

2 *Ibid.*, p. 127.

3 Borica to Branciforte, Monterey, November 5, 1796, Provincias Internas (originals, A.G.P.M.), Vol. VI, No. 16.

4 Additional important references concerning the *Otter* follow: Macario de Castro, "Diario de novedades," Monterey, October 27—November 7, 1796, State Papers, Sacramento (transcripts, B.L.), VI, 86–87; Branciforte to Borica, Orizaba, February 3, 1798, Provincial State Papers (transcripts, B.L.), XVII, 17.

5 J. & T. H. Perkins & Co. to James Rowan, Boston, August 8, 1798, in Lloyd Vernon Briggs, *History and Genealogy of the Cabot Family* (Boston, 1927), I, 392.

6 Important references for the *Eliza* follow: William Sturgis, Journal of the *Eliza*, February 13—May 17, 1799 (original, M.H.S.); Rowan to Pedro Alberin, San Francisco, May 27, 1799, Provincial State Papers, XVII, 206–7; Borica to Miguel José de Azanza, Monterey, June 3, 1799, Provincial Records (transcripts, B.L.), VI, 125; Azanza to Langara, Mexico, August 9, 1799, Correspondencia de los virreyes (originals, A.G.P.M.), Vol. CXCVIII, No. 131.

7 The fiscal to Sagarzureta, Mexico, February 14, 1801, transcript, B.L. Other important accounts of the *Betsy* follow: José Joaquín de Arrillaga to Manuel Rodríguez, Loreto, September 29, and October 28, 1800, Provincial Records, XII, 6; Arrillaga to Félix Berenguer de Marquina, Loreto, December 6, 1800, Provincias Internas, Vol. XIX, No. 5.

8 Important references for the *Enterprise* follow: supplies given to the *Enterprise*, Tepic, December 26, 1800, January —, 1801, Californias (originals, A.G.P.M.), Vol. XLI; Francisco de Eliza to José García, Tepic, December 25, and December 26, 1800, January 1, 1801, *ibid.*; Rodríguez to Arrillaga, San Diego, July 11, 1801, *ibid.*; Arrillaga to Berenguer de Marquina, Loreto, September 11, and September 20, 1801, *ibid.*

9 For the *Alexander*, see the following: John Stoughton, Boston, July 19, 1802, Provincias Internas, Vol. XVIII, No. 1; Rodríguez to Arrillaga, San Diego, March 10, 1803, *ibid.*; Inquiry into the *Alexander* Case, San Diego, March 10, 1803, *ibid.*

10 Richard Jeffry Cleveland, *A Narrative of Voyages* (Cambridge, 1842), I, 212.

11 Onofre Villaoa to Arrillaga, San Diego, March 12, 1803, Provincial State Papers, XVIII, 261.

12 Arrillaga to Rodríguez, Loreto, April 21, 1803, Provincial Records, XII, 20. A long legal action centered around the 491 confiscated skins. Before it was settled, the skins spoiled and had to be thrown into the sea. Borbón to the fiscal, Mexico, July 19, 1803, Provincias Internas, Vol. XVIII, No. 1; Rodríguez to Arrillaga, San Diego, June 20, 1806, Provincial State Papers, XIX, 156.

13 Rodríguez to Arrillaga, San Diego, March 10, 1803, Provincias Internas, Vol. XVIII, No. 1.

14 Cleveland, *loc. cit.*

[15] There is some discrepancy between the Spanish and American accounts of what happened as the *Lelia Byrd* left San Diego. Rodríguez to Arrillaga, San Diego, April 10, 1803, Provincial State Papers, XVIII, 252–58, 261–66, 307; Cleveland, *Narrative*, I, 213–17; Cleveland to ——, San Quintín, April —, 1803, Departmental State 'Papers (transcripts, B.L.), III, 205–6.

[16] Castro to Arrillaga, San Jose, September 30, 1804, Provincial State Papers, XVIII, 403–4.

[17] Braulio de Otalora y Oguendo to the commander of San Blas, Monterey, September 2, 1803, Californias, Vol. LXII.

[18] Additional accounts of the *Alexander* follow: Arrillaga to Rodríguez, Loreto, June 6, 1803, Provincial Records, XII, 21; Arrillaga to José Darío Argüello, Loreto, July 15, 1803, *ibid.*, p. 249; Otalora to the commander of San Blas, August 31, 1803, Californias, Vol. LXII.

[19] Otalora to the commander of San Blas, Monterey, September 2, 1803, *ibid.*

[20] Rowan to Argüello, San Francisco, August 12, 1803, State Papers, Missions and Colonization (transcripts, B.L.), I, 88.

[21] Additional accounts of the *Hazard* in 1803 follow: Rowan to Raymundo Carrillo, Santa Barbara, August 23, 1803, Californias, Vol. LXII; Carrillo to Rowan, Santa Barbara, August 23, 1803, *ibid.;* Luis Antonio Argüello to Arrillaga, San Francisco, August 26, 1803, State Papers, Missions and Colonization, I, 84–87; Carrillo to Arrillaga, Santa Barbara, September 2, 1803, Californias, Vol. LXII.

[22] Expediente on the *Enterprise*, Mexico, March 15, 1803, *ibid.*, Vol. XLI, No. 11; José de Iturrigaray to Arrillaga, Mexico, December 23, 1803, State Papers, Sacramento, V, 83.

[23] Otalora to the commander of San Blas, Mexico, November 26, 1803, Californias, Vol. LXII; Arrillaga to Iturrigaray, Loreto, July 5, 1804, *ibid.*

[24] Iturrigaray to Arrillaga, Mexico, December 23, 1803, State Papers, Sacramento, VIII, 73; Iturrigaray to Cevallos, Mexico, July 27, 1804, Correspondencia de los virreyes, Vol. CCXXII.

[25] Notes on Missions, 1803–1804, Archivo de la misión de Santa Barbara (transcripts, B.L.) XII, 72; Arrillaga to the padres of San Juan Bautista, Loreto, May 7, 1805, Provincial Records, VI, 22.

[26] Arrillaga to Iturrigaray, Loreto, July 4, 1804, Californias, Vol. XLII.

[27] The most important of the many accounts of the 1804 voyage of the *Hazard* follow: Rowan to José Darío Argüello, San Francisco, January 30, 1804, *ibid.;* Luis Peralta, certification of inspection of the *Hazard*, San Francisco, February 3, 1804, Provincial State Papers, XVIII, 377; Rodríguez to the corporals of San Miguel and Santo Tomás, San Diego, September 6, 1804, Californias, Vol. LXII; Arrillaga to Iturrigaray, Loreto, October 26, 1804, *ibid.*

[28] William Shaler, "Journal of a Voyage between China and the Northwest Coast of America," *The American Register*, III (1808), 143; Arrillaga to Carrillo, Loreto, August 11, 1804, Provincial Records, XI, 101.

[29] Shaler, p. 147.

[30] Arrillaga to the padres of San Juan Bautista, Loreto, May 7, 1804, Provincial Records, VI, 22.

[31] Shaler, p. 147.

[32] *Ibid.*, p. 171; Spanish accounts of the *Lelia Byrd* in 1804 follow: Rodríguez to Arrillaga, San Diego, April 9, 1805, Californias, Vol. LXII; Arrillaga to Iturrigaray, Loreto, July 29, 1805, *ibid.;* González to Arrillaga, Mexico, September 24, 1805, Provincial State Papers, XIX, 74.

[33] Cleveland, *Narrative*, I, 245–47; Arrillaga to Iturrigaray, Monterey, February 26, and June 30, 1806, Californias, Vol. LXII; Rodríguez to Arrillaga, San Diego, April 1, and June 20, 1806, Provincial State Papers, XIX, 153, 169.

[34] Presentation by Domingo Rivas, 1814, in Mexico, Secretaría de hacienda, archivo y biblioteca, *Colección de documentos* (Mexico, 1914), II, 145–49; Arrillaga to Iturrigaray, San Francisco, May 24, 1806, transcript, B.L.; Luis Sales, *Noticias*, p. 32.

NOTES TO CHAPTER IV

RUSSIAN OTTER HUNTING IN SPANISH CALIFORNIA

[1] The main body of this chapter has been published under title of "Russian Sea-Otter and Seal Hunting on the California Coast, 1803–1841," California Historical Society, *Quarterly*, XII (September, 1933), 217–39.

[2] The word "Aleut" in the Russian documents is applied not only to the natives of the Aleutian archipelago, but also to those on Kodiak Island and the southeastern shores of Alaska. In this account, therefore, the same word will be used to describe the hunters of the Northwest Coast, unless documents from other sources reveal their geographical identity.

[3] P. Tikhmenev, "Historical Review," Russian America (transcripts, B.L.), Vol. II, Pt. 1, p. 835; Kiril Khlebnikov, "Letters on America," *ibid.*, Vol. III, Pt. 3, p. 12.

[4] Hubert Howe Bancroft, *History of Alaska* (San Francisco, 1886), chap. 19.

[5] Kiril Khlebnikov, "Biography of Alexander Baranoff," Russian America, Vol. IV, Pt. 4, pp. 65–66; Khlebnikov, "Letters," pp. 12–13. For a description of the outfitting of an otter-hunting expedition, see Tikhmenev, "Historical Review," pp. 259–61.

[6] Arrillaga to Iturrigaray, Loreto, March 2, 1804, Californias (originals, A.G.P.M.), Vol. L, No. 8.

[7] Some additional accounts of the *O'Cain* in 1803 follow: Arrillaga to Rodríguez, Loreto, January 12, 1804, Provincial Records (transcripts, B.L.), XII, 27–30; José Manuel Ruiz to Arrillaga, San Vicente, February 10, 1804, Californias, Vol. L, No. 8; Arrillaga to Iturrigaray, Loreto, July 10, 1804, *ibid.*

[8] A main objective of Baranov was to create a great Russian commercial empire in the North Pacific. John William Stanton, "The Foundations of Russian Foreign Policy in the Far East, 1847–1875," Ph.D. dissertation, University of California, 1932, p. 485.

Concerning Baranov's purpose in extending hunting activities to new fields because of the decreasing number of otters in the Northwest, Captain Lütke stated, "Of some assistance in this pursuit were the California sea otters" ("Extracts from the Writings of Captain Lütke," Russian America, Vol. III, Pt. 4, p. 164).

[9] Nikolai Petrovich Rezanov to the minister of commerce, Sitka, June 17, 1806, Appendix of Tikhmenev, "Historical Review," p. 837.

Important accounts of the *Peacock* on its 1806 voyage follow: Rodríguez to Arrillaga, San Diego, March 2, April 1, and April 30, 1806, Provincial State Papers (transcripts, B.L.), XIX, 181, 155, 174; Rodríguez to Arrillaga, May 4, 1806, Provincias Internas (originals, A.G.P.M.), Vol. XVIII, No. 9; Oliver Kimball to Padre Rosnande and the governor (no place or date), *ibid.*

[10] William Dane Phelps, "Solid Men of Boston in the Northwest" (original, B.L.), pp. 4, 15; Khlebnikov, "Biography of Baranoff," p. 94; Khlebnikov, "Letters," pp. 13, 203–4; Tikhmenev, "Historical Review," p. 184.

[11] Phelps, "Solid Men of Boston," p. 15.

[12] *Ibid.*, p. 19.

[13] Important accounts of the *Eclipse* in 1806 are as follows: Rodríguez to Arrillaga, San Diego, June 23, 1806, Provincial State Papers, XIX, 136–38; Rodríguez to Arrillaga, San Diego, July 5 and July 25, 1806, Californias, Vol. LXII; Ruiz to Rodríguez, San Vicente, July 12, 1806, *ibid.*

[14] Tikhmenev, "Historical Review," p. 188.

[15] Georg Heinrich von Langsdorff, *Voyages*, II, 180.

[16] References for the 1807 voyage of the *Peacock* follow: Luis Antonio Argüello to Arrillaga, San Francisco, March 31 and May 15, 1807, Californias, Vol. LI, No. 12; José Ignacio Arce to Ruiz, Santo Domingo, June 2, 1807, *ibid.*, Vol. LXII; Khlebnikov, "Letters," p. 14; Tikhmenev, "Historical Review," p. 844.

[17] Phelps, "Solid Men of Boston," pp. 21–22.

[18] Khlebnikov, "Biography of Baranoff," pp. 94–95; Khlebnikov, "Letters," pp. 14, 203–4; Tikhmenev, "Historical Review," p. 185.

[19] Arrillaga to Luis Antonio Argüello, Santa Barbara, February 14, 1807, Provincial Records, XII, 269; Arrillaga to Iturrigaray, Santa Barbara, February 28, 1807, Californias, Vol. LXII; Arce to Ruiz, Santo Domingo, March 20, 1807, *ibid.*

[20] Arce to Ruiz, Santo Domingo, May 4 and June 2, 1807, *ibid.*

[21] Phelps, "Solid Men of Boston," p. 24.

[22] Khlebnikov, "Letters," p. 14.

[23] George Washington Eayrs to Benjamin W. Lamb, San Diego, March 9, 1814, *Mercury* Case Documents (originals, L.P.L.).

[24] Important references to the *Mercury* in 1806 and 1807 follow: Ruiz to Goycoechea, San Vicente, January 9, 1807, Californias, Vol. LXII; Arrillaga to Iturrigaray, Santa Barbara, February 18, 1807, *ibid.*; Goycoechea to Iturrigaray, Santa Ana, February 20, 1807, *ibid.*

[25] Alvarado to Eayrs, Los Angeles, May 14, 1809, *Mercury* Case Documents.

[26] Important accounts of the *Mercury* in 1808–1809 follow: Arrillaga to Pedro de Garibay, Monterey, December 30, 1808, Californias, Vol. LXII; Khlebnikov, "Biography of Baranoff," pp. 106–8; Khlebnikov, "Letters," pp. 14–15.

[27] Eayrs to the viceroy, San Diego, February 17, 1814, *Mercury* Case Documents.

Other important references to the 1809–1810 voyage of the vessel follow: notes of goods and skins, November and December, 1809, *ibid.*; declaration of captured sailors, Santa Barbara, January 16, 1810, Provincias Internas, Vol. XIX, No. 3; declaration of Julian Pedro, San Blas, January 18, 1814, *Mercury* Case Documents.

[28] Khlebnikov, "Biography of Baranoff," p. 129; Khlebnikov, "Letters," p. 15.

[29] For the operations of the *Isabella* along the coast in 1809, see the following: Enrique Cota to Ruiz, Santo Domingo, July 30, 1809, Californias, Vol. LXII; Goycoechea to Garibay, Loreto, August 23, 1809, *ibid.*; John Ebbets to John Jacob Astor, Macao, January 11, 1811, John Jacob Astor Collection (originals, Baker Library, H.S.B.A.).

[30] Eayrs to Félix María Calleja, San Diego, February 17, 1814, *Mercury* Case Documents; Declaration of Julian Pedro, San Blas, January 18, 1814, *ibid.*

[31] Phelps, "Solid Men of Boston," p. 52.

[32] *Loc. cit.*; Khlebnikov, "Biography of Baranoff," p. 129; Khlebnikov, "Letters," p. 15.

[33] Difficulties between Aleuts and Spaniards in the latter part of 1810 are mentioned in the following: Luis Antonio Argüello to Arrillaga, San Francisco, September 19 and September 20, 1810, Provincial State Papers, XIX,

275–76; Gabriel Moraga, "Diario de su expedición al puerto de Bodega," San Francisco, October 3, 1810, *ibid.*, p. 276; Arrillaga to Francisco Javier de Venegas, Monterey, October 20, 1810, Provincial Records, IX, 125.

[34] Luis Antonio Argüello to Arrillaga, San Francisco, November 26, 1810, Provincial State Papers, XIX, 280–81.

[35] Phelps, "Solid Men of Boston," p. 53.

[36] *Ibid.*, p. 54.

[37] Luis Antonio Argüello to Arrillaga, San Francisco, May 30, 1811, Provincial State Papers, XIX, 307–8.

[38] Khlebnikov, "Letters," pp. 17, 205.

[39] Osio, "Historia de California" (original, B.L.), pp. 14–15, 24–25.

[40] Phelps, "Solid Men of Boston," p. 54.

[41] *Ibid.*, p. 57; Khlebnikov, "Biography of Baranoff," p. 129; Khlebnikov, "Letters," p. 15.

In addition to its share of otter skins, the *Albatross* had as the result of its California voyage 74,526 sealskins taken entirely apart from the Russian contract.

[42] Alexander Baranov to Astor, Sitka, August 13/15, 1811, Astor Collection.

[43] Testimonies of John Dillaway and Pedro, San Blas, January 16, 1814, *Mercury* Case Documents; Khlebnikov, "Biography of Baranoff," p. 129; Khlebnikov, "Letters," p. 15.

[44] Testimony of Dillaway, Santa Barbara, June 19, 1813, *Mercury* Case Documents; Phelps, "Solid Men of Boston," p. 62; Khlebnikov, "Biography of Baranoff," p. 129.

[45] *Loc. cit.;* Khlebnikov, "Letters," p. 15.

[46] Langsdorff, *op. cit.*, p. 221.

[47] Tikhmenev, "Historical Review," p. 254; *Overland Monthly*, LXVI (December, 1915), 522–24.

[48] The policies of Rezanov, Russian foreign ministers, and other officials were all directed toward checking encroachments in the North Pacific. A few references on these policies follow: Bancroft, *History of Alaska*, p. 481; Kenneth Wiggins Porter, *John Jacob Astor* (Cambridge, 1931), I, 171–72, 180; Tikhmenev, "Historical Review," p. 190.

[49] Lütke, "Extracts," p. 164. This statement is also supported by Khlebnikov's analysis of the reasons for Baranov's instructions to Shvetsov in 1803. "He wanted to get acquainted with the inhabitants of California . . . and, above all, he wanted to discover how far the influence of the Americans extended over the Californians and the savages on other portions of the Northwest Coast of America" (Khlebnikov, "Biography of Baranoff," pp. 64–65).

[50] Khlebnikov, "Letters," p. 16.

[51] Langsdorff, *op. cit.*, p. 185.

[52] Luis Antonio Argüello to Arrillaga, San Francisco, February 16, 1809, Provincial State Papers, XIX, 266–67.

Other Spanish records of the voyage of the *Kodiak* are as follows: Arrillaga to Argüello, Monterey, February 9, March 29, and April 5, 1809, Provincial Records, XII, 286–87. Russian references follow: Khlebnikov, "Biography of Baranoff," pp. 110–11; Khlebnikov, "Letters," pp. 16, 204; Tikhmenev, "Historical Review," pp. 200–202.

[53] Khlebnikov, "Letters," p. 205.

[54] *Loc. cit.*

[55] All Russian accounts of the establishment of Fort Ross mention the strictness of Spanish law enforcement in San Francisco Bay and the effect it had upon Russian otter hunting.

[56] Khlebnikov, "Letters," p. 207.

[57] Some Russian writers place otter hunting as first among the purposes of the Ross settlement. Vasilii Golovnin, "Extracts from a Description of a Voyage round the World," Russian America, Vol. III, Pt. 4, p. 84; Lütke, "Extracts," p. 165.

[58] Enrique Cerruti, "Establecimientos rusos en California" (original, B.L.), p. 1; Khlebnikov, "Biography of Baranoff," p. 128; Khlebnikov, "Letters," pp. 205–7; Tikhmenev, "Historical Review," pp. 202–6.

[59] Gaspar de Maguna to Labayen, San Blas, January 14, 1814, original, S.G.M., 52–6–6–1.

[60] Khlebnikov, "Letters," p. 211.

[61] Ivan Kuskov to Luis Antonio Argüello, Fort Ross, June 20, 1814, Provincial State Papers, XIX, 365.

[62] Vasilii Petrovich Tarakanov, "Statement," Russian America, Vol. II, Pt. 2, p. 5.

[63] Kuskov to Luis Antonio Argüello, Fort Ross, June 9, 1814, Provincial State Papers, XIX, 365.

[64] The main account of the 1814 voyage of the *Ilmen* is the "Statement" of Tarakanov. This is not dated and the names of geographical points are not mentioned. Although the circumstances of Tarakanov's seizure correspond in many details to those of the party under John Elliot d'Castro of the *Ilmen* at San Luis Obispo in September, 1815, there are enough differences to make it clear that it was not the same affair. A few important accounts of the *Ilmen* follow: Guillermo Cota to José de la Guerra y Noriega, Los Angeles, September 22, 1815, original, S.G.M., 52–6–6–2; Khlebnikov, "Letters," p. 18; Tikhmenev, "Historical Review," p. 210.

[65] José Luyando to Calleja, Madrid, February 4, 1814, original, S.G.M., 52–6–6–9.

[66] Cota to de la Guerra, Los Angeles, September 22, 1815, original, S.G.M., 52–6–6–2.

[67] Cota to de la Guerra, Los Angeles, September 19, 1815, original, S.G.M., 52–6–6–2. Bancroft wrongly states that Tarakanov was head of the party seized at San Pedro, September, 1815. Tarakanov at that time was working at Santa Barbara Mission. When Tarakanov was safely aboard the *Rurick* in November, 1816, Boris Tarasov was in Tepic, Mexico, trying to obtain permission to return to Europe. Tarasov to Juan Ruiz de Apodaca, Tepic, February 21, 1817, original, S.G.M., 52–6–6–5.

[68] Cota to de la Guerra, Los Angeles, September 22, 1815, original, S.G.M., 52–6–6–2; Tarasov to Pablo Vicente de Solá, Monterey, October 15, 1815, Provincial State Papers, Benicia, Military (transcripts, B.L.), XLVI, 41–42; declaration of Tarasov, San Blas, February 1, 1816, original, S.G.M., 52–6–6–4.

[69] De la Guerra to Solá, Santa Barbara, September 24, 1815, original, S.G.M., 52–6–6–2.

[70] The Russian accounts of the *Ilmen* at Refugio are the same as those cited in note 64. A complete Spanish correspondence is contained in the *expediente*, "Prisión de varios individuos del establecimiento ruso," original, S.G.M., 52–6–6–2.

There is a wealth of correspondence on the subject of the treatment and return of the Russian and Aleutian prisoners taken in 1814 and 1815. Such letters may be found in the following: Documentos para la historia de México (originals, B.N.M.), Vol. IV, No. 8; Provincial State Papers, Vols. XIX, XX; José de la Guerra y Noriega, Documentos para la historia de California (transcripts, B.L.), Vols. II, III.

[71] Gervasio Argüello to Solá, San Francisco, October 21, 1816, Provincial State Papers, XX, 26–28.

[72] Ludovik Choris, *Voyage pittoresque autour du monde* (Paris, 1822), Pt. 3, p. 8.

[73] Zakahar Chichinov, "Adventures" (original, B.L.), p. 5.

[74] Golovnin, "Extracts," p. 70.

[75] *Loc. cit.*

[76] Chichinov, p. 9.

[77] Golovnin, "Extracts," p. 70.

[78] Solá to Baranov, Monterey, May 5, 1817, Mariano Guadalupe Vallejo, Documentos para la historia de California (originals, B.L.), IV, 206–10; Tikhmenev, "Historical Review," pp. 214–15.

[79] W. Potekhin, "Settlement of Ross," Russian America, Vol. V, Pt. 2, fol. 12.

[80] *Loc. cit.;* Khlebnikov, "Letters," pp. 211–12; Tikhmenev, "Historical Review," pp. 216–19.

[81] Semen Yanovski to Solá, Novo-Arkhangelsk, June 1/13, 1820, State Papers, Sacramento (transcripts, B.L.), VIII, 58–60.

[82] Solá to Yanovski, Monterey, August 2, 1820, *ibid.*, pp. 60–61.

[83] Yanovski to Solá, Novo-Arkhangelsk, June 1/13, 1820, *ibid.*, pp. 58–60.

[84] Potekhin, "Settlement of Ross," fol. 13; Tikhmenev, "Historical Review," pp. 222–23.

[85] See next chapter.

NOTES TO CHAPTER V

LATER YANKEE ENTERPRISE IN THE OTTER TRADE

[1] Whereas 1,600 California skins were reported at San Blas in 1803, the numbers sent on any one of the supply ships from 1803 to 1810 never totaled more than 300. Richard Jeffry Cleveland, *A Narrative of Voyages*, I, 200; *Gazetas de México*, XII (1804), 475–76; XVII (1808), 39–40.

[2] Eayrs to Calleja, San Diego, February 17, 1814, *Mercury* Case Documents (originals, L.P.L.).

[3] Declaration of Pedro, San Blas, January 18, 1814, *ibid.*

[4] José Bartolomé Tapia to Eayrs (no place or date), *ibid.*

[5] Padre Luis to Eayrs (no place or date), *ibid.*

[6] José Caulas to Eayrs, Rosario, May 7, 1812, *ibid.*

[7] Additional accounts of the 1812 voyage of the *Mercury* follow: declaration of Manuel Vicente Navarro, Santa Barbara, June 19, 1813, *ibid.;* declaration of Dillaway, San Blas, January 16, 1814, *ibid.*

[8] Main accounts of the 1813 voyage of the *Mercury* follow: testimonies of Eayrs, Navarro, Dillaway, Thomas Jones, Santa Barbara, June 18, 1813, *ibid.;* Eayrs to Calleja, San Diego, October 8, 1813, *ibid.;* declaration of Pedro, San Blas, January 18, 1814, *ibid.;* Eayrs to Calleja, San Diego, February 17, 1814, *ibid.;* Eayrs to Lamb, San Diego, March 9, 1814, *ibid.*

[9] Declaration of Nicolás Noé, San Blas, January 12, 1814, *ibid.*

[10] José Darío Argüello to Arrillaga, Santa Barbara, June 26, 1813, Provincial State Papers (transcripts, B.L.), XIX, 351–52.

[11] Arrillaga to José Darío Argüello, Monterey, June 8, 1813, *ibid.*, p. 352.

[12] Declaration of Eayrs, Santa Barbara, June 18, 1813, *Mercury* Case Documents.

[13] Declaration of Dillaway, Santa Barbara, January 16, 1813, *ibid.*

[14] Eayrs to Lamb, San Diego, March 9, 1814, *ibid.*

[15] Declaration of Eayrs, Santa Barbara, June 19, 1813, *ibid.*

[16] Eayrs to Calleja, San Diego, October 8, 1813, *ibid.*

[17] Eayrs to Lamb, San Diego, March 9, 1814, *ibid.* There is a large correspondence on the handling of the *Mercury* case in Mexico. Most of these letters are in the *Mercury* Case Documents. Proceedings dragged on for years. In November, 1817, an order permitted Eayrs to take goods from a Mexican ship in California to the value of those seized on the *Mercury*. Whether the smuggler was finally compensated for his losses is not known.

[18] Ebbets to Astor, Macao, January 11, 1811, in Kenneth Wiggins Porter, *John Jacob Astor*, I, 176.

[19] William Pigot to Ebbets, Coast of California, March 22, 1814, John Jacob Astor Collection (originals, H.S.B.A.).

[20] Of the 5,000 sealskins which Pigot took to Sitka, 3,400 were purchased at Bodega. The source of the remainder is evident. Porter, *op. cit.*, II, 643.

[21] Pigot to Ebbets, Coast of California, March 22, 1814, Astor Collection.

[22] Porter, *loc. cit.*

[23] For the *Pedler* affair see, "Diligencias sobre Pedler," Santa Barbara, September 10, 1814, Provincial State Papers, Benicia, Military (transcripts, B.L.), XLV, 3–6.

[24] Pigot to Ebbets, St. Peter and St. Paul, January 7, 1817, Astor Collection; Porter, *John Jacob Astor*, II, 641–42.

[25] William DeWitt Alexander, "The Relations between the Hawaiian Islands and Spanish America," Hawaiian Historical Society, *Papers*, No. 1 (1892), p. 8.

[26] Gabriel Franchère, *Narrative of a Voyage to the Northwest Coast of America* (New York, 1854), p. 288.

[27] Log of the *Atahualpa* (original, M.H.S.), Oahu, November 7, 1813.

[28] *Ibid.*, Atooi, July 9, 1814; Eayrs to Lamb, San Diego, March 9, 1814, *Mercury* Case Documents.

[29] P. Tikhmenev, "Historical Review," Russian America (transcripts, B.L.), Vol. I, Pt. 1, pp. 189–91.

[30] Pigot to Ebbets, St. Peter and St. Paul, January 7, 1817, Astor Collection.

[31] Tikhmenev, "Historical Review," pp. 189–91.

[32] De la Guerra to Solá, Rancho del Refugio, January 16, 1816, José de la Guerra y Noriega, Documentos para la historia de California (transcripts, B.L.), II, 101–4.

[33] De la Guerra to Solá, Santa Barbara, January 13, 1816, *ibid.*, pp. 96–98.

[34] De la Guerra to Solá, Rancho del Refugio, January 16, 1816, *ibid.*, pp. 99–101.

[35] William Smith to Solá, Santa Barbara, January [*sic*] 7, 1816, Departmental State Papers, Custom House, Benicia (transcripts, B.L.), I, 7.

[36] Accounts of the voyage and seizure of the *Lydia* follow: de la Guerra to Solá, Rancho del Refugio, January 16, 1816, de la Guerra, Documentos, II, 101–4; Arrillaga to de la Guerra, Monterey, January 18, 1816, Provincial Records (transcripts, B.L.), XI, 29; de la Guerra to Solá, Santa Barbara, January 22, 1816, de la Guerra, Documentos, II, 104–12; testimonies of sailors and Henry Gyzelaar, Monterey, February 19, 1816, Archives of California, Miscellany (transcripts, B.L.), Pt. 1, Vol. I, pp. 51–63.

[37] List of prisoners from the *Lydia* and *Albatross*, Santa Barbara, February 3, 1816, Departmental State Papers, Custom House, Benicia, I, 3.

[38] Gyzelaar to Solá, Santa Barbara, January 22, 1816, *ibid.*, p. 6; Gyzelaar and other sailors, Coast of Santa Barbara, January 17, 1816, *ibid.*, p. 5.

[39] Smith to Solá, Santa Barbara, February 2, 1816, Archives of California, Miscellany, Pt. 1, Vol. II, pp. 11–13.

[40] De la Guerra to Solá, Santa Barbara, January 21 and February 3, 1816, de la Guerra, Documentos, II, 104, 114–16; Arrillaga to de la Guerra, Monterey, January 25, 1816, Provincial Records, XI, 30.

[41] Solá to de la Guerra, Monterey, March 9, 1816, de la Guerra, Documentos, III, 224–25.

[42] Arrillaga to de la Guerra, Monterey, March 10, 1816, Provincial Records, XI, 32; de la Guerra to Solá, Santa Barbara, March 18, 1816, Provincial State Papers, XX, 116–17.

[43] "Extracts from an Ancient Log," *Hawaiian Almanac and Annual* (1906), p. 67; Judge Frederick William Howay, "A List of Trading Vessels," The Royal Society of Canada, *Proceedings*, Ser. 3, Vol. XXVII, sec. 2 (May, 1933), pp. 123–24; Egor Nikolaevich Sheffer, "Les russes aux îles Hawaïennes" (transcripts, B.L.), p. 27.

[44] De la Guerra to Solá, Santa Barbara, July 7, 1816, Provincial State Papers, XX, 109; Solá to de la Guerra, Monterey, July 27, 1816, de la Guerra, Documentos, II, 231; Solá to Apodaca, Monterey, August 3, 1816, Provincial Records, IX, 141.

[45] Solá to de la Guerra, Monterey, December 3, 1816, *ibid.*, XI, 43.

[46] James Hunnewell, "Voyage in the Brig *Bordeaux Packet*," Hawaiian Historical Society, *Papers*, No. 8 (1895), p. 7.

[47] Otto von Kotzebue, *A Voyage of Discovery* (London, 1821), I, 326.

[48] Joaquín Pascual Nuez to de la Guerra, Mission San Gabriel, March 17, 1817, transcript, B.L.

[49] James Smith Wilcocks to Solá, Monterey, June 11, 1817, Provincial State Papers, XX, 160.

[50] José Joaquín de la Torre to de la Guerra, Monterey, December 30, 1821, Documentos para la historia de California (originals, B.L.), IV, 561–63; Eliab Grimes, Logbook of the *Eagle*, 1821–1822 (original, U.C.L.), October 12, 1821.

[51] Camille de Roquefeuil, *A Voyage round the World, between the Years 1816–1819* (London, 1823), p. 24.

[52] Solá to de la Guerra, Monterey, December 22, 1817, transcript, B.L.

[53] Wilcocks to Antonio Cordera, Guaymas, December 8, 1817, Provincial State Papers, XX, 164–71.

Other main references to Wilcocks follow: de la Guerra to ———, Santa Barbara (January 9, 1817), de la Guerra, Documentos, III, 71–72; Solá to de la Guerra, Monterey, January 24, 1817, Provincial Records, XI, 45; Solá to Wilcocks, San Antonio, June 13, 1817, Provincial State Papers, XX, 161–62; Cordera to Solá, Loreto, January 7, 1818, *ibid.*, p. 219.

[54] William Heath Davis, *Sixty Years in California* (San Francisco, 1889), p. 302.

[55] Howay, *op. cit.*, p. 137; Hunnewell, *op. cit.*, p. 8.

[56] Davis, *op. cit.*, p. 301.

[57] *Ibid.*, p. 302.

[58] *Loc. cit.*

[59] Davis, p. 298.

[60] *Ibid.*, p. 299.

[61] William Dane Phelps to Joseph B. Eaton, Lexington, November 17, 1868, William Dane Phelps Collection (originals, W.M.L.). Other accounts of the *Clarion*, 1818, follow: de la Guerra to Solá, Santa Barbara, October 6 and October 16, 1818, transcripts, B.L.; Solá to Apodaca, Monterey, November 4, 1818, transcript, B.L.

[62] Howay, *op. cit.*, p. 136. References for these ships are numerous. Important ones follow: For the *Avon:* Solá to de la Guerra, Monterey, January 20 and February 5, 1817, Provincial Records, XI, 44, 46; "Extracts from an Ancient Log," *Hawaiian Almanac and Annual*, p. 72. For the *Enterprise:* Kotzebue, *op. cit.*, II, 198. For the *Ship:* de la Guerra to Solá, Santa Barbara, July 20, 1818, de la Guerra, Documentos, III, 89–90. For unnamed vessels: Antonio Rodríguez to Solá, San Luis Obispo, January 31, 1819, Archivo del arzobispado (transcripts, B.L.), Vol. III, Pt. 2, pp. 55–56.

[63] Except where other references are cited, all information for the voyage of the *Eagle*, 1821–22, is taken from its log.

[64] John Coffin Jones to Josiah Marshall and Dixey Wildes, Oahu, November 20, 1821, Josiah Marshall Collection (originals and transcripts, W.M.L.); also see Jones to Marshall, Oahu, October 5, 1821, *ibid.*

[65] Solá to the commanders of Santa Barbara and San Diego, Monterey, September 7, 1821, Provincial State Papers, XX, 295.

[66] Torre to de la Guerra, Monterey, December 30, 1821, Documentos para la historia de California, IV, 561–63.

[67] José María Estudillo to de la Guerra, San Diego, September 15 and 26, 1821, *ibid.*, pp. 547, 549–51.

[68] Anastacio Carrillo to de la Guerra, Los Angeles, November 9, 1821, de la Guerra, Documentos, V, 156–58.

[69] *Loc. cit.* Bancroft, basing his description of the incident on Spanish documents alone, stated that whether the affair took place with the *Eagle* or some other schooner "it is impossible to say" (Hubert Howe Bancroft, *History of California* [San Francisco, 1884–90], II, 441). The log of the vessel concerned clears up the story.

[70] Grimes to Marshall & Wildes, Tongass, July 8, 1822, Marshall Collection.

[71] Solá, report on judicial proceedings, Monterey, December 14, 1821, Provincial State Papers, Benicia, Military, LII, 9–10.

[70] Grimes to Marshall & Wildes, Tuongass, July 8, 1822, Marshall Collection. lection; also, Jones to Marshall & Wildes, Oahu, December 23, 1821, *ibid.*

[73] José de Jesús Vallejo, "Reminiscencias históricas de California" (original, B.L.), pp. 13–14.

[74] William Heath Davis, *Seventy-five Years in California* (San Francisco, 1929), p. 252; also, p. 200.

[75] Among the numerous references describing conditions on the Northwest Coast after 1820 the following are important: Bernard du Hautcilly, *Voyage* (Paris, 1834–35), II, 320–22; Otto von Kotzebue, *A New Voyage* (London, 1830), I, 1–2, II, 32, 121; Logbook of the *Arab* (original, B.L.), November 23, 1822; "Dr. John Scouler's Journal of a Voyage to N. W. America," Oregon Historical Society, *Quarterly*, VI (June, 1905), 191–92; Grimes to Marshall, Oahu, July 5, 1821, Marshall Collection; Grimes to Marshall & Wildes, Tongass, July 8, 1822, *ibid.;* Amelius Simpson to John McLoughlin, on the *Cadboro*, October 1, 1829, in Sir George Simpson, *Fur Trade and Empire* (Cambridge, 1931); Hunnewell to Bryant & Sturgis, Oahu, December 15, 1829, James Hunnewell Collection (originals, H.U.L.).

[76] Frederick William Beechey, *Narrative of a Voyage to the Pacific and Beering's Strait* (London, 1831), II, 99; Jones to Marshall & Wildes, Oahu, July 6, October 5, and December 23, 1821, January —, 1823, Marshall Collection.

[77] Kiril Khlebnikov, "Letters," Russian America, Vol. III, Pt. 3, p. 118.

[78] Grimes to Marshall & Wildes, Oahu (December 24, 1821), Marshall Collection.

[79] *Ibid.*

[80] *Ibid.*

[81] Brown to Marshall, Canton, March 22, 1822, *ibid.*

[82] Grimes to Marshall & Wildes, Oahu (December 24, 1821), *ibid.*

[83] Important references for the *Owhyhee*, 1822, are as follows: Grimes, Logbook of the *Eagle;* Jones to Marshall & Wildes, Oahu, December 23 and (December 24), 1821, December 21, 1822, Marshall Collection; Grimes to Marshall & Wildes, Tongass, July 8, 1822, *ibid.;* duties of the *Owhyhee*, San Francisco, November 20, 1822, Mariano Guadalupe Vallejo, Documentos para la historia de California (originals, B.L.), XVII, 99–101; Grimes to Marshall & Wildes, Santa Barbara, November 30, 1822, Marshall Collection.

[84] Important references for the 1823 voyage of the *Mentor* follow: Luis Antonio Argüello to Ignacio Martínez, Monterey, November 12, 1823, Departmental Records (transcripts, B.L.), I, 76; duties of the *Mentor*, San Francisco, November 17, 1823, Vallejo, Documentos, XVII, 229–30; John Rogers Cooper to Hunnewell, Monterey, December 29, 1823, Hunnewell Collection; Khlebnikov, "Letters," p. 118.

[85] Important references for the 1824 voyage of the *Mentor* follow: Jones to Marshall, Canton, March 13, 1824, Marshall Collection; duties of the *Mentor*, San Francisco, July 16, 1824, Vallejo, Documentos, XVII, 43–46; Luis Antonio Argüello to Romero, Monterey, September 23, 1824, Departmental Records, I, 85–87; Khlebnikov, "Letters," p. 118.

[86] Jones to Marshall, Canton, February 19, 1824, Marshall Collection.

[87] Important references for the 1824 voyage of the *Owhyhee* follow: Wildes to Marshall, Oahu, March 12 and July 21, 1824, *ibid.*; Martínez to Luis Antonio Argüello, San Francisco, May 5, 1824, Departmental State Papers, Monterey (transcripts, B.L.), IV, 87; duties of the *Owhyhee*, San Francisco, May 8, 1824, Vallejo, Documentos, XVIII, 5, 31–33; John Kelly to Marshall, Mazatlan, July 17, 1824, Marshall Collection.

[88] Wildes to Marshall, Oahu, November 5, 1824, *ibid.*

[89] Important references to the 1824 voyage of the *Washington* follow: Wildes to Marshall, Oahu, July 21 and November 5, 1824, *ibid.*; Robert Elwell to Marshall, Monterey, September 4, 1824, *ibid.*; Elwell to Marshall, San Luis Obispo, September 13, 1824, *ibid.*; Khlebnikov, "Letters," p. 118.

[90] See list of vessels in Appendix.

[91] Wildes to Marshall, Canton, March 27, 1825, Marshall Collection; Jones to Marshall, Oahu, June 18 and August 10, 1826, June 29, 1827, *ibid.*

[92] Jones to Marshall, Oahu, June 29, 1827, *ibid.*

[93] McNeil to Marshall, Oahu, January 10, 1826, *ibid.*

[94] Wildes to Marshall, Oahu, December 7, 1825, *ibid.*

[95] McNeil to Marshall, Oahu, January 10, 1826; *ibid.*; Alpheus Basil Thompson to Marshall, Oahu, January 20, 1826, *ibid.*; Logbook of the *Owhyhee* (original, C.H.S.), San Francisco, June 20 and June 26, 1827.

[96] George Newell to Perkins & Co., Sonsonate, January 20, 1826, James Perkins Collection (originals, M.H.S.).

[97] Robert Forbes to Perkins & Co., at sea, January 20, 1826, *ibid.*; also, José María Herrera to the *comisario provisional*, Monterey, June 28, 1826, Departmental State Papers, Benicia, Commissary and Treasury (transcripts, B.L.), I, 43.

[98] Important references for the *Waverly*, 1827–1828, follow: Hunnewell to Bryant & Sturgis, Oahu, May 19, 1827, Hunnewell Collection; William Goodwin Dana to Cooper, Santa Barbara, May 12 and October 28, 1828, Vallejo, Documentos, XXIX, 220, 286; Dana to Cooper, San Buenaventura, July 13, 1828, *ibid.*, p. 256; Logbook of the *Waverly*, 1828–1829 (original, B.L.).

[99] Important references for French's vessels follow: Dana to Cooper, Oahu, March 6, 1827, Vallejo, Documentos, XXIX, 119; William French to Cooper, Monterey, July 6, 1827, *ibid.*, pp. 137–38; Jones to Marshall, Oahu, November 30, 1827, Marshall Collection; John Temple to Hunnewell, Los Angeles, January 4, 1829, Hunnewell Collection.

[100] Jones to Cooper, Monterey, May 6, 1830, Vallejo, Documentos, XXX, 55.

[101] Hunnewell to Cooper, Oahu, August 17, 1830, Hunnewell Collection.

[102] Cooper to Hunnewell, Monterey, April 22, 1833, *ibid.*

[103] Grimes to Thompson, Oahu, February 27, 1831, Alpheus Basil Thompson Collection (originals, owned by Mrs. John M. Williamson, Carpinteria); French to Thompson, Oahu, February 28, 1831, *ibid.*; Jones to Thompson, Oahu, March 2, 1831, *ibid.*

[104] Thompson in account with Cooper, Monterey, October 12, 1831, Vallejo, Documentos, XXX, 259.

[105] David Spence and Juan Malarin to Jones and Thompson, Monterey, August 14, 1832, Thompson Collection.

[106] French to Cooper, Oahu, February 28, 1831, Vallejo, Documentos, XXX, 185.

[107] References for vessels of Jones, Thompson, and French in 1833 follow: Davis, *Seventy-Five Years*, p. 206; documents relative to the seizure of the *Loriot*, Department of State, Consular Letters, Honolulu (originals, L.C.), Vol. I; Jones in agreement with Cooper, Monterey, October 4, 1833, Vallejo, Documentos, XXXI, 45; Ebbets to Thomas Oliver Larkin, San Diego, November 15, 1833, *ibid.*, p. 50; Jones to Larkin, Oahu, April 20 and December 17, 1834, *ibid.*, p. 143.

[108] Accounts of Hinckley's ships, 1832–1835, follow: William Sturgis Hinckley in account with Nathan Spear, 1833, 1835–1836, Spear Account Book (original, B.L.); arrivals and departures of ships, 1834, Rafael Pinto, Documentos para la historia de California (originals, B.L.), I, 29; Hinckley to (Spear), Santa Barbara, October 30, 1835, original, B.L.

[109] Henry Augustus Peirce, "Memoranda" (original, B.L.), pp. 15–16.

[110] William Gale to Cooper, San Luis Rey, October 6, 1829, Vallejo, Documentos, XXIX, 434.

[111] Some accounts of the *Brookline*'s otter collections follow: Journal of the *Brookline* (original, owned by A. Porter Robinson, San Francisco), August 19, 1829; Robinson to Russell & Co., Santa Barbara, July 31, 1831, Alfred Robinson Collection (originals, owned by A. Porter Robinson, San Francisco); Peirce to Hunnewell, Oahu, September 25, 1831, Hunnewell Collection.

[112] Robinson to Bryant & Sturgis, Santa Barbara, October 23, 1832, Robinson Collection; Peirce to Hunnewell, Oahu, December 6, 1832, Hunnewell Collection.

[113] Robinson to Peirce, Santa Barbara, December 20, 1833, Robinson Collection; Robinson to Russell & Co., Santa Barbara, December 20, 1833, *ibid.*

NOTES TO CHAPTER VI

OTTER HUNTING UNDER THE MEXICAN REGIME

[1] José María Narváez to Antonio Valdés, Guadalajara, January 7, 1822, Californias (originals, A.G.P.M.), Vol. XLV.

[2] George Tays, "Revolutionary California," Ph.D. dissertation, University of California, 1932, pp. 56–58.

[3] Certificate of registry, Boston, May 15, 1822, Mariano Guadalupe Vallejo, Documentos para la historia de California (originals, B.L.), XXVIII, 143.

[4] John Rogers Cooper, Logbook of the *Rover*, 1822–1826 (original, owned by Miss Frances Molera, San Francisco), Monterey, June 24, 1823; Estudillo to José María Echeandía, Monterey, August 3, 1826, Departmental State Papers (transcripts, B.L.), I, 160–61.

[5] José Señan to Argüello, San Buenaventura, August 5, 1823, Archivo del arzobispado (transcripts, B.L.), Vol. IV, Pt. 2, p. 12.

[6] Andrew Lozarev, "Extracts from the Description of a Voyage around the World," Russian America (transcripts, B.L.), Vol. III, Pt. 4, p. 108.

[7] Argüello to Ruiz, Monterey, August 9, 1824, Departmental Records (transcripts, B.L.), I, 155.

[8] José Fernández, "Cosas de California" (original, B.L.), pp. 25–26; Kiril Khlebnikov, "Letters," Russian America, Vol. III, Pt. 3, pp. 212–13.

[9] Important references for the Argüello-Cooper agreement of 1823 follow: Cooper to Hunnewell, Monterey, December 24, 1823, James Hunnewell Collection (originals, H.U.L.); bill of sale of *Rover*, Monterey, December 29, 1823, Vallejo, Documentos, XXVIII, 143; provincial deputation, Monterey, January 29, 1824, Legislative Records (transcripts, B.L.), I, 28; Wildes to Marshall, Oahu, November 5, 1824, Josiah Marshall Collection (originals and transcripts, W.M.L.).

[10] Argüello to Martínez, Monterey, January 12, 1824, Departmental Records, I, 76; Martínez to Argüello, San Francisco, January 22, 1824, State Papers, Sacramento (transcripts, B.L.), XIV, 4; Khlebnikov, "Letters," p. 214.

[11] Accounts of skin collections for the *Rover* follow: Cooper, Logbook of the *Rover*, January 22 and 28, March 16, 1824, *et seq.*; account of Cooper and the Province, Canton, June 20, 1824, Vallejo, Documentos, XXVIII, 369; Khlebnikov, "Letters," p. 214.

[12] Martínez to Argüello, San Francisco, February 5, 1824, State Papers, Sacramento, XIV, 4.

[13] Khlebnikov, "Letters," p. 214.

[14] *Ibid.*; Otto von Kotzebue, *A New Voyage*, II, 136; Martínez to Argüello, San Francisco, December 17, 1824, State Papers, Sacramento, XIV, 6.

[15] Cooper, Logbook of the *Rover*, April 25—July 1, 1824.

[16] Important references for the commercial accounts for the *Rover's* 1824 voyage are as follows: Manila, May 13, 1824, Vallejo, Documentos, XXVIII, 360; Canton, June 20, 1824, *ibid.*, p. 369; Monterey, September 22, 1824, *ibid.*, p. 404; Monterey, November 4, 1824, Departmental State Papers, Benicia, Military (transcripts, B.L.), LXII, 22–23.

[17] Cooper to Khlebnikov (San Francisco) (December 1, 1824—January 5, 1825), Valentín Alviso, Documentos para la historia de California (originals, B.L.), No. 189. Place and approximate date of above letter may be determined from the log of the *Rover*.

[18] Important references on the 1825–1826 voyage of the *Rover* follow: Cooper, Logbook of the *Rover;* shipment by Cooper on *Tartar,* Oahu, May 16, 1825, Vallejo, Documentos, XXVIII, 454; commercial accounts, Lintin, October 2, 1825, Canton, October, 1825, *ibid.,* p. 507.

[19] Cooper to Sturgis, Monterey, July 30, 1828, *ibid.,* XXIX, 387. There is a great quantity of correspondence on the *Rover* case which will not be cited here. Perhaps the most important document is Antonio José Cot and William Hartnell, "Arbitration of the Case of the *Rover,*" Monterey, April 20, 1827 (original, B.L.).

[20] Hartnell to de la Guerra, Monterey, December 9, 1825, Hartnell Letter Book (original, B.L.), p. 154.

[21] Echeandía to the minister of war, San Diego, April 22, 1826, State Papers, Sacramento, XIX, 27–31.

[22] Khlebnikov, "Letters," p. 215.

[23] Echeandía to the minister of war, San Diego, April 22, 1826, State Papers, Sacramento, XIX, 27–31.

[24] Echeandía to Khlebnikov (no place or date), *ibid.,* XI, 13–14.

[25] Hartnell to de la Guerra, Monterey, December 9, 1825, Hartnell Letter Book, p. 154.

[26] Hartnell to de la Guerra, Monterey, February 26, 1826, de la Guerra y Noriega, Documentos para la historia de California (transcripts, B.L.), V, 93–95.

[27] Hartnell to de la Guerra, Monterey, April 5, 1826, transcript, B.L.

[28] Peter Egorovich Chistiakov to Echeandía, Sitka, October 13, 1828, Departmental State Papers, II, 65–67.

[29] Echeandía to Adolf Karlovich Etolin, San Diego, December 10, 1828, original, S.G.; Echeandía to the minister of war, San Diego, May 14, 1829, original, S.G.

[30] Extract from the log of the *Baikal,* undated, José Joaquín Estudillo, Documentos para la historia de California (originals, B.L.), II, 166. The only means of identification of this extract is the mention of "Capt. D. Aduelfo," the month and day of the year, and the activity of the crew.

[31] Khlebnikov, "Letters," p. 215.

[32] Mexico, Ministerio de relaciones exteriores, *Memoria de los ramos del ministerio de relaciones interiores y esteriores de la república* (Mexico, 1829), p. 22; Riesgo to Herrera, Rosario, August 7, 1828, Departmental State Papers, Benicia, Commissary and Treasury (transcripts, B.L.), I, 106.

[33] Juan de Dios Cañedo to Echeandía, Mexico, August 6, 1828, Vallejo, Documentos, XXIX, 268.

[34] José Ignacio Esteva to the secretary of relations, Mexico, September 23, 1828, original, S.G.

[35] Minister of relations to Echeandía, Mexico, September 27, 1828, original, S.G.

[36] Mariano Guadalupe Vallejo, "Historia de California" (original, B.L.), II, 125; also see Juan Bautista Alvarado, "Historia de California" (original, B.L.), II, 128–29.

[37] Echeandía to the minister of relations, San Diego, May 14 and 22, 1829, originals, S.G.

[38] G. Pedraza to the commanders of the marine, Mexico, January 26 and 28, 1825, Mexico, *Ordenes y circulares espedidas por el supremo gobierno* (Mexico, 1830), pp. 1–3; "Arancel para las aduanas marítimas," Manuel Dublán and José María Lozana, eds., *Legislación mexicana* (Mexico, 1876–1913), II, 26.

[39] Tays, "Revolutionary California," pp. 102, 108.

[40] Enrique Eduardo Virmond to Cooper, San Diego, January 20, 1831, Vallejo, Documentos, XXX, 177.

[41] Ferdinand Petrovich Wrangel to Manuel Victoria, Sitka, October 20, 1831, ibid., p. 138.

[42] Victoria to Wrangel, Monterey, March 5, 1831, ibid., p. 189.

[43] J. A. Facio to the commanders of the two departments, Mexico, July 1, 1830, Ordenes y circulares, p. 7; Facio to the secretary of relations, Mexico, July 23, 1830, ibid., pp. 8–9.

[44] Victoria to Lucas Alamán, Monterey, April 13, 1831, Departmental Records, IX, 121–22.

[45] Decree of Echeandía, San Diego, June 13, 1826, ibid., IV, 48; Echeandía to Luis Bringas, San Diego, December 6, 1826, ibid., p. 20; Echeandía to J. B. López, Monterey, June 30, 1830, ibid., VIII, 52; Echeandía to the comisario subalterno of Monterey, Monterey, September 24, 1830, ibid., p. 102; Echeandía, license for Eugenio Morillo, Monterey, December 14, 1830, ibid., p. 131.

[46] Charles Lewis Camp, "The Chronicles of George C. Yount," California Historical Society, Quarterly, II (April, 1923), 46.

[47] Echeandía to Romualdo Pacheco, Monterey, December 9, 1830, Departmental Records, VIII, 130.

[48] Pacheco to Victoria, Santa Barbara, April 17, 1831, Departmental State Papers, Benicia (transcripts, B.L.), II, 5; Antonio Carrillo to ———, Santa Barbara, April 17, 1831, Departmental State Papers, Benicia, Commissary and Treasury, II, 17.

[49] Victoria, license, Monterey, March, 1831, Departmental Records, IX, 94. Bancroft presents this document as a general decree of Victoria's on otter hunting and states that San Francisco was the northern limit of hunting (Bancroft, History of California, III, 374). The contents of the document indicate its temporary and special nature.

[50] References to the Alvarado-Castro hunting of 1831 follow: Alvarado, "Historia," II, 39–40; Salvador Vallejo, "Notas históricas sobre California" (original, B.L.), p. 36; Alvarado to Cooper, San Francisco, April 3, 1831, Vallejo, Documentos, XXX, 200.

[51] "Letter from Mr. Wallace," Hayes Scrap Books, XLVII, 53–54.

[52] James Ohio Pattie, Narrative (Cincinnati, 1833), p. 387.

[53] Yount's account of his experiences has been published by Camp, op. cit., pp. 44–49. The vessel seen by Yount was probably the Griffon, Captain Taylor, which was on the coast, July–September, 1831. See next chapter.

[54] Jonathan Trumbull Warner, "Reminiscences of Early California" (original, B.L.), p. 63; Henry Dwight Barrows, "William Wolfskill, the Pioneer," Historical Society of Southern California, Publications, V (1902), 287–94.

[55] Victoria to Vicente Sánchez, Monterey, February 19, 1831, Departmental Records, IX, 92.

[56] Warner, p. 65.

[57] Important references for the Wolfskill expedition, 1831–1832, follow: Warner, pp. 63–67; "Letter from Mr. Wallace," Hayes Scrap Books, XLVII, 54; José Figueroa to William Wolfskill, Santa Barbara, October 9, 1833, Departmental State Papers, III, 173.

[58] Alfred Robinson, Life in California (San Francisco, 1891), pp. 140–41.

[50] Accounts of Young's otter hunting follow: Warner, pp. 13–19; Joseph John Hill, "Ewing Young in the Fur Trade of the Far Southwest, 1822–1834," Oregon Historical Society, *Quarterly*, XXIV (March, 1923), 1–35.

[60] "Recollections of a Pioneer of California," Santa Cruz *Sentinel*, May 15, 1869, No. 49; also see, Job Francis Dye, "Recollections" (original, B.L.).

[61] —— to ——, Monterey, August 5, 1834, Vallejo, Documentos, XXXI, 113.

[62] George Nidever, "Life and Adventures" (original, B.L.), p. 67. This manuscript has been published by William Henry Ellison, *The Life and Adventures of George Nidever, 1802–1883* (Berkeley, 1937). All page references given here are to the manuscript.

[63] Isaac J. Sparks to Nidever, Santa Barbara, September 14, 1835, Thompson Collection (originals, owned by Mrs. John M. Williamson, Carpinteria). Other accounts of Sparks, 1832–1835, follow: Mrs. F. H. Day, "Sketches of the Early Settlers of California—Isaac J. Sparks," *The Hesperian*, II (July, 1859), 198; Nidever, pp. 67, 82. In the first part of his narrative, Nidever is a year late in his dates.

[64] Camp, *op. cit.*, p. 50.

[65] Nidever, p. 63. The time in the narrative is 1835. However, the Walker party arrived in November, 1833.

[66] Charles Brown, "Statement of Recollections" (original, B.L.), p. 28. Brown states the time as "1835 or thereabouts."

[67] Nidever, p. 66.

[68] *Ibid.*, pp. 66–67. The date of the narrative is 1835. However, the *California*, Captain Robinson, upon which Nidever sailed, left San Francisco for Santa Barbara on April 21, 1834.

[69] *Ibid.*, pp. 72–73.

[70] *Ibid.*, pp. 73, 85. Just before his 1835 trip, Sparks had returned from removing the last of the Indians from San Nicolas Island, the famous one woman excepted.

[71] *Ibid.*, p. 85.

[72] It is not clear whether Yount or Sparks had licenses on their smaller expeditions. Other foreigners in addition to those mentioned in this chapter are known to have engaged in hunting, but under what circumstances is not known. Such for example were Isaac Williams, Timothy Murphy, Francis Branch, John Forster, and Cyrus Alexander.

[73] Victoria to Eduarda Osuna, Monterey, October 30, 1831, Departmental Records, IX, 118. Also see the following: Victoria to María Josefa Boronda, Monterey, October 22, 1831, *ibid.*, p. 117; Warner, "Reminiscences," p. 65.

[74] Echeandía, representation against Joaquín Ortega, Monterey, January 15, 1831, Departmental Records, IX, 80; Echeandía to Martínez, Monterey, January 15, 1831, *ibid.*, p. 81; Victoria to Martínez, Monterey, February 1, 1831, *ibid.*, p. 1; Victoria to Sánchez, Monterey, March 6, 1831, *ibid.*, p. 93.

[75] José Antonio Carrillo to ——, Los Angeles, September 13, 1833, Departmental State Papers, Benicia, *prefecturas y juzgados* (transcripts, B.L.), II, 24; legal procedure, Monterey, September 2, 1833, Monterey Archives (transcripts, B.L.), I, 29.

[76] Two original licenses may be found in the Spanish records; the others as recorded are only brief summaries. Figueroa, license to Cooper, Monterey, June 20, 1833, Vallejo, Documentos, XXXI, 18; Figueroa, license to Ortega, Monterey, January 21, 1834, *ibid.*, p. 61.

[77] Important references from the many on the question of duties on otter skins, 1830–1834, follow: Spanish law on the subject, April 16, 1811, Dublán and Lozano, eds., *Legislación mexicana*, I, 341; Victoria to the minister of relations, Monterey, April 16 and June 7, 1831, Departmental Records, IX, 124, 135–36; Agustín Zamorano to José Antonio Sánchez, Monterey, September 8, 1832, Vallejo, Documentos, I, 323; *bando* of Figueroa, Monterey, August 6, 1834, Departmental State Papers, Monterey (transcripts, B.L.), III, 27–28.

[78] Accounts of the Castro hunting of 1832 follow: James William Weeks, "Reminiscences" (original, B.L.), p. 63; Zamorano to Sánchez, Monterey, September 8, 1832, Vallejo, Documentos, I, 323.

[79] José Castro and José Ramón Estrada to Figueroa, Monterey, January 24, 1833, *ibid.*, XXXI, 3.

[80] Figueroa, license to Castro and Estrada, Monterey, January 25, 1833, Departmental State Papers, III, 76.

[81] Cooper to Hunnewell, Monterey, April 22, 1833, Hunnewell Collection; Cooper to Figueroa, Monterey, June 18, 1833, January 4, 1834, Departmental State Papers, III, 138, 158; Figueroa, license to Cooper, Monterey, June 20, 1833, Vallejo, Documentos, XXXI, 18; Figueroa to Cooper, Monterey, January 14, 1834, Departmental State Papers, III, 144.

[82] Figueroa to Ortega, Monterey, December 5, 1833, August 21, 1834, *ibid.*, pp. 172, 204; Figueroa, license to Ortega, Monterey, January 21, 1834, Vallejo, Documentos, XXI, 61.

[83] Licenses for men listed may be found in the following: Departmental State Papers, III, 92–93, 126, 144–47, 157–58, 171, 174, 187–89; Departmental Records, IX, 117.

[84] Wrangel to the secretary of foreign relations, Mexico, February 28, 1836, original, S.R.E., 5–8–7978; W. Potekhin, "Settlement of Ross," Russian America, Vol. V, Pt. 2, fol. 12.

[85] Wrangel to the governor of California, Fort Ross, July 24, 1833, State Papers, Sacramento, X, 85–87. In the 1831 edition of Beechey there is only one sentence directed against the Russians. Frederick William Beechey, *Narrative* (London, 1831), II, 69. Wrangel may have been referring to some other account by the same captain.

[86] Secretary of foreign relations to Wrangel, Mexico, March 12, 1836, original, S.R.E., 5–8–7978; also see, Potekhin, "Settlement of Ross," fols. 17–18.

[87] George Simpson to the governor, deputy governor, and committee of the Hudson's Bay Company, Honolulu, March 1, 1842, *American Historical Review*, XIV (October, 1908), 85; Enrique Cerruti, "Establecimientos rusos" (original, B.L.), p. 6; Potekhin, "Settlement of Ross," fols. 19–20.

NOTES TO CHAPTER VII

CONTRABANDIST AND CAPITALIST IN SEA OTTER FIELDS

[1] Peirce to Hunnewell, Oahu, September 25, 1831, James Hunnewell Collection (originals, H.U.L.). Other important accounts of the *Griffon*, 1831, follow: Peirce to Hunnewell, Oahu, September 25, 1831, *ibid.;* Pablo de la Portilla to Ignacio del Valle, San Diego, October 27, 1831, Departmental State Papers, Benicia, Military (transcripts, B.L.), LXXIII, 12–13.

[2] Peirce to Hunnewell, Oahu, September 19, 1832, Hunnewell Collection. Also see Peirce to Hunnewell, Oahu, May 21, 1832, *ibid.*

[3] Cooper and Jones, Monterey, April 23, 1830, Mariano Guadalupe Vallejo, Documentos para la historia de California (originals, B.L.), XXX, 45.

[4] Jones to Cooper, Oahu, March 1, 1831, *ibid.*, p. 186.

[5] Thompson and Cooper, Monterey, May 30, 1831, *ibid.*, p. 214.

[6] J. A. Facio to the commanders of the marine department, Mexico, August 16, 1830, Mexico, *Ordenes y circulares* (Mexico, 1830), pp. 9–17.

[7] Jones to Cooper, San Diego, August 22, 1831, Vallejo, Documentos, XXX, 239.

[8] Jones to Cooper, Oahu, October 28, 1831, *ibid.*, p. 264.

[9] Abel Stearns and Thompson (no place), September 22, 1831, original, owned by Henry Raup Wagner, San Marino.

[10] Thompson to Stearns, Monterey, September 22, 1831, Historical Society of Southern California, *Publications*, VII (1907–1908), 205.

[11] Peirce to Hunnewell, Oahu, April 10, and September 19, 1832, Hunnewell Collection; Francis A. Thompson to Mrs. Thompson, Santa Barbara, October 27, 1832, Alpheus Basil Thompson Collection (originals, owned by Mrs. John M. Williamson, Carpinteria).

[12] Peirce to Hunnewell, Oahu, November 13, 1832, Hunnewell Collection. Other references follow: Peirce to Hunnewell, Oahu, August 19, 1833, *ibid.;* Peirce to Hunnewell, on the *Becket*, January 26, 1834, *ibid.*

[13] Victoria to the minister of relations, Monterey, June 7, 1831, Departmental Records (transcripts, B.L.), IX, 135–36.

[14] Figueroa to the receptor, San Diego, July 30, 1833, Archives of San Diego (transcripts, B.L.), p. 2.

[15] Nicolás Gutiérrez to Edmund P. Kennedy, Monterey, October 28, 1836, original, S.G.M., 52–8–7–1.

[16] *Ibid.* The letters at the Secretaría de Guerra y de Marina concerning this case have been translated and published by George Tays, "Commodore Edmund B. Kennedy, U.S.N., versus Governor Nicolás Gutiérrez, an Incident of 1836," California Historical Society, *Quarterly*, XII (June, 1933), 137–46.

[17] Cooper to Hunnewell, Monterey, April 22, 1833, Hunnewell Collection.

[18] *Loc. cit.*

[19] George Nidever, "Life and Adventures" (original, B.L.), p. 82.

[20] *Ibid.*, p. 75.

[21] *Ibid.*, pp. 67–68.

[22] Mariano Chico to the minister of war and marine, Monterey, July 22, 1836, original, S.G.M., 52–8–7–1. Other important references to contrabandists, 1834–1836, follow: Hudson's Bay Company, Journal at Fort Simpson (transcript, B.L.), pp. 1, 7; Antonio María Osio to Alvarado, Los Angeles, January 12, 1835, Departmental State Papers, Angeles (transcripts, B.L.), II, 11;

arrivals of vessels, Oahu, 1836, A. de La Salle, *Relation du voyage* (Paris, 1845–52), II, 398–99; Stephen Reynolds to Spear, Oahu, July 4, 1836, original, B.L.

[23] Vasilii Sokolov, "The Voyage of Alexander Markoff" (original, B.L.), pp. 5–6.

[24] Figueroa to Wrangel, Monterey, December 23, 1833, State Papers, Sacramento (transcripts, B.L.), XIX, 15–18.

[25] Figueroa to the secretary of war and marine, Monterey, December 10, 1834, original, S.G.M., 52–6–6–11.

[26] Chico to the minister of war and marine, Monterey, July 22, 1836, original, S.G.M., 52–8–7–1.

[27] The full details of this episode are given in Nidever, pp. 75–81.

[28] For identification of this vessel, see Nidever, p. 83; outfitting and sales accounts of the *Convoy*, 1835–1837, Thompson Collection; Richard Henry Dana, *Two Years before the Mast* (Boston, 1873), p. 279.

[29] Shipping list, *The Hawaiian Spectator*, Vol. I (1838), No. 2, pp. 102–3; *ibid.*, Vol. II (1839), No. 1, pp. 118–19; quotation from Fort Simpson Journal, Hubert Howe Bancroft, *History of the Northwest Coast* (San Francisco, 1884), II, 606.

[30] Accounts of this voyage of the *Lama* follow: Hubert Howe Bancroft, *California*, IV, 90–91; Bancroft, *Northwest Coast*, II, 604–7; Faxon Dean Atherton to Larkin, Honolulu, January 13, 1839, Thomas Oliver Larkin, Documents for the History of California (originals, B.L.), I, 1; J. Molteno to Grimes, Brig *Lama*, January, 1839, *The Hawaiian Spectator*, Vol. II, No. 2, pp. 236–38.

[31] *Ibid.*, p. 237.

[32] *Ibid.*, pp. 237–38.

[33] *Ibid.*, p. 238. Some time later the Kaiganies brought their California skins to Fort Simpson for sale. Bancroft, *Northwest Coast*, II, 607.

[34] Atherton to Larkin, Honolulu, January 13, 1839, Larkin, Documents, I, 1.

[35] Alvarado to Antonio Rodríguez, Santa Barbara, January 25, 1839, Departmental State Papers (transcripts, B.L.), XVIII, 58; Alvarado to Allen Light, Santa Barbara, January 27, 1839, San Diego Archives (transcripts, B.L.), p. 218.

[36] Testimonies, Santa Barbara, January 25, 28, and 29, 1839, Departmental State Papers, XVIII, 58, 60; Alvarado to ———, Santa Barbara, January 27, 1839, *ibid.*, p. 59.

[37] Alvarado to Light, Santa Barbara, January 27, 1839, San Diego Archives, p. 218.

Light was not appointed as "commissary general" of a "national armada," as stated in Bancroft, but was authorized to get the *Lama* if he could, since he was "*compromosiario pral*," "principal representative," or the principal one engaged in "the national armada" of otter-hunting boats.

[38] Romero to the minister of war, Mexico, December 3, 1837, original, S.G.M., 52–6–9–2.

[39] William Heath Davis, *Sixty Years in California*, p. 136.

[40] Cooper to Vallejo, Santa Cruz, September 3, 1840, Vallejo, Documentos, IX, 236.

[41] Pesado to Alvarado, Mexico, July 20, 1838, State Papers, Missions and Colonization (transcripts, B.L.), II, 287; Alvarado to the departmental *junta*, Monterey, February 27, 1840, *ibid.*, p. 391.

[42] Accounts of the contrabandists, 1839–1841, follow: Eugène Duflot de Mofras, *Exploration* (Paris, 1844), I, 483; Tiburcio Tapia to the mayordomos of San Juan Capistrano, San Luis Rey, and the judge of San Diego, Los Angeles, December 21, 1840, Departmental State Papers, Angeles, I, 37; Jules Dudoit to Hunnewell, Oahu, December 14, 1841, Hunnewell Collection; Bancroft, *Northwest Coast*, II, 605.

[43] Atherton to Larkin, Honolulu, January 13, 1839, Larkin, Documents, I, 1.

[44] Accounts of hunting on the upper coast, 1837–1841, are as follows: Nidever, Life and Adventures, pp. 88, 101, 108; William Dane Phelps, Logbook of the *Alert* (original, W.M.L.), September 28, 1840; certification by Spence, Monterey, August 5, 1839, San Diego Archives, p. 218; judge of first instance to the prefect of Santa Barbara, Santa Barbara, March 25, 1841, Archivo de Santa Barbara (transcripts, B.L.), p. 17; Jones to Larkin, Santa Barbara, July 21, 1841, Larkin, Documents, I, 136.

[45] Nidever, p. 101.

[46] For accounts of the 1840 expedition see the following references: *ibid.*, pp. 103–9; Departmental Government to Sparks, Santa Barbara, February 8, 1840, José de la Guerra y Noriega, Documentos para la historia de California (transcripts, B.L.), V, 298–99. Nidever must have been in San Diego between August 24 and 28 when the *Alert* was in harbor.

[47] Accounts of the 1842 expedition follow: José de la Guerra y Carrillo to ———, Santa Barbara, April 4, 1842, Departmental State Papers, Angeles, VI, 115; Phelps, Logbook of the *Alert*, October 29, 1842; William Dane Phelps, *Fore and Aft* (Boston, 1871), pp. 262–64.

[48] John Wilson to Larkin, San Francisco, December 6, 1841, Larkin, Documents, I, 192. Other accounts of the Wilson expedition of 1841 follow: Nidever, p. 107; Pico to the prefect of the first district, Santa Barbara, October 22, 1841, Departmental State Papers, VI, 70; Jones to Larkin, Santa Barbara, November 20, 1841, Larkin, Documents, I, 189.

[49] Jones to Thompson, Santa Barbara, September 11, 1843, Thompson Collection.

[50] *Loc. cit.*

[51] Jones to Thompson, Santa Barbara, October 2, 1843, Thompson Collection.

[52] Nidever, p. 109; receipts from canoe men, Santa Barbara, November 18, 1843, Thompson Collection.

[53] Thompson to Henry Fitch, San Pedro, December 25, 1843, *ibid.*

[54] Roderick to Green, Brig *Oajaca*, January 17, 1844, Larkin, Documents, II, 57.

[55] Thompson to Larkin, Santa Barbara, April 16, 1845, *ibid.*, III, 112.

[56] References for 1845 hunting follow: Carl Dittmann, "Narrative of a Sea-Faring Life from 1844" (original, B.L.), pp. 15–19; Nidever, pp. 109–10.

[57] Names of those in Lower California from whom Fitch collected skins are Santiago Arce, William Ames, Martain Morino, and padres Duarto, Mansilla, and Poneia. Some important references to Fitch's otter business follow: Argüello to the *jueces de paz* of Los Angeles, Los Angeles, May 17, 1841, Departmental State Papers, Angeles, VI, 28–29; Mansilla to Fitch, Santo Tomás, January 5, 1842, February 1, 1843, Henry Fitch, Documentos para la historia de California (originals, B.L.), Nos. 191, 245; Robert Robertson to Fitch, San Diego, August 10, 1843, *ibid.*, No. 267.

[58] *Ibid.*

[59] Edward Stokes to Fitch, Rancho de Santa Maria, April 24, 1844, *ibid.*, No. 301.

[60] Thompson to Lawrence Carmichael, San Francisco, July 11, 1842, Thompson Collection; Warner to the prefect of the district, Los Angeles, January 7, 1843, Archives of Los Angeles (transcripts, B.L.), II, 317–18; Manuel Micheltorena to Manuel Casarin Jimeno, Los Angeles, January 27, 1843, *ibid.*, pp. 324–25; Teodoro González, certificate, Monterey, May 15, 1843, Monterey Archives (transcripts, B.L.), XI, 7.

[61] Henry J. Dally, "Narrative" (original, B.L.), pp. 19–23.

[62] Dittmann, pp. 20–37; Nidever, pp. 111–13; Phelps, *Fore and Aft*, p. 263; Pio Pico to Thompson, Santa Barbara, June 30, 1846, Departmental State Papers, VII, 31.

[63] Argüello to the *jueces de paz* of Los Angeles, Los Angeles, May 17, 1841, Departmental State Papers, Angeles, VI, 28–29.

[64] Jimeno to the prefect of the second district, Monterey, March 9, 1842, Departmental Records, XIII, 28.

[65] Important references on the question of duties follow: Pico to the prefect of the second district, Santa Barbara, October 22, 1841, Departmental State Papers, VI, 70; José de la Guerra y Carrillo, license to Sparks, Santa Barbara, April 4, 1842, Departmental State Papers, Angeles, VI, 115; Estanislao Armentos, certificate, San Vicente, October 31, 1841, *ibid.*, VII, 16; Redington, receipt, San Diego, May 10, 1844, *ibid.*, VIII, 17.

[66] Dittmann, pp. 41–43.

[67] Henry Mellus to William Appleton & Co., Los Angeles, May 3, 1848, Gordon Dexter Collection (originals, Baker Library, H.S.B.A.).

[68] Nidever, pp. 136–37.

[69] Dittmann, pp. 45–47.

[70] Nidever, p. 137.

NOTES TO CHAPTER VIII

A GENERAL SURVEY OF THE SEA OTTER TRADE

[1] In this chapter no attempt will be made to cite authorities for numbers of otters except for direct or indirect quotation.

[2] Ludovik Choris, *Voyage pittoresque* (Paris, 1822), Pt. 3, p. 7.

[3] P. Tikhmenev, "Historical Review," Russian America (transcripts, B.L.), Vol. I, Pt. 1, p. 206

[4] Otto von Kotzebue, *A New Voyage* (London, 1830), II, 121.

[5] Frederick William Beechey, *Narrative* (London, 1831), II, 80.

[6] Auguste Bernard du Hautcilly, *Voyage* (Paris, 1834–35), II, 74.

[7] Charles Lewis Camp, "The Chronicles of George C. Yount," The California Historical Society, *Quarterly*, II, 46.

[8] Juan Bautista Alvarado, "Historia de California" (original, B.L.), II, 7; José Fernández, "Cosas de California" (original, B.L.), p. 26.

[9] William Dane Phelps, *Fore and Aft* (Boston, 1871), p. 263.

[10] Cooper to Hunnewell, Monterey, April 22, 1833, James Hunnewell Collection (originals, H.U.L.).

[11] Charles Wilkes, *Narrative of the United States Exploring Expedition* (Philadelphia, 1844), V, 169.

[12] George Nidever, "Life and Adventures" (original, B.L.), p. 110.

[13] Carl Dittmann, "Narrative" (original, B.L.), pp. 23–25; Phelps, *op. cit.*, p. 263.

[14] Nidever, pp. 77–78.

[15] William Heath Davis, *Sixty Years in California* (San Francisco, 1889), p. 24.

[16] Nidever, p. 103.

[17] John James Audubon and John Bachman, *The Quadrupeds of North America* (New York, 1849–54), III, 173.

[18] Charles Melville Scammon, *Marine Mammals* (San Francisco, 1874), p. 171.

[19] Camp, *op. cit.*, p. 47.

[20] Henry James Snow, *In Forbidden Seas* (London, 1910), p. 42.

[21] Mrs. F. H. Day, "Isaac J. Sparks," *The Hesperian*, II, 199.

[22] For an account of sea otters found recently on the coast, see Grinnell, *Fur-Bearing Mammals of California*, I, 290. In 1890 sea otters were taken just south of San Francisco and near San Miguel Island. In 1906, a few lived around the islands off Lower California. In 1908 one was taken off Point Sur. In 1916 thirty-one were seen south of Catalina Island, and about the same time as many as forty were seen between San Luis Obispo and Point Sur. In 1917 two were seen off Del Monte.

[23] Jones to Larkin, Oahu, December 17, 1834, Mariano Guadalupe Vallejo, Documentos para la historia de California (originals, B.L.), XXXI, 143.

[24] Reynolds to Spear, Oahu, July 28, 1836, original, B.L.

[25] Bryant, Sturgis, & Co. to Thomas B. Park and Mellus, Boston, June 11, 1838, Bryant, Sturgis, & Co., Letter Book (original, W.M.L.).

[26] French to Thompson, Oahu, February 7, 1837, Alpheus Basil Thompson Collection (originals, owned by Mrs. J. M. Williamson, Carpinteria). See also the following: Reynolds to Spear, Oahu, March 16, May 7, and July 28, 1836, originals, B.L.; Stephen Mackintosh to Thompson, Honolulu, April 8, 1837, Thompson Collection; French to Thompson, Oahu, April 8, 1837, *ibid.*

[27] Hinckley in account with J. Mellish, Santa Cruz, July 24, 1836, original, B.L.; Spear in account with Hinckley, Monterey, September 13, 1836, original, B.L.

[28] References for Reynolds' interest in otter skins follow: Reynolds to Spear, Oahu, March 16, 1836, January 22, and May (10), 1837, May 15, 1838, originals, B.L.; Spear to Reynolds, Monterey, June 4, 1836, original, B.L.

[29] Reynolds to Thompson, Oahu, September 16, 1837, Thompson Collection.

[30] Peirce and Brewer to Thompson, Oahu, August 9 and September 30, 1837, ibid.

[31] Reynolds to Thompson, Oahu, May —, 1838, ibid.

[32] Thompson to Reynolds, San Pedro, October 8, 1840, ibid. See also the following: Nidever, "Life and Adventures," p. 88; Fitch in account with José Antonio Aguirre, 1838, Henry Fitch, Documentos para la historia de California (originals, B.L.), No. 42; John Daniel Meyer to Stearns, San Jose, November 23, 1839, Abel Stearns Collection (originals, H.L.).

[33] Important references for otter trade with Mexico, 1840–1846, follow: manifest of Nymph, San Diego, December 16, 1840, Fitch, Documentos, No. 148; Robert Dare, petition, San Diego, December 16, 1840, Archives of San Diego (transcripts, B.L.), Commerce and Revenues, 1820–1843, No. 6; Meyer, petition, San Diego, December 17, 1840, ibid.; Wilson to Larkin, San Francisco, December 6, 1841, Thomas Oliver Larkin, Documents for the History of California (originals, B.L.), I, 192; Henry Dalton to William Alexander Leidesdorff, Mazatlan, June 25, 1844, Leidesdorff Collection (originals, H.L.); accounts of the Nymph, June 8, 1845, Fitch, Documentos, Nos. 344, 345.

[34] Elliott C. Cowdin, "The Northwest Fur Trade," The Merchants' Magazine, XIV, 536.

[35] William Dane Phelps, Logbook of the Alert (original, W.M.L.), April 7, 1841; ibid., April 20, 1841.

[36] Appleton & Co. to Mellus, Boston, August 22, 1843, Gordon Dexter Collection (originals, H.S.B.A.).

[37] Loc. cit.

[38] Mellus to Appleton & Co., Monterey, April 10, 1844, Dexter Collection.

[39] Mellus to Appleton & Co., Monterey, June 18, 1844, ibid.

[40] Mellus to Appleton & Co., San Diego, December 18, 1844, ibid.; manifest of the Barnstable, Boston, February 4, 1842, ibid.

[41] Appleton & Co. to Mellus, Boston, April 28, 1845, ibid.

[42] Appleton & Co., to Mellus, Boston, October 21, 1845, ibid.

[43] Appleton & Co. to Mellus, Boston, November 10, 1845, ibid.

[44] Mellus to Appleton & Co., San Francisco, October 10, 1845, ibid.

[45] References for 1845–1846 follow: recapitulation of purchases, Admittance and Tasso, 1846, ibid.; invoice of hides on Admittance, San Diego, January 14, 1846, ibid.; sales of cargo of Admittance, Boston, June, 1846, ibid.

[46] Arther to Fitch, San Francisco, March 6, 1847, Fitch, Documentos, No. 427; see also Robert Robertson to Fitch, San Diego, August 10, 1843, ibid., No. 267.

[47] References for otter shipments, 1847, follow: Invoice of Sterling, San Francisco, March 1, 1847, William Dane Phelps Collection (originals, W.M.L.); invoice of goods shipped on the Loo Choo, San Diego, June 22, 1847, Dexter Collection; sales of cargo of Loo Choo, Boston, January 20, 1848, ibid.; Davis, Sixty Years in California, p. 211.

[48] Jones to W. C. B. Finch, Honolulu, October 30, 1829, in Charles Samuel Stewart, A Visit to the South Seas (New York, 1831), II, 219.

[49] See Chapter VII.

[50] Warner to Martin Van Buren, Hadlyme, Connecticut, September 21, 1840, Department of State, Consular letters, Monterey, 1837–1848 (originals, L.C.).

[51] Robert Glass Cleland, "Asiatic Trade and American Occupation of the Pacific Coast," The American Historical Association, *Annual Report*, I (1914), 281–89; Cleland, *The Early Sentiment for the Annexation of California* (Austin, 1915); Rayner Wickersham Kelsey, *The United States Consulate in California* (Berkeley, 1910); George Lockhart Rives, *The United States and Mexico, 1821–1848* (New York, 1913); Justin Harvey Smith, *The War with Mexico* (New York, 1919).

BIBLIOGRAPHY

BIBLIOGRAPHY

FOR PRACTICAL PURPOSES, the following bibliography is limited to materials cited in the notes. Exceptions are a few general reference books. When the depository of the originals of transcripts is evident from the title, it is not repeated. The following classification is used:

A. Manuscript materials

    1. Correspondence and official documents
    2. Logbooks and journals
    3. Contemporary histories and reminiscences
    4. Unpublished theses

B. Printed materials

    1. Books
    2. Periodical literature
    3. Newspapers and newspaper articles

A. MANUSCRIPT MATERIALS

1. CORRESPONDENCE AND OFFICIAL DOCUMENTS

Alviso, Valentín. Documentos para la historia de California, 1817–1849. Originals, in Bancroft Library, University of California.

Archives of Los Angeles, Miscellaneous Papers, 1821–1850. 5 vols. Transcripts, in Bancroft Library, University of California.

Archives of Monterey County, Miscellaneous Documents. 16 vols. in 1. Transcripts, in Bancroft Library, University of California.

Archives of San Diego, 1826–1850. Transcripts, in Bancroft Library, University of California.

Archivo de California. Transcripts of documents in the United States Surveyor General's Office at San Francisco, destroyed in 1906; in Bancroft Library, University of California.
Archives of California, Miscellany. 1 vol. in 4 parts.
    Part 1. Provincial State Papers, Benicia, 2 vols.
    Part 2. Register of Brands and Marks.
    Part 3. Mexican Archives, Lower California, 1847–1848.
    Part 4. State Papers, Benicia, Miscellaneous, 1773–1829.
Departmental Records, 1822–1845. 14 vols. in 4.
Departmental State Papers, 1821–1846. 20 vols. in 7.
Departmental State Papers, Angeles, 1825–1847. 12 vols. in 4.
Departmental State Papers, Benicia, 1821–1846. 5 vols. in 2.

Departmental State Papers, Benicia, Commissary and Treasury, 1825–1842. 5 vols. in 1.

Departmental State Papers, Benicia, Custom House, 1816–1848. 8 vols. in 1.

Departmental State Papers, Benicia, Military, 1772–1846. 36 vols. in 3.
    Vols. LIII–LXXXVIII continued from Provincial State Papers, Benicia, Military.

Departmental State Papers, Benicia, *prefecturas y juzgados*, 1828–1846. 6 vols. in 1.

Departmental State Papers, Monterey, 1777–1845. 8 vols. in 1.

Legislative Records, 1822–1846. 4 vols. in 3.

Provincial Records, 1775–1822. 12 vols. in 5.

Provincial State Papers, 1767–1822. 22 vols. in 14.

Provincial State Papers, Benicia, Military, 1767–1822. 52 vols. in 3.

State Papers, Missions and Colonization, 1787–1845. 2 vols.

State Papers, Sacramento, 1770–1845. 19 vols. in 3.

Archivo del arzobispado, cartas de los misioneros de California, 1772–1839. 5 vols. in 3.
    Transcripts, in Bancroft Library, University of California.

Archivo de la misión de Santa Barbara, 1768–1836. 12 vols.
    Transcripts, in Bancroft Library, University of California.

Archivo de Santa Barbara, 1839–1853.
    Transcripts, in Bancroft Library, University of California.

Astor, John Jacob. Collection of manuscripts.
    Originals, in Baker Library, Harvard School of Business Administration, Boston.

Bryant, Sturgis, & Co. Collection of manuscripts, 1811–1871. 10 vols.
    Originals and transcripts, in Widener Memorial Library, Harvard University, Cambridge.

Californias, 1634–1835. 81 vols.
    Originals, in Archivo General y Público de la Nación, Mexico City.

CERRUTI, ENRIQUE. "Establecimientos rusos en California. Datos sacados por Enrique Cerruti de documentos en poder del General Mariano Guadalupe Vallejo."
    Original, in Bancroft Library, University of California, Berkeley.

Correspondencia de los virreyes, 1755–1821. 344 vols.
    Originals, in Archivo General y Público de la Nación, Mexico City.

COT, ANTONIO JOSÉ, and HARTNELL, WILLIAM EDWARD PETTY. "Arbitration of the Case of the *Rover*, 1827."
    Original, deposited by Ana Zabala and Teresa Zabala, Monterey, in Bancroft Library, University of California.

Council of the Indies. Consulta sobre proyecto de Vicente Basadre para comerciar pieles de nutria, June 22, 1791.
    Transcript from the Archivo General de Indias, Seville, in Bancroft Library, University of California.

Department of State, Washington, D. C., Consular Letters, Honolulu.
Originals, in Library of Congress, Washington, D. C.

Department of State, Washington, D. C., Consular Letters, Monterey, 1837–1848.
Originals, in Library of Congress, Washington, D. C.

Dexter, Gordon. Collection of William Appleton & Co. manuscripts.
Originals, in Baker Library, Harvard School of Business Administration, Boston.

Documentos para la historia de California, 1770–1875. 4 vols.
Originals, in Bancroft Library, University of California.

Documentos para la historia de México. 4 vols.
Originals, in Biblioteca Nacional, Mexico City.

Documentos relativos á las misiones de California. 4 vols.
Originals, in Museo Nacional, Mexico City.

Estudillo, José Joaquín. Documentos para la historia de California, 1776–1850. 2 vols.
Originals, in Bancroft Library, University of California.

Expediente sobre establecer por la Compañia de Filipinas un comercio de pieles de nutrias, castores, y lobos marinos de la costa de California, promovido por el intendente de exercito y real hacienda de aquellas islas Don Ciriaco González de Carbajal, en que demuestra el medio y reglas que deben observarse para un establecimiento y utilidades que de el resultarán á las mismas islas, 1786–1788.
Transcripts from the Archivo General de Indias, Seville, in Bancroft Library, University of California.

Expediente sobre proyecto de Basadre para cambiar azogue de la China por pieles de Californias, 1784–1790.
Transcripts, from the Archivo General de Indias, Seville, in Library of Congress, Washington, D. C.

Fitch, Henry. Documentos para la historia de California, 1827–1856.
Original, in Bancroft Library, University of California.

Guerra y Noriega, José de la. Documentos para la historia de California. 7 vols.
Transcripts, from the de la Guerra collection owned by Miss Delfina de la Guerra, Santa Barbara, in Bancroft Library, University of California.

Hartnell, William Edward Petty. Letter Book, 1823–1831.
Original, deposited by Ana Zabala and Teresa Zabala, Monterey, in Bancroft Library, University of California.

Hunnewell, James. Collection of manuscripts, 1809–1869.
Originals, in Harvard University Library, Cambridge.

Larkin, Thomas Oliver. Documents for the History of California, 1839–1856. 9 vols.
Originals, in Bancroft Library, University of California.

Leidesdorff, William Alexander. Collection of manuscripts.
Originals, in Huntington Library, San Marino.

MALASPINA, ALEJANDRO. "Examen político de las costas del NO. de la América, 1791."
Transcript, from the Archivo General de Indias, Seville, in Bancroft Library, University of California.

Marshall, Josiah. Collection of manuscripts, 1818–1841.
Originals and transcripts, in Widener Memorial Library, Harvard University, Cambridge.

Mercury Case Documents.
Originals, in Los Angeles Public Library.

Original manuscripts, unbound correspondence.
In Bancroft Library, University of California. Letters cited, William Sturgis Hinckley, Stephen Reynolds, Nathan Spear, 1836.
In Secretaría de Gobernación, Mexico City. Documents cited, 1828–1829, in Indiferente, Legajos 5, 16.
In Secretaría de Guerra y Marina, Mexico City. Documents cited, 1813–1836, in 52–6–6–1, 52–6–6–2, 52–6–6–5, 52–6–6–9, 52–6–6–11, 52–6–9–2, 52–8–7–1.
In Secretaría de Relaciones Exteriores, Mexico City. Documents cited, 1836, in 5–8–7978.

Perkins, James, and Perkins, Thomas Handasyd. Collection of manuscripts.
Originals, Massachusetts Historical Society, Boston.

Phelps, William Dane. Collection of manuscripts, 1828–1873.
Originals and transcripts, in Widener Memorial Library, Harvard University, Cambridge.

Pinto, Rafael. Documentos para la historia de California, 1823–1878. 2 vols.
Originals, in Bancroft Library, University of California.

Provincias Internas. 254 vols.
Originals, in Archivo General y Público de la Nación, Mexico City.

Robinson, Alfred. Collection of manuscripts.
Originals, owned by A. Porter Robinson, San Francisco.

SHEFFER, EGOR NIKOLAEVICH. "Les russes aux îles Hawaïennes."
Transcripts, in Bancroft Library, University of California.

Spear, Nathan. Account book, 1833–1836.
Original, in Bancroft Library, University of California.

Stearns, Abel. Collection of manuscripts.
Originals, in Huntington Library, San Marino.

Stearns, Abel, and Thompson, Alpheus Basil. Contract, September 22, 1831.
Original, owned by Henry Raup Wagner, San Marino.

Thompson, Alpheus Basil. Collection of manuscripts.
Originals, owned by Mrs. John M. Williamson, Carpinteria.

Transcripts, unbound correspondence, in Bancroft Library, University of California.
From the Archivo General de Indias, Seville. Letters cited: José Joaquín

de Arrillaga, 1806; Alejandro Malaspina, 1791; Conde de Revilla Gigedo, 1789–1791.

From the de la Guerra collection owned by Miss Delfina de la Guerra, Santa Barbara. Letters cited, José de la Guerra y Noriega, 1817–1826.

Vallejo, Mariano Guadalupe. Documentos para la historia de California, 1713–1851. 36 vols.

Originals, in Bancroft Library, University of California.

VASADRE Y VEGA, VICENTE. "Informe sobre perjuicios en la comisión que se le dió de conducir á la China pieles de nutria. April 11, 1791."

Transcript, from the Archivo General de Indias, Seville, in Bancroft Library, University of California.

2. LOGBOOKS AND JOURNALS

BODEGA Y CUADRA, JUAN FRANCISCO DE LA. Logbook of the *Sonora*, 1775.

Transcript from the Archivo General de Indias, Seville, in Bancroft Library, University of California.

CAAMAÑO, JACINTO. Logbook of the *Aranzazu*, 1792.

Transcript from the Archivo General de Indias, Seville, in Bancroft Library, University of California.

CAMPA, MIGUEL DE LA. Logbook of the *Santiago*, 1775.

Transcript from the Archivo General de Indias, Seville, in Bancroft Library, University of California.

COOPER, JOHN ROGERS. Logbooks of the *Rover*, 1822–1826.

Originals, owned by Miss Frances Molera, San Francisco.

CRESPI, JUAN. Logbook of the *Santiago*, 1774.

Transcript from the Archivo General de Indias, Seville, in Bancroft Library, University of California.

GRIMES, ELIAB. Logbook of the *Eagle*, 1820–1822, Berkeley.

Original, in University of California Library.

Hudson's Bay Company, Journal at Fort Simpson, 1834–1837.

Transcript, in Bancroft Library, University of California.

Logbook of the *Arab*, 1821–1825.

Original, in Bancroft Library, University of California.

Logbook of the *Atahualpa*, 1811–1814.

Original, Massachusetts Historical Society, Boston.

Logbook of the *Owhyhee*, 1827.

Original, California Historical Society, San Francisco.

Logbook of the *Waverly*, 1828–1829.

Original, in Bancroft Library, University of California.

MARTÍNEZ, ESTEBAN JOSÉ. Logbook of the *Princesa*, 1789.

Transcript from the Archivo General de Indias, Seville, in Bancroft Library, University of California.

——. Logbook of the *Santiago*, 1774.
Transcript from the Archivo General de Indias, Seville, in Bancroft Library, University of California.

MOURELLE, FRANCISCO ANTONIO. Logbook of the *Favorita*, 1779.
Transcript from the Archivo General de Indias, Seville, in Bancroft Library, University of California.

PANTOJA Y ARRIAGA, JUAN. Logbook of the *Princesa*, 1779.
Transcript from the Archivo General de Indias, Seville, in Bancroft Library, University of California.

PEÑA, TOMÁS DE LA. Logbook of the *Santiago*, 1774.
Transcript from the Archivo General de Indias, Seville, in Bancroft Library, University of California.

PHELPS, WILLIAM DANE. Logbooks of the *Alert*, 1840–1843.
Originals, in Widener Memorial Library, Harvard University, Cambridge.

——. "Solid Men of Boston in the Northwest."
Original, in Bancroft Library, University of California.

ROBINSON, ALFRED. Journal of the *Brookline*, 1829.
Original, owned by A. Porter Robinson, San Francisco.

STURGIS, WILLIAM. Journal of the *Eliza*, 1799.
Original, Massachusetts Historical Society, Boston.

3. CONTEMPORARY HISTORIES AND REMINISCENCES

ALVARADO, JUAN BAUTISTA. "Historia de California, 1769–1847." 5 vols.
Original, in Bancroft Library, University of California.

BROWN, CHARLES. "Statement of Recollections of Early Events in California."
Original, in Bancroft Library, University of California.

CHICHINOV, ZAKAHAR. "Adventures of Zakahar Tchitchinoff, an Employee of the Russian American Fur Company, 1802–1878."
Original, in Bancroft Library, University of California.

DALLY, HENRY J. "Narrative from 1843."
Original, in Bancroft Library, University of California.

DITTMANN, CARL. "Narrative of a Sea-Faring Life from 1844."
Original, in Bancroft Library, University of California.

DYE, JOB FRANCIS. "Recollections of California."
Original, in Bancroft Library, University of California.

FERNÁNDEZ, JOSÉ. "Cosas de California."
Original, in Bancroft Library, University of California.

GOLOVNIN, VASILII. "Extracts from a Description of a Voyage round the World by Captain Golovnin of the Sloop *Kamchatka*, 1817–1819."
Part 4 of "Material for the History of the Russian Settlements on the Shores of the Eastern Ocean," Russian America, Vol. III, Pt. 4, pp. 47–92.
Transcript and translation, in Bancroft Library, University of California.

KHLEBNIKOV, KIRIL. "Biography of Alexander Andreievitch Baranoff."
Russian America, Vol. IV, Pt. 4, pp. 1–185. Transcript and translation, in
Bancroft Library, University of California.

——. "Letters of K. Khlebnikoff on America."
Part 3 of "Materials for the History of the Russian Settlements on the
Shores of the Eastern Ocean," Russian America, Vol. III, Pt. 3, pp. 1–261.
Transcript and translation, in Bancroft Library, University of California.

LOZAREV, ANDREW. "Extracts from the Description of a Voyage around the
World by Captain A. Lozareff on the Sloop Ladoga, 1822–1824."
Part 4 of "Materials for the History of the Russian Settlements on the
Shores of the Eastern Ocean," Russian America, III, Pt. 4, pp. 93–108.
Transcript and translation, in Bancroft Library, University of California.

LÜTKE, CAPTAIN. "Extracts from the Writings of Captain Lütke During his
Journey on the Sloop Seniavin, 1826–1829."
Part 4 of "Materials for the History of the Russian Settlements on the
Shores of the Eastern Ocean," Russian America, Vol. III, Pt. 4, pp. 109–89.
Transcript and translation, in Bancroft Library, University of California.

MARKOV, ALEXANDER. "Journey of Alexander Markoff."
Russian America, Vol. VII, Pt. 1, pp. 1–205. Transcript and translation,
in Bancroft Library, University of California.

NIDEVER, GEORGE. "Life and Adventures of George Nidever."
Original, in Bancroft Library, University of California.

OSIO, ANTONIO MARÍA. "Historia de la California, 1815–1848."
Original, in Bancroft Library, University of California.

PEIRCE, HENRY AUGUSTUS. "Memoranda of Past Events."
Original, in Bancroft Library, University of California.

POTEKHIN, W. "Settlement of Ross."
Russian America, Vol. V, Pt. 2, fols. 1–21. Transcript and translation, in
Bancroft Library, University of California.

SOKOLOV, VASILII. "The Voyage of Alexander Markoff from Okhotsk to California and Mazatlan in 1835."
Original, in Bancroft Library, University of California.

TARAKANOV, VASILII PETROVICH. "Statement."
Russian America, Vol. II, Pt. 2, pp. 1–42. Transcript and translation, in
Bancroft Library, University of California.

TIKHMENEV, P. "Historical Review of the Origin of the Russian American
Company."
Russian America, Vol. I, Pt. 1, pp. 1–451, Pt. 2, pp. 1–220, Vol. II, Pt. 2,
pp. 222–853. Transcript and translation, in Bancroft Library, University of
California.

VALLEJO, JOSÉ DE JESÚS. "Reminiscencias históricas de California."
Original, in Bancroft Library, University of California.

VALLEJO, MARIANO GUADALUPE. "Historia de California. Recuerdos históricos y personales tocante á la California, 1769–1848." 5 vols.
Original, in Bancroft Library, University of California.

VALLEJO, SALVADOR. "Notas históricas sobre California."
Original, in Bancroft Library, University of California.

WARNER, JONATHAN TRUMBULL. "Reminiscences of Early California."
Original, in Bancroft Library, University of California.

WEEKS, JAMES FRANCIS. "Reminiscences."
Original, in Bancroft Library, University of California.

4. UNPUBLISHED THESES

STANTON, JOHN WILLIAM. "The Foundations of Russian Foreign Policy in the Far East, 1847–1875."
Ph.D. dissertation in history, University of California, 1932.

STEWART, CHARLES LOCKWOOD. "Martínez and López de Haro on the Northwest Coast, 1788–1789."
Ph.D. dissertation in history, University of California, 1936.

TAYS, GEORGE. "Revolutionary California: the Political History of California During the Mexican Period, 1822–1846."
Ph.D. dissertation in history, University of California, 1932.

B. PRINTED MATERIALS
1. BOOKS

AUDUBON, JOHN JAMES and BACHMAN, JOHN. The Quadrupeds of North America. 3 vols. New York, 1849–1854.

BANCROFT, HUBERT HOWE. History of Alaska, 1730–1885. San Francisco, 1886.

———. History of California. 7 vols. San Francisco, 1884–1890.

———. History of the Northwest Coast. 2 vols. San Francisco, 1884.

BEECHEY, FREDERICK WILLIAM. Narrative of a Voyage to the Pacific and Beering's Strait, to Coöperate with the Polar Expeditions: Performed in His Majesty's Ship "Blossom," under the Command of Captain F. W. Beechey . . . in the Years 1825, 26, 27, 28. . . . 2 vols. London, 1831.

BERESFORD, WILLIAM. A Voyage round the World; but More Particularly to the Northwest Coast of America; Performed in 1785, 1786, 1787, and 1788, in the "King George" and "Queen Charlotte," Captains Portlock and Dixon. Edited by Captain George Dixon. London, 1789.

BERNARD DU HAUTCILLY, AUGUSTE. Voyage autour du monde, principalement à la Californie et aux îles Sandwich, pendant les années 1826, 1827, 1828, et 1829. 2 vols. Paris, 1834–1835.

BOLTON, HERBERT EUGENE. Guide to Materials for the History of the United States in the Principal Archives of Mexico. Washington, 1913.

BRIGGS, LLOYD VERNON. *History and Genealogy of the Cabot Family.* Boston, 1927.

CHAPMAN, CHARLES EDWARD. *A History of California: the Spanish Period.* New York, 1921.

CHORIS, LUDOVIK. *Voyage pittoresque autour du monde, avec des portraits de sauvages d'Amérique, d'Asie, d'Afrique, et des îles du grand océan; des paysages, des vues maritimes, et plusieurs objets d'histoire naturelle. . . .* Paris, 1822.

CLELAND, ROBERT GLASS. "Asiatic Trade and American Occupation of the Pacific Coast," American Historical Association, *Annual Report of the American Historical Association for the Year 1914* (Washington, 1916), I, 281–89.

CLEVELAND, RICHARD JEFFRY. *A Narrative of Voyages and Commercial Enterprises.* 2 vols. Cambridge, 1842.

COUES, ELLIOTT. *Fur-Bearing Animals: a Monograph of North American Mustelidae, in Which an Account of the Wolverene, the Martens or Sables, the Ermine, the Mink and Various Other Kinds of Weasels, Several Species of Skunks, the Badger, the Land and Sea Otters, and Numerous Exotic Allies of These Animals, Is Contributed to the History of North American Mammals,* U. S. Geological and Geographical Survey of the Territories, *Miscellaneous Publications,* No. 8. Washington, 1877.

DANA, RICHARD HENRY. *Two Years before the Mast. A Personal Narrative by Richard Henry Dana, Jr.* Boston, 1873.

DAVIS, WILLIAM HEATH. *Seventy-Five Years . . . a Re-issue and Enlarged Illustrated Edition of "Sixty Years in California," to Which Much New Matter by Its Author Has Been Added Which He Contemplated Publishing under the Present Title at the Time of his Death. . . .* Edited by Douglas S. Watson. San Francisco, 1929.

——. *Sixty Years in California, a History of Events and Life in California; Personal, Political and Military, under the Mexican Regime; during the Quasi-Military Government of the Territory by the United States, and after the Admission of the State into the Union, Being a Compilation by a Witness of the Events Described.* San Francisco, 1889.

DUBLÁN, MANUEL and LOZANA, JOSÉ MARÍA, eds. *Legislación mexicana ó Colección completa de las disposiciones legislativas expedidas desde la República.* 44 vols. Mexico, 1876–1913.

DUFLOT DE MOFRAS, EUGÈNE. *Exploration du territoire de l'Orégon, des Californies et de la Mer Vermeille, exécutée pendant les années 1840, 1841, et 1842, par M. Duflot de Mofras.* 2 vols. Paris, 1844.

ELLIOTT, HENRY WOOD. *A Report upon the Condition of Affairs in the Territory of Alaska.* Washington, 1875.

ELLISON, WILLIAM HENRY, ed. *The Life and Adventures of George Nidever, 1802–1883.* Berkeley, 1937.

FLEURIEU, CHARLES PIERRE CLARET DE. *A Voyage round the World, Performed during the Years 1790, 1791, and 1792, by Etienne Marchand, Preceded by a Historical Introduction, and Illustrated by Charts, etc.* Translated from the French. 2 vols. London, 1801.

FONSECA, FABIÁN DE and URRUTIA, CARLOS DE. *Historia general de real hacienda escrita por D. Fabian de Fonseca y D. Carlos de Urrutia, por orden del virey, conde de Revillagigedo. Obra hasta ahora inédita y que se imprime con permiso del supremo gobierno.* 6 vols. Mexico, 1845–1853.

FRANCHÈRE, GABRIEL. *Narrative of a Voyage to the Northwest Coast of America in the Years 1811, 1812, 1813, and 1814; or The First American Settlement on the Pacific.* Translated from the French and edited by Jedediah Vincent Huntington. New York, 1854.

GRINNELL, JOSEPH, DIXON, JOSEPH S., and LINSDALE, JEAN M. *Fur-Bearing Mammals of California, Their Natural History, Systematic Status, and Relations to Man.* 2 vols. Berkeley, 1937.

JEWITT, JOHN R. *A Narrative of the Adventures and Sufferings of John R. Jewitt; Only Survivor of the Crew of the Ship "Boston," during a Captivity of Nearly Three Years among the Savages of Nootka Sound: with an Account of the Manners, Mode of Living, and Religious Opinions of the Natives.* New York, 1816.

KELSEY, RAYNER WICKERSHAM. *The United States Consulate in California.* Berkeley, 1910.

KOTZEBUE, OTTO VON. *A New Voyage round the World, in the Years 1823, 24, 25, and 26.* London, 1830.

——. *A Voyage of Discovery, into the South Sea and Beering's Straits, for the Purpose of Exploring a Northeast Passage, Undertaken in the Years 1815–1818, at the Expense of His Highness . . . Count Romanzoff, in the Ship "Rurick," under the Command of the Lieutenant in the Russian Imperial Navy, Otto von Kotzebue.* Translated from the German by Hannibal Evans Lloyd. 3 vols. London, 1821.

KRASHENINNIKOV, STEPAN PETROVICH. *The History of Kamtschatka, and the Kurilski Islands, with the Countries Adjacent; Illustrated with Maps and Cuts.* Translated from the Russian by James Grieve. Glocester and London, 1764.

LANGSDORFF, GEORG HEINRICH VON. *Voyages and Travels in Various Parts of the World, during the Years 1803, 1804, 1805, 1806, and 1807.* Translated from the German. 2 vols. in 1. London, 1813–1814.

LAPÉROUSE, JEAN FRANÇOIS DE GALAUP DE. *A Voyage round the World, in the Years 1785, 1786, 1787 and 1788.* Edited by Louis Marie Antoine Destouff, Baron de Milet de Mureau, and translated from the French. 3 vols. London, 1798.

LA SALLE, A. DE. *Relation du voyage, par A. de La Salle.* 3 vols. Paris, 1845–1852.

LISIANSKY, UREY FEDOROVICH. *A Voyage round the World, in the Years 1803, 4, 5, & 6; Performed, by Order of His Imperial Majesty Alexander the First, Emperor of Russia, in the Ship "Neva" by Urey Lisiansky*. London, 1814.

MEARES, JOHN. *Voyages Made in the Years 1788 and 1789, from China to the N.W. Coast of America: with an Introductory Narrative of a Voyage Performed in 1786, from Bengal, in the Ship "Nootka." To Which Are Annexed Observations on the Probable Existence of a North West Passage. And Some Account of the Trade between the North West Coast of America and China; and the Latter Country and Great Britain*. 2 vols. London, 1791.

Mexico, Ministerio de relaciones exteriores. *Memoria* . . . (title varies). 22 vols. in 8. Mexico, 1822–1852.

Mexico, Laws and statutes. *Ordenes y circulares espedidas por el supremo gobierno desde el año de 1825 hasta la fecha, para el arreglo y legitimidad del comercio marítimo nacional*. Mexico, 1830.

Mexico, Secretaría de hacienda, archivo y biblioteca. *Colección de documentos históricos*. 2 vols. Mexico, 1914.

NAVARRETE, MARTÍN FERNÁNDEZ DE. *Examen histórico-crítico, de los viajes y descubrimientos apócrifos del capitán Lorenzo Ferrer Maldonado, de Juan de Fuca y del almirante Bartolomé de Fonte. Memoria comenzada por D. Martín Fernández de Navarrete, y arreglada y concluida por D. Estaquio Fernández de Navarrete, año de 1848*, in Miguel Salvá and Pedro Sainz, eds., *Colección de documentos inéditos para la historia de España*, XV (Madrid, 1849), 5–363.

——. *Relación del viage hecho por las goletas "Sutil" y "Mexicana" en el año de 1792, para reconocer el estrecho de Fuca; con una introducción en que se da noticia de las expediciones executadas anteriormente por los españoles en busca del paso del noroeste de la América*. Madrid, 1802.

PATTIE, JAMES OHIO. *The Personal Narrative of James O. Pattie, of Kentucky, during an Expedition from St. Louis, through the Vast Regions between That Place and the Pacific Ocean, and Thence Back through the City of Mexico to Vera Cruz, during Journeyings of Six Years*. . . . Edited by Timothy Flint. Cincinnati, 1833.

PENNANT, THOMAS. *Arctic Zoölogy*. 2 vols. London, 1784–1785.

PÉRON, ——. *Mémoires du capitaine Péron, sur ses voyages aux côtes d'Afrique, en Arabie, à l'île d'Amsterdam, aux îles d'Anjouan et de Mayotte, aux côtes nord-ouest de l'Amérique, aux îles Sandwich, à la Chine, etc*. . . . 2 vols. Paris, 1824.

PHELPS, WILLIAM DANE. *Fore and Aft; or Leaves from the Life of an Old Sailor*. Boston, 1871.

PORTER, KENNETH WIGGINS. *John Jacob Astor, Business Man*. 2 vols. Cambridge, 1931.

PRIESTLEY, HERBERT INGRAM. *The Coming of the White Man, 1492–1848*. New York, 1929.

REVILLA GIGEDO, JUAN VICENTE GUÉMEZ PACHECO DE PADILLA HORCASITAS Y AGUAYO, CONDE DE. "El virey . . . recopila en este difuso informe los sucesos ocurridos en la península de Californias y departamento de S. Blas, desde el año de 1768, proponiendo lo que considera conveniente," in Carlos María de Bustamente, *Suplemento á la historia de los tres siglos de México durante el govierno español. Escrita por el padre Andrés Cavo* (Mexico, 1836), III, 112–64.

RIVES, GEORGE LOCKHART. *The United States and Mexico, 1821–1848; a History of the Relations between the Two Countries from the Independence of Mexico to the Close of the War with the United States.* 2 vols. New York, 1913.

ROBINSON, ALFRED. *Life in California during a Residence of Several Years in that Territory. Comprising a Description of the Country and the Missionary Establishments, with Incidents, Observations, etc., by Alfred Robinson. With an Appendix, Bringing Forward the Narrative from 1846, to the Occupation of the Country by the United States.* San Francisco, 1891.

SALES, LUIS. *Noticias de la provincia de Californias en tres cartas de un sacerdote religioso hijo del real convento de predicadores de Valencia a un amigo suyo.* Valencia, 1794.

SAUER, MARTIN. *An Account of a Geographical and Astronomical Expedition to the Northern Parts of Russia, for Ascertaining the Degrees of Latitude and Longitude of the Mouth of the River Kovima; of the Whole Coast of the Tshutski, to East Cape; and of the Islands in the Eastern Ocean, Stretching to the American Coast. Performed . . . by Commodore Joseph Billings, in the Years 1785 & to 1794. The Whole Narrated from the Original Papers, by Martin Sauer. . . .* London, 1802

SCAMMON, CHARLES MELVILLE. *The Marine Mammals of the Northwestern Coast of North America, Described and Illustrated: Together with an Account of the American Whale-Fishery.* San Francisco and New York, 1874.

SIMPSON, SIR GEORGE. *Fur Trade and Empire; George Simpson's Journal; Remarks Connected with the Fur Trade in the Course of a Voyage from York Factory to Fort George and Back to York Factory 1824–1825; Together with Accompanying Documents.* Edited by Frederick Merk. Cambridge, 1931.

SMITH, JUSTIN HARVEY. *The War with Mexico.* 2 vols. New York, 1919.

SNOW, HENRY JAMES. *In Forbidden Seas. Recollections of Sea-Otter Hunting in the Kurils.* London, 1910.

STEJNEGER, LEONHARD HESS. *Georg Wilhelm Steller, the Pioneer of Alaskan Natural History.* Cambridge, 1936.

STELLER, GEORG WILHELM. "The Early History of the Northern Fur Seals," translated by Walter Miller, in U. S. Treasury Department, Commission on Fur-Seal Investigations, *The Fur-Seals and Fur-Seal Islands of the North Pacific Ocean* (Washington, 1898–1899), III, 179–218.

STEPHENS, FRANK. *California Mammals.* San Diego, 1906.

STEVENSON, CHARLES H. "Utilization of the Skins of Aquatic Animals," U. S. Bureau of Fisheries, *Report of the Commissioner for the Year Ending June 30, 1902* (Washington, 1904), pp. 283–352.

STEWART, CHARLES SAMUEL. *A Visit to the South Seas in the U. S. Ship "Vincennes," during the Years 1829 and 1830, with Scenes in Brazil, Peru, Manilla, the Cape of Good Hope, and St. Helena.* 2 vols. New York, 1831.

VANCOUVER, GEORGE. *A Voyage of Discovery to the North Pacific Ocean, and round the World; in Which the Coast of Northwestern America Has Been Carefully Examined and Accurately Surveyed. Undertaken by His Majesty's Command, Principally with a View to Ascertain the Existence of Any Navigable Communication between the North Pacific and North Atlantic Oceans: and Performed in the Years 1790, 1791, 1792, 1793, 1794, and 1795, in the "Discovery," Sloop of War, and Armed Tender "Chatham," under the Command of Captain George Vancouver.* 3 vols. London, 1798.

WAGNER, HENRY RAUP. *Spanish Explorations in the Strait of Juan de Fuca.* Santa Ana, 1933.

WILKES, CHARLES. *Narrative of the United States Exploring Expedition. During the Years 1838, 1839, 1840, 1841, 1842. By Charles Wilkes, U.S.N., Commander of the Expedition.* 5 vols. Philadelphia, 1844.

2. PERIODICAL LITERATURE

ALEXANDER, WILLIAM DEWITT. "The Relations between the Hawaiian Islands and Spanish America in Early Times," Hawaiian Historical Society, *Papers*, No. 1 (1892), pp. 1–11.

BARANOV, ALEXANDER. "The Spirit of Russian Hunters Devised," edited and translated by Henry Wood Elliott, *Overland Monthly*, LXVI (December, 1915), 522–24.

BARROWS, HENRY DWIGHT. "William Wolfskill, the Pioneer," Historical Society of Southern California, *Publications*, V (1902), 287–94.

CAMP, CHARLES LEWIS. "The Chronicles of George C. Yount," California Historical Society, *Quarterly*, II (April, 1923), 3–66.

CHASE, A. W. "The Sea-Lion at Home," *Overland Monthly*, III (October, 1869), 350–54.

CLELAND, ROBERT GLASS. "The Early Sentiment for the Annexation of California: an Account of the Growth of American Interest in California, 1835–1846," *Southwestern Historical Quarterly*, XVIII (July and October, 1914, January, 1915), 1–40, 121–61, 231–60.

COWDIN, ELLIOT C. "The Northwest Fur Trade," *The Merchants' Magazine*, XIV (June, 1846), 532–39.

DAY, MRS. F. H. "Sketches of the Early Settlers of California, Isaac J. Sparks," *The Hesperian*, II (July, 1859), 193–200.

"Dr. John Scouler's Journal of a Voyage to N. W. America, 1824, '25, '26," Oregon Historical Society, *Quarterly*, VI (June, 1905), 54–76, 159–205, 276–89.

"Extracts from an Ancient Log," *Hawaiian Almanac and Annual. The Reference Book of Information and Statistics Relating to the Territory of Hawaii, of Value to Merchants, Tourists, and Others* (1906), pp. 66–74.

HILL, JOSEPH JOHN. "Ewing Young in the Fur Trade of the Far Southwest, 1822–1834," Oregon Historical Society, *Quarterly*, XXIV (March, 1923), 1–35.

HOWAY, JUDGE FREDERICK WILLIAM. "A List of Trading Vessels in the Maritime Fur Trade," 1785–1825, The Royal Society of Canada, *Proceedings and Transactions*, Third Series, Vol. XXIV (1930), sec. 2, pp. 111–34; Vol. XXV (1931), sec. 2, pp. 117–49; Vol. XXVI (1932), sec. 2, pp. 43–86; Vol. XXVII (1933), sec. 2, pp. 119–47; Vol. XXVIII (1934), sec. 2, pp. 11–49.

HUNNEWELL, JAMES. "Voyage in the Brig *Bordeaux Packet*, Boston to Honolulu, 1817, and Residence in Honolulu, 1817–1818," Hawaiian Historical Society, *Papers*, No. 8 (1895).

OGDEN, ADELE. "Russian Sea-Otter and Seal Hunting on the California Coast, 1803–1841," California Historical Society, *Quarterly*, XII (September, 1933), 217–39.

———. "The Californias in Spain's Pacific Otter Trade, 1775–1795," *The Pacific Historical Review*, I (December, 1932), 444–69.

SHALER, WILLIAM. "Journal of a Voyage between China and the Northwest Coast, Made in 1804," *The American Register, or General Repository of History, Politics and Science*, III (1808), 137–75.

Shipping lists, *The Hawaiian Spectator*, Vol. I (1838), No. 2, pp. 102–3; Vol. II (1839), No. 1, pp. 118–19.

TAYS, GEORGE. "Commodore Edmund B. Kennedy, U.S.N., versus Governor Nicolás Gutiérrez, an Incident of 1836," California Historical Society, *Quarterly*, XII (June, 1933), 137–46.

THOMPSON, ALPHEUS BASIL. Letter to Abel Stearns, September 22, 1831, Historical Society of Southern California, *Publications*, VII (1907–1908), 205.

3. NEWSPAPERS AND NEWSPAPER ARTICLES

Gazetas de México. 44 vols. Mexico, 1784–1821.

"Letters from Mr. Wallace," in *Benjamin Hayes Scrap Books*, LXVII, 53–55.

"Recollections of a Pioneer of California," Santa Cruz *Sentinel*, May 15, 1869, No. 49.

INDEX

INDEX

Abalone, food of sea otters, 8; shells, use in fur trade, 2, 28, 29, 30
Acapulco, 2, 15, 19, 23, 31, 157, 169, 174
Activo (brig), 159, 160
Adams, Captain Alexander, 71, 165, 166
Adamson, Captain John William, 156
Admittance (ship), 149, 150, 181
Aguardiente, consignment of, 92
Alaska, 57. *See also* Aleuts, Kodiaks, Russians, Sitka
Albatross (ship), 53–55, 72–75, 162–166
Alciope (ship), 180
Alert (ship), 133, 134, 148
Aleutian Islands, Russians on, 2
Aleuts, as sea otter hunters, 6, 45, 46, 47, 50, 51, 53, 54, 55, 57, 58, 59, 60, 62, 63, 64, 65, 96, 97, 99, 100, 102, 105, 140, 143, 144, 158, 165, 168, 169, 174; method of hunting otters by, 11–14; need of Americans for, 45, 76; in San Francisco Bay, 50, 60; at San Francisco presidio, 54, 59, 60; at Fort Ross, 60, 63; forced to work at Santa Barbara, 61; seized at Refugio, 62; word as used in documents, 195 (note 2). *See also* Fort Ross; San Francisco Bay; Seizure; Shooting
Alexander (ship), 36–37, 39–40, 158
Alvarado, Juan Bautista, quoted, 12; hunting policy of, 106–107, 115, 130, 131, 137; statement by, concerning numbers of otters, 142
Amador, José María, statement of, 142
American (citizens, consul, traders, vessels). *See also* New England; United States
Amethyst (ship), 57, 164
Angel Island, 59
Anglo-Americans, 47, 48. *See also* New England and United States (citizens, traders, vessels)
Ann (schooner), 170
Appendix, pp. 155–182
Appleton & Co., William, 149, 150, 181, 182

Arab (brig), 79, 172
Aranzazu (frigate), 30, 156
Arce, Joaquín, 37
Arce, José Ignacio, 51
Argüello, Gervasio, 63
Argüello, José Dario, commander of San Francisco presidio, 39, 40, 48, 55, 56, 60; governor, 66, 71
Argüello, Luis Antonio, commander of San Francisco presidio, 54, 80; governor, 95, 96, 98, 99, 103, 104
Argüello, Santiago, *alférez*, 101
Arrillaga, José Joaquín, governor, 36, 37, 41, 46–47, 51
Arther, Captain James P., 150, 181, 182
Articles of trade, 18, 28, 29, 52, 67, 75, 86, 88, 91–94 *passim*, 99. *See also* Hide-and-tallow trade; Horses
Astor, John Jacob, 56, 69, 87, 90, 168, 172, 173
Astoria, 69, 70, 72
Atala (ship), 75, 166
Avon (brig), 79, 93, 178, 180

Baidarkas (bidarkas, kayaks): structure of, 11–12; method of hunting in, 12–13; hunting in, 46, 48, 50, 51, 53, 54, 55, 56, 57, 58, 59, 60, 61, 62, 63, 96, 97, 100, 101, 102, 105, 107, 109, 116, 120, 124, 125, 128, 129, 140, 141, 158, 159, 160, 174. *See also* Canoes
Baikal (brig), 99–100, 102, 105, 172, 174
Baker & Co., William, 92
Balguerie, Jr., ———, 167
Ballast Point (San Diego), 35, 46, 48
Bancroft, Captain John, 128–129, 130, 178, 179
Baranov, Alexander, 45, 46, 47, 48, 49, 50, 52, 53, 56, 57–58, 59, 64, 65, 67, 70, 72, 164, 165, 195 (note 3), 197 (note 49)
Baridon, Captain Francisco, 159
Barnstable (ship), 138, 149, 150, 181
Bass & Co., Henry, 36, 158
Beads, for California Indians, 18; used in fur trade, 29; delivered to Russian vessel, 71

[237]